CW00945350

Francis Bacon

Also by Andrew Sinclair

FICTION

The Breaking of Bumbo
My Friend Judas
The Project
The Hallelujah Bum
The Raker
A Patriot for Hire
The Facts in the Case of E. A. Poe
Beau Bumbo
Gog
Magog
King Ludd

NONFICTION

Prohibition: the Era of Excess
The Better Half: the Emancipation of the American Woman
The Available Man: Warren Gamaliel Harding
The Concise History of the United States
Che Guevara
The Last of the Best
The Savage
Dylan: Poet of His People
Jack London
John Ford
Corsair: the Life of J. P. Morgan
The Other Victoria
Sir Walter Raleigh and the Age of Discovery
The Red and the Blue
Spiegel: the Man Behind the Pictures
War like a Wasp: the Lost Decade of the Forties
The Sword and the Grail

DRAMA

Adventures in the Skin Trade (play)
Under Milk Wood (screenplay)

TRANSLATION

The Greek Anthology

FRANCIS BACON

His Life and Violent Times

ANDREW SINCLAIR

SINCLAIR-STEVENSON

First published in Great Britain in 1993
by Sinclair-Stevenson
an imprint of Reed Consumer Books Ltd
Michelin House, 81 Fulham Road, London SW3 6RB
and Auckland, Melbourne, Singapore and Toronto

A CIP catalogue record for this book
is available at the British Library
ISBN 1 85619 310 1

Typeset by CentraCet, Cambridge
Printed and bound in Great Britain
by Clays Ltd, St Ives plc

To Sonia and Pandora
and the life of the artist

'Between birth and death it's always been the same thing. It is what it is. It is the violence of life.'

Francis Bacon, *the painter*

Contents

List of Illustrations

Acknowledgements

The author and publishers would like to thank all the writers, publishers, and literary representatives, who have given permission for reprinting quoted material. In some instances it has been difficult to track down copyright holders and the publishers will be glad to make good any omissions in future editions. Writers whose work has been quoted are listed in order of first appearance below.

Michael McConville: extract from *Ascendency to Oblivion: the Story of the Anglo-Irish*, Quartet Books, 1986. C. S. Andrews: extract from *Dublin Made Me*, The Talbot Press, 1930. L. MacManus: extract from *White Light and Flame: Memories of the Irish Literary Revival and the Anglo-Irish War*, The Talbot Press, 1924. L. E. O. Charlton: extract from *War over England*, Longman's Green, 1938. Extract from *'I.O.' The Administration of Ireland*, 1920, Philip Allan and Co, 1921. Joice M. Nankivell and Syndey Lock: extract *Ireland in Travail*, John Murray, 1922. W. Alison Phillips: extract from *The Revolution in Ireland, 1906–23*, Longmans Green and Co., 1923. Christopher Isherwood: extracts from *Christopher and his Kind*, Eyre Methuen, 1977. René Gimpel: extract from *Diary of an Art Dealer*, Calmann-Lévy, Paris, 1963. Ernst Toller: extract from *Broken Brow*, Hogarth Press, 1928. Billy Klüver and Julie Martin: extracts from *Kiki's Paris: Artists and Lovers, 1900–1930*,Harry N. Abrams, New York, 1989. Brassaï: extract from *The Secret Paris of the 30's*, Thames & Hudson, 1976. Patrick White: extracts from *Flaws in the Glass*, Random House, 1981. Valentine Cummingham: extract from *British Writers of the 'Thirties*, Oxford University Press, 1988. John Rothenstein: extracts from *Modern English Painters*, Eyre & Spottiswoode, 1956. William Sansom: extract from *Westminster at War*, Faber & Faber,

1947. Stephen Spender: extract from *World Within World*, Hamish Hamilton, 1951. John Lehmann: extract from *In the Purely Pagan Sense*, G. M. P., 1976. Quentin Crisp: extract from *The Naked Civil Servant*, Fontana, 1968. T. S. Eliot: extracts from 'The Waste Land' and 'Sweeney Among the Nightingales,' reprinted by permission of Faber & Faber and Harcourt Brace. Hugh Davies: extracts from *Francis Bacon: The Early and Middle Years*, Garland Press, 1978. Colin MacInnes: extract from *England, Half English*, by permission of the estate of the author and Chatto & Windus. Michael Wishart: extracts from *High Diver*, by permission of the author. Michael Ayrton: extract from *The Rudiments of Paradise*, Secker & Warburg, 1971. Ted Morgan: extracts from Literary Outlaw: *The Life and Times of William S. Burroughs*, Random House, 1991. John Rothenstein: extracts from *Time's Thievish Progress, Vol. III*, Eyre & Spottiswoode, 1970. Keith Vaughan: extracts from his *Journals 1939–1977*, John Murray, 1989. Stephen Spender: extracts from his *Journals 1939–1983*, Faber & Faber, 1986. Extracts from *Self Portrait with Friends: The Selected Diaries of Cecil Beaton*, by permission of Weidenfeld & Nicholson. John Ashbery: extracts from his copyright *Reported Sightings: Art Chronicles: 1957–1987*, Random House, 1989. Bryan Appleyard: extract from *The Pleasures of Peace: Art and Imagination in Post-War Britain*, Faber and Faber, 1989. Lorenza Trucchi: extracts *Francis Bacon*, Harry N. Abrams, 1975. Joan Wyndham: extract from *Anything Once*, Sinclair-Stevenson, 1991. Peter Fuller: extract from *The Cambridge Guide to the Arts in Britain: Vol. 9: Since the Second World War*, Cambridge University Press, 1988.

The author and publishers would also like to thank the following institutions, publishers, magazines and newspapers, which have given permission for reprinting quoted material. Permission from the Tate Gallery to reprint extracts from Francis Bacon's introduction to the catalogue of the Matthew Smith retrospective exhibition of 1953 and from John Rothenstein's introduction to the catalogue of the Francis Bacon retrospective exhibition of 1962. Permission from the Fortune Press to reprint an extract from Christopher Lee's poem, 'A. R. P.', from *The Secret Field*. Permission from *Encounter* to reprint Lawrence Raab's copyright poem, 'Figure with Hypodermic Syringe'. Permission from Thames & Hudson to reprint the following copyright material: extracts from John Russell, *Francis Bacon*, 1978; from Andrew Forge and Dawn Ades, *Francis Bacon*, 1985; fromn Michel Leiris, *Francis Bacon*, 1988; from Sam Hunter and Lawrence Gowing, *Francis Bacon*, 1989; and from Robert Hughes, *The Shock of the New*, 1991. Permissions from *The Burlington Magazine* to reprint Anita Brookner's criticism of a Francis Bacon exhibition of July, 1962, and from *The Radio Times* for extracts from Brian Sewell, 'The Loaded Brush', of 10 November 1984. Permission from *The Times* to reprint the following copyright material: extracts from Richard Cork's analysis of Bacon's first Triptych of the Crucifixion hanging in the Tate Gallery, printed on 8 May 1992, and from his interview with Francis Bacon in October, 1972; also extracts from Pierre Schneider's piece on Francis Bacon, printed on 7 November 1971. Permission from the *Evening Standard* to reprint a copyright extract from Brian Sewell's article on Francis Bacon, printed on 28 April 1992. Permission from the *Observer* to reprint a copyright extract from Nigel Gosling's article on Francis Bacon, printed on 5 March, 1967. Permission from the *Daily Telegraph* to reprint a copyright extract from Richard Dorment's piece on Francis Bacon, printed on 3 February 1989. And permission from the *Sunday Telegraph* to reprint copyright extracts from John McEwan on Francis Bacon, printed on 3 May 1992.

Prologue

Because he did not go to Moscow, Francis Bacon was able to see me. He came into The Groucho on the balls of his feet with the spring and the bounce in his step of a young man. He was nearly eighty years old, but his round face with taut skin and imperious green gaze was that of a young commander. After the inquisition of his eyes, the gestures illustrated the artist. The hands were those of a worker, square with strong fingers, but he used them to demonstrate the points of his piercing intelligence as if he were a French logician. His clothes were casual and elegant and practical; he might have been a yachtsman come to port in Soho. Hypnotic as the Ancient Mariner, he told me something of his life.

We spent four hours together and consumed four bottles of champagne. Although I managed to pay for one, the rest were his gift to our interview. He settled the bill with fifty pound notes taken from a roll in his pocket. He was prodigal in his generosity and impatient of his time. Trying and failing to connect at the beginning, he consulted his watch every few minutes, as though he had to leap up and go. But as he grew interested in the war culture of the 1940s, the subject of my book, and in the Greek dramatists and in reminiscences of Soho and Limehouse, where I had also lived, he forgot the passing hours and spoke with amazing fluency and frankness, with only a slight lisp or momentary stutter making him pause upon a syllable – which, on one occasion, caused me to misquote his quotation from Aeschylus about blood smiling rather than blood spilling.

For he allowed me to take notes as he spoke, a rarity with him and a sign of trust. He had appreciated some of my books and knew of me as a neighbour at times, and a social historian. His easy manner and deprecating charm did not hide an incisive wit and adamant philosophy. He had reached the ultimate stage in life when he knew what he was doing and described precisely why he did it. His 'ordered chaos' and 'rules of chance' in the sensation of painting reminded me strongly of Baudelaire and Verlaine and Rimbaud, all of whom he admired, with their 'fixing of vertigos' and 'the reasoned unreason of the senses'. As he talked of Michelangelo and Ingres, and of trying to recreate the voluptuous feeling of male flesh, I remembered Baudelaire's call for '*luxe, calme et volupté*'. Bacon told me that he had achieved that, in his last love, in his optimism about nothing and in exhilarated despair – practised phrases that he had used with other people. He really seemed not only the supreme master of the use of paint of his age, but also the captain at last of his long yawing about the futility of life. If his answer to dying was hard work and hedonism, he was holding the Grim Reaper in perpetual check.

He changed my life as he had those of many other people. It was not so much his pictures, although they captured in his snare of the moment both the history of his time and his autobiography, which could translate in images his personal feelings into the private survivals of countless millions of his viewers. Those transcendent Baconian figures of the twentieth century meant less to me than this dominant little man, whose courage in his honest and reckless pursuit of the life of the *artiste damné*, and his fierce dedication to the fact of his work, reminded me of the clarion call of my young days, the men sitting round a table in *The Plague* by Camus, discussing what a *métier* was. The *métier* was the only reason to live when the plague came. Yet Bacon went further than *The Plague*. He reminded me of what Camus had written about Meursault, the hero of *The Outsider*: 'For me, Meursault is not a reject, but a poor and naked man, in love with a sun that casts no shadows. Far from lacking all sensibility, he is driven by a tenacious and therefore profound passion, the passion for an absolute and for truth. This truth is as yet a negative one, a truth born of living and feeling, but without which no triumph over the self or over the world will ever be possible.'

To me, as to everyone else in his later life, Bacon denied that there was any message in his pictures. He painted by instinct, by feeling, by hazard. What appeared was not a conscious work of art. Bacon did not lie, he was openness itself. But he chose to deny the directive of the unconscious, the sorting-house of the mind in the selection of the remembered image, the imperative of the sifting of time past at the moment that his hand moved the brush. When I pointed out to Bacon that some critics had even called him a mannerist within the formal European tradition, he laughed and said, with the self-mockery of the Anglo-Irish gentleman he was, 'Well, they would say that of me, wouldn't they? The English, they've always hated my pictures over here.'

I have never spent a more illuminating four hours in my life. Although I met Bacon on many other occasions, this was the only time we talked at length and in depth. We corresponded, and he liked the historian and classicist in me. Although he did not want his biography written for reasons that will be explained, we were both concerned in depicting the history of our times. That was our common ground. Just before his death I had written to him, enclosing a copy of my translations from *The Greek Anthology* and asking to meet him again as I was writing the account of his life and times. Tragically, there was no response. He died in Madrid.

It is a failure of writers that they cannot paint. A close friend and rival of Bacon's for the affections of the Australian painter Roy de Maistre, the novelist Patrick White, described how he always wanted to be an artist and not have to sit in front of a grey blank piece of paper every morning. Action was all, the smearing of the paint on the canvas, as Bacon triumphantly demonstrated. I also had tried to be an artist. In fact at school, another enthusiast for Bacon, Lord Gowrie, had bought one of my early paintings and declared that I should have been a painter, not a writer. I should probably have been neither, but it is too late now. I have my *métier*, as Bacon most certainly had his. My unique job is to try and describe the history and violent life of this genius, the supreme painter of the century.

I

An Awareness of War

> A man that is young in years may be old in hours, if he have lost no time. But that happeneth rarely. Generally, youth is like the first cogitations, not so wise as the second. For there is a youth in thoughts as well as in ages. And yet the invention of young men is more lively than that of the old; and imaginations stream into their minds better, and as it were more divinely. Natures that have much heat, and great and violent desires and perturbations, are not ripe for action till they have passed the meridian of their years.
>
> 'Of Youth and Age'
> by Francis Bacon, Lord Verulam,
> Viscount St. Albans

'The mind is like a sieve,' the painter, Francis Bacon, once said. That sieve he used to strain from his memory the grit and splinters of a violent age. The structure of the human brain makes us record each and every image that we see. Yet our recollection is the mesh on which those million on million pictures of the past are sifted for the benefit of the conscious present. Our intelligence chooses one image among a multitude to describe or to depict. 'We saw that,' we say. Or we draw it, if we have the gift. Francis Bacon selected and set down the fear and the aggression of his century, so much out of kelter and true.

The first memory that he relished was of painting as war and deceit. He came to live in London at the age of five, where he remembered his father telling him that the First World War had begun. His father had a job in the War Office. They lived near Hyde Park at Westbourne Terrace, and Francis Bacon remembered that military men would spray the ground with something phosphorescent out of watering-cans, so that the grass glittered in zig-zags on the rough blades. When a black-out was enforced, this device was meant to persuade the German Zeppelins and Gothas into thinking that the luminous Park was a residential area which had left its lights on. Then the bombs would rain down on the innocent worms. This camouflage did not work, although its memory was to recur in Bacon's later use of rough canvas and paint.

A still earlier memory was of a British cavalry regiment galloping up the drive of his father's training establishment near the Curragh just before the outbreak of the First World War. The horsemen were on manoeuvres, waiting to mobilize for that conflict in Europe or to intervene in Ulster, which was already preparing for a civil war in Ireland. Bacon's father, Anthony Edward Mortimer Bacon, had started his army career not as a mounted soldier, but as an infantryman. He had been born in Adelaide in South Australia in 1870, the son of Alice Lawrence of that city and Captain Edward Bacon of Eyewood in Herefordshire, whose father had been urged by Queen Victoria to take up the lapsed title of Lord Oxford. The title came, by direct descent, from the original philosopher and statesman Francis Bacon, Lord Verulam – only he could not afford it. Anthony Bacon had been educated at the semi-military public school of Wellington and had joined the Durham Light Infantry. He rose to the rank of lieutenant and accompanied his regiment to Buttevant in County Cork, where he had his first taste of Irish hunting with the Duhallow Hounds. Later, the regiment was posted to Dublin, where Anthony Bacon became a close friend of Captain James Barry, the ADC to Earl Cadogan, then Lord Lieutenant of Ireland, and the son of the Lord Justice of Appeal who styled himself the O'Barrymore of the Galtees. The Barrys were 'Castle Catholics', content to co-operate with members of the Protestant Ascendancy such as Anthony Bacon, who took up Barry's passion for horses and hunting.

The Boer War, however, proved the climacteric time in the life of Francis Bacon's father. Now gazetted a captain, he was shipped with his battalion to South Africa in 1902 to avenge the defeats at Colenso and Spion Kop. Ladysmith was still under siege, and more bloody fighting was necessary to break the Boer defences on the way there. General Redvers Buller launched the Durham Light Infantry on a frontal attack on the ridge at Vaal Krantz that proved as desperate a charge for the regiment as its assault at Inkerman in the Crimean War. The soldiers had to attack over a pontoon bridge that crossed the Tugela River. 'It was rather a stiff job,' the commander of the Light Brigade wrote in understatement, 'and the Durham Light Infantry at first were a bit staggered at the heavy fire which greeted them. But they pulled themselves together, and covered by accurate shelling and closely supported by the Rifle Brigade, they breasted the hill splendidly.' The infantry had to spend the night in shallow trenches or *schanzes*, bombarded by pom-poms and fusillades of Mauser rifle fire. The next day, they beat off the Boer counter-attacks through burning grass, until they were withdrawn that evening. The action had been useless, although General Buller thought the retreat was done 'uncommonly well'. Twenty officers and men were killed, seventy-six wounded, while Captain Bacon was unhurt. He would speak of his service under fire to his sons.

In the following assault on Terrace Hill, it was the turn of Hart's Irish Brigade to be shattered. It took five hundred casualties, but the advance was held 'by the eyelids' by the Durham Light Infantry, digging into the forward positions. The regiment played little further part in the actual Relief of Ladysmith and was then relegated to serve as the guardian of the railway lines from Natal to Transvaal, where the British armies were bent on the capture of the Boer capital at Pretoria. But when the Boer commanders refused to surrender with the British annexation of their Republic, Captain Bacon found himself transposed to the role of a mounted soldier, on trek for month after month, living in the saddle, sleeping on the *veldt* under a blanket and the stars, pursuing the elusive guerillas. Many of the Durham Light Infantry had been miners and had learned to ride on pit ponies. And so they could ride with their Captain, already used to stirrup and reins from his Irish hunting experience. To him, the horse became war and the pursuit of life.

At the end of the conflict, Captain Bacon found himself in the Fourth Militia Battalion of his regiment on training duties back at the depot in Newcastle-on-Tyne. There he met and married

Winifred Christina Loxley Firth. He was thirty-four years old, while she was only twenty, an heiress to a steel business and a Northumberland colliery, for her Scottish and French grandmother had married a mine-owner called Watson. The family looks came from the grandmother, who was strikingly beautiful with black hair and blue eyes and high cheekbones. She was also astute and insisted that all her children became directors of the Watson coal mines. Some of these royalties would even pass down to the grandchildren, who were partially to live on the black gold of the underground.

From her mother, Winifred Christina would also inherit an interest in the knives, forks and spoons made by the Firth company in Sheffield. Now only the façade of the business stands with a wasteland of industry behind its grinning open windows and doorless exterior. Yet in its thriving time, it was luxuriant with one ill legacy. The soot and grime of Sheffield were held to give the Firth children 'a weak chest': recent discoveries of radon, a radioactive gas within the geology of Derbyshire, revealed what affected the lungs of generations of householders in the city. Certainly the boys were afflicted, although the girls did not appear to suffer so much from bronchial problems. One of Winifred Christina's sons would die young from his bad lungs, while another, Francis Bacon, would suffer from debilitating and desperate asthma all his born days.

Winifred Christina was connected to more fortune. She was the niece of Highat Mitchell, the wife of Charles William Mitchell of Jesmond Towers, a house which Francis Bacon was to remember as not much smaller than the Palace of Westminster at the end of the tram tracks, out of the city. Her dowry and inheritance were put in trust and would keep the Bacon family together. It could hardly have existed on the pay of a junior army officer. Her mother, Winifred Margaret Firth, was also wealthy and, in 1899, had remarried a rich young man of twenty-two, Walter Loraine Bell, who was also devoted to horses and hunting and carried the horn in Devonshire.

Anthony Bacon now left the army, taking on the eventual position of Honorary Major with permission to retain and wear the prescribed uniform of scarlet with dark green facings and bugle badge. He settled in a rented property called Canney Court near Brannockstown village in County Kildare. Situated near the army barracks at the Curragh, it was a racing and horse-breeding establishment for the British cavalry, a plain square house with extensive stables and quarters for the grooms. Bacon now registered his racing colours and was to win occasionally at the Punchestown Races with his wife's brother, 'Ginger' Leslie Loxley Firth, in the saddle. His first son, Harley Bacon, was born in a nursing home in Dublin in 1905. And Anthony Bacon's friend, James Barry, persuaded his wife's mother, Winifred Bell, and her rich young husband to move into the family country house, Lismany near Ballinasloe, where Walter Loraine Bell became Master of the East Galway Hounds. Barry could now ride with his friend Bacon and his mother-in-law to the meets with the Earl of Clancarty, then under the protection of the bankruptcy courts, and his Countess, who had been Belle Bilton of the Empire Theatre. Lismany was a two-storey great house with an irregular façade of gables and Tudor-Revival and Georgian windows with rusticated surrounds and three-sided bow fronts. The estate was large, some twenty-nine thousand acres, and Mrs Bell was famous for the children's parties she gave for Harley and his friends.

In 1908, Walter Loraine Bell became the Joint Master of the Duhallow Hunt which Anthony Bacon had followed on his first posting to Ireland. The Bells moved to a rented house called Belleview near Mallow in County Cork. A year later on the 28th of October, Winifred Christina Bacon bore her second son, Francis, during the week of the Dublin Horse Show in a nursing home at 63 Lower Baggot Street, in the capital. 'It is as natural to die as to be born,' his distant ancestor Francis Bacon, Lord Verulam, had written in his *Essays*, 'and to a little infant, perhaps, the one is as painful as the other.' The place of the infant's birth was, indeed, a route to stealthy murder, which he later heard told as a child. In 1920 on Bloody Sunday in November, during the time of the troubles before the independence of Ireland, Sinn Fein gunmen killed fourteen British undercover officers in Dublin in their lodgings or in their beds or at their breakfast. At 92 Lower Baggot Street, a dozen armed men pistolled Captain Newbury, a Court Martial Officer, as he was climbing out of the bedroom window. His body lay half in and half out of the room in front of his pregnant wife, who later gave birth to a still-born child. At 119, another Court Martial Officer, who had been a prosecutor under the Restoration of Order in Ireland Regulations, Captain Baggally, was also shot at dawn. He had lost a leg in the First World War, and his disability became his death in the street of the English painter's first breath.

The baby boy was taken to his father's horse training establishment at Canney Court in the parish of Giltown in County Kildare, and he was baptised in the nearby St. Patrick's Church in Canalway, where his uncle 'Ginger' had the Lodge. Before the child was two years old, his father filled in the Census return for the household. He detailed the many people needed to run the great houses of Ireland in the days when horses were still the main means of transport, recreation and war. As the house and the grooms' quarters were joined under one roof, the full complement was listed:

Anthony Bacon aged 41 Capt. late Durham Light Infantry, born Australia
Winifred Bacon aged 27 born England, married 7 years, 2 children
Harley Bacon aged 6 born Dublin city
Francis Bacon aged 1 born Dublin city
Reginald Bora aged 24 C. of E. groom born England
Delia Murray aged 27 R.C. parlour maid born Co. Westmeath
Mary Flynn aged 26 R.C. housemaid born Co. Wicklow
Annie Gahan aged 20 R.C. cook born Co. Louth
Jessie Lightfoot aged 34 C. of E. nurse born England
John Boylan aged 50 R.C. head groom single born Co. Kerry
George Blong aged 46 R.C. groom married born King's County
Thomas Lynch aged 17 R.C. groom single born Co. Kildare
Robert Bell aged 24 R.C. groom single born Co. Kildare
Thomas Carey aged 20 R.C. groom single born King's County
Daniel Meany aged 19 R.C. groom single born Co. Kildare
Joseph Bagghall aged 19 R.C. groom single born Dublin city
Conrad Blackwell aged 17 C. of E. groom single born England
Joseph Goodchild aged 19 C. of E. groom single born England

From his cradle, Francis Bacon was brought up in sight of the rearing of horses and the culture of the stable. Before the division of Ireland that began in the Protestant uprising in Ulster in 1913, the great houses mixed Roman Catholic and Church of England believers with abandon. The thing was for servants to believe, and so serve and obey. The two housemaids and the cook were Catholic, the nurse an English Protestant. Seven Catholic grooms were matched by three young English grooms. The Protestant Ascendancy had ruled in Ireland for two-hundred-and-fifty years since Cromwell's ruthless invasion and the Battle of the Boyne, and the flight to France of the 'Wild Geese' Catholic army after the fall of Limerick. Now the Protestants held most of the land, certainly within the Pale around Dublin, where Ireland was ruled from the Castle. Home Rule seemed far better than Independence to most of the governing classes. 'In Ireland there was a common Irishness,' a historian of the Anglo-Irish, Michael McConville, has written, 'but one part of the country looked upon the other as "garrison" and the "garrison" regarded the other part with at best a superior benevolent affection, laced with a standing suspicion that it was superstitious and unreliable.' The centre of upper-level Anglo-Irish and Unionist social life was the Kildare Street Club in Dublin, and there Honorary Major Anthony Bacon could meet like minds, since nearly everybody had served in the army at one time or another and knew that a show of force was necessary to keep a potential Irish rebellion down. A period of military service in India generally took the place of a university in Irish county family life, while the classics in the libraries of the great houses were replaced with books on field sports and memoirs of obscure colonial campaigns.

'From childhood', C. S. Andrews, the author of *Dublin Made Me*, asserted, 'I was aware that there were two separate and immiscible kinds of citizens: the Catholics of whom I was one, and the Protestants, who were as remote and different from us as if they had been blacks and we whites. We were not acquainted with Protestants but we knew that they were there – a hostile element in the community, vaguely menacing to us.' And they did become positively menacing in 1913, when the Ulster Volunteers were organised to protest against a new Home Rule Bill which was said to mean Rome Rule. Twenty-thousand modern rifles from Germany were landed the next year at Larne in the north of Ireland, soon matched by a consignment of fifteen-hundred Mauser rifles for the Irish Volunteers, shipped by private yacht to Howth Bay in the south. Rumours of plots to seize army munitions at Armagh and Omagh and other barracks bedevilled the messes. Orders for the troops at the Curragh to move to protect military depots were misinterpreted as a surprise attack on Protestant Ulster. Brigadier-General Hubert Gough and sixty-four other cavalry officers, whose mounts were sometimes supplied by Honorary Major Bacon, sent a memorandum to Command Headquarters that they would 'respectfully and under protest prefer to be dismissed', if ordered to move north against Ulster. They were not dismissed, but there appeared to be a sort of private bargain, between the Government in London and the rebellious officers, to ignore the mutiny. This resulted in the resignation of the Secretary of State and the Prime Minister felt obliged to take over the Seals of the War Office in such a 'great public emergency'. Ireland seemed on the brink of civil conflict, although the army there was to mobilise for another one, the First World War.

That mobilisation and the Cavalry manoeuvres preceding it were among the first long-held memories of the four-year-old Francis Bacon at Canney Court, only fifteen miles from the Curragh. There were the sounds of hooves galloping in the woods nearby, the rattle of gunfire at night. But this was a distant menace, a violence that was not seen. His grandmother's husband, Walter Loraine Bell, had left the Duhallow country and had taken the Leix hounds for two seasons before the First World War. The child was terrified at Bell stringing up cats when he was drunk and making his grandmother and his mother and her brother Peter lock themselves in cupboards when the Master of the Hunt approached. He put them onto unbroken horses, so that they rode in fear of their lives. He was not only a sadist and a bully to humans, but he was known as 'Cat' Bell for his appalling cruelty to these unfortunate animals. He would throw them to the Leix Hounds in order to give the dogs a taste for blood. First, he would put the cats in sacks, and when their claws showed through, he would cut these off so that the cats could not scratch the hounds at the moment of death. Such mutilation of the flesh forever remained in the mind of the small boy, who later heard that his beloved grandmother had to divorce 'Cat' Bell for cruelty. Yet she always rode superbly, kept the same straight back and figure at fifty years old as at seventeen, and was made formidable by the hard knocks inflicted by her second husband.

The Bells had leased for eight years a large place at Farmleigh near Abbeyleix. The little Francis remembered the semi-circular bow windows and the wide view over open country. He was always to like great houses and their spaciousness, the large rooms leading through to the arc of the view outside. He later thought that perhaps it was one of the reasons why he often used curved backgrounds in his triptych paintings. The visiting of each other's houses, so important in Anglo-Irish society, also gave the child a sense of rootlessness and a taste for encounter and strange places. His mother was sociable, although his cantankerous father could keep few friends outside the Bells and the Barrys and the Firths. His rare supporter in County Kildare was Mrs 'Cub' Kennedy, who married a bloodstock breeder, and the agent of the Earl of Clonmel. She had been Doris Lumsdaine of Sydney and had known Francis Bacon's Australian grandmother. When Lord Clonmel died after being carried round each window of his stately home to say, 'Goodbye Bishopcourt', the Kennedys moved in and helped to bring up Harley and Francis Bacon with their own children. Bishopcourt, Farmleigh, Canalway Lodge and Canney Court were the four poles of the existence of the child who would be an artist.

The Kennedy daughter remembered the boy Francis. While the men said that he was rather a sissy and did not like horses, she recalled that 'we adored dressing up and talking about clothes'. His softness and sensitivity brought out the worst in his own father, who was rigid and narrow-minded and opinionated. His niece, Pamela Firth, found that he had a crushing force of personality and flew into violent rages if anything in his structured life went wrong. He would throw his boots around if they were not polished to perfection and curse at all the world. As his son Francis was to observe, he was 'an intelligent man who never developed his intellect at all'. He believed in training his children as he did his horses for an army career. In fact, Francis only appeared to dislike the discipline and bigotry of his male parent. He would later recognise that he felt a sexual attraction to his father when he was a child.

The boy loved his mother, who was warm and outgoing, although as conventional as his father. She was excessively tidy, even dusting the tops of doors. She always remained cool and upright and unflustered, detaching herself from her husband's wrath. She never moved her neck, but turned her whole body to look round or to speak. 'My dear, you are making a *big* mistake . . .' was her favourite phrase. She was not maternal to Francis, but shared her love between him, his elder brother Harley and younger one, Edward, who was to die early, at the age of four years old, from his weak chest. This death caused the only display of emotion that Francis ever saw in his father, who loved his smallest son – perhaps because Edward was at the age where he could only give love without conditions and in ignorance. Edward was buried in Kildare near his grandmother's house. But Francis's elder brother Harley was a kind of protection, and the first happy memory recorded by Francis was parading along an avenue of cypresses, enveloped in the snuggery of his brother's bicycling cape, unusual comfort in a hostile world.

The mobilisation in Ireland for the First World War led to an upheaval in the life of the Bacon family. Something like a wave of relief and patriotism swept the country. It was no longer to be a war of brother against brother in Ireland, but a united stand against the despotic Hun, who had occupied little Belgium as the English had Ireland. Among the allies over the water was Catholic France, where the Wild Geese had fled more than two centuries before in order to continue their long struggle against the English. But this time, outside the Irish Volunteers and the nascent Irish Republican Army, there was a flocking to the colours. In the eighteenth century, almost half-a-million Irishmen crossed the seas to serve in foreign wars, and fifty thousand fell in battles such as Fontenoy, fighting the English. In the First World War, another half-million Irishmen fought for the British Army and another fifty-thousand were killed over four years in that decimation. As the song went:

For we carried our packs for Marshal Saxe
When Louis was our King,
But Douglas Haig's our marshal now
And we're King George's men,
And after a hundred and seventy years
We're fighting for France again.

The Irish had long tolerated the presence of the occupying British Army rather as the Jews tolerated the Roman legions in the Holy Land at the time of Christ. For generations, many families had sent their sons to serve in that army from tradition and economic necessity. Ireland was administered as one of seven commands that covered the British Isles. The regular establishment was thirty-thousand men, consisting of two regular infantry divisions and a cavalry brigade, concentrated mainly on Dublin and Cork and the Curragh. The 3rd Cavalry Brigade, which performed its manoeuvres in the woods near Canney Court, had its headquarters at the Curragh and two of its regiments, the 16th Lancers and the 4th Hussars, while the third regiment of the 5th Lancers was at Marlborough Barracks in Dublin. Included in the Formation was a brigade of the Royal Horse Artillery with two batteries, one field troop of signals and one of engineers. These batteries were the first rumble of big guns that the child Francis Bacon heard in the prelude to the First World War.

The mobilisation of the British Army in the United Kingdom and Ireland was ordered on Tuesday afternoon, 4 August 1914. Although the Galway Races were proceeding, the officers and men had been kept in the barracks over the Bank Holiday weekend against such an eventuality. 'It was a warm, calm evening,' the commander of the Connaught Rangers recalled, 'a veritable calm before the storm. After years of work we could set all this machinery in motion by one word, "mobilise".' That machinery and that mobilisation ended the effective presence of the British Army in Ireland, except for Ulster in the north. The regular establishment was reduced to a few thousand men, while another three divisions were authorised by Lord Kitchener to be recruited, one in Ulster and two in the South. 'The stoutest men from hill, valley, and town came pressing into the British Army,' Sean O'Casey noted. 'Long columns of armed Irishmen went swinging past Liberty Hall down to the ships at the quays waiting to take them to a poppy-mobbed grave in Flanders.' The Connaught Rangers marched out of Boulogne towards their end in the trenches singing an unknown song called *Tipperary*, which became the nostalgic refrain of the war.

The child Francis Bacon watched the soldiers leave the Curragh for Flanders, the cavalry and the 14th Infantry Brigade, the Suffolks and the East Surreys, the Manchester Regiment and the Duke of Cornwall's Light Infantry. But his father could not join them, much as he wanted to serve, particularly in the regiments which sometimes rode the horses he bred. Honorary Major Bacon was too old, at forty-four, to be required to fight in Flanders, and he had quarrelled with too many of the cavalry officers and his neighbours to be thought a desirable recruit. The only post he was offered was at the Territorial Force Records Office at London Wall, where he would serve under a retired Colonel Adamson and administer the organisation of the London and City of London Territorials, a job which suited his rigorous and limited mind. It was hardly a heroic role for the Boer War veteran, but it put him in uniform at a time when to be out of it appeared to be cowardice. On the Army List, he was given the title of Temporary Captain, also Honorary Major retired, Special Reserve. At least, he was again serving his country in some capacity.

Like so many of the terraces of London, Westbourne Terrace was a series of oblong boxes, like gigantic coffins stacked one on top of the other to the height of four storeys – in a sense a mausoleum for the living. Francis Bacon's father rented a house there for his family, while he worked at the War Office. There were no large views over the rolling green fields, only the wide black trench of the street. Along that rut, the double-decker motor-buses ran, the same as those which had brought soldiers to the defence of Paris at the Marne, also a few private motor-cars with monstrous flapping bags of coal-gas attached to their roofs for fuel; and increasingly the mud-coloured ambulances stained with their red crosses – the image of blood against the ochre of earth – ferrying the wounded to hospital from nearby Paddington Station.

There was an escape and an excitement for the child Francis, pretty now at the age of six, with fair hair and pouting lips, but very small and over-sensitive: a silent boy who took in all he saw. To him, the curves of the great grimy glass roof of Paddington Station, on its wrought-iron ribs, was another transparent curvature in front of the sky – like the bay back windows of Farmleigh. Only all was in soft focus now, the steam rising from the panting engines, the soot and the grime floating in the air and coating clothes and bricks and carriages. The vast station hall was not an enclosure before a bright country, but a barrier against an enveloping darkness. And from the trains, the troops came out in their drab new colours, the khaki adopted by the Tommies in the Boer War, and the blue-black uniforms and *képis* of the Belgians. They emerged from crowded compartments as long and narrow as the rooms of Westbourne Terrace. Their rifles drew hard lines against the right angles and edges of the steam engines and carriages. Their packs were square hunchbacks. Their faces and bodies materialised from an obscurity and gloom, and they returned to that same murk. As one traveller from Dublin noted after a journey on the mail-boat *Ulster*, zig-zagging across the Irish Sea to avoid German submarines, 'In London I came into the penumbra, the partial shadow, the shadow behind the shadow . . . At night the shadow thickened. You moved through dark streets, peered into shaded shops, as into caverns of light, went on again in the darkness, looked up at a sky that no longer held the glare of a city.'

Yet the London stations were also the escape route to the north and Jesmond Towers, where the young Francis first wondered at art and paintings. His wealthy great-aunt Highat Mitchell had married an enthusiast for the Pre-Raphaelites; her husband Charles Mitchell himself imitated their style in his own pictures, which he hung with other Victorian masterpieces in the enormous ballroom of the mansion. There the small boy could see the defined flow and rich, sombre colours of the Pre-Raphaelite school, and he would first understand that paintings could be a part of family being, not just the still lives that hung dead on museum walls, where his philistine father hardly took him. Life at Jesmond Towers was luxurious and grand. Mrs Mitchell rented Bamburgh Castle one summer and asked all her relatives to stay with her in that stronghold for the impressionable young. What with the grandeur of the northern mansion and fortress, the small Francis acquired a Gothic sense of opulence and ruin on a larger scale even than he had seen in the great houses of Ireland.

The Park at the bottom of Westbourne Terrace, however, was the daily delight and panorama of the small boy. He recorded the military efforts to camouflage the grass and create the illusion of city lights where none were. Another effort to deceive enemy bombers was an equal failure. The lake in St. James's Park was drained and dried out so that the reflection from the water might not signal to the skies nearby Buckingham Palace and Whitehall. The bed of the lake was even covered with huts to house civil servants, whose job was to prevent trading with the enemy. But the Thames could not be drained, and as its glistening serpentine skin was inscribed on every German raider's map, no removal of the sheen of water could prevent an aerial navigator from finding the heart of the metropolis by following the bends of the river, especially as the shining railway tracks also led straight from the counties into Euston and Paddington, Victoria and Waterloo.

Along the Thames and in Hyde Park itself, barrages and lines of shell bursts were set up for anti-aircraft guns. These deterrents against bombers were given fancy names such as 'The Ace of Spades' and 'Mary Jane' and 'No Trumps' and 'Cold Feet'. They were ineffective against the first raiders, the gas-filled Zeppelins, which flew with impunity at an altitude of twenty-thousand feet. In fact, the ineffective anti-aircraft batteries caused more damage to the people of London than they ever inflicted on German dirigibles and aeroplanes. The London guns could fire as many as forty-thousand 3-inch shells in a single night against the high-flying Germans. Of the fifteen-hundred civilians killed by air raids in the whole First World War, one-third of the casualties resulted from the half-a-million fair-sized pieces of metal that rained down from the heavens when the mighty barrages were let loose. Winston Churchill denounced the defence system of the capital as the instruments of self-bombardment. These shell fragments and shrapnel were collected by the child Francis in Hyde Park near the Hotchkiss six-pounder in the wide open space to the east, and below the searchlight on the top of the gate at Hyde Park Corner, or on the emergency landing strip cleared for fighter planes. They were souvenirs to swap with his brother Harley and the other boys, but also a reminder for life of how easily and at random death might topple from above.

Yet the most enduring image of war in the boy's mind was the unnecessary defence against low-flying aircraft installed in the Park.

Square struts with cross-bars were erected to grid the atmosphere, to confine the air. They trailed high wires in a see-through skirt. This balloon apron was indelibly printed on the child's memory as a box against existence, a futile sketch in metal versus an invisible foe. Steel nets were also draped over the National Gallery and the War Office and Buckingham Palace, although Queen Mary thought the flimsy mesh no better than the wire round a poultry run. As useless as the balloon apron, the steel nets did portray the city snared and trapped within a delusion of precaution. The statue of Charles the First in Trafalgar Square was surrounded by a cube of sandbags, as were the tombs of the kings and queens in Westminster Abbey. So would the future artist Francis Bacon imprison his screaming pope.

Perhaps most real and most deceptive to Francis were the exhibition trenches dug in Kensington Gardens to boost morale on the home front. They were clean and dry with squared sides and sandbags stacked in regular rows. Those who had been in the trenches in Flanders, such as the poet Wilfred Owen, called the Park trenches 'the laughing stock of the army'. The actual ones were crooked, improvised and dark, muddy and smelly with the reek of decay. And young as he was, Francis Bacon would have noticed the subterfuge. For he was truly a child of the twentieth century, the heir of the newsreel and the photograph. He saw the truth of trench warfare in black and white, the haphazard and the ramshackle structures, the mud and the danger and the dying. From that awareness, he would often choose the monochrome and the snapshot as an insight into reality rather than the many-coloured surface of what he could see, which might be only propaganda.

The warnings of air raids further unsettled the boy in Westbourne Terrace. At the beginning of the war, the only alarms were sounded by constables on foot or bicycle, ringing bells with TAKE COVER placards hanging round their necks. They would reappear at the end of the air raid with ALL CLEAR on the signs, while Boy Scouts and the Church Lads Brigade sounded bugle calls of relief, and the engine-drivers played cock-a-doodle-do on their train whistles in Paddington Station. But after a while, maroons were set off, their series of bangs making noises like the bomb explosions which they were meant to announce. Then there would be the rolling drum taps and dull chatter of the distant anti-aircraft barrages and the louder thumps of the Hyde Park battery. And even more frightening was the fizz and high-pitched whine of a dropping bomb and the curious soft thud of its explosion nearby. And worst of all for a child – until then reared in the country – would be the barking of dogs and screech of cats, who sensed the hum of the engines of the bombers before the humans heard and voiced their shrill fear of death to come.

The boy had the opportunity to inspect some of the damage in central London, for the local devastation became the favoured tour of the sightseer and the curious. There was the bomb from the notorious Silent Raid by a Zeppelin, which blew a hole twelve-feet deep outside Swan and Edgar's in Piccadilly Circus, and blasted the famous actor Charles Hawtrey, then playing in *The Saving Grace* at the Garrick Theatre, clean through the door of the Trocadero. There were the exposed girders of the explosion at the Odham's Printing Works, and the black square holes of the stage doors blown away at the back of the Strand Theatre. The bombs eviscerated houses and exposed the innards of family lives. But most bizarre were the twisted pipes and intestines of underground London, visible on the Embankment in the early September of 1917, with slabs and blocks of stone strewn up to the pedestal on which a Sphinx lay with her inscrutable smile looking along the raiders' path down the Thames.

From the windows of Westbourne Terrace, however, the nights were the most illuminating and unforgettable. For the beams of the searchlights would criss-cross the sky and score the darkness in triangles and lozenges and sharp, shifting patterns. It was a geometry of brightness, a light show that encased the dark briefly. And the moon itself was at first the defender and then the instigator of the air raids. The Zeppelins were afraid of it, because they became too visible as they sailed sky-high and mute above the metropolis. But the moon was the friend of the bi-plane Gothas and Giants, which followed the huge dirigibles in their assault on the capital. They would drop their bombs more accurately during the periods of the Hunter's Moon and the September Harvest Moon, when they killed and wounded ninety people in front of the main entrance to the

Bedford Hotel in Southampton Row and on the full moon, when a large bomb of 660 pounds destroyed the basement beneath Odham's in Long Acre, crowded with Londoners seeking shelter there. The bright sky was the signal of mass murder.

Yet perhaps for the child, the black-out was the ultimate fear, a daily terror that lasted all the years of the long world war. Street lights were reduced and shaded. The interiors of trains and buses were darkened into a miasma. Blinds had to be drawn across windows before lights were switched on inside houses. Time seemed to have stopped in the evenings and the early hours. Even the face of Big Ben was kept sombre, and the counting of the ominous hours over London could no longer be seen. There was only a dull gleam on the pavement on starry nights, and the road was no brighter than a country lane. Bodies of people would loom out of the obscurity and disappear again. Throughout the future portraits by Francis Bacon, distorted figures would emerge from a fearful night, as sudden and grotesque as the strangers glimpsed in the dim streets of London in the black-out.

However, the keenest horror and the most terrible bogey was the Zeppelin. As Air Commodore L. E. O. Charlton testified, for the better part of two years the whole country suffered under a Zeppelin psychosis. 'Not a Zeppy night tonight, thank God,' people would say, scanning the bright sky, which they thought would protect them from the murderous dragon above:

> The Zeppelins were our tyranny during the War. On their account men showed fear before their fellow-men and were not ashamed. They laid bare our moral bones. Lacking the strength afforded by discipline and training, such as belongs to the fighting man proper, we were liable to confusion and panic. The airship approach was furtive, essentially that of a night animal, and much more unmanning than the full-speed dash of the Gotha and the Giant which tipped and ran. There was black magic in the monosyllable 'Zep,' and just as mothers would say 'Napoleon' to make their children good a century ago, so now did they modernize the threat. The airship could be noisy or silent at will, motionless or swiftly moving. Once seen, or vividly described, their monster bulk, ominously

shaped and evil looking, could obsess the mind and endow them with a fabulous power of destruction.

Seen from far below, the Zeppelins seemed like silver worms as they emerged from their cloud cover or writhed on top of a cone of searchlights. Later, their underbellies were painted black to diminish their visibility. But the children who watched them over London forever remembered the high serpent of the air and the terror that dropped from it. The Gothas and the Giants, however, looked no more threatening than flights of moths or shoals of flying fish. When the first Zeppelin was brought down in September, 1916, it burst into flames and exploded, its remnants crashing to earth near Enfield. Tens of thousands went to see the charred bodies in the wreckage: it was like Derby Day. Later that month, three more Zeppelins were brought down by fighters, one in flames over Potter's Bar. Its destruction interrupted the philosopher Bertrand Russell's first night with Lady Constance Malleson. He heard 'a shout of bestial triumph in the streets', leapt out of bed and saw the falling fiery worm illuminate the night sky. If the boy Francis was fast asleep at the time, he would have seen the pictures of the crashes or the display of Zeppelin trophies, which was put on show in Finsbury. Among them was one of the 'spy baskets' which hung below the doomed dirigibles. It looked like a torpedo with two observation windows and tail fins. It was another indelible image of war.

With the present bombardment of the senses by pictures of conflict and atrocity from television screen, magazine and tabloid newspaper, it is difficult to assess the effect of the first newsreels of war and occasional photographs of the Western Front on the mind of a hyper-sensitive boy at his most impressionable age. The present-day barrages of information and images are as useless and damaging as the half-a-million pieces of shrapnel which fell from the sky on the heads of the Londoners after an anti-aircraft fusillade. But the few black and white prints or moving pictures of war which Francis Bacon saw, for the first time between the ages of six and eight years old in London during its first blitz, imposed their impressions forever on his receptive senses. He would always see much of the truth of life in fear and wailing, darkness and bloat, distortion and violence.

As he later said, 'I was made aware of what is called the possibility of danger even at a very young age.'

His father resigned from his job at the War Office after the Armistice and took the family back to Ireland to resume his horse-training business, first at Canney Court and then at Farmleigh in County Leix, which he now rented from his wife's mother. She was an eccentric woman, in Francis Bacon's opinion, forever changing houses. 'She had a very curious relationship with my father. I think he disliked her very much, but nevertheless they were always exchanging houses.' His cousin, Pamela Firth, thought that the Bacons were always moving, always visiting. A terrible restlessness infused them all.

Yet this was no longer the Irish county society which Honorary Major Bacon had left. The Easter Rebellion of 1916 had created martyrs for Irish independence; sixteen of the leaders were executed and another thirty-five-hundred sympathisers were arrested. The battle-lines between Catholic and Church of Ireland believers were drawn. The era of the Protestant Ascendancy was ending and of the Irish rebellion beginning. Anthony Bacon was still an Honorary Major on the Special Reserve, and he may have played a part in the formation of the counter-insurgency Black and Tans, which were largely formed from those who had been Territorials, to fight the Sinn Fein and the Irish Republican Army. Certainly, his wife's mother had desperately compromised the Bacon family by taking, as her third husband, Kerry Leyne Supple, in 1917. He was the District Inspector of Police for County Kildare, one of the most dangerous and unpopular duties in all Ireland.

As Francis Bacon left his boyhood and approached puberty, his personal turmoils were played out in a land and time of troubles. 'Life is violent, though,' he said as a mature artist. 'Just the fact of being born is a ferocious event.' He grew up in Ireland with the Sinn Fein movement and lived through two world wars. 'I suppose all that leaves some impression. You can't separate life from suffering and despair.'

2

A Time of Troubles

These things are commonly not observed, but left to take their chance.

'Of the True Greatness of Kingdoms'
by Francis Bacon, Lord Verulam,
Viscount St. Albans

'I had no upbringing at all,' Francis Bacon told John Rothenstein, then Director of the Tate Gallery, in 1962, 'and I used simply to work on my father's farm near Dublin. I read almost nothing as a child – as for pictures, I was hardly aware that they existed.' Yet his asthma, an affliction he had suffered all his life, drove him to become an artist. He could breathe in, but he could not exhale. The air was trapped inside him, he could not get it out. His cousin Pamela Firth would view him fighting for breath in his bedroom, throwing his head around on the pillow, painful to watch. He was so ill from his weak chest as a child that nobody in the family expected him to live to the age of twenty-one. 'He would gasp and heave, and it was in the age before allergies were known.' It proved in the end that Francis was allergic to horses and dogs, exactly the animals which surrounded him in Ireland. What he did not yet know was that the grimy air of cities would suit his lungs better. He could breathe where others choked. 'It was his tremendous drive and defiance,' Pamela said later of him. 'He had to rebel against his family and background.' One of his fondest memories was to be those times when he was allowed morphine by his father to quiet his asthma. It gave him, with all his nervous energy, the only true relaxation he was to know lifelong, but he was never given enough to turn him into an addict.

Asthma is mainly a symptom of stress, and Francis Bacon was distressed by his rootless and dangerous childhood, and above all, by his love and hatred of his nervous and dictatorial father. 'He certainly didn't get on with his children,' Francis said, and he himself was the most unpopular of all, a silent sissy with observant eyes. He bottled up his inner resistance and could not open it. The father was so dominant in his life that the early paintings by the son were either detached abstracts or crucifixions, a testament to personal mute suffering. Only after his father's death in 1940 was Francis Bacon able to transmute his own early repression into images of universal grief. Although he remained asthmatic, he found a release from his breathlessness, as Proust did, in creation in cities. It was an expression of what was life to him.

The asthma of the child prevented his acceptance by his father, who merely thought the affliction was a weakness of character. He was forced astride a pony and made to go fox-hunting. But when he reached the meet, he started to choke on his allergy to horses and blood sports. Later in his middle age, he was to demonstrate to Lady Caroline Blackwood, then the wife of the painter Lucian Freud, that the memory still agitated him. Recalling it, he would tug at his collar as if he were trying to loosen a choking noose and he resembled 'the agonised figures in his paintings whose faces turn a truly dangerous shade of indigo purple as they go into the last stages of strangulation'. She was also told by a homosexual friend of Bacon's that he had admitted to being systematically and viciously horsewhipped by the Irish grooms in front of the father he feared and loved. This parental sadism was to haunt his sexual life. 'Surely there's nothing worse', he was to say to Lady Caroline, 'than the dusty saddle lying in the hall.'

The recurrent bouts of asthma also prevented his formal education, which was hardly helped by the nomadic style of his family, who thought that a home was like a field – the next one always greener. Although later he would say he was not in the least religious and that Christianity was a ridiculous harness to put on people, he did admit that he was 'brought up in the Protestant faith and went to church as a child'. This act was, as he later knew, a public protest against Catholicism – 'and we all *had* to go to church'. His only tutor was Lionel Fletcher, the Church of Ireland chaplain at the great house of Straffan, where his father's supporter Doris 'Cub' Kennedy stayed with her Barton relations. Francis's grandmother Winifred, now Mrs Kerry Supple, lived at Straffan Lodge with her husband, the Kildare District Inspector of the Royal Irish Constabulary. As the Reverend Fletcher was also a successful horse-dealer, the tutoring of the boy was as much in horses as Homer, although Francis did acquire a taste for Greek drama. In later life, he always expressed the regret that he had not learned ancient Greek, but his passion for Aeschylus remained. He claimed the Greek playwright was the source of his first masterpiece. Fletcher's niece was to be the mother of Lord Gowrie, who became the artist's friend in later years and claimed to share the same roots in the village in County Kildare. Francis admitted to Grey Gowrie that the memory of Ireland was both important and traumatic for him and that it did affect the paintings.

Brought up between Farmleigh with his father, Canalway Lodge with the Firths, and Straffan Lodge with his grandmother, Francis had many opportunities to fear and see the Irish rebellion which was to end with independence for all Ireland except Ulster. 'My parents were the enemy of the Sinn Fein,' he said later. 'I remember my father saying: "If they come tonight, keep quiet and say nothing."' His father did not fear being shot, but looted, with his motor-car and horses appropriated for the good of the Irish Republican Army. 'He expected to be attacked, and on all the trees you'd see the green, white and gold of the Sinn Fein flags. All the houses in our neighbourhood were being attacked.'

It was still more terrifying at Straffan Lodge. 'My grandmother was married to the Chief of Police in County Kildare and used to live with sandbagged windows and ditches dug on the road to ambush cars.' The young Francis had to be driven round the ditches through the fields to reach the Lodge. He was told that snipers would be waiting on the edges. 'I lived with my grandmother a lot. I grew up in an atmosphere of threat for a long time.' One night, he was driving with his step-grandfather Kerry Supple, when the motor-car became stuck in the Bog of Allen. Lamps flashed like will o' the wisps all around them, banshee cries sounded from one rebel band to another at the sight of their prey. The child and the police inspector had to abandon their broken-down vehicle and squelch their way to the nearest Big House. There, they were only taken inside by the owners after being vetted at the point of a gun.

To be in the Royal Irish Constabulary had been a matter of honour and prestige. Before the First World War, there had been a hundred applicants for each vacancy. The ten-thousand officers and constables were the forces of law and order, but they had local knowledge and respect. They were armed and operated from barracks and posts, but they were a recognised part of the community. The Irish rebellion changed all that. Its propagandist and guerilla leader, Michael Collins, saw that the countryside could become the property of the rebels if the Royal Irish Constabulary was frightened and humiliated. For it was mostly drawn from the Roman Catholic small farmers who occupied the land.

An anathema was passed on the police force by the Sinn Fein and its women's arm, the Cumann-na-mBan. At Mass, nobody would sit in a pew occupied by a 'peeler'. A woman who went with a policeman had her hair shaven. One woman had pig's rings put in her buttocks for supplying milk to a police barracks, and a donkey was stabbed in the forehead for carting turf there. No tradesman or farmer dared to supply the barracks. The old weapon of the boycott was enhanced by intermittent intimidation. The constable's life was spent

> in constant apprehension of danger. If he would go out of barracks, he was compelled to do so as one of a party operating in practically an enemy's country. He could never predict the moment when a hail of bullets would burst upon him from a carefully prepared ambush, his assailants being the apparently harmless citizens who surrounded him every day. Every means was employed to tempt him from his allegiance. Letters reached him warning him to resign if he wished to escape the death penalty.

The Cumann-na-mBan cursed the police with the *Aceldama* or *Field of Blood*:

> For money their hands are dipped in the blood of their people . . .
> They are the eyes and ears of the enemy.
> Let those eyes and ears know no friendship.
> Let them be outcasts in their own land.
> The blood of the martyrs shall be on them and their children's children, and they shall curse the mothers that bring them forth.

The rebellion began with sporadic assaults on the scattered police barracks, some of which were only stockades held by a dozen men. The attacks spread from the south and west to cover all Ireland. Constables were murdered on duty and off-duty, and they began to retire to their fortified district headquarters. By August 1920, a thousand constables had resigned, a tenth of the force. Meanwhile, in commemoration of the Easter Rising, Michael Collins ordered the abandoned barracks to be put to the torch, and a hundred-and-eighty-two were set ablaze. To this day, outside almost every town and many a village in Ireland stands a ruin of recent date, the quarters of the Royal Irish Constabulary.

The riposte of the British was to recruit auxiliaries for the police. The first of these took the nickname of the 'Black and Tans', later to be known by the regular British Army as the 'Blacks and Scum'. They wore the black jacket of the Royal Irish Constabulary over the khaki trousers of the Tommy, but these colours were also those of the Limerick Hunt, called the Black and Tans. This débris of the First World War treated Ireland as an occupied country to loot and terrify, while all Irishmen were murderers or 'Shinners'. Their ranks were supplemented by the more disciplined and formidable auxiliaries, who had been army officers with good records. These recruits were trained in police work at the Curragh and wore a dark green uniform with a tam o'shanter and crowned harp badge. Mobile in their armoured cars and tenders, they were intended to answer the flying columns of Michael Collins the length and breadth of Ireland.

Although the new Chief of Police, General Tudor, rearmed the Royal Irish Constabulary with rifles and machine guns, and also had the barracks fortified with steel shutters, there was a mutiny of the force at Listowel. The constables refused to hand over their quarters to the military and take up dangerous positions in the outlying countryside. And then and there, the war of atrocity was declared official by a one-armed veteran, Colonel Smyth, the Divisional Commander for Munster. 'Now, men,' he announced, 'Sinn Fein has had all the sport up to the present, and we are going to have the sport now . . . If a police barracks is burned or if the barracks already occupied is not suitable, then the best house in the locality is to be commandeered, the occupants thrown into the gutter. Let them die there – the more the merrier. Police and military will patrol the country at least five nights a week. They are not to confine themselves to the main roads, but make across the country, lie in ambush and when civilians are seen approaching, shout "Hands up!". Should the order be not immediately obeyed, shoot and shoot with effect. If the persons approaching carry their hands in their pockets, or are in any way suspicious-looking, shoot them down.' At the end of this speech, five more constables resigned from the force.

Atrocity was now matched by atrocity, ambush by ambush. Eighty victims had been detailed by Michael Collins to be killed on Bloody Sunday, and a force of Irish Volunteers gathered on Baggot Street Bridge for this purpose; but only fourteen British officers were murdered, two in Baggot Street where Francis Bacon was born. A seventy-year-old woman, Mrs Lindsay, was torn to pieces by women of the Cumann-na-mBan for informing the British forces of an ambush. A Resident Magistrate was buried up to the neck in sand at low tide to watch the sea-water rising to drown him. Between April and June 1920, some sixty towns and villages were 'fired up' or partially wrecked by British soldiers and auxiliaries. At Templemore, the Northamptonshires raided a drink shop and a draper's, dressed in women's blouses, and burned and sacked the town. Eventually, Cork itself was put to the flame in an orgy of destruction. Curiously, the general who had led the mutiny at the Curragh before the First World War, Sir Hubert Gough, warned against government policy: 'I don't think any truthful or sane person can avoid the conclusion that the authorities are deliberately encouraging and, what is more, actually screening reprisals and "counter murder" by the armed forces of the Crown.'

Worse than the actual atrocities – for hardly more than a thousand people were killed on both sides in the rebellion and damage to property was assessed at only five-and-a-half million pounds – far worse were the rumours and fears of violence. In the words of one witness:

> Terrible tales were whispered in those final weeks of the dying year. Tales of frenzied men hunted by bloodhounds. Tales of pitiless ambushes, of police slaughtered to a man, and the bodies hacked to pieces with axes. Tales of savage reprisal followed on shameful deed, of burned shops, of deserted farms, of peasants gone to couch with fox and hare. Tales of new proclamations and new restrictions falling alike on guilty and innocent . . . Tales of gross murder of isolated police replied to by tales of blindfolded prisoners taken at dead of night to lonely places and there told they were to die, made to kneel praying and listen while a grave was dug, and this play-acting done, the victim promised life if he would say was his neighbour, the butcher, a peaceful citizen or a follower of Sinn Fein . . . Tales that the golden age of robbery had come.

As well as the tales, pictures of the atrocities were widely circulated. The same witness was shown negatives of the outrages.

> The publication of these negatives no Irish firm would risk; in fact, had their mere existence been known to the perpetrators, death would have been the certain fate of their possessor. In one, the Irish wife of a British officer, about to become a mother, was shown shot to death in the stomach. In another, an Irish girl, who had accompanied a British officer to a tennis party, lay by the roadside, her white dress drenched with blood; in his car, a few feet away, could be seen the body of her escort, riddled through and through with bullets.

These were the tales and images of the war in Ireland which Francis Bacon would have heard and seen, while he was staying with his grandmother and her police officer husband in fortified Straffan Lodge. They were even more terrifying than the images of the First World War, because this was a civil war which shattered the boy's memories of his early years before he had heard the manoeuvres and the guns of the Lancers in the dark wood. Even in Kildare, the situation had worsened. In 1919 the Sinn Fein could be countered at the elections by the Hunt Club stopping Punchestown Races, the County's great holiday, and the course where Bacon's father and uncle had so often run their horses. But by the time the boy reached twelve and the fratricidal war was being fought to a ferocious stalemate and a bitter Treaty, there was bad blood in every head and evil memories of that time. Later, Francis Bacon was to recall one incident in particular which was to influence his pictures of dead meat hanging in a butcher's shop. He retained the image of men's bodies hanging on a gate. In fact, he did not see it, he heard of it from the Supples. Every evening, a guard of members of the Royal Irish Constabulary would arrive to watch over Straffan Lodge. One dusk they failed to appear. They had been ambushed outside the great house of Lord Mayo. As they tried to escape by clambering over his locked iron gates, they were shot in the back and left to hang there.

Francis Bacon heard other tales from the maids at the Supple house. His grandmother had lost nearly all of her hair and had to wear a wig, while her husband had lost all of his. One night, the Shinners did evade the guards and reach the dining-room, where the police officer was eating with his wife. The gunmen made a noise and the couple dived under the table. Two bald heads confronted the would-be killers, who were local men and knew the Supples well. 'We can't risk shooting the lady,' they are supposed to have said before disappearing into the darkness. Hanging on the walls behind the terrified couple were the linen sheets decorated by his grandmother in her endless crewel stitch – the oblongs and lines of cages with which Francis would frame the hunted creatures of his later paintings.

There was more evidence of war in the countryside. Trees were felled across the road to stop the passage of the armoured cars. Walls were tumbled to the ground and made into pyramids of masonry to halt the police tenders. And little movable bridges were erected over the trenches dug across the highway, so that the lorries of auxiliaries could still pass through. But most horrifying were the engines of military transport, the heavy waggons filled with soldiers in tin hats, and the Crossley tenders packed with the Black and Tans. Soon the backs of the lorries were caged with wire netting as the buildings in

London had been, to protect the soldiers from lobbed grenades. In Dublin and the cities, the rebel children cried 'Chook, chook, chook!' as the police passed under their mesh. And the word was, 'The Boers put them in khaki, the Germans put the tin hats on them; but it took the Sinn Feiners to put them into cages.'

The cage round the body of the screaming pope has been a primal image in the paintings of Francis Bacon, although it is hard to tell whether the pope is shouting at the cage of his Holy Office or protesting at the cage of belief he has set about his worshippers. Bacon himself saw the cages in Hyde Park and around the monuments of London, threatened with German bombs, and he also saw the cages round the British troops and auxiliaries in Ireland. He heard of the internment camps for the Catholics at Ballykinler, where eighteen-hundred men were held in 'two big enclosures they call cages'. He knew of the Pale in which they lived, that invisible enclave around Dublin which represented Protestant rule over rebellious Catholicism. He knew of the result of the Treaty of early 1922, which caused another civil war among the Irish rebels because of the partition of the island between Ulster and Eire. He did admit to having been very interested in religious things when he was young, and he would have imbibed the Protestant bigotry against the despotic Pope, longing to oppress Protestant freedom within the power of Rome. Equally, he could see the Catholics imprisoned by the oppression of the Protestant minority and screaming to get out, as the women had in their hundreds outside the walls of Mountjoy, when the Irish captives went on hunger-strike until death. And above all, Francis Bacon screamed to liberate himself as well as those who were caged by religion or colonialism or history or war. His censorious father had set a trap about his nature and his impulses, and he howled in silence to kick free.

He could see that the great houses which he loved in Ireland were doomed along with the Protestant Ascendancy and its stern morality. The civil war between the two factions of the triumphant rebels was nastier and bloodier than the rebellion had been. The British troops handed over the Curragh and their other barracks, their armoured cars and their horses and their guns, to the forces of the Provisional Government, and then they trained their old enemies to defeat the

Irish Republican Army – a thing which they had not achieved. As Lord Birkenhead declared when he wished success in arms to the Provisional Government which had accepted the Partition Treaty, 'I would far rather that they were undertaking that task than we were . . . it will result in an economy of British lives.' Although the government army had enlisted some members of Sinn Fein who believed it was a stepping-stone to power, most of its members were demobilised regular soldiers from the First World War, armed with British weaponry and led by commanders who had fought for the British in France. By 1923, the new National Army reached a strength of sixty-thousand men, twice the size of the British Establishment keeping down Ireland at the beginning of the century. With this superiority, it did reduce the Irish Republican Army to a nuisance and only a permanent threat to partitioned Ulster. Ironically, the same heavy lorries covered with mesh and Crossley tenders would leave the fortified cities to hunt down the elusive guerillas, just as the British had done. Yet now, it was a war of the green against the green.

From Straffan Lodge and Farmleigh, the adolescent Francis Bacon watched this tragedy of internecine independence. He also watched the beginning of the end of the great houses of Ireland. The Sinn Fein gave the Firths three days to quit Canalway Lodge before they burned it. The family fled to Dublin Castle, where an uncle was in command of troops, and then on to a Georgian mansion, Cavendish Hall in an English village in Suffolk. In fact, Canalway Lodge was occupied, not burned down. But between January and November 1922, fifty country houses and mansions were destroyed. By the early spring of the next year when the Irish civil war came to an end, another eighty-nine had gone to waste and fire. The question of the protection of Loyalist houses had been asked before the Irish civil war had increased the destruction of the great houses. 'If the military reprisals go on, there will be no Loyalist houses left. How can you quell a rebellion by burning a farmer's house worth £800 when he can burn a landlord's mansion worth £20,000?' Both in the rebellion and the civil war, the guerillas revised the old system of 'coyne and livery'. Like the gallowglasses and kernes of the ancient kings of Ireland, the armed bands scoured the countryside, living free on the inhabitants, requisitioning food and money and motor-cars, driving away the cattle and looting the houses, which were also burned down. One family's house in Cork was raided on no less than seventy nights by armed youths who wore no uniform and used it as a supply base. As a contemporary Irish historian wrote:

> The motives behind these burnings were also various. Some were punishments decreed by the Irregular Executive against any who dared to serve the 'usurping Government.' Others were the work of mere bands of robbers; others again that of peasants who, on pretext of reprisals for the execution of rebels, burned down the mansion and then seized and divided up the demesne. But what was perhaps the most sinister in its significance was that, not only did the people reputed respectable in the countryside – small farmers and others – do nothing to stop these outrages, but that they often crowded to share in the plunder. As General Mulcahy said in the Dail, 'Everybody minds his business and many people take their little bit when it comes their way.'

A genealogist and chronicler of the great houses in Ireland saw in their destruction the end of many centres of civilisation and culture, such as the library containing Gaelic manuscripts in Marfield in Tipperary, the Palladian house of Summerhill in Meath once rented by Elizabeth Empress of Austria for the hunting, Desart in Kilkenny where the few salvaged treasures were looted at a road-block. 'The ruined Big House became part of the Irish landscape, best known to followers of hounds who rode across country. The Land Commission divided lawn and parkland into smallholdings of thirty acres. There was an air of triumphalism about their work, which continued for many years.' Bacon himself, at the age of ten, remembered spending a night in a haunted Irish Big House, half-mad with fear at its ghosts and impending doom.

With the levelling of the great house came the lessening of the Protestant Ascendancy. It was not wholly despoiled, but it became as irrelevant as the French aristocracy had in that sister Republic. There was emigration back to England. In 1911, there were a quarter of a million people on the rolls of the Church of Ireland; by 1926, half that number; fifty years later, less than half that. Ironically, in the twenty years after the Irish Free State was liberated from the British yoke, nearly one-third of its Catholic population also emigrated to oppressive Britain. It was hard to see what the troubles and the fight for freedom had been about.

Yet for the young Francis Bacon, also soon to return to England with his family, the turbulent days were over. He had enjoyed the visiting of the great houses, their strangeness and their style, and now they were diminished. He always kept with him, however, a picture of their extravagance and their welcome, their excess and their humour. But it was in his father's establishment at Farmleigh that he had to face his own nature in the culture of the stables, a recognition that would lead him into a bohemian way of life in those wayward quarters of cities, which hardly found his behaviour criminal or queer.

Francis Bacon said that it was only later, through the grooms and the people in the stables he had affairs with, that he realised he was sexually drawn towards his martinet of a father. While he was still a minor and an adolescent, he was made conscious of his homosexuality. It was not the usual homo-erotic fondlings of the English public school of the period. In his erratic education, Francis only attended one small public school, Dean Close in Cheltenham, for one year, and he ran away so frequently that he was not made to return. But his prettiness and smallness and love of dress and quiet ways made him an easy mark of desire to the Irish grooms, who took him as easily and brutally as a stallion might a mare. There is a rampant sexuality in a horse-breeding establishment: all is stamp and rut and whinny. It was as hard for Francis to avoid the evidence of the nature around him as it was for him to recognise the truth of his own nature.

The problem was his guilt. He knew that his father, who secretly attracted him, must never know. Or the punishment would be terrible. He was still religious at that young age and the anathema of the Church against sodomy was utter. And so was the penalty of the law. The fate of Oscar Wilde still reverberated through society on both sides of the Irish Channel. And though a quick sexual encounter was the most natural thing in the world in a place designed to breed horses, the young Francis feared the verdict of his father and the law and the Bible.

Wilde had been the Faust and the Mephistopheles of homosexuality. As Faust, he was doomed for flouting society and parading his taste for stable-boys and guttersnipes. As Mephistopheles, he was judged for enticing the young Lord Alfred Douglas and Robert Ross and other leading members of society. Before Sigmund Freud's *Three Essays on a Theory of Sexuality* of 1905 became widely read in Britain after the First World War, homosexuality was considered a disease as well as a crime. Wilde's oblique defence of it in *The Picture of Dorian Gray* was, as his leading biographer said, 'a negative version' of Wilde's own homosexual existence. The desire of boys and men for each other was seen as dangerous and evil and destructive. So the adolescent Francis Bacon saw himself, another Dorian Gray, in his early affairs.

The First World War was also fought on the home front against homosexuality. Lord Alfred Douglas himself proved particularly treacherous in equating a homosexual with a traitor. 'It is just as important to civilization', he wrote, 'that Literary England should be cleansed of sex-mongers and pedlars of the perverse, as that Flanders should be cleared of Germans.' His strictures were backed up by the *Manual of Military Law*, which set two years' imprisonment for any act of gross indecency by a male in public or in private, and ten years to life as the sentence for sodomy. During the course of the War nearly three hundred officers and men were court-martialled for indecency, including an officer in the Grenadier Guards, who was denounced by a nephew of Robert Ross. In a sense, art had been on trial in the case of Oscar Wilde, and the decadent upper-class was judged in the case of the Grenadier Officer. The equation was made plainer by the vicious antics of a Member of Parliament, Noel Billing, who claimed, as the late Senator McCarthy would with his list of American Communists, to have a Black List of 47,000 perverts reaching up to Prime Minister Asquith himself – all of them capable of treachery through blackmail by the German Secret Service. He attacked a new production of Oscar Wilde's play *Salome*, which he called 'The Cult of the Clitoris' and declared a vehicle for sexual perverts, sodomites and lesbians. It was being put on when national existence was at stake. He was sued for libel in the same way as Oscar Wilde had ill-advisedly sued the father of Lord Alfred Douglas. The trial was another trial of Wilde and had nothing to do with justice. In his summing-up, Mr Justice Darling, himself named in the Black List as a pervert, declared: 'Oscar Wilde wrote filthy works, as you know: he was guilty of filthy practices: he was convicted in this Court and suffered imprisonment, and social extinction, and death in due course . . . Well, gentlemen, it is possible to regard him as a great artiste, but he certainly was a great beast; there is no doubt about that.' The patriotic jury, confusing every issue, returned to find the Member of Parliament innocent of all charges.

The long grim war had made Wilde and decadent art and homosexuality come to seem a form of treason in most British and Irish eyes. Duff-Cooper wrote to his wife Diana that nobody at the front in Flanders spoke or thought of anything but the Billing case. She replied that Lord Albemarle had walked in to the Turf Club and had said that he had never heard 'of this Greek chap *Clitoris* they are all talking of'. But at the front, in a womanless world, the love of men for men was normal – a mere extension of the homoeroticism of the public school. So many of the leading literary figures in pre-War days had been passive or active homosexuals along with Wilde – Samuel Butler and Lord Alfred Douglas, Edward FitzGerald and A. E. Housman, John Addington Symonds and Lytton Strachey, John Maynard Keynes and Hugh Walpole, Edward Carpenter and Montague Summers, E. M. Forster and J. R. Ackerley – that the mutual love of men and boys seemed acceptable among small côteries in London.

In his confessional, *My Father and Myself*, Ackerley wrote that the army with its male relationships was simply an extension of his public school, although he never met a recognisable or self-confessed adult homosexual during the War. The penalties were simply too severe. But even the heterosexual Robert Graves in his obscure play, *But It Still Goes On*, made his hero confess to the love of men for a good-looking officer. 'He's a being apart: an officer's uniform is most attractive compared with the rough shapeless private's uniform. He becomes a sort of military queen-bee.' And then he agrees that the officer drilling the men encourages the feeling, although 'they don't realise exactly what's happening, neither does he; but it's a very strong romantic link'.

This was the strong unconscious feeling which Francis Bacon had for his father in uniform who drilled him in his early days. His escape was to the rough embrace of the grooms and stable-boys in whose arms he could indulge his love for the father he thought he hated. But he was too vulnerable not to feel guilt. He feared exposure and expulsion and even imprisonment. Especially sensitive and observant, he particularly felt as an adolescent the four crosses of the homosexual at that time – isolation and illegality, insecurity and guilt. To the end of his days, Francis Bacon would tell some friends that homosexuality was an affliction and a tragedy. At one point, it turned him into a liar and a crook. He could not talk about his homosexuality, but only conceal it. That was its shame, the acts that homosexuals were made to do by the vengeance of society, not the sexual act itself.

Two girls were born to the Bacon family in Ireland, Ianthe at Farmleigh in the March of 1919, and Winifred Kerry in August two years later at Straffan Lodge. The youngest and most unfortunate of the members of the Bacon family was named after her mother and her grandmother, and after her grandmother's third and last husband, Kerry Supple, who died that same year in 1921 of natural causes, not from the gunshot wounds of the Sinn Fein or the Irish Republican Army. Twelve years older than Ianthe and fourteen years older than Winifred Kerry, their brother Francis was hardly to have any relationship with his young sisters, except in later years to pay for the care of Winifred when she contracted multiple sclerosis and to look after Ianthe in her old age in South Africa. Generous as always, but growing distant from his kin, Francis Bacon's rift with his past began to widen with his adolescence. In later years, he would never visit Ireland again, because the memory of the turmoils of his youth and his allergies to dogs and horses brought on such severe attacks of asthma that he was likely to choke to death.

His habit of dressing up as a girl with his playmates continued. On a visit to the Firth family at Cavendish Hall with his parents, he chose as his fancy dress to be a flapper of the 'twenties. 'He was very distinctive,' Pamela Firth remembered. 'He never copied anyone.'

This time, he had his hair cut in an Eton crop, wore a beaded dress dropping straight down to his knees, put on hanging ear-rings and lipstick and high heels, and rolled his eyes while flourishing a cigarette-holder a foot long. 'Isn't Francis wonderful?' Pamela's mother said. 'Isn't he just like a girl?' But even as a child of ten years old, Pamela thought her cousin Francis was enjoying the role a little too much. And his father was simmering with fury.

The explosion happened because Francis continued to try on his mother's clothes in secret. His father discovered his son, dressed only in his wife's underwear. There was a terrible outburst of rage, which was compounded by the fact that Francis announced that he wanted 'to do nothing' at all, or if he did anything, he wanted to be an artist. It seemed to his parents that they had a small Oscar Wilde on their hands, in the conventional and patriotic equation of art and decadence and deviant behaviour. Later Bacon was to say that he had never got on with his mother or his father. 'They didn't want me to be a painter, they thought I was just a drifter, especially my mother.' There was no tradition in the family of anyone being an artist, except the amateur Charles Mitchell of Jesmond Towers, and his mother and father thought it was a form of eccentricity at the best. He would never earn a living as a painter, but equally they could not stand having a pervert in their unhappy home. So, at the age of sixteen, Francis was turned out of the Bacon house with an allowance from his mother's trust fund from the Firth Steel business of three pounds a week, enough to scrape an existence in those louche quarters of large cities which would tolerate him. Later he would say that Ireland was, anyway, a country of literature, not of paint. 'It's because of the Church, of course, that people like Joyce and, for a great deal of his time, Yeats, had to live out of Ireland.'

Rootlessness had been his way of life. His grandmother and his parents had always been changing homes, drifting from one place to another. 'My father and mother were never satisfied with where they were,' he said. They moved back to England to Linton Hall on the borders of Gloucestershire and Herefordshire, then back to Straffan Lodge, where Bacon's elder brother Harley took up permanent residence and trained horses like his father, before leaving for South Africa. The Bacons then moved back to England again to an old rectory at Bradford Peverell near Dorchester, for the Protestant Ascendancy was truly over and the great houses were withering on their foundations. Anthony Bacon's best friend, James Barry, had been a Major in the 5th Royal Irish Lancers during the War, but he still lived from hand to mouth, although he often visited his daughter at Castle Martin in Kildare near Canney Court. He himself had become a marginal figure with the collapse of Anglo-Irish society, and he could not prevent his friend Bacon from making a final return to England. Castle Martin, indeed, was left to Grey Gowrie and preserved his relationship with Francis Bacon, who never would go back to Ireland again, particularly when the last member of his family that he truly loved, his grandmother Winifred Supple, died in the grand manner during a performance of *Aida* in the Metropolitan Opera House in New York, where she was visiting her son Peter, who had fled to the United States to escape his creditors. So spendthrift and hospitable was she to the last that her estate was worth less than a thousand pounds.

In a way, his lack of formal education and his nomadic way of life had prepared the adolescent Francis Bacon for a wandering existence in the jungles of cities. He was not trained to a code or to a system of ethics. He was unused to any pattern in his life. He had hardly ever answered a roll-call or slept in a dormitory. He had served in no ranks and had never been regimented. He had preserved that curiosity and questing innocence that is the great gift of childhood. Above all, his creative growth had not been stunted by the regime of the classroom, and his extraordinary powers of observation were untrammelled by any of the blinkers which art school or college may put over young eyes in the name of a classical tradition. He had a free vision and a long insight. And he was, as Walt Whitman once wrote, 'as lawless as snowflakes'.

His father had bequeathed him one instinct: a fondness for gambling. As a child, he used to be sent to the Post Office to place a last bet before 'the off'. 'In Ireland', he said, 'there were professional gamblers who made a living out of it, but then they had very good inside information.' He himself disliked the horses and would take up playing roulette at casinos. Although it was the most stupid form of gambling, it did depend entirely on chance – an important element in the future painter's life. It was 'the peculiar feeling that the gods are with you and you are going to win.' He did not go to a casino thinking he would lose. It was the same all his life: an optimistic gamble that each occasion might turn up his lucky number – and that life was an improvisation and a bet on another day.

Moving from one rented room to another in London, often skipping without paying the landlady when his allowance ran out, Francis Bacon existed in the obscure streets of that metropolis for more than two years, still following the demands of his sexual nature that led him to the existence of an urban gypsy. He read a little Nietschze and lost the last shreds of his religious faith while contemplating some dog shit on a pavement. That was how life was, unless he made something remarkable out of it. And then one of his last connections with Irish life appeared late in 1927 to take him away to a wilder life in Berlin. He said that his patron was a 'sporting uncle', one of his father's friends, who knew of his reputation. He also said on another occasion that his father sent him to an old army friend in London, whom he hoped would teach his son to become a man. Ironically, as Bacon told it later, the ex-officer fell in love with his charge and ran off with him to Berlin. It would not have been James Barry, who was wild, but poor and heterosexual. The only relation he had with the means and the inclination to take him to Berlin was Sir Percy Loraine, who was the kinsman of Walter Loraine Bell, the second husband of Francis Bacon's grandmother. The baronet had a long connection with racing in Ireland and the army, and must have known Francis's father. Although he married briefly in 1924, it was not a success, and he left alone to serve as High Commissioner for Egypt and the Sudan. On one of his leaves, he probably took his 'nephew' of eighteen to Berlin. To this day, he is remembered for liking young men and low life, and he would have extended the experience and observation of Francis Bacon.

3
Prick in Some Flowers

> Travel, in the younger sort, is a part of education; in the elder, a part of experience . . . Let it appear that he doth not change his country manners for those of foreign parts; but only prick in some flowers of that he hath learned abroad into the customs of his own country.
>
> 'Of Travel'
> by Francis Bacon, Lord Verulam,
> Viscount St. Albans

Francis Bacon was always conscious that his ancestor and namesake, the Lord Chancellor of the reign of King James the First, was, in John Aubrey's words, a pederast. 'His Ganimeds and Favourites tooke Bribes; but his Lordship always gave Judgement *secundum aequum et bonum*': according to the just and the good. Both Francis Bacons had 'a delicate, lively, hazel Eie . . . like the Eie of a viper'. They would hold a gaze until the prey submitted. Yet the eye of the artist was that of a true chameleon spotting a fly: it would change from hazel to green to brown to blue in the light of the day. Both Bacons also shared the same pessimism about living. After looking at the dog shit on the pavement and considering the futility of living, the modern Bacon came to accept that he was alive, 'existing for a second, brushed off like flies on the wall'. It had been the same for his namesake, the Lord Chancellor, who declared in one of his poems:

> The world's a Bubble, and the life of man
> Less than a span;

In his conception wretched, from the wombe
   So to the tombe;
Curst from his cradle, and brought up to yeares
   With cares and feares.
Who then to frail mortality shall trust
But limmes in water or but writes in dust . . .

Our owne affections still at home to please
   Is a disease;
To crosse the sea to any foreine soyle,
   Perills and toyle;
Warres with their noise affright us; when they cease
   W' are worse in peace.
What then remaines? but that we still should cry
Not to be borne, or, being borne, to dye.

The nascent artist Francis Bacon did not trust to frail mortality, even at an early age, nor would he 'limme' or paint in water. But he had crossed the sea to a foreign soil with its perils and toil. It was a choice taken at the same time by other young English poets and writers, chiefly Wystan Auden, Christopher Isherwood and Stephen Spender, while one of Francis's future friends and rivals was already living there, Lucian Freud, before he came to England. The motive of the flight to Berlin was, in Auden's case, the fact that it was a homosexual Mecca, where working-class blond boys could be picked up at The Cosy Corner café at the cost of a few marks. This was also its attraction for Isherwood, who had been warned against it by an elderly relative, who said it was the vilest place since Sodom: 'For months I had been day-dreaming of it as unrealistically as a child dreams of the jungle; he hopes to meet tigers and pythons there, but doesn't expect them to hurt him. A favourite line of mine at that time – I chose to take it altogether out of the context of the play – was Iago's:

There's many a beast then, in a populous city,
And many a civil monster.

I arrived in Berlin on the lookout for civil monsters.'

He and Auden met their civil monsters, particularly Gerald

Hamilton, whom Isherwood was to immortalise in his novel, *Mr Norris Changes Trains*, with his comment that 'beauty was only *sin*-deep.' A journalist for *The Times* and a blackmailer, Hamilton had been imprisoned twice in the First World War, once for an act of gross indecency with a male, and once for anti-British activities. But as Stephen Spender wrote in his preface to his homosexual novel about Germany, *The Temple*, which he did not risk publishing in England until sixty years later when homosexuality between consenting adults was legal, young English writers and artists in the late 'twenties were more concerned with censorship than with politics. These were the last years of 'that strange Indian summer – the Weimar Republic . . . Germany seemed a paradise where there was no censorship and young Germans enjoyed extraordinary freedom in their lives.' In England, James Joyce's *Ulysses* was banned as was Radclyffe Hall's lesbian novel *The Well of Loneliness*, while D. H. Lawrence's sexually explicit paintings and drawings were removed from a London gallery wall by order of a magistrate. As young Americans such as Scott Fitzgerald and Ernest Hemingway went to France to escape Prohibition, so young English writers were fleeing repression by going to Germany. 'For them, drink; for us, sex.' Isherwood even wrote back to a woman friend in England, boasting that he was 'doing what Henry James would have done, if he had had the guts'.

There was almost an obsession among the refugee writers and artists, as Spender showed in writing *The Temple*, to describe the forbidden and the illegal, openly on show in Berlin in the clubs and the cinemas and the galleries. During the Weimar years, there was an extraordinary pricking in of the flowers of creativity. *The Douino Elegies* and *The Magic Mountain* and *Steppenwolf* and *Wozzeck* and *The Threepenny Opera* were written. *The Cabinet of Dr Caligari* and *Pandora's Box* were filmed, there were theatre productions by Piscator and Jessner and Reinhardt, while the works of George Grosz and Otto Dix were widely disseminated and Bauhaus architecture and design announced a new age of materials and the machine. There were new arts and a new language and new ideas, particularly on sexual liberation.

Another motive for Isherwood's visit to Berlin was to meet a

Jungian analyst who preached, 'There is only one sin: disobedience to the inner law of our own nature. This disobedience is the fault of those who teach us, as children, to control God (our desires) instead of giving Him room to grow.' In Isherwood's case, as he later professed in *Christopher and his Kind*, he resisted the dictates of the State and the Church and the Law to marry a woman and breed. '*My* will is to live according to my nature, and to find a place where I can be what I am . . . If boys didn't exist, I should have to invent them.'

Isherwood ended his Berlin days living with an English homosexual archaeologist suffering from syphilis, and lodging next door to Dr Magnus Hirschfield's famous Institute for Sexual Science. Its museum contained the whips and chains, decorated boots and lacy underwear of the fetishists, also photographs of perverse practices and famous homosexual couples such as Oscar Wilde and Lord Alfred Douglas. The French writer and friend of Wilde, André Gide, came to see the exhibits with Isherwood and was shown a live one of a young man with two perfect female breasts. Later the American writers, Paul and Jane Bowles, appeared, who would make Tangier their home before Francis Bacon arrived there. Dr Hirschfield campaigned for the repeal of Paragraph 175 of the German Penal Code, which officially punished homosexual acts as English law did – only it was honoured in the breach rather than in the enforcement. A Penal Reform Bill was even drafted in the Reichstag in 1929, but it was shelved because of the stock market crash and the rise of the Nazi party which was to burn the Reichstag itself and put homosexuals in concentration camps.

In the days of the Weimar Republic, in the late 'twenties, however, the attraction of Berlin was its licence. Auden mocked Isherwood in his dedication to him of his first book of poems, many written in Berlin:

Let us honour if we can
The vertical man
Though we value none
But the horizontal one.

He himself suffered from a rectal fissure dug out of his backside in the homosexual trenches of Berlin. In his poems and plays, it is called 'The Wound', as though it were contracted in the true fighting of a war.

Francis Bacon remembered Berlin in 1928 as a wide open city, but already very violent. The night life was exciting to his eyes, because he had come straight from Britain, but the violence was even more shocking as it was *emotional* violence, not the military violence he had experienced in Ireland. He described walking at night down a main street lined with side shows. It was a sexual circus. Hawkers sold the skin play inside the booths to those who could pay, while men and women mimed what might be seen inside to attract the customers. Although Bacon did not stay in Berlin for more than three months and did not see, as Isherwood did, the destruction of the Weimar Republic by the rise of Hitler, he did observe the initial clashes of the Nazis and the Communists, recalling 'there was already an atmosphere of tension and unease'.

He had only gone to Berlin, however, because he had been picked up by his 'sporting uncle'. 'One is always helped when one is young,' he said disarmingly, 'because people always like you when you are young.' He was 'what you call pretty' when he was young and had 'no trouble getting around and getting money'. He did not stay in the working-class quarters of the Hallesches Tor, where Auden and Isherwood frequented the male brothels and homosexual cafés, and he would not meet Auden until thirty years later in Rome. He stayed at the luxurious Adlon Hotel, where he remembered swans' necks arching from the four corners of the trolley as it was wheeled in for breakfast. A photograph taken of him at the time, in the gardens of Schloss Nymphenburg, shows him wearing a formal striped suit, a high collar, knotted tie and dark homburg hat. He was dressed conventionally in an erotic gymnasium. Yet 'Bacon knew a Berlin that was laid out on its back', his friend and critic John Russell wrote, 'and asked only to be pleasured over and over again'.

With his wealthy patron, Bacon did not visit The Cosy Corner, but the high-class bars of the West End. 'Here, screaming boys in drag and monocled Eton-cropped girls in dinner-jackets play-acted the high jinks of Sodom and Gomorrah,' Isherwood wrote, 'horrifying the onlookers and reassuring them that Berlin was still the most decadent city in Europe.' But there was no threat of arrest, even under paragraph 175 of the Criminal Code. The Berlin police tolerated the places. 'No customer risked arrest simply for being in them. When the bars were raided, which didn't happen often, it was only the boys who were required to show their papers.' The famous transvestite bar, the Eldorado, which Otto Dix painted in 1927, was the rage of Berlin society, and the *Berliner Journal* reported the guessing game of who was who and which sex was which: 'They don't always guess right. The techniques of dressing up, doing one's hair and make-up have achieved undreamed perfection.' Only when his patron ran off with a woman after a week did Bacon see anything of Berlin low life. He remembered particularly the cafés where a client could telephone from table to table to fix an anonymous rendez-vous.

In his most famous phrase from his *Berlin Diary*, Isherwood wrote, 'I am a camera with its shutter open, quite passive, recording, not thinking . . . Some day, all this will have to be developed, carefully printed, fixed.' It was, through the young Bacon's recording eyes and the images of the Expressionist and Weimar artists. He did not escape from the influence of Edvard Munch, whose woodcut and painting, 'The Cry', proved almost as indelible a memory as the nurse crying out with her face bloodied and glasses shattered in the Odessa Steps sequence of Eisenstein's film *The Battleship Potemkin*, which Bacon saw for the first time. His very process of detached assimilation was that of the *Neue Sachlichkeit*, or New Objectivity school of painting, which was led by Otto Dix and Christian Schad, important in Bacon's early work and in the whole work of Lucian Freud, with its meticulous depiction of every wrinkle and rib and pubic hair on the human body. One painting by Schad, his 'Woman of Berlin' of 1928, eerily forecast Bacon's later use of Cubist shapes around his portrait heads, as she looks forward from cones of lighting that make an abstract halo of angels and thorns behind her.

To see the German art of the time was also to see violence. Two years before Bacon reached the German capital, the French art dealer and friend of Proust, René Gimpel, visited Berlin and wrote in his diary that the modern artist did not 'have to understand the whole past, since his art contains it in its entirety'. Rembrandt had expressed his time: reflective, powerful, rich. Manet's pictures showed the absolute present. And as the French art dealer viewed modern painting in Berlin, he saw the present-day sensibility of Germany and future disaster. 'Furious, violent heads, drunk with blood, murderous, demonic, and not in the ancient manner but the modern: replete with the scientific, with poison gases.' The world of hate was a modern invention, laid bare on these canvases, the paintings in which the young Francis Bacon would also begin to discern the imagery which would make him the particular recorder of the violence of his century. 'The demons in the Gothic pictures are child's play beside these human, or rather these inhuman, heads of a turbulent humanity, avid for devastation, which line the walls, baring their black teeth, teeth of steel, eyes bordered by live coals, blood-tinged nostrils. They'll revel in cutting into living flesh, the Germans of tomorrow!'

This was the first modern art that Bacon saw when he went to Berlin, although the work of the German Expressionists came to his vision mainly through posters and illustrations in magazines. It would inform his own later pictures. And photography, which was always to fascinate him, was informing figurative painting. Otto Dix and Christian Schad were creating pictures that were almost clinically accurate, cloaking a vision in technical perfection. 'Photography can never record more than a moment (and then purely from the outside),' Dix once declared. 'It can never create forms which are specific and personal, for this capacity depends on the artistic powers and intuition of the painter. And so a hundred photographs of a person would produce merely a hundred different momentary views, but never the miracle of the totality.'

The year that Bacon stayed briefly in Berlin was the year that Dix painted his masterpiece, his triptych of 'Metropolis' – a form that Bacon was to use in his own depictions of human violence and corruption. In Dix's triptych, he appears himself as a war cripple hobbling into the German capital to meet a snarling dog and a row of enticing prostitutes. The central panel shows a West End night-club playing American jazz at full blast to lurid women of riches or from the streets. The musicians with their thrusting instruments dominate this dance of living death. The panel on the right portrays prostitutes in a row, flaunting themselves in front of a Baroque building, the rotten modern on parade in front of the irrelevant and flamboyant old, emphasised by a war cripple who gives an ironic salute above the severed stumps of his legs.

George Grosz's scenes of Berlin life were less detached, more a vicious comment on the human degradation inflicted by the lost World War and the following rampant inflation, a process which had culminated in the hedonistic sexuality and exhibitionism of the late 'twenties. As one commentator noted, 'By making vice safe for democracy, in the laudable effort to allow all and sundry pleasures of the more expensive kind hitherto reserved for gentlemen, the Weimar Republic focused the world's attention on Berlin as a city not of dreadful, but of disgraceful, night.' George Grosz's savage line and images that bordered on caricature were *moral* invective, a shock of awareness of the truth. In Ernst Toller's *Brokenbrow*, his drawings of Berlin street life complemented the excoriating speech of the Showman, who explained what life was all about in the city of sexual booths, which Bacon had seen.

> You must see the War's back number now. Peepshow 'the horrors of the war' won't earn sixpence. Nowadays Progress is the word. Hundred per cent. All the rage. Full steam ahead and pat me on the back. Look about you, man. Got to make good nowadays. Show your paces. Spirit of the age. Doesn't matter what it is: boxing, politics, stock exchange, golf champion, copper king, movie star, prophet, jockey, antisemite, agitator, advertising man. Business booming. Take time by the forelock. No pitch so black it won't wash off. Morality: free sample given away with every packet.

Grosz's brutal brush and pen were counterpointed by the spare and harsh lyrics sung in the night-clubs which Bacon attended with his Irish 'uncle'. There was one song which attacked the New Objectivity and the triumph of the Machine Age.

> Tomorrow they will build houses bare, wholly and utterly without façades.
> We are sick of trifling rubbish. Far too much is superfluous.

> Get rid of the furniture in the flat. Get rid of anything out of place.
> We declare without mercy, every person who happens to be there is in the way.

This criticism of the New Objectivity and the Bauhaus design of machine-made furniture, which was a factor in mass unemployment among the crafts, was not lost on Francis Bacon. Curiously enough, he liked the Bauhaus style and in his early career as an interior decorator he would adopt many of its functional principles. His chairs of steel tube and leather would be very similar in style to the current Bauhaus style of Marcel Breuer and the seat on which the 'Young Aesthete' is sitting in Karl Rössing's woodcut of 1929. Bacon was still shy and confined within many of his own repressions, and the cool and detached New Objectivity of Berlin art and the Bauhaus was attractive to him in his adolescence. He was too young and too insecure to achieve what Otto Dix had achieved in the new era, when technology and photography were being incorporated into art. Although Dix despised the age of the machine, he made himself into a machine of precision. As one critic said, 'He records the unpredictability, the diversity, the horrible violence and the grotesque grandeur of human nature, things which are of no interest to the objectively-minded businessman, engineer or surgeon. This is what was meant by the difference between style and state of mind.' Francis Bacon was introduced to the style of the New Objectivity with its precision and its detached recording of horror and violence. But as yet he would only comprehend the outward clinical lines and objects, not yet the defined technique for encapsulating all the fear and shock and loathing of the mass murder of the First World War within a formal framework.

Otto Dix had been a machine-gunner at the front, which he depicted in the same spirit of removed detail as he did himself following a tart upstairs in Brussels. Before the Nazis denounced his degenerate art, he was twice prosecuted during the Weimar years for pornography and lascivious imagery and sedition, and twice acquitted, something which would not have happened in contemporary England. Over there, nudity and homosexuality were banned from the cinema and the stage, in spite of an occasional performance of plays such as J. R. Ackerley's *The Prisoners of War*, which starred Raymond Massey in a drama which one critic noted was 'not one of depression but of repression'. In Berlin, as Christopher Isherwood saw at a costume ball, only for men and female impersonators, the great film star Conrad Veidt sat apart in tails. He had already appeared in two homosexual films, *Anders als die Andern* (*Different from the Others*) in 1919 and *Gesetze der Liebe* (*Laws of Love*) in 1927. Now he seemed 'a supernatural figure, the guardian god of these festivities, who was graciously manifesting himself to his devotees'.

This was the Berlin world of sexual liberty and new vision and detached style to which Francis Bacon was taken. He only stayed there for three months before leaving for another louche and artistic urban jungle in Paris, where he would learn the style of living as an artist and a bohemian. Yet it was in Berlin that he first encountered the gay and abandoned ways of the refugee Anglo-American writers and artists, who fled to Europe from the repressions of their own countries, to enjoy the cabaret songs and nude dances of those whom Dix painted, Anita Berber with her drug addiction and Ilse Bois, who sang:

> Without shame and without pang
> I sleep with the whole gang,
> Not just with a single gent.
> No holds barred is the modern bent.

As Bacon recalled at the end of his life, 'Berlin was a very violent place – emotionally violent, not physically – and that certainly had its effect on me.' He then denied the effect on his unconscious vision which German Expressionism had had on him. 'I wasn't the slightest bit interested in art until about 1930. I lived a very indolent life. I was absolutely free. I drifted for years.'

'If there be fuel prepared', the Lord Chancellor Bacon wrote, 'it is hard to tell whence the spark shall come that will set it on fire.' The young Francis Bacon never spoke much about the two years which he spent in Paris at the end of the 'twenties, nor about what he took away from the experience, except for an abiding love of France, particularly its food and wine and speech. He arrived at the end of October and on his nineteenth birthday he went to Montmartre in a party with the leading Chanel model, Toto Koopman. He spent the first three months of his stay living with a family in Chantilly to the north of Paris, trying to learn the language. His great-grandmother had been partially French, and he was conscious that the Paris of the time exceeded even Berlin as a refuge for British and American artists on the run, as well as a stimulant for the avant-garde.

While he was still staying at Chantilly and trying to exist on his allowance of three pounds a week from his mother, Francis would often visit the local Musée Condé. There he would stare at Poussin's 'Massacre of the Innocents'. Although the picture was celebrated at the time for its control over disturbing images of violence, Bacon was struck by 'probably the best human cry in painting'. It seemed to him then, with the victim before the massacre screaming mutely with open mouth for an impossible mercy, and dilating two pairs of eyelids to the size of begging lips, that this silent and useless protest put in paint what was shown in black and white in Munch's woodcut of 'The Cry' and the images of revolt and yelling in the film of *The Battleship Potemkin*. The latter played regularly in that *cinéaste* city, where the Surreal Cinema of Buñuel would pluck out the images of the subconscious and make them available to the mind's eye.

One other inescapable influence in the Paris of the time was acknowledged by Francis Bacon. It was Picasso, whose show he viewed at the Paul Rosenberg Gallery. 'That's when I first thought about painting,' he told his cousin Diana Watson. 'There were some very decorative still lives at that time which I liked.' The awkward and bulbous people in the Dinard bathing pictures, that floated by the beach huts, also opened his eyes to the 'possibilities of painting'. Although he did not meet either Picasso or his later friend Giacometti at that time, as he did not move in their circles, he was conscious of who they were and how artists lived their lives in Montparnasse. As John Russell wrote, he was deeply affected by the Parisian *ambience*, which largely came to an end with the financial crash of 1929. People were left alone to be themselves and life was improvisation in an age of increasing standardisation. Also, Paris was cerebral to him in the way that Berlin had been visceral.

Curiously enough, Bacon himself was studying furniture design and interior decoration more than painting. The angular furniture of Dufet and Breuer and Pierre Chareau, the lighting marketed by Damon and particularly Le Corbusier's chaise-longue of 1928, designed with Jeanneret and Perriand in hide and leather and steel, all impressed him. So did the asceptic white architecture of Le Corbusier and Chareau, Mallet-Stevens in the Seizième district and André Lurçat, whose brother Jean's geonometrical designs for rugs were also a profound influence. More than the style of Lázló Moholy-Nagy from the Bauhaus, Le Corbusier and Jean Lurçat, with their clean lines and striking colours, influenced the young Bacon in Paris.

Yet Picasso dominated the city and was to possess the first paintings of Francis Bacon. To his contemporaries, Picasso was a demi-urge, the creator of his time. For Maurice Sachs, who wrote *The Decade of Illusion*, about Paris in the 'twenties, Picasso rediscovered painting as Chaplin discovered the cinema. In the world after Freud was widely read, Picasso gave the abstract a concrete form. He realised dreams in Cubism and progressed from it to an inner realism. The unconscious flowed into the conscious to produce a visible thing; the external appearance was discarded to show an internal truth. The discoveries of Freud, the Russian Revolution, and Cubism – these gave the twentieth century unshakable foundations for future building. 'I do not seek,' Picasso said, 'I find.' This is exactly what Bacon would do in his major works, which found in flayed figures wrenched from the guts, and in screaming popes, the internal truths of his century.

In another way, Picasso's technique informed Bacon: his use of chance to reach the final result. Jean Cocteau told of him designing the stage-set for *Antigone*. Picasso had painted masks, which Cocteau had hung, but they wondered what to do with a white panel below, 'how to indicate on this surface the meaning of a chance *décor*'. Picasso rubbed a stick of red chalk over the uneven wood, which then looked like marble. With a bottle of ink, he traced designs and blackened a few spaces and three columns appeared so instantaneously that the watchers burst into applause. Picasso admitted to Cocteau that he had been surprised himself at their sudden appearance, but that 'one always calculates without realising it'. It was to be the method of Francis Bacon in his art, the use of rough surfaces and chance brush strokes to achieve the calculations he had not anticipated. It was also the method of the French bohemian poets whom he admired – Baudelaire, Verlaine and Rimbaud – to fix the vertigos, to pursue the rational unreason of the senses. Nadar's famous photograph of Baudelaire would be pinned in pride of place beside clippings of Himmler and Goëbbels from *Picture Post*, and a reproduction of Velasquez's painting of Pope Innocent X, in Bacon's later London studio.

One stage-set and artist that did appear to influence Francis Bacon in one of the first paintings that he was to sell, was André Masson's Surreal design for the Russian Ballet of *Les Présages*. The stick-like limbs of a luminous and fantastic insect were superimposed by Bacon onto a Crucifixion. As he was to say later, he wanted his pictures to look as if a human being had passed between them like a snail, leaving a trail of slime. The Surrealists believed in the vision of instinct, the choice of the unconscious. The mentor of the movement, André Breton, in his *Surrealism and Painting* of 1928, declared that 'the eye exists in a savage state.' The artist should view the world without the blinkers of convention with untamed vision and liberty to pick and discard at will. The painter should refer to interior landscapes and the inner eye. The artist's drive was for his own emancipation beyond painting. And for inspiration, he should depend on the *objet trouvé*, the random thing or postcard or photograph, which was made into a work of art itself by the artist's choice of it. Bacon always remembered his ambles along the *quais* among the booksellers from whom he bought a second-hand medical manual with beautiful hand-coloured plates of diseases of the mouth. These obsessed him as much as the screams in Poussin's painting and the film of *The Battleship Potemkin*, and he would paint studies of false teeth for months on his return to London. As a later critic of his early painting was to surmise, the first twenty years of Bacon's career as an artist was an attempt to resolve and assimilate the difference between the New Objectivity of Berlin and the Surrealism of Paris.

Although Bacon had left Berlin before the street violence had initiated the collapse of the Weimar Republic, he was in Paris when the economic crash of 1929 heralded the decline of the Decade of Illusion. He saw enough of the artists' life in Montparnasse, that swirled round The Dôme and The Rotonde, The Select and The Coupole, to know that he would like to lead it when he could afford it: a daily meeting with friends after work in the studio to drink the night away. In 1929, Alice Prin, the model and singer who was the acknowledged Queen of Montparnasse under the name of 'Kiki', wrote her memoirs at the age of twenty-eight as a valedictory to that style of life, which the refugee American writers and artists were already deserting after the Great Crash of Wall Street.

'Montparnasse, so picturesque, so colourful', she wrote. 'All the people of the earth pitched their tents here like one big family. In the morning you can see young fellows in wide trousers and fresh-cheeked young girls hurrying to the academies: Watteau, Colarossi, Grande Chaumière ... Later the *terrasses* of the cafés fill up, the porridge of the pretty Americans sits side by side with the French lemon-pickers. One looks for a ray of sunlight at The Dôme, at The Select. The models meet each other there. They are true to their trade: Aicha, Bouboule, Clara ...' And herself. And Hemingway corroborated her view of Montparnasse. The difference between the workers and the visiting bums was that the latter appeared at the cafés before noon. 'The worker goes to the café with the lonesomeness that a writer or painter has after he has worked all day and does not want to think about it until the next day but instead see people and talk about anything that is not serious and drink a little before supper. And maybe during and after supper too.'

Kiki particularly modelled for Man Ray, when he gave up painting for photography and became her lover. 'His stare is lost in pieces of crystal – in imagination – or dreaming about new photographic devices.' He and her other artist patrons, Foujita and Derain and Desnos and Kisling and Pascin, were the friends who had made the reputation of Montparnasse – then the art dealers had sustained it. 'To make a long story short, Montparnasse is a village that's as round as a circus. You get into it and you don't know just how, but getting out of it again is not so easy.'

Francis Bacon, at the age of eighteen and nineteen, was too shy to get into the life of Montparnasse, but he did observe it. His sense of isolation was only increased by taking in the easy intimacy of the artistic côteries. He did learn, however, from Man Ray and Max Ernst, of the importance of the photograph to the painter: both of them took to the camera as a relief from the palette. Even Léger had been a photographic retoucher to earn a living and had done photo montage. In 1927, the pioneer of French photography had died, Eugène Atget. His documentation over fifty years of street life had been of 'beggars, hand-organ players, shop-fronts of literally all the *métiers*, horses, women's hats, shoes, fashions in fish, in civic and military uniform'. The plates had been saved and were put on exhibition by an American photographer and commemorated by the ubiquitous American reporter of Paris, Janet Flanner, who wrote her fortnightly 'Letter from Paris' to *The New Yorker*, under the name of Genêt. She claimed that Atget was the first to show the beauty of the empty street, although Utrillo made it fashionable and used Atget's photographs to paint his canvases – complaining of their lack of perspective. That use of photographs was to be a technique of Francis Bacon's.

Another remarkable photographer, Brassaï, who was called 'the eye of Paris' by his friend and fellow night-stroller Henry Miller, examined and published the images of the hidden world of Paris. He would go, with his camera, to the brothels, gay balls and criminal bars of the city, take one picture, and toss the camera to an assistant, who would run for it while he stayed to be beaten up. His account of the 'Magic City' showed its attraction to Francis Bacon. It was there that he first met the liberated members of an international set of patrons, who would finance him to begin his career as an interior decorator. As Brassaï described them, they were Proustian characters:

> The Baron de Charlus and the tailor Jupien, every Albert and André metamorphosed for this great night into Andrée and Albertine . . .

> They arrived in small groups, after having emptied the closets of the fairer sex: dresses and corsets, hats, lingerie, wigs, jewelry, necklaces, mascara, creams and perfumes . . . Everyone wore silk flowers, garlands, ropes of pearls, feathers, trinkets . . . Of course most of them were in dressmaking, lacemaking, furs, hairdressing – creators of hats, ribbons, embroidery, fabrics, laces . . . Almost all of them had devoted their lives to dressing, beautifying, deifying women, making them seductive and attractive for others to love – for they certainly didn't.
>
> Every entrance and every costume gave rise to shrieks of surprise, cries of astonishment, of joy. They embraced, they showered each other with compliments, they admired and kissed. They camped and teased each other with squeals of delight. An immense, warm, impulsive fraternity. There were monstrous couples, grotesque couples, some were surprising and even heartwarming. Two young men wrapped in each other's arms had – to demonstrate the perfect union of their souls, their bodies – dressed in a single suit: one was wearing the jacket, with his legs and buttocks naked; the other wore the pants, his torso and feet bare, since he had given his boyfriend the only pair of shoes.
>
> Most of the couples were less well matched, however. Mature men accompanied by youths in drag were the rule . . . And I saw many enigmatic, unidentifiable creatures, floating between the poorly drawn barrier between the sexes in a sort of no man's land. There were long, fragile necks, smooth doll-like faces, peaches-and-cream complexions, platinum hair set off by a camellia or a red carnation . . .
>
> There was no ban on homosexuality in France, and the police were fairly tolerant toward 'special' night clubs. So long as the customers maintained a minimum of decent behaviour and the management kept out minors and prohibited overly blatant cruising, the police left such places alone. However, though women had always been allowed to dance together, men doing so was one of the forbidden pleasures. It's odd that in French literature, Sapphic love has always been allowed a certain dispensation, whereas up until Gide and Proust, there was a ban on love between men.

Later talking to Grey Gowrie, Francis Bacon said that he liked Proust and the beginning of 'Cities of the Plain' said all that needed to be said about being homosexual. Bacon was still trying to escape his attraction for the father he disliked, but he had not yet found a father in another man. He told Gowrie that Picasso and Yeats were the great artists of the century, and revealed that France had given him his taste for fine claret. 'Taking Francis out was, financially,' Gowrie wrote, 'like buying one of his paintings. He could be polite about anything other than Petrus, Mouton, Cheval Blanc, Margaux, Lafite, but only just.' As an older man, he worked on 'an almost Proustian sequence of paintings' about his own life, but he did not complete it, as he considered that painting and sculpture were more limited than writing and the film.

Before he returned to London from Paris in 1930, however, Francis Bacon recorded in his mind's eye the most sensational images of the cinema of his time, those created by Louis Buñuel in *Un Chien Andalou* and *L'Age d'Or*. The second film created a public outrage when it was shown in the year of Bacon's departure. Already Eisenstein's film, *The General Line*, had been banned by the Board of Censors, although *The Battleship Potemkin* was not. A new bigotry seemed to be born. A Surrealist Manifesto accompanied *L'Age d'Or*, signed by Aragon and Breton, Dali and Tzara, with drawings by Max Ernst and Miró, Man Ray and Tanguy. Its message would have pleased the young rebel in Bacon:

> It is *Love* which brings about the transition from permission to action; Love, denounced in the bourgeois demonology as the root of all evil. For Love demands the sacrifice of every other value: status, family and honour. And the failure of Love within the social framework leads to Revolt . . . In this age of so-called prosperity, the social function of *L'Age d'Or* must be to urge the oppressed to satisfy their hunger for destruction and perhaps even to cater for the masochism of the oppressor.

It was certainly homosexual love which had taken Francis Bacon to Berlin and Paris, and had made him reject the bourgeois and conventional life of his parents in Ireland and England. The images which he was to carry away from the European capitals of Germany and France were those of violence and protest and destruction, the cry and the carcass,the scream and the anger. In Buñuel's first film, *Un Chien Andalou*, the opening images showed the director himself sharpening a razor to cut open the eyeball of a young woman. Matter ran out of the sliced eyeball into its lower lid. Later, the young woman poked in the gutter with a walking-stick at a severed hand, while ants crawled out of a wound in the palm of another hand crushed in a door. But most haunting for the young artist, who was becoming anti-religious and had observed as closely as Soutine the bloody meat hanging from the hooks in the butchers' shops of Paris, was the sequence of the young lover dragging behind him a grand piano with a dead and gashed donkey lying on top, over the keyboard, and a couple of live priests: a savage eye commenting on music and the flesh and the faith. Although Bacon's early paintings were not to be accepted for the International Surrealist Exhibition in London in June, 1936, the violence of Buñuel's pictures of passion and destruction would trouble him all his life.

However attractive and relatively cheap life was in Paris, Francis Bacon found that he could not make a living there. With some knowledge of modern interior decoration and an inner vision of extreme urban images, he returned to London to earn money and find a patron and a father figure. Later he claimed that he had carried out commissions in design in Berlin and Paris. The truth is that these were the streets of his visual education. In spite of the criminality of homosexuality in London, the young artist would find there what he sought, a mentor and a marginal way of existence. He would prick in some flowers of that he had learned abroad.

4
The Chair and the Crucifixion

> Love is ever matter of comedies, and now and then of tragedies: but in life it doth much mischief; sometimes like a siren, sometimes like a fury.
>
> 'Of Love'
> by Francis Bacon, Lord Verulam,
> Viscount St. Albans

Francis Bacon was conscious that he had lived all the distorted years of the 'thirties. He had always existed through forms of violence. But the violence of life was very different from the violence in painting. 'When talking about the violence of paint, it's nothing to do with the violence of war.' It had to do with 'an attempt to remake the violence of reality itself'.

The mentor whom Francis met on his return to London had actually worked on colour combinations which might help the deranged victims of war to achieve some peace of mind. Roy de Maistre had escaped from a background of horse-breeding and a lack of early formal education as had his young protégé. Brought up on an Australian ranch by his patriarchal and wealthy father and adoring mother, Roy was the ninth child and sixth son of a large family. He had always been the sole artistic odd one out, and he was remembered as a prissy little boy who always wore a bow-tie at play and wheeled his pram of dolls through the paddocks. He was allowed to take up the study of music and art. Unable to serve long in the Australian Army during the War because of weakness and debility, he invented patterns of sky-blue and primrose and dark green floors to put shell-shocked soldiers in Red Cross Nerve Hospitals to sleep. He progressed from a psychiatry of colour to a melody of colour, in which the seven shades of the rainbow were laid against the notes of the scale. These correspondences of hues and tones were used to decorate the wards of the Nerve Hospitals and were later developed by Roy de Maistre into his schemes of interior decoration and a patented Colour Harmonising Disc to facilitate the work of artists and designers.

He sailed to Europe, to Montparnasse in Paris and to Kensington in London, where he met the young Bacon. They moved into a converted garage in 7 Queensberry Mews West in South Kensington, where Bacon had already held his first design show of furniture and rugs. In a second joint show, in the November of 1929, Bacon's tentative watercolours and gouaches hung alongside de Maistre's oils and circular wall mirrors of clear and opaque glass, while painted screens were set on polished wooden floorboards with ruches of rubber sheeting suspended over the windows. Later he would admit that his furniture was totally influenced by Le Corbusier, and he would say, 'I loathe my own furniture. I think it absolutely horrible . . . I never want to see it again.'

Roy de Maistre was unprepossessing, but highly seductive. Two of his influential friends, the art historian and Director of the Tate Gallery – John Rothenstein – and the novelist Patrick White, have left testimonies to his powers of attraction. At this time, he was plump and balding, small and diabetic. Despite his social graces and exposure to French culture, he remained stubbornly Australian. He seemed to Rothenstein a reticent and deeply civilised painter with an advanced personality, aggressive to the point of harshness. His attitude was contradicted by his appearance. He looked neat, Edwardian and fastidious: he had urbane manners; in his hallway, a collapsible opera-hat lay beside a Roman Catholic missal and pieces of antique French porcelain. 'Roy's studio was a work of art,' Rothenstein wrote of his friend, 'and, like Courbet's, a repertory of his whole life.' He chose to cultivate friendships rather than social relations which might be casual or fortuitous. Although he believed in being gentle and forbearing in life, the conduct of art was quite different. 'It is often necessary, for instance,' he told Rothenstein, 'to give the spectator an ugly left uppercut.' When Patrick White met de Maistre in 1936 because he had been told by old ladies in Australia that the artist used to trim hats, he found him melancholy and snobbish with loyal friends, somebody who dressed like a bank manager and worked in an embroidered smock. But like Francis Bacon before him, White was looking for a father and a mentor, an elder man who 'held a sort of secret knowledge of the details of living that was very important to me'.

The details of living and the introductions to patrons of the arts were the contribution of Roy de Maistre, whom Francis Bacon revered as he could not his father. Both of them had a patriarchal and horse-mad male parent and a fond mother; but Roy also had the gift of attracting wealthy men and women and art critics, something which the shy Francis, at twenty years of age, still had to learn. He did not really know yet that he even wanted to be a painter. He was a late starter in everything. He had become an interior decorator and designer because of the influence that Berlin and Paris had on him. He said that the analytic side of his brain did not develop until he was nearly thirty years old. Only then could he begin to open out. The truth was that his emancipation did not begin until his true father was to die in 1940. Until then, he would look for and find two other fathers and teachers and patrons, Roy de Maistre and afterwards Eric Hall, an intelligent and sensitive civil servant.

De Maistre provided Bacon with enough money to manufacture more rugs and furniture. His major patron would be met through an admirer of de Maistre, Samuel Courtauld, a formidable collector of post-Impressionist art, whose daughter was married to the rising Conservative politician and future Under-Secretary of State for Foreign Affairs, R. A. Butler. Butler commissioned from Bacon a glass and metal dining-table and a set of stools for his house in Smith Square. Malcolm Sargent never liked the transparent table, because he could not 'play footsie-footsie' under it; but both Bacon and de Maistre became family friends of the Butlers. Their furniture was later to be bought by Patrick White and sold again to disappear in time; but its style can be deduced from a photograph and a note on Bacon's work in *Studio* magazine in 1930 on the 'Look in British Decoration'. Tubular steel and chromium plate stools with arched rests and spotted hide seats are depicted, with round glass table-tops set on white-painted steel frames, and a circular and an oval mirror hung over a dressing-table made from wooden blocks and cubes. Rugs in square and oblong and angular shapes lie on the floor or hang on the walls. There is a cocktail bracket of steel and glass – a device to save space. The colours are beige and grey, pink and black and white. The style is highly derivative of the Bauhaus and contemporary French design, particularly that of Lurçat and Jeanneret and Le Corbusier. All is spare and cornered and spartan, the imitative inhibition on display of a shy young artist raging to break out. As *Studio* wrote, the inspiration for his pieces 'springs from nothing Oriental or traditional – they are purely thought forms'.

The early Bacon paintings which were seen by Rothenstein showed the predominant influence of Picasso, also of the mechanism of Léger and the Surrealism of Max Ernst. Roy de Maistre painted Bacon's studio in 1934, when he had moved to 71 Royal Hospital Road in Chelsea. Against bare boards and angular white surfaces, canvases are stacked, two turned towards the painter's brush, one of a skeletal and feathered bird, another of the quartered outline of a horse or dragon – the start of a movement from geonometric abstraction towards a more organic image. But these are works of transition, those of an embryo trying to flesh itself. 'People – when you are young – influence you a great deal,' Bacon later admitted. ' – perhaps I was in love.' Certainly de Maistre recorded the change of his protégé from interior decorator to painter, his furniture left behind him.

The problem of the exhibition in Queensberry Mews was that the Cubist furniture and rugs of Francis Bacon appealed, while the paintings of Roy de Maistre did not. The Crucifixion and the *Pietà* were very much the subjects of the elder painter, who was a convert to Catholicism; and in their austere and fractured angularity, they were an example to the young Bacon. De Maistre made a living chiefly on his portraits and still lives and flower paintings, which appealed to his circle of elderly women friends, such as the Princess Galatzine. But these were not the principles of painting which he taught to Francis, his young lover. He found him ignorant of almost everything. He told Rothenstein that Bacon had only scrutinised reproductions, knew nothing whatever about the techniques of art and had hardly drawn at all. The Crucifixion paintings by Cimabue and Grünewald in reproduction had particularly affected him. It was amusing that a young man of such rare intelligence, who had understood the Picasso exhibition in Paris, should 'ask questions a schoolchild might have answered'. This tentative start led to Bacon painting his 'diluted Picassos', a style in which he was not to persist, and 'dead pale trees in landscape'. There were also watercolours and gouaches of temples and columns, that evoked Giorgio de Chirico and the Surreal scenes of Paul Nash. But for Francis Bacon this was a dead end.

The first exhibition of Bacon and de Maistre in their Kensington garage was sufficiently successful for the fledgling Cork Street gallery of Freddie Mayor, a convinced advocate of modern art, to offer them another show in April 1933, in an exhibition of recent paintings by English, French and German artists. Bacon showed a painting, 'Women in the Sunlight', which has now disappeared, but which provoked *Time and Tide* to call it 'a little tiny piece of red mouse-cheese on the end of a stick for a head' and *Harper's Bazaar* 'a glass of champagne which denotes a woman'. The earliest of Francis Bacon's paintings to survive was also shown there, a portrait of a man with full lips and close-set eyes and diseased appearance. It was bought by his second cousin and close friend, Diana Watson, who confirmed to Rothenstein that Francis had never from his childhood spoken of becoming a painter until after the Picasso exhibition he had seen in Paris. She was rich by inheritance, but she remained single. She had an affinity with her relative Francis, who was hardly more interested in marriage than she was.

Yet the second most influential critic after the doyen of Bloomsbury, Roger Fry, was Herbert Read, and he included a Crucifixion painted by Francis Bacon in his influential *Art Now: An Introduction to the Theory of Modern Painting and Sculpture* of 1933. Bacon's Crucifixion was shown without commentary after works by Henry Moore and Zadkine and Kirschner and Picasso. Later, a painting by de Maistre was reproduced of a phallic shape seen as the top of a tower penetrating vague buttocks and ending in a lighthouse balcony. Mayor now put on a show of the artists featured in *Art Now*, including Bacon, and Sir Michael Sadler bought his Crucifixion by telegram because of the reproduction in the book. It was the ectoplasmic and etiolated spectre derived from the Surrealist work of Masson and Ernst. Sadler was then the leading collector of contemporary art, and he purchased two further Crucifixions from Bacon. The second was set behind the bars of a prison while a figure with imploring feet put the lance into the Saviour's side on the Cross like the Roman centurion Saint Longinus. The third Crucifixion depicted a warped and angular being starting forward from his swept-back and pinioned arms. To this picture, Bacon had added an impression of an X-ray, which Sadler had sent him of his own skull. In his method of mocking the hand which fed him, Bacon added fleshy pink lips to the transparent skull, riddled with nerves, as though greed prefigured thought, the body came before the mind. These three Crucifixions, each in an isolated space, prophesied the triptych, 'Three Studies for Figures at the Base of a Crucifixion', which would make Bacon's reputation eleven years later at the end of the Second World War. Another picture of the dead and bandaged body of Christ laid on a table, was destroyed by the artist.

At this second Mayor Gallery exhibition, which also showed four carvings by Henry Moore and works by Picasso and Masson and Ernst and Arp and Klee, success went to de Maistre as well as to his protégé. He was taken up by one of the proprietors of the gallery, another Australian expatriate, Douglas Cooper, gay and bitchy and wealthy from the proceeds of a useful Sheep Dip. He converted the family fortune into one of the finer collections of Cubist works in the world, particularly those of Picasso and Braque, Gris and Léger. At this time, Cooper signed his articles on art under the pseudonym of Douglas Lord, a homage to Lord Alfred Douglas, the friend of Oscar Wilde. His house, at 8 Groom Place, was decorated for a time by the furniture designed by Francis Bacon, which Cooper was later to use with cruel effect against the artist, when the two of them fell out. He was a great connoisseur, but jealous, competitive and vindictive, although he remained friends with de Maistre and Patrick White, who found him 'loyal once he takes to you'.

The patronage of Sadler and de Maistre and the Butlers and now Douglas Cooper was the introduction of Francis Bacon into a monied world which, especially in the Great Depression, could afford to buy what he designed or painted. He was introduced to fine and discriminating minds. He was learning the techniques and tricks of a new trade. And his homosexuality was no longer a hindrance, but a help. In his important book on the 'thirties, Julian Symons called the period the homosexual decade. In those years, the practice became accepted as a personal idiosyncrasy as well as a sort of password to success in the arts. With the demand for unlimited personal liberty, there was a conscious revolt against the standards of society. What the English expatriate writers had experienced in Weimar Berlin before they ran from the rise of Fascism was transferred to Fitzrovia and Hampstead in London. 'The unique contribution made by the intelligentsia in the 'thirties to the change in our sexual ethic rested in the attitude they adopted, by which the assertion of sexual freedom appeared to be a social duty . . . Every illicit sexual act seemed a blow struck in aid of an ideal theoretical freedom.'

Patrick White clearly expressed the feelings of the shy artists of his persuasion; he blamed his sense of isolation and self-pity on his homosexual temperament.

> [It was] forced at that period anyway to surround itself with secrecy, rather than on the instinctive need to protect my creative core from intrusion and abuse.
>
> The repression society demands of homosexuals obviously reduces them to some extent as members of that society, but if we can quench our fears the perception gained through our temperament strengthens our hand as man, woman, artist, whichever it may be – or all in one. Homosexual society as such has never had much appeal for me. Those who discuss the homosexual condition with endless hysterical delight as though it had not existed, except in theory, before they discovered their own, have always struck me as colossal bores. So I avoid them, and no doubt I am branded as a closet queen. I see myself not so much a homosexual as a mind possessed by the spirit of man or woman . . . I don't set myself up as an intellectual. What drives me is sensual, emotional, instinctive. At the same time I like to think creative reason reins me in as I reach the edge of disaster.

He might have been writing for the feelings of Francis Bacon, whose affections he was to inherit from the gentlemanly de Maistre through whom White and Bacon met. It was a common feeling among those who had escaped a moralistic and moral childhood, as all three of those artists had done. All of them had also had strong fathers and remembered the attractions of the khaki and male presences of the First World War. In his analysis of British writers of the 'thirties, Valentine Cunningham found that homosexual life in that decade did have a way of turning into a curiously welcomed parody of that conflict. For E. M. Forster, anyone in a uniform would do, bus conductors and train-drivers and especially policemen. 'Homosexuality being illegal, to consort sexually with a policeman was to be engaged dangerously and literally with the enemy, and an enemy never entirely pacified even within the close-knit bonds of the uniformed lovers' world . . . The whole thing was as enticingly risky in fact as having a German boyfriend was outrageous to decent British opinion.' That was the choice of those who had gone to Berlin, such as Spender, Auden, Isherwood and the adolescent Bacon, 'the boyfriend defiantly sought among the recent wartime foe . . . A period controlled by memories, fantasies, the language of the War, the 'thirties is commanded obsessively by a violence – its images, its tone, its horrors, its pleasures – that one wants to keep tracing back to the First World War.'

Yet Francis Bacon did not turn to the images of war in his paintings of that time. He took up de Maistre's theme of the Crucifixion, of a man or God suffering for all men. Although the young artist was turning away from religion in spite of de Maistre's convictions, he still saw in the martyrdom of Christ his own suffering from his secret sexuality and his poverty. He would deny later any religious impulse in his paintings, saying that he was merely fascinated by the human body raised on high. Its elevation made it more formal and abstract. But he had his own reasons to paint as he did – de Maistre's teaching and his rebellion from his own education. Curiously enough, the illustration of Bacon's Crucifixion became the most thumbed page in Graham Sutherland's copy of *Art Now*, and he became an admirer of his fellow artist.

Yet as Bacon tasted early success, he would fail and be unable to bear this failure. The following year, he arranged for an exhibition of seven oils and six gouaches in the Transition Gallery, a name he gave to the basement of Sunderland House in Curzon Street, which had been taken for him by his friend, the art patron Arundell Clarke. Although he repudiated and later destroyed all the works except for two which were put on show there, he recalled one of them with regret to John Russell. It was named 'Wound for a Crucifixion' and was set in a hospital ward like those which his lover de Maistre had decorated, with the same dark green of the floors painted to waist-height, with a dark line dividing the picture to a cream above. Presented forward was a large piece of human flesh and 'a very beautiful wound'. It was a portent, suffering flesh inside an enclosure pushed to its limit within the frame of the picture.

The show in Sunderland House was poorly attended in the depths of the Depression and no pictures were sold. *The Times* wondered about the difficulty of the paintings, whether they were artistic expressions or 'the mere unloading on canvas and paper of what used to be called the subconscious mind'. Bacon now hung up his brushes and painted little else for a decade. Of the fifteen surviving early Bacon pictures, all but one were collected by Sir Michael Sadler and Diana Watson and Eric Alden, a friend and supporter. Later Bacon said he didn't want to paint much, he preferred to enjoy himself. He was growing apart from de Maistre, who now had a studio in Ebury Street which looked like a white ship's cabin with minimal furniture. De Maistre would soon be presented by the Butlers with the lease of an adjoining house in 13 Eccleston Street, where he set up a studio at the back of what had formerly been a restaurant on the ground floor. Bacon took up a vagrant and a rootless existence, becoming a bohemian in his clothes and style of life, perhaps as a reaction from the precious de Maistre. He lived on his wits, renting a series of studios in the Fulham and the Cromwell Roads and then at 1 Glebe Place in Chelsea, where he painted on the top floor. He admitted to stealing from his father whenever he could, and to leaving his rooms and studios without paying the rent. 'In those days, I managed to get by on petty theft and on living off people.' He was to be caught shoplifting in his favourite store, Harrod's, which he was to adore for the hanging, bloody carcasses in its butcher's shop. However rich he might grow to be, he was never to be allowed an account at Harrod's. But his crime was committed in his young days. His virtue was to increase with his means and his generosity. In his early years, he had believed with many artists, both socialists and anarchists, that property was theft. That did not mean, of course, that theft was necessarily property, as Harrod's had to caution him. But he was to return to favour when he could afford their prices and his morality, giving the great emporium his infinite custom.

Occasional commissions for making furniture continued to come in. A yellow sofa of his stood in pride of place in Roy de Maistre's living-room, backed by a screen which Bacon had painted. There he was to meet Patrick White, who was to become the lover of the ageing painter. For these two young artists, de Maistre was tutor. When White was introduced to abstract painting, he began 'to write from the inside out . . . it was like jumping into space, and finding nothing there at first . . . Then gradually one saw it was possible to weave about freely on different levels, at one and the same time.' De Maistre was also an entry to the social and artistic world of London. He had a talent for important friendships, White's biographer explained. 'His circle included poets and critics, musicians, politicians and royalty. In country houses, he was thought "great fun, and like Creevey was always a *most* welcome guest". He never travelled without letters of introduction.'

White's affair with de Maistre was not to last long. De Maistre told him that he was 'trying to recover from something unhappy', but that he was twenty years older than White, so the relationship could not work. He was also fifteen years older than Francis Bacon, who remained friendly with him, but was already moving toward a love affair with the civil servant, Eric Hall, who was as reticent as he was, but so sympathetic towards the arts that he was to become the young artist's new counsellor and adviser. Like Bacon, Patrick White always remained the friend of de Maistre, who had the extraordinary talent of converting his seductions into amity, his passions into fatherliness. 'We were both too irritable and unyielding,' White said of his affair and took the guilt of the collapse upon himself by admitting that he was hoping consciously to consummate his stifled love for his father, who was everything that de Maistre was not. 'My failure depressed me as much as my failure to communicate with my actual father.'

Bacon had also seen in his love of the older painter a stifled love for his father, who was everything that his lover was not. Yet he became friendly with his supplanter, the writer from Australia, who was allowed by de Maistre to meet other English artists including Henry Moore and Graham Sutherland. Otherwise de Maistre lived his life in watertight compartments, particularly his homosexual one. White was offered the two top floors of 13 Eccleston Street to rent as a flat. He shuddered at the cost, but accepted. He wanted modern furniture and asked Francis Bacon to make it for him. One magnificent desk was designed with wide, shallow, wooden drawers and a top of red linoleum. The rest of the furniture was bought from R. A. Butler, who found that the modern Baconian style of glass and steel and hide was too much for his politician's dining-room at Smith Street. Perhaps the negotiations at Munich with Hitler and Chamberlain did not quite suit designs derived from the Bauhaus and the Weimar Republic.

Once they had established a friendly distance from de Maistre, White and Bacon learned to appreciate one another. As a novelist of genius, White gave the first revealing portrait in words of Francis Bacon:

> I got to know Francis when he designed some furniture for my Eccleston Street flat. I like to remember his beautiful pansy-shaped face, sometimes with too much lipstick on it. He opened my eyes to a thing or two. One afternoon at Battersea, crossing the river together by a temporary footbridge while the permanent structure was under repair, he became entranced by the abstract graffiti scribbled in pencil on its timbered sides. Alone, I don't expect I would have noticed the effortless convolutions of line he pointed out for me to admire. To discover something as subtle as it was simple made me feel quite elated. In those days Francis was living at the end of Ebury Street, across the Pimlico Road, within a stone's throw of the Mozart-Sackville brothel. He had an old nanny who used to go out shoplifting whenever they were hard up, and as lover there was an alderman.

What White particularly noticed in Bacon and de Maistre was their mutual love of the snapshot and the newsreel. Their odd passion 'for newspaper photographs was one that White came to share. Each collected them; the painters took them as starting points for abstract exercises . . . for these figures exposed so incongruously to public scrutiny.' Bacon now scrutinised the *March of Time* and the available newsreels which displayed the Fascist monsters of Europe, Mussolini and Hitler and their cohorts. At one time, Bacon bought a Sickert painting of a woman leaning on a bed and of a man sitting on a chest, taken from a photograph as the Edwardian artist often used to do. Bacon also studied Eadweard Muybridge's pioneering photographic Victorian volumes of *The Human Figure in Motion* and *Animals in Motion*. Victorian painters had subscribed to Muybridge's volumes: in England, Watts and Holman Hunt and Millais and Whistler and Sargent; in France, Bougereau and Rodin. There, his rival, Etienne-Jules Marey, had produced more beautiful images of motion, but these influenced Bacon less. He found Muybridge more stimulating because of his 'raw statements of movement'.

Bacon had to study Muybridge's volumes in the nearby Victoria and Albert Museum before he could afford to buy reproductions of them. In these, Muybridge used a trip-thread technique in his photography to expose in a series of frames the exact motions of human beings and animals at play and in action. To Bacon, these were as revealing as the unstudied pictures taken by press photographers of the great and the unsavoury. As John Rothenstein, his early patron and most sympathetic critic, explained of his fascination for the captured instant of the camera eye:

> The photograph has had another effect on the art of Bacon besides providing points of departure for his imagery. In the traditional portrait there is a direct relation between the painter and his subject: sometimes they look at each other; sometimes the subject looks elsewhere, but he or she is aware of the presence of the painter and, however informally, is posing for him. The modern photographer – the earlier worked under the influence of painting – catches people when they are unaware of his presence; off balance, when they are not in the poses which they think most dignified and attractive, nor wearing their 'Sunday Best'. Pho-

tography of this order has done much to foster in Bacon his predilection for portraying people as though they were alone, unaware of any other presence.

'What modern man wants', Bacon said to Rothenstein, quoting Valéry, 'is the grin without the cat; that is, the sensation without the boredom of its conveyance.' He meant that the painter's job was to remove the essence of the picture out of the exactitude of the camera. A sweep of the brush would eliminate the unnecessary detail. A stroke of the mind would demolish in a photograph the intrusion of a whip or a sock, a hat or a truncheon. While Muybridge might portray absolute reality by his exposures of mammals in motion caught at each two-thousandth of a second, Francis Bacon's perceptions of the active flesh would be captured on canvas at the very moment of violence and desire. There stood the abyss between the technician and the artist, the instrument and the seer.

Bacon was aware of his distortions of the recorded image. He even painted portraits from photographs rather than from the sitter. 'But who can I tear to pieces', he asked, 'if not my friends?' They would understand his need to distance himself from reality by photography in order to produce his inner vision of the truth beneath the body. His pictures were always to be those of a surgeon, not the cosmetic variety but the visceral. As he told John Russell, the news-photograph of the 'thirties was his education in painting. It formalised disrespect. It wrenched the figures of authority out of their high places. It caught them unguarded and inconsequent, 'racked by tics, their faces distorted, their clothes in disorder, their bodies off balance'. It was the new school of truth and intrusion, which coincided with the arrival of Isherwood's civil monsters.

Bacon recorded in his mind's eye the leprosy of his time, but he did not paint it. Yet he did base one unfinished painting on a photograph of Hitler getting out of his car at a Nuremberg rally – a painting which was abandoned before the start of the Second World War and revised after the victory as 'Landscape with Car', before it was left incomplete. It showed originally a loathsome reptile, dangling and snarling over the windscreen of a car, and leaning to speak into a battery of three microphones. He resurrected the concept in another post-War picture, 'Figure in a Landscape', which showed the shape of Eric Hall asleep in a London park on a deckchair instead of in a car, his body deconstructed to gristle and hair, while the Nuremberg background was replaced with harsh grass and branches as if to celebrate the rigours of victory. Hall's suit was actually painted in a thin grey wash, thickened with dust from the floor. The dust lasted well and did not change its colour. This particular vision was to surface again as one inspiration for the centrepiece of Bacon's first triptych of the screaming and mutilated Eumenides or Furies.

To the retina of his eye and the camera of his mind, the photographs of his violent times and newsreel images were more important to Francis Bacon than any influences he might have derived from the paintings of German Expressionism, New Objectivity, French Cubism or Surrealism. He had shown some pictures at the Mayor Gallery along with members of 'Unit One', a group headed by Paul Nash and Henry Moore, which included Surreal works by Dali, Miró and Ernst. But when asked to contribute more pictures to the International Surrealist Exhibition in the June of 1936, Bacon found his works rejected for not being Surreal enough. Two of the judges, Herbert Read and Roland Penrose, visited his studio at Glebe Place and viewed three or four large canvases including one with a grandfather clock. These were turned down, although Penrose said later that Bacon had destroyed much from that time and had 'become more Surreal in his later work' – a judgement that Bacon wholly rejected. He recalled Penrose declaring, on his abortive Chelsea visit, 'Mr Bacon, don't you realise a lot has happened in painting since the Impressionists?' Moore and Sutherland and Nash did show their creations at the International Surrealist Exhibition, even though Herbert Read had declared, 'Surrealism in general is the romantic principle in art.' Romanticism was never a principle in Bacon's art. He was later to say that the *conscious* mystery was the boring side of Surrealism. 'The only true mystery is the way you bring the image about.'

With his contacts of importance, Roy de Maistre secured Bacon his last showing in 1937 at Thomas Agnew and Sons in Bond Street. An idea had been floated that an artists' co-operative should be founded, similar to the Bloomsbury London Artists' Association formed in 1925 by Maynard Keynes and Samuel Courtauld. De Maistre, the Butlers, Kenneth Clark and Lord Balniel were consulted, as well as Keynes and Courtauld, about raising capital for the venture. The money was not forthcoming. The Agnew's exhibition was the only benefit for the associated artists. None of the thirty-six works on show cost more than forty guineas, and they included four paintings by Sutherland and three by Bacon. One of these, 'Figures in a Garden' or 'Seated Figure', was bought by Bacon's cousin, Diana Watson, and was shown later in an Arts Council touring exhibition. Another, called 'Abstraction from the Human Form', was seen by John Rothenstein before Bacon destroyed it – as he destroyed all his early work when he could get a knife to it. He was not unique in that. Degas and Monet used to destroy their past work and especially Soutine, who influenced Bacon, and Giacometti, who would become Bacon's friend after the end of the Second World War and share in his belief that his works of art were mainly unfinished failures. 'Oh, to be able to say', Giacometti would protest, 'that's it, I cannot do more.' Both he and Bacon rarely thought they had come to the end of a painting, which sometimes had to be ripped, dripping, off their easels by their gallery owners to reach a conclusion.

Rothenstein considered that 'Abstraction' was another inspiration for the central panel of Bacon's 'Three Studies for Figures at the Base of a Crucifixion', painted at the end of the Second World War after 'an almost complete break of seven or eight years . . . It is as though he was picking up where he left off.' The break from the end of the 'thirties through the first years of the Second World War was prolonged, indeed. Bacon even refused to design the scenery for a production of *The School for Scandal*, which Rupert Doone proposed to put on at the fashionable Group Theatre. Doone had worked as a dancer with Diaghilev and with Reinhardt in Berlin. His lover and his usual costume and mask designer was the painter Robert Medley: he put on the plays of the Berlin expatriates, Spender's *Trial of a Judge* and Auden and Isherwood's *The Dog Beneath the Skin*, *The Ascent of F6* and *On the Frontier*. But Bacon was no joiner of côteries or causes. The fashionable Communism of the middle-class radicals who supported the Group Theatre had no appeal for him. He remained on his own or with the few he knew well. Privacy was his desire. 'Taking no part in society's rituals, observing none of its canons or taboos', John Russell wrote of his friend, 'he just went on as if none of them existed.'

The surviving originals and photographs of Bacon's work of the 'thirties show a young painter struggling to overcome the overpowering influence of Picasso, and to a lesser extent the style of German New Objectivity and French Surrealism, also the designs of the Bauhaus and Le Corbusier. A painting by de Maistre of the studio in Queensberry Mews shows Cubist rugs and a powerful abstract figure painted on the central panel of a screen. Seven of the rugs designed and signed by Bacon still exist: they were so like paintings, with multiple angular perspectives and apparent depths in space, that they were hung as tapestries as often as they were used to cover the floor. His painted screens had three tall oblong figures standing on sentry duty by Grecian pillars as unfathomable as those painted by Giorgio de Chirico. The triple screen shape appears again in front of a dead tree in one of his paintings shown in Queensberry Mews, while his 'Interior of a Room', bought by his cousin Diana Watson in 1933, 'Corner of the Studio' and 'Studio Interior' of the following year, are the transitional pieces of an interior decorator becoming a painter, with the sprawl of his menacing shapes either cut off by floral screens or shadowing floorboards and wallpaper and door with their implacable presence. 'Corner of the Studio', indeed, was bought by a woman who had hired Bacon to decorate and design the furniture for her London flat. But the most individual of the surviving pictures of that decade was also bought by Diana Watson, 'Figures in a Garden' of 1936, sometimes known as 'The Fox and the Grapes' or even 'Goëring and his Lion Cub'. In it, a feral creature bares its teeth at a squat and skeletal tree trunk which suggests a howling face, while a harsh line divides the background as night from day. As John Rothenstein wrote about Bacon's early works, however, he obviously had an extraordinary natural talent without any of the conventional armoury of the painter, and so he did not yet have the means 'of projecting an imagination of terrifying power and extreme sophistication'.

That imagination and sophistication was being developed by Bacon's new mentor, Eric Hall, whom Patrick White called the 'alderman'. Hall was intelligent and had a great influence on the wayward Bacon, who was taught 'the value of things', such as 'what decent food was'. Bacon had not learned that in Ireland, only the value of things abroad. When one of his pieces of furniture reached County Kildare, it became a subject of shocked surprise and was known for fifty years as 'The Chair', as though it were as dangerous as the electric one on Death Row in America. His cousin, Pamela Firth, saw one of his tables at Straffan Lodge – half a looking-glass and half a transparent plate glass with a tubular steel support. From Eric Hall, Bacon could accept an education which he had missed all his life – in food and drink and behaviour, in reading the classics and in the appreciation of music and dance, as well as art. Although he remained a bohemian, he was led by Hall into a double life of dinner-parties and concerts and viewing galleries with the cognoscenti of the metropolis. Hall was Bacon's Dante, his guide through the hell and purgatory of the city. While Bacon's own father was soon to die in 1940 and unlock his son's last inhibitions, the death of Eric Hall after the Second World War would be the first of many tragedies of love in the painter's life.

A friend of his, the art historian John Richardson, said that Bacon, at this period, liked being kept by respectable middle-class gentlemen in pin-striped suits with a perverse streak. 'What would really excite me', he told Richardson, 'is a middle-aged Belgian commercial traveller with hairy wrists – and a marquesite watch embedded in that hair.' He loved an illicit stuffiness, a slightly criminal respectability. 'A fustian thing turned him on,' Richardson has said, and has showed how the rabid beast in the genteel background occurs in so many of his paintings, as in the transmutation of Eric Hall asleep in his deckchair in the Park to a raw and wounded thing of slavering menace in such a normal setting.

Meanwhile, the problem for the young artist was present existence. Another one of his protectors took him into the Bath Club, among the aristocrats, and installed his lover there as a telephone operator. Such a penetration of the respectable façade of London life appealed to Bacon, but the switchboard job did not. He worked in various offices doing odd jobs, and for a time in the rag trade in a wholesale shop in Poland Street, Soho, where he had to answer the telephone again 'and that was about all'. He became a gentleman's gentleman, advertising himself under the name of John Lightfoot, which implied that he would not stay in any position for very long. He forged a set of references, and so became the cook and manservant of a solicitor who lived in Mecklenburgh Square. His situation did not last, but nothing did at that time of transience. Later, he would tell two stories of his departure. In one, his employer saw him dining with Eric Hall at the next table at the Ritz on his evening off and immediately asked him to be off for ever. In another, he could not stand his menial role any more and gave in his notice, only to hear the rejoinder, 'I can't understand why he's leaving because he doesn't do anything.'

He drifted into the bohemian world of Chelsea and Fitzrovia and Soho, where art and homosexuality were tolerated and even welcomed. It was the ambience of Augustus John and Dylan Thomas, of the patron Peter Watson and the itinerant editors and writers and artists. The radical political life of Britain was still being managed from Bloomsbury and Holborn and Covent Garden east of Fitzrovia, where the bohemians and misfits gathered in the shadows of the approaching World War. In his *Memoirs of a Public Baby*, one of the regulars, Philip O'Connor, remembered how the artists tried to exploit those who were slumming in the hope of meeting artists. Income was the frontier. To him, 'Fitzrovia was a national social garbage centre. But its inhabitants had the sweetness as well as the gameness of humanity gone off. They lived a life of pretence among themselves, and the successful ones pretended also to become outsiders, leaving the district to slander it.'

Francis Bacon was truly an outsider before he came to Fitzrovia and Soho, and he established his favourite haunts there, the French Pub of Gaston Berlemont in Dean Street, Wheeler's Fish Restaurant in Old Compton Street, and when he could afford it, the Gargoyle night-club with its décor by Matisse himself, where the dandy Brian Howard once dismissed a heterosexual poet with the words, 'The trouble, my dear, is that you're not one of *us*.' Through Roy de Maistre and Eric Hall, Bacon had already achieved an *entrée* to many of the wealthy patrons of the arts, who enjoyed playing at being bohemian and visiting the pubs of Fitzrovia, like the editor John Lehmann in search of male flesh and talent for his *New Writing*. From the time of Oscar Wilde onwards, Soho and its environs had attracted those who wished to mix art and sex with compliance, without discovery and disgrace. Although class barriers and expectations still divided the rich from the poor bohemians, this area in Central London was one place where they might forget nightly their frontiers and their differences.

Machiavelli wrote that half of a man's life was his *vertù*, his skill as well as his virtue, and half was chance, but when necessity came, he had to bow his head. Bacon followed Machiavelli in his existence, for chance and the skill at exploiting chance were always a theme in his life. Like Nathan Detroit in *Guys and Dolls*, he set up a moveable and illegal gambling game. He had brought over from Ireland an old nanny, and she used to act as a door-minder and hat-and-coat taker, while Francis ran the roulette wheel and *vingt-et-un* games in the inner room. As long as he took the house percentage and did not hold the bank, Bacon made money on his gambling operations, but usually he plunged as much as he plundered. His disdain for his brief gains was legendary. He wasted what he had with a reckless prodigality. The young Jeffrey Bernard, who was to become a drinking companion of his in Soho, remembered their first meeting, introduced by the painter John Minton, who then was supporting Bernard in the hope of the use of his body. In a smart new suit from Savile Row, Bacon perched at the top of a step-ladder, painting the studio ceiling pure white. He spattered himself in paint with complete indifference. House decorating was not his forte. When Bernard asked him how he could ruin clothes that cost a hundred pounds, he laughed. 'He threw it away like one of his one-liners.'

Bacon's awareness of decay and death was already set against the improvisation of his life. He lived by his wit and his wits, from hand to mouth, from night to day. Although intensely private, he cultivated a growing circle of influential friends in the arts, who admired his independence and his gay abandon. The coming of the War would both convert his bohemian society into the core of artistic activity in Britain and recreate and hone the images of horror and destruction that the boy had seen near Paddington Station and in the Park and the cinema during the First World War. The blitz and the later photographs of the concentration camps in Europe would score and scratch more mutilations on the preserved memories of the child, whose asthma would still keep him as an adult from any real participation in the Second World War. And while he waited for the declaration of it, the parks of London were already being gouged open again in preparation for a more terrible and probable rain of death. Christopher Lee wrote of the urban landscape of 1939:

> Great stripes, banks, mounds
> across placid green of London commons, gravel
> dumped sand, planks, bricks
> ousting bright boats, cricket-bats and kites.
>
> Needed perhaps, these shelters
> for life and limb's sake, and their skelter of stuff
> fantastic patterns, or strict beauty
> like farmed, reclaimed land won from rough ground.
>
> Yet walks, rides, nostalgic pond
> which were themselves a shelter in quieter war
> of relentless industry, of London,
> must be given back to boats, clerks, factory hands.

5
Come to the Execution

> For when things are once come to the execution, there is no secrecy comparable to celerity; like the motion of a bullet in the air, which flieth so swift as it outruns the eye.
>
> 'Of Delay'
> by Francis Bacon, Lord Verulam,
> Viscount St. Albans

Like a watched kettle, the War did not come to the boil for a year after its declaration. In the September of 1939, Londoners had expected an immediate destruction from Nazi dive-bombers, the agony of Guernica in the Spanish Civil War, that was commemorated in Picasso's painting. Yet during the winter and the spring of the next year, nothing much happened in a Phoney or Bore War before the evacuation of the British Expeditionary Force from Dunkirk in France. In the words of Malcolm Muggeridge:

> Every circumstance of war was present except warfare. Armies existed, apparently in battle-array; uniforms were worn, both at home and abroad; fortifications were dug, passwords were exchanged, trumpets were sounded, canteens were organized, songs were sung – Washing to be hung on the Siegfried Line, Rabbit to be made to run, run, run, or of the tenderer sort, Somewhere in France with you ... So strange a situation has rarely existed. Clouds were dark and menacing; the wind had dropped and there was the stillness which precedes a mighty storm, and still the first heavy drops of rain did not fall, still it seemed that, after all, no storm might come.

The artists and writers in London moved about in a state of intense hallucination. Many of them joined the Auxiliary and later the National Fire Service, among them Stephen Spender, Henry Green, William Sansom and Leonard Rosoman, the painter. Others became air-raid wardens or worked in the control rooms of the fire services or on anti-aircraft or barrage balloon units. Food and clothes rationing were universal and accepted, black-out regulations necessary and unpopular. Excepting a few insiders and profiteers, everybody had to put up with it. Civilians had to register at shops to receive their variable weekly average of two shillings' worth of meat, four ounces of bacon and cheese and fat and tea, eight ounces of sugar and two eggs. Clothes coupons had to be hoarded to buy a coat, while petrol was practically invisible outside the black market.

The black-out turned familiar streets into dark ravines with shaded traffic-lights, buses creeping along like dimly lit monsters, taxis all sombre inside and cars with headlamps no brighter than cats' eyes. As Mass-Observation discovered: 'Nothing, no amount of experience, makes you really used to the black-out. And however little it may change your habits, the consciousness of it, waiting for you out there, behind the black material on the window, is a threat to any of the pre-War happy-go-lucky. Each evening expedition is now an event, maybe a dangerous adventure.' Mass-Observation also noted that lovers and prostitutes liked the black-out. It conferred on everybody an equality of clandestine anonymity before the radiance of the incendiaries that were to come from the sky.

In the pubs and in the streets, in the defence units and in the factories where men and women were drafted because of special skills or disabilities which kept them from the armed forces, there was little antagonism of class or background. It did seem a people's war on the Home Front, and authority lay in a local warden or policeman or fireman, wearing a tin hat or a helmet or an armband. Francis Bacon was prevented from joining up by his sense of detachment and his asthma and sinus trouble. He had already had an operation on the roof of his mouth several years before, but it had not improved his sinus condition, which was only kept under control by large doses of the drug M and B, that panacea before the age of antibiotics. 'If I hadn't been asthmatic,' Bacon once said, 'I might

1 Francis Bacon's grandmother and mother, Winifred Christina Firth.

2 Major Edward Bacon, the father of the artist.

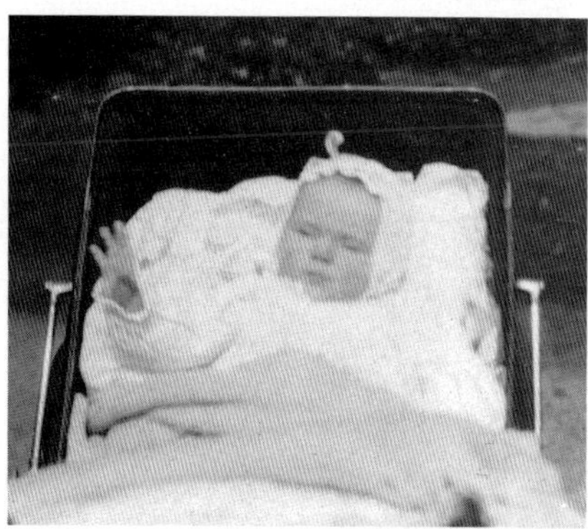

3 Francis Bacon as a baby, his father's 'second string'.

4 Francis Bacon with his elder brother, Harley.

5 Thames Embankment with Sphinx after an aeroplane raid, 4–5 September 1917.

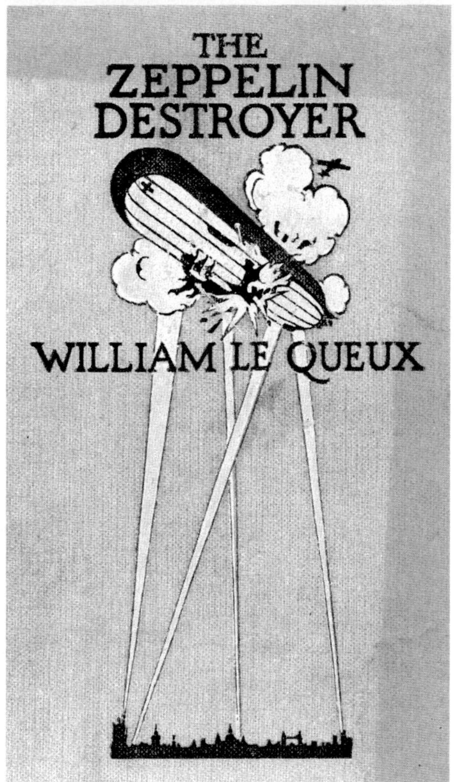

6 A child's vision of a Zeppelin raid.

7 Mr and Mrs Kerry Supple.

8 Farmleigh, near Abbeyleix, the last home of the Bacon family in Ireland.

9 Edward Bacon leads in 'Ginger' Firth after another sporting victory.

10 Francis Bacon at the age of nineteen, taken in Berlin.

11 Francis Bacon at Schloss Nymphenberg.

12 'Street Scene, Berlin' by George Grosz, from *Brokenbrow*.

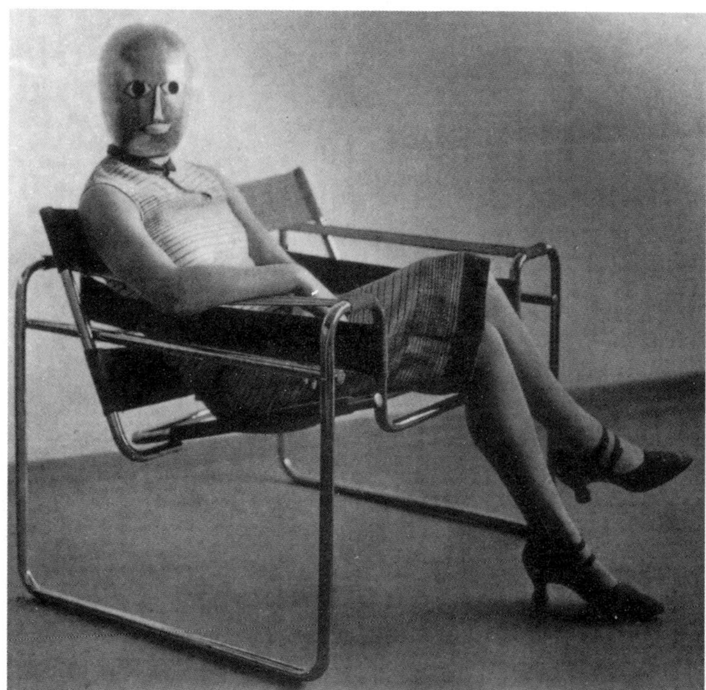

13 Bauhaus chair with dummy model.

14 'Junger Ästhet' by Karl Rössing, 1929.

15 'A Woman of Berlin' by Christian Schad, 1928.

16 'The Scream' by Edvard Munch, 1894.

17 & 18 Screaming mouths from Eisenstein's film of *The Battleship Potemkin*.

19, 20 & 21 Scenes from Buñuel's film of *Un Chien Andalou*.

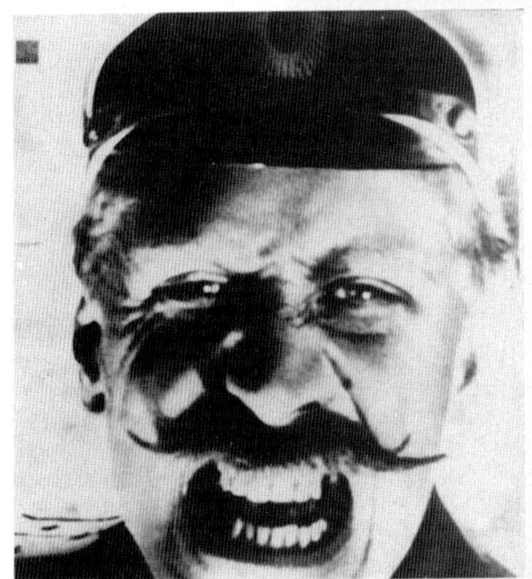

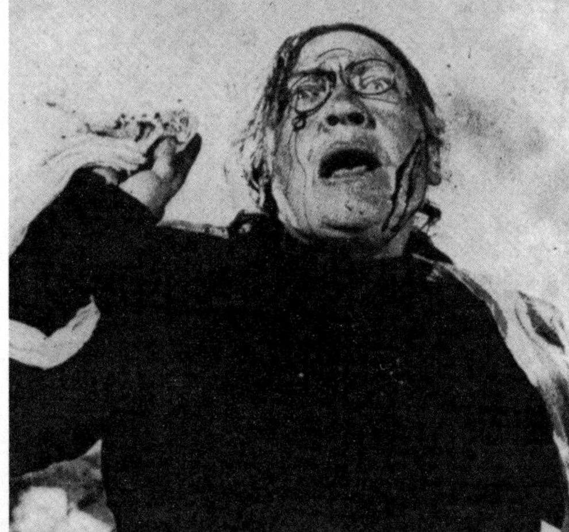

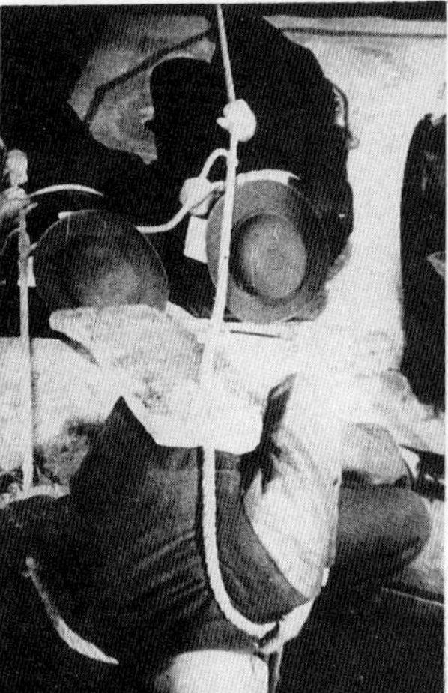

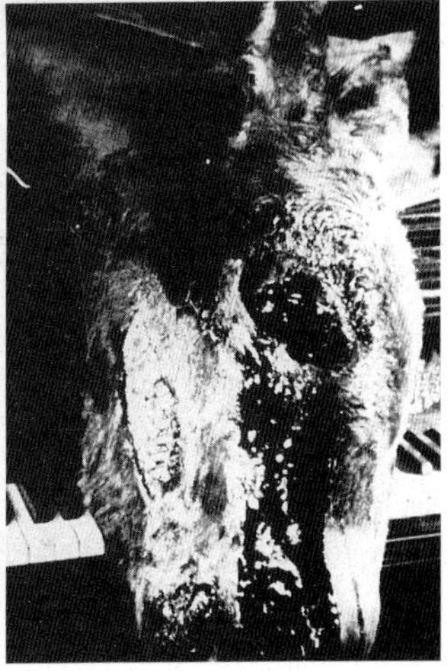

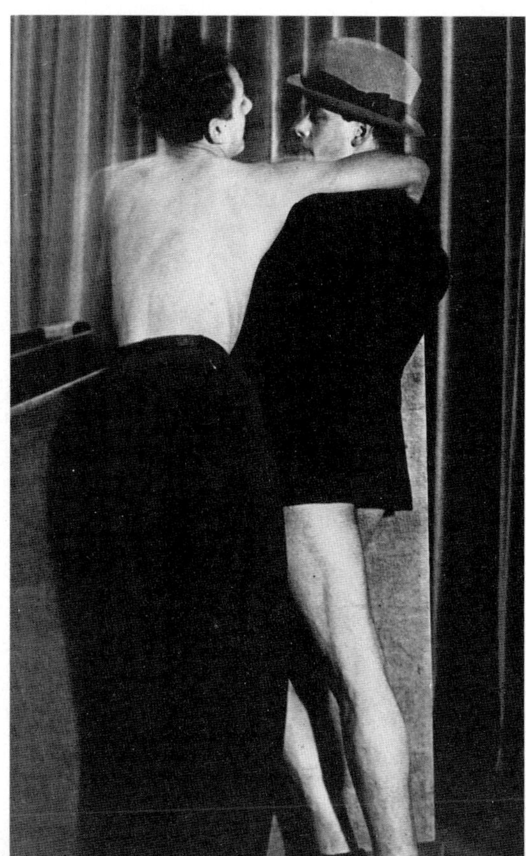

22 Two young men wearing one suit at a drag ball in Paris, by Georges Brassaï.

23 Francis Bacon's furniture designs, including his desk.

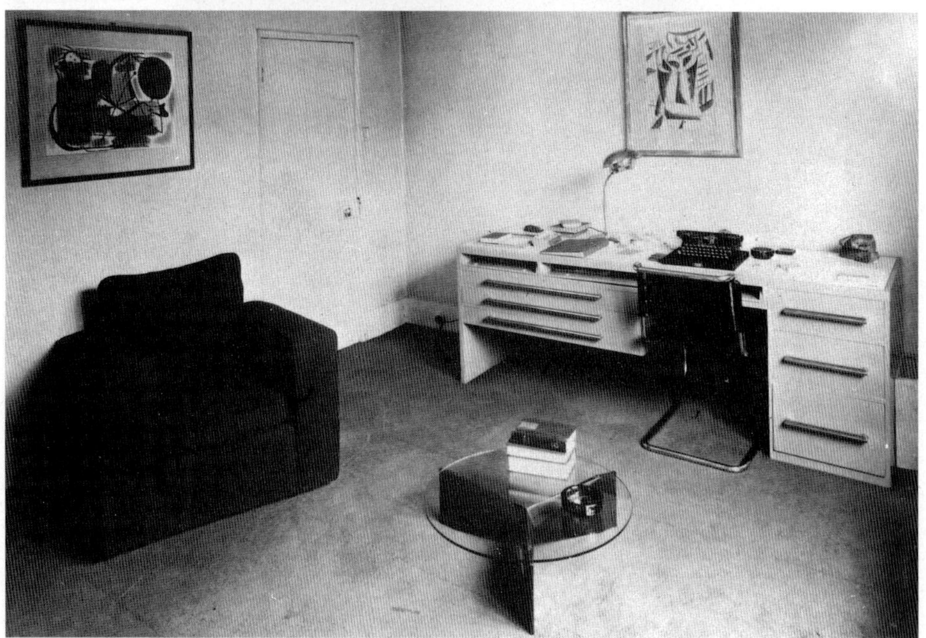

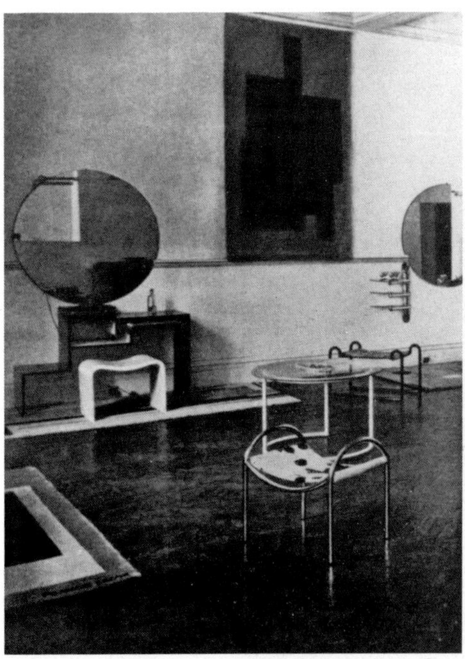

24 Francis Bacon's furniture and rugs on display in Queensberry Mews, London, from *Studio*, August 1930.

25 Francis Bacon's studio, painted by Roy de Maistre, 1930.

26 'Corner of the Studio' by Francis Bacon, 1934.

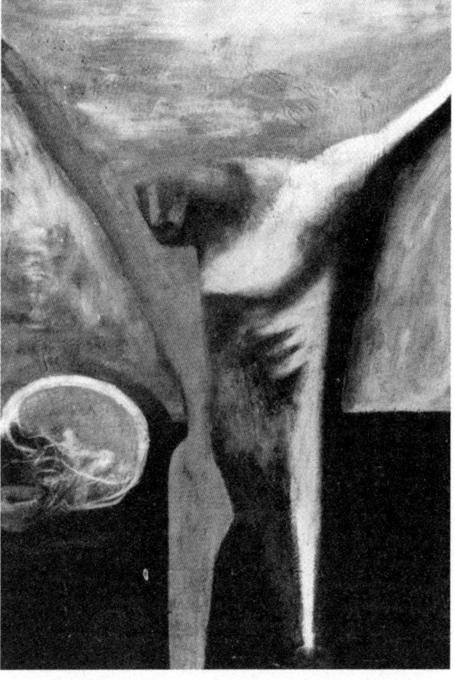

27 'Crucifixion' by Francis Bacon, 1933.

never have gone on painting at all.' He knew that many artists had suffered from asthma, Proust especially, but he could not assess just how much asthma affected him. 'One can't account for the deformations in the make-up of one's character as they are part of one's whole make-up.' He was not conscious of asthma affecting his War. To say it did, would be to falsify it, as far as he knew. Yet he would also claim that he had become aware of his allergy to dogs, hired an Alsatian from Harrods, slept next to it overnight, and was so choked in the morning at his medical that he was classified as unfit for military service.

However, his affliction did affect his life during the blitz. When the bombs began to rain from the sky, Bacon fled to the countryside along with millions of other refugees from the metropolis. He lived with his old nanny from Ireland, in a cottage in Petersfield in Hampshire, which was rented for him by Eric Hall, and where he began to paint again. One of his few surviving figurative works of that period, 'Man in a Cap', shows the yelling mouth of authority under a peaked officer's cap, the body suggested as a crouched beast squatting on a bar inside a cage. Bacon stayed in the country until 1942, when the pollen became almost as bad as poison gas and the worst of the air raids seemed to be over. He then returned to London and he bought the bombed studio of the Pre-Raphaelite painter, Sir John Millais, at 7 Cromwell Place, South Kensington. There his old nanny slept on the table, muttering about her obsession, the need for capital punishment. The whole roof of the studio had been blown in by a bomb, but Bacon lived and painted in the enormous billiard room at the back. He was now obliged to serve sporadically in the ARP Rescue Service, until once again severe attacks of asthma brought about his discharge from the force. 'Anyone', he said later, 'who lived through the European wars was affected by them.' They affected his whole psyche, because he had 'to live continuously under an atmosphere of tension and threat'.

He had been liberated during the Phoney War by the death of his father, Anthony Bacon, who expired on 1 June 1940, at The Old Rectory in Bradford Peverell, near Dorchester. Although the son had drifted apart from the sire, he had not escaped from his love and loathing of his parent. His brother Harley had emigrated to South

Africa and had joined the Rhodesian Police, where he contracted tetanus while trying to cross the flooded Zambesi River and died of lockjaw. This death so haunted Francis that a decade later, when he gashed his finger while slicing chips to fry with his fish, he turned white and almost fainted with fear of poisoning. 'These are South African potatoes,' he said. Francis was the only one of the three Bacon brothers to reach the age of thirty and was named in his father's will as his sole Trustee and Executor, a fact that argued that there was no absolute estrangement. The will left to the wife, Winifred Christina, her marriage settlement, now in trust, to Francis the sum of fifty pounds and equal shares in the residue of the estate with his younger sister Winifred, although the probate declared the total value of the effects to be a mere three-hundred-and-forty-four pounds, five shillings and eightpence – not a fortune at the end of a long military and horse-racing career. Anthony Bacon had sold most of the plates printed with the family crest and two letters from the famous Francis, Lord Verulam, Viscount St. Albans, to the Duke of Portland to pay some of his gambling debts. His painter son and heir would say of his genealogy and inheritance that he was called Francis Bacon and was uncertain whether he was really a descendant. His namesake had no children and was a homosexual. Whether his brothers perhaps had children, the artist was unsure, but if so, this made him an heir of the great philosopher and statesman.

Excluded from the will was the eldest daughter Ianthe, who had gone to South Africa to work as a volunteer nurse. Included, however, was her younger sister Winifred, although she had made a most unsuitable marriage to a lorry driver in the first flush of the War. She was to have two children before her husband left her. Following that she met a second man, who almost immediately went to gaol. She would not give him up, but waited for his release, keeping a house for paying guests with her mother off the Cromwell Road in London. When he was let out, he disappeared, and Winifred was to contract a form of paralysis which developed into multiple sclerosis. Like his own asthma, the paralysis of his sister horrified Bacon emotionally, but intrigued him intellectually. The connection between the mind and the body, where stress induced a malady, fascinated him. His own sickness and those of his siblings, the asthma and the lockjaw and the paralysis, were to be reflected in his portraits of diseased and suffering humanity.

Bacon's own nervous system was hardly improved by his service in civil defence, although he did experience the terrible beauty of the blitz, which his fellow fire-fighter William Sansom described in *Westminster in War*: the yellow flash of gunfire, the whitish-green hiss of incendiaries, the copper-red reflection of the flames, the criss-cross hatching of the searchlights, and in the streets of Pimlico and Soho:

> . . . the high scarfing columns of naked gas flame flaring like some giant idealization of the naphtha flames that through the years had lit their fairs and their stalls.
>
> These were the lights – but there were also dark streets, streets where suddenly a house of blackness collapsed with a roar, shifting down heavily like some bricked elephant lumbering to its knees, thickening the darkness with a poisonous cloud of dust, shrouding the moment after its fall with a fearful empty silence broken only by small sounds, the whispering of broken water pipes, slight shiftings of debris, moans and little cries of the injured; then into the torch-light of the wardens there would stagger those untrapped, lonely figures in the dust-fog bleached grey with powder and streaked and patched with black blood; or – there would be nobody, and not a sound, only a living silence in the knowledge that under a smoking, spawning mass of timber and brick and dust there lay pressed and stifled bodies of warm people whose minutes were slowly ticking away, whose rescue was absurdly blocked . . .

The worst elements of the bombed streets were the rank smells and the rabid cats. A raw and harsh stink pervaded the air, a compound of soot and dust, cinder and the lingering acidity of high explosive. Gas escaping from broken pipes tweaked at the nostrils, and the sweet reek of blood and corpses made the lungs retch. Meanwhile, hordes of mad cats leapt and screeched, trying to find their old snug-holes in the rubble of their owners' houses. Light as birds on the treacherous debris, the cats often led the firemen to burned bodies. And on the streets, glass glittered like frost on grass and broke underfoot in a strange grinding twinkle.

The morning after the raids revealed the houses disembowelled, the intimacies of private lives broadcast to the glare of the day. The writer and artist Mervyn Peake served as a sapper in a bomb disposal group. To him, the ruined houses were not skeletons, but opened bodies showing their coloured muscles and burst skin, vacant wombs and organs as rubble. Yet the very extent of the destruction also revealed the old anatomy of London itself. On a December night on Ludgate Hill, James Monahan could serve as the coroner of chaos and see among the desolation the sinews and ligaments of the ancient roads and patterns of the city, 'each criss-cross, curve, each cul-de-sac, each square, a blueprint magical across the waste'. The heart of history was still beating, the dome of St. Paul's still stood serene above the autopsy performed by a blitz that had sliced open the fundamental design of bygone London.

So the general devastation changed the perceptions and the visions of artists and transients in the capital. This evisceration of people and houses and streets, the display of the entrails of bodies and places, these sights affected the art of Francis Bacon. The bombs also stimulated the senses, awoke the eye. Men and women, after all, were alive and aware, while bricks and plaster were not. The arts revived with a fresh significance. 'This arose spontaneously and simply,' Stephen Spender wrote, 'because people felt that music, the ballet, poetry and painting were concerned with a seriousness of living and dying with which they themselves had suddenly been confronted . . . A little island of civilisation surrounded by burning churches – that was how the arts seemed in England during the War.' The troops and the displaced still swarmed to that last centre of civilisation despite its battered geography and nightly mayhem.

Francis Bacon's own withdrawal from art was matched by the National Gallery, which had removed its masterpieces for safe storage into disused mine shafts. The empty spaces on the walls encouraged the showing of the art of the people. In December, 1939, the Royal Academy had given its first open show of contemporary art with more than two-thousand exhibits, including a portrait in feathers of the young Princess Elizabeth. One leading painter, John Piper, suggested that this might kill art with kindness. When an exhibition by members of the armed forces was assembled to hang on the bare walls of the National Gallery, Herbert Read fulminated:

'Even a worm could lift his head above this level. What stretches before us is the sordid scum left by a receding civilisation. Aesthetic criticism has no function here: it is an affair for the social pathologist. But to that science the art critic is inevitably driven day by day, and I doubt whether the War has left him with any other relevant basis.'

Read had been influential in shifting the emphasis of British art from the stifling formalism and classicism beloved by Roger Fry and the Bloomsbury Group towards a neo-Romantic vision of painting, its distant roots in the Celtic and Gothic past, in Fuseli and William Blake and Samuel Palmer, but its modern stimulation in the apocalypse of a world war. Peter Watson, the patron of *Horizon* and *Poetry London*, financed the young neo-Romantic painters, the Scottish lovers Robert Colquhoun and Robert MacBryde, along with Lucian Freud and John Craxton, to whom he wrote, 'Nostalgia for the past is not a valid vehicle for art now, I am sure of that.'

As in the First World War, artists were now commissioned by the Government, which bought their canvases and drawings. The better of the established Surreal and neo-Romantic painters produced major work as a contribution to the struggle. Henry Moore would become obsessed by the sleepers in the underground stations, trying to avoid the bombs, the masses of the people camping deep under the earth. Widely admired for their coherence and actuality, Moore's Shelter sketches looked to Bacon like 'knitting when he's dropped the stitches in the wrong place'. He refused the role of official war artist which so many other painters took, such as his future jealous friend, Graham Sutherland, who painted aircraft and tin-mines and steel furnaces and open-cast coal operations as well as bomb damage in London – 'perspectives of destruction seeming to recede into infinity'. John Piper also would paint bomb damage in addition to the stylised control rooms of regional quarters of ARP command posts and the Cardiff docks, which he sketched from the top of a refrigerated warehouse, a sinister place of eighteen storeys of nothing but meat, covered with icicles. 'One knew one was alone with all those thousands of frozen carcases – very Kafka-esque,' Piper wrote, 'Francis Bacon might have made something of it, but it didn't appeal to me.' Another of Bacon's Soho friends, John Minton, would make blitzed dockland the home of ghostly haunted children. And Paul

Nash converted the flying dreams of his childhood into pictures of downed German aeroplanes that did not please his superiors in the Air Ministry. A drawing of the wreck of an enemy machine on the ground 'was rather like shooting at a sitting bird. In the slang of the moment, they took a poor view of it'.

The dead sea of dumped German aeroplanes which Paul Nash called *Totes Meer* was the supreme fusion of the Romantic vision and the facts of the fighting – the best War picture so far, Sir Kenneth Clark considered in 1941. Without a doubt, employment as war artists did stimulate the leading neo-Romantics, who were shocked into a perception of the truth of conflict that wonderfully concentrated their minds and defined their paintings. 'Apart from any blockages and the tendency to self-destruction they shared with the other war-babies . . .' the Irish critic Anthony Cronin observed, 'the English Romantics belonged to the War and immediate post-War.' Too soon they were too late. The one genius among them, Francis Bacon, did not look to the Celtic past or to his London contemporaries for his inspiration. 'How can you find the techniques of putting over the eternal realities so that they shine violently as reality?' he asked. Realities had to be renewed, while the basics were always the same. The ways of conveying them became very tired. 'That is why I hate all the late Romantics'. In answer to the calamities of his time – holocaust and fire raid and nuclear fission – he would turn to the imprisonment of power in Velázquez and to the scream against atrocity of Goya. His confined and flayed shapes caged in curtains and boxes would have holes for mouths. They would howl dumbly to be freed from pain and canvas, as the tens of millions of the dead groaned in silence from their untoward mass graves. Bacon's art proved the flaw in the nationalism of the neo-Romantics. The long experience of Europe in its interminable internecine strife informed the truest painter of his age.

One of the 'Lost Girls' of the time, Theodora Fitzgibbon, used to drink with Bacon and the other young painters in the Horseshoe or the Mandrake. She was delighted to have her looks compared to his. They had both been brought up in the same part of Ireland. She knew him for being a brilliant painter, working under great difficulties, but praised his lack of malice and his 'gay equanimity; his troubles were not brought out for drinks'. At the time, his poverty led him to painting with one-inch thick brushes bought from ironmongers. The War was hell on artists' materials. They had to paint as they could in the colours they could find. 'London was dirty, chaotic and dangerous,' John Craxton said. 'People were just about managing to keep things ticking over. It was unbearable. I started to read the works of several contemporary European writers and I often thought how Kafka-esque London was during that period.'

Yet as in Kafka's constructions, there were strange connections between people and places in wartime London. For painters, Fitzrovia was a castle of the arts, where pub rooms led to parties and commissions from a hidden bureaucracy and a transient plutocracy. There were jobs to be found not only from the War Artists' Advisory Committee, but also from editors and theatre managers and film companies as well as from private patrons. Particularly, the patronage of Peter Watson was the gluepot of the Fitzrovian painters. 'He was a man everyone was in love with,' Stephen Spender remembered. 'He paid for everything.' Although he was a depressive and meeting people was agony for him, he had the rare elegance of a Beau Brummel, 'which is to say by elimination'. Or so the young painter Michael Wishart thought, pitying Watson for spending so much time in the pursuit of love, 'a thankless task for so fastidious a homosexual, despite his haunted beauty'. The first and last of his objects of passion were homicidal and larcenous, dissipating the collections of modern paintings entrusted by Watson to their care. Through his art editorship of *Horizon*, he introduced its readers to the best of modern British painting, educating a generation during the 'forties. In its last issue at the end of the decade, *Horizon* would praise the transcendent power of the art of Francis Bacon.

Watson's little flat in Palace Gate was a refuge and a café of European taste. He bought works and subsidised painting trips for John Minton and Francis Bacon as well as the older artists Graham Sutherland and John Piper, while secretly giving money to the poets David Gascoyne and Dylan Thomas, who made it all disappear 'quick as a sardine'. He set up John Craxton in a studio with Lucian Freud, who had spent five months as a seaman on the dangerous Atlantic convoy run, and he bought the works of both of the young painters. He was admirable in his reserve, his tact, his generosity, his lack of ostentation and his taste in modern art. He used the bounty of his fortune from margarine to ease the lives of his talented friends. He seemed to Stephen Spender almost American, 'extraordinarily chic, like a character from Henry James'. He was the last of the true private patrons of the arts before the coming of state aid for them. Under the pretence of retouching it, Francis Bacon destroyed the picture which Watson bought off him, as he did with all of his early work when he could get his hands back on it.

The cauldron and melting-pot of Soho and Fitzrovia in the War led to intense friendships and passing encounters. The editor of Penguin *New Writing*, John Lehmann, plunged into the urban underworld that brought together soldiers and sailors and men of letters and artists in an erotic transience more charged than the bars and the sexual booths of Weimar Berlin.

> The black-out heightened the sense of adventure as one slipped into pub after pub. My sexual hunger was as avid as it was with so many others at a time when death seemed to tease us with forebodings of liquidation in terrors still undeclared. One curious manifestation of this was in the public urinals. As never before, and with the advantage of the black-out, a number of these, scattered all over London, became notorious for homosexual activities . . . This was not my scene, but the pubs frequented by the soldiery were: those caverns of light and potential sensuous adventure that hid behind the blacked-out windows and the heavy double curtains of the doorway, in a totally darkened though sometimes moon-dramatised cliff landscape. Faceless uniformed figures passed me, fingers brushed my fingers, but I hurried on, ignoring the solicitations of blindfold Eros until I was in a place where I could see and choose for myself . . . An atmosphere of heightened emotion dominated; kisses were exchanged with those one would never in normal times have reached the point of kissing; declarations of devotion and admiration were made that might never have come to the surface otherwise; vows to keep in touch, to form closer and more meaningful alliances when peace returned.

So *In the Purely Pagan Sense* described the encounters of young serving men with a leading literary editor in the first year of the War.

A Fitzrovia regular and artists' model with hennaed hair, Quentin Crisp, agreed. Along with some of the younger painters, he had been exempted from military service as an overt homosexual, said to suffer from sexual perversion although he gloried in it. He lived in the world of bookies and burglars, artists and actresses, poets and prostitutes who haunted Fitzrovia. These were now joined by the War deserters, who existed in the cafés and stayed for weeks on end in a cellar called The Low Dive, until the military police swooped on them. Crisp liked the time because the women had gone butch and took to uniforms, and he could at last wear women's trousers and black, lace-up shoes with firm, medium heels. London by night became 'one of those dimly-lit parties that their hosts hope are slightly wicked'. But when bombs started to fall, 'the city became like a paved double bed. Voices whispered suggestively to you as you walked along; hands reached out if you stood still and in dimly lit trains people carried on as they had once behaved only in taxis'. Railway carriages were the playground of exhibitionists. 'The whole of London was one long towpath, one vast movie house.' This was 'the feast of love and death that St. Adolf had set before the palates of the English – parched these long dark twenty-five years. And along Piccadilly, the regular tarts still walked their beats, carrying gas masks, which seemed to offer a grim sort of sex, a threat of terminal disease behind the smiling question, "Hallo, dearie – want a little love?" '

This was the wartime London at night of Francis Bacon, who was attracted to Soho as the stimulus and rendez-vous for artists and homosexuals like himself. His chief port of call was the York Minster or French Pub run by Gaston Berlemont, whose father Victor once had the cellar fixed as a ring for the use of the great French boxer Carpentier. He was no regular at the two gay pubs, the Golden Lion and the Fitzroy Tavern, but he always tried to eat well to anchor the alcohol swilling inside him, particularly at Wheeler's in Old Compton Street round the corner from the French Pub. Something that Bacon had learned from his regular lover, Eric Hall, was that good food would prolong a life spent drinking too much good wine. Depending on the state of his finances and those of his friends, he would also drink in the Gargoyle along with fellow artists such as John Minton and Lucian Freud, who was introduced to Bacon by Graham Sutherland in 1943 as a 'fantastic painter, like a cross between Vuillard and Picasso'. Bacon found the Gargoyle 'a wonderful club' and after drifting in, he would go to a lean-to café on a bomb-site in Dean Street, 'where about four o'clock in the morning you could go and have tea and bacon sandwiches. It was a kind of all-night thing – it was a lovely life.'

In spite of his small production and destroyed works, Bacon already had influence over Sutherland and Freud, who was to paint the portrait of him that hung in the Tate Gallery before it was stolen in Berlin, and also intensely to admire the evocative power of his friend's handling of paint. Until then, as John Rothenstein recorded, Freud had drawn constantly in the confidence that his pen or pencil could express his ideas fully. But seeing Bacon's flow with a brush, he was made 'aware, as never before, of his need to represent *volume*, more naturally fulfilled by the brush than the pencil'. In order to stimulate his urge to paint as fluently as Bacon, Freud now denied himself the delight of drawing. He found Bacon 'the wildest and wisest' person he had ever met. And he was to do more than was expected of him. 'Opinion was divided as to whether he would have a career comparable to that of the young Rimbaud, or whether he would turn out to be one of the doomed youths who cross the firmament of British art like rockets soon to be spent.'

Bacon did not spend all his time drinking or cruising in what George Melly has described as the classless or class-aphrodisiac acceptance of pre-War and wartime homosexual circles, 'their belief in the self-sufficiency of the chic, the "amusing", the new; the love of glitter and danger; the belief in hard work at the service of sensation'. For he had learned his own concentration on hard work from his first tutor Roy de Maistre, as Patrick White had along with him. In White's words:

> He also taught me to discipline myself as an artist. I had seen him close his door in the faces of casual callers. I thought it a cranky joke. I did not really get the message till I found he did not discriminate. It hurt at first. I saw him as a sour old bastard. Nowadays when I close the door on some importunate, destroyed

> face I feel as though the spirit of Roy de Maistre is at my elbow supporting me. His work was what mattered, much as he enjoyed social occasions when the ingredients were sympathetic.

Bacon also began to concentrate and to exclude, to put work before drinking with his friends. He still lived marginally from his illegal gambling sessions, but he took more and more to the brush again, as if his father's death and the daily menace of war had loosed his inhibitions and set him free. For the first time as an artist, he could say, as his great ancestor Francis Bacon had said about his philosophy, that his painting 'came as a guest, not as an enemy'. He began to record his fears and his nightmares, his visions and his observances, as three Furies or Eumenides, screaming at the cataclysm of this world.

Many of Bacon's influences were literary. He read deeply, but not widely. He could not say, as the philosopher Francis Bacon had written, 'I have taken all knowledge to be my province'. He plumbed some knowledge to its profundities. Yet he could claim as his own the title of one of his ancestor's works, *Cogitata et Visa*. He had considered and *seen* the abyss of himself and his age. In *The Waste Land* by T. S. Eliot, he discerned his bleak views:

> I will show you fear in a handful of dust . . .
>
> But at my back in a cold blast I hear
> The rattle of the bones, and chuckle spread from ear to ear.

His favourite line of Aeschylus, that he would endlessly repeat, was, 'The reek of human blood smiles out of him.' Shakespeare also was his study, particularly for the images that rose in his mind after reading the soliloquies of Hamlet or the horrors of *King Lear*, when Gloucester is blinded to Cornwall's words, 'Out, vile jelly! Where is thy lustre now?', and gives the answer, 'All dark and comfortless'. But in his 'Three Studies for Figures at the Base of a Crucifixion' Bacon's inspiration was the Greece of Sophocles and Pericles, when the Furies were loosed on the land by the insane long struggle between Athens and Sparta. These were the three divine avengers which he painted during the Second World War, to express his protest at its dread carnality.

'Each panel represented a horrific creature, half human and half animal,' John Rothenstein wrote of the triptych before Eric Hall presented it to the Tate Gallery – extremely angrily because his offer to do so had been ignored for several months. 'That on the left hand is tensely bowed as though for beheading; that in the centre, a defeathered ostrich, with a mouth in place of a head, emerging from a bandage; and that on the right, a long-necked creature with a huge open mouth, screaming, with ears but faceless, yet voracious, infinitely malignant.' These were the paintings in embryo which Sir Kenneth Clark saw when Graham Sutherland took him to Bacon's studio at Cromwell Place, along with the unfinished, reptilian 'Figure in a Landscape', which Bacon would complete from a snapshot of Eric Hall asleep in the Park. Acting then as Director of the National Gallery as well as Chairman of the War Artists' Advisory Committee, the urbane Clark glanced over Bacon's few canvases and said, 'Interesting, yes. What extraordinary times we live in.' Then he walked out of the studio.

Bacon was understandably annoyed. He turned to Sutherland, who had been telling him not to work in a vacuum, but to meet important people in society, and he said: 'You see, you're surrounded by cretins.' But later that evening when Sutherland dined with Clark, he heard something which excited his jealousy about his fellow artist. 'You and I may be in a minority of two,' Clark said, 'but we may still be right in thinking that Francis Bacon has genius.' He did not add that he thought Sutherland had genius as well, although he was to buy his work, and not Bacon's, still too raw as yet for his taste. Sutherland did, however, bring Bacon's paintings to the attention of Sir Colin Anderson, who was to buy his 'Study for a Crucifixion' of 1933 from the Redfern Gallery thirteen years after it was painted, and later 'Owls' from the Hanover Gallery in the 'fifties. And Eric Hall was to foster Rothenstein's interest in Bacon's art, presenting pictures he had bought from his lover to the Tate Gallery with a declaration from the Athenaeum that one of them was among 'the best paintings Bacon has painted and I have known his works for twenty years.'

Bacon entertained the conventional Graham Sutherland and his wife Kathleen to dinner almost every week in Cromwell Place. The salad bowl often had paint in it, but the wine and food were good in spite of rationing, and the conversation was even better. Certainly the influence of Bacon on Sutherland was pervasive, but unrecognised even by Sutherland himself, who disapproved of Bacon's spasmodic life, as Rothenstein called it – 'first a painting spasm, then a drinking or social spasm. He liked the hazards of Soho by night and was by nature a gambler.'

'Three Studies for Figures at the Base of a Crucifixion' was being hung in the Lefevre Gallery with works by Henry Moore and Matthew Smith and other British artists in April, 1945, one month before the Nazi surrender in Berlin. It seemed to howl against the massacre of the twenty million dead and more in the conflict, just as the nation was about to celebrate a victory that seemed to be justice. Bacon had worked on a triptych in the last years of the War, his traumas put on board with rough strokes. He admitted to the influence of Picasso's work in the 'twenties, but he had gone further in distorting the organic form that related to the human image. After his death in 1992, Richard Cork was to suggest the continuing impact of 'this howl of peace at a universe so meaningless that humanity is reduced to the level of a gruesome accident'.

> The triptych arrangement enabled him to join three repugnant creatures in one work. At the same time, it isolates each presence within gilt frames so that none can alleviate the other's torment. The female figure on the left, saddled with a pair of limp feelers hanging from her shoulder-stumps, cranes forward.
>
> She seems to be trying to slide off her perch and discover what is happening in the central panel, but cannot move. Paralysis also affects the monster on the right, a hump-back oddity with starved ribs who can only stretch out its distended neck and utter a helpless roar.
>
> The realistic human ear attached to this screaming head clashes with the animality of its body. And the same principle of shock through contrast applies to the patch of grass growing so unexpectedly in the orange ground which gives the whole triptych such a parched and eye-smarting air.
>
> The impulsive handling of paint and pastel, smeared, scraped,

> slashed and dragged over the hardboard rather than applied with conventional refinement, shows the urgency with which Bacon set down this atheistic vision of hell. But discipline counters the rhetoric wherever you look.
>
> Spare black outlines brushed in behind the figures lend order to the triptych, and direct our attention towards the middle. Here, the focal image offers no trace of a body on a cross. Instead, a beast as brutish as its companions bares jagged teeth at us.
>
> The beast could be growling, like an enraged dog warning strangers not to get too close. Or it might be yelling because its eyes, like poor Gloucester's in *King Lear*, have been put out. The ambiguity is left exposed, for Bacon understands that a cry can signify aggression just as easily as pain.

The triptych was to receive some hostility for its ferocity, one critic writing that Bacon had discovered 'in the art of painting the felicities of the death warrant [and] covered the lamp-shades of his immediate predecessors with human skins.' He did shock, he did strike for the bowels, the inner nerve. Yet alone, on the verge of the discovery of the holocaust and the use of atomic fission to decompose human beings and their cities, Bacon realised his three Furies in appropriate images for the terrible end of the Second World War. As he once said to Francis Russell, 'I think of myself as a kind of pulverizing machine into which everything I look at and feel is fed.' He read the entrails of his half century, pulverised them and vomited his three Eumenides in paint.

6

A Commendable Prodigality

> None can character him to the life, save himself . . . He and his servants had all in common, the men never wanting what their master had, and thus what came flowing in unto him was sent flying away from him, who in giving of rewards knew no bounds but the bottom of his own purse. Wherefore when King James heard that he had given ten pounds to an underkeeper by whom he had sent him a buck, the King said merrily, 'I and he shall both die Beggars', which was commendable prodigality in a subject.
>
> Thomas Fuller on Francis Bacon,
> Lord Verulam, Viscount St. Albans
> from *The Church-History of Britain*, 1655.

The feeling of mental and physical exhaustion at the end of the War among British artists was allied to a sense of powerlessness. The monstrous regimentation of the War was only to become worse in the state socialism of the peace. And from that lassitude and impotence, a myth and a justification would grow that would become a truism of art and literary history. The events of the War were too appalling to describe or depict. They were beyond the capacity of the artist, who would never comprehend the long agony of the holocaust nor the obliteration by the atom bomb. In his own reaction from his memory of tossing his 'bricks' of fire and annihilating all living things on a Proustian beach and watching the destruction of his fellow rocket-ships off Walcheren, William Golding later wrote a full assertion about the impossibility of bearing witness: 'The experiences of Hamburg and Belsen, Hiroshima and Dachau cannot be imagined. We have gone to war and beggared description all over again. These experiences are like the black holes in space. Nothing can get out to let us know what it was like inside. It was like what it was like and on the other hand it was like nothing else whatsoever. We stand before a gap in history. We have discovered a limit to literature.'

Francis Bacon would prove that there was no limit to painting. And Golding bypassed his limit to literature in many of his own novels; their sense of moral evil and human frailty reek of his experience of war. Although Golding personally avoided Belsen and Hiroshima, he could not avoid the pictures and descriptions of them. In point of fact, the direct experience of Belsen, along with the photographs and newsreels taken by the Americans of the concentration camps, did change British painting, while the age of nuclear fission decomposed the arts. Mervyn Peake was then beginning to write his three eerie and Gothic illustrated manuscripts, *Titus Groan* and *Gormenghast* and *Titus Alone*, the best of their kind since the works of Thomas Love Peacock. In 1945 he was sent to Belsen to prepare a series of drawings for the *Leader* magazine. He had already foreseen what he would witness in his *chef d'oeuvre*, his drawings for Coleridge's 'The Rime of the Ancient Mariner'. His 'Nightmare Life-in-Death' was Belsen incarnate. When he returned from the camp, his wife found he looked inward, 'as if he had lost, during that month in Germany, his confidence in life itself'.

Graham Sutherland had felt some compunction about drawing the victims of the blitz and had often taken photographs of the destruction rather than sketch the sufferers among the ruins. He experienced the horrors of war directly, when his last assignment as a war artist was to depict the wrecked flying-bomb launching sites north-west of Paris. He found a panoramic devastation, houses reduced to black spokes, and in the caves the fragments of bodies, which he drew, but which were not exhibited by his state employers. He never saw the concentration camps, although he said that in some ways he would have liked to have seen them. 'I remember receiving a black-covered American Central Office of Information book dealing with the camps. It was a kind of funeral book. In it were the most terrible photographs of Belsen, Auschwitz and Buchenwald . . . The whole idea of the depiction of Christ crucified became more real to me after having seen this book and it seemed to be possible to do this subject again.'

Sutherland thought that the disasters of the time did affect painters, who were a kind of blotting paper, bound to soak up the implications of modern chaos. At the Lefevre Gallery show of April, 1945, five of his paintings were hung with Francis Bacon's seminal triptych, of his howling Furies. Influenced by Bacon's work and the Grünewald altarpiece of the Isenheim Christ that had inspired the Expressionists, and by his own studies of twisted trees and thorns in Wales, Sutherland set about his magnificent 'Crucifixion' for St. Matthew's Church in Northampton. His agonised Christ was pierced with thorns of light and caged with bars and arcs of wire. To Sutherland, the thorns were the cruelty, while the tortured body of the Saviour was derived from Grünewald and the Belsen dead who looked 'like figures deposed from crosses'. They seemed eternal and classic beside 'the continuing beastliness and cruelty of mankind, amounting at times to madness'.

Francis Bacon collected newspaper and magazine photographs of Adolf Hitler and the Nazi leaders, and he saw the newsreels of Belsen at the Rialto Cinema by the bombed Café de Paris. Unlike the ordered and accurate Sutherland, the anarchic Bacon would never admit to his direct influences, claiming sometimes to work while drunk and at other times saying that chance made him paint as he did. In a discussion with this author, he admitted to the direct influence of the Belsen newsreels, but only through 'an intense, active unconsciousness. I see the violence of existence. We must recall it.' Technique was all to him. He did not draw, but painted direct on to the coarse side of the canvas. As it happens, he did do a series of concentration camp pictures, which were owned by Keith Lichtenstein, once the proprietor of the Gigolo café in Chelsea. They showed the horror of the Holocaust, but they do not appear in the present catalogues of Bacon's paintings, so many of which he has destroyed himself. The gaping mouths of his figures in torment, the white streaks that enclose them like torture cages, the distorted bodies swollen by death or greed, these did derive, as did the drawings of Goya, from images of human bestiality which Bacon saw in blurred photographs and moving pictures from the War.

Bacon denied that his aggression in painting had anything to do with the aggression of fighting. He had been accustomed to living through forms of violence which had offended him – the military violence of his Irish boyhood and brutal early affairs with the grooms in his father's stables, the emotional violence of his life in Weimar Berlin and Paris in the 'thirties and wartime London. Yet he looked beyond the violence of war 'to remake the violence of reality itself ... the brutality of fact'. Although contemporary pictures of pain and wounds influenced his images, he wanted to create a universal statement about the suffering of man. His human corpses, his figures of Christ hung like mutton in a butcher's shop, showed a belief in the absolute mortality of man without hope of redemption. 'Of course, we are meat, we are potential carcasses.'

Worse was to happen in the early August of 1945. The atomic bombs were dropped at Hiroshima and Nagasaki in Japan. The War in the Pacific was, indeed, over. 'This has killed a beautiful subject,' the leading Australian physicist said; but a hundred and fifty thousand civilians had also been killed, and perhaps twice that number were to rot and peel and erode over the next forty years, while their children would be born maimed and deformed. The sight of the explosion on the newsreels, a fireball depending on the stem of a cloud toadstool sixty-thousand feet high, seemed to signify the end of the Second World War, and perhaps of all war. But for the survivors of the explosion, only a slow and pained decomposition was left for them. Even some physicists such as Isador Rabi felt that an ancient equilibrium in nature had been upset. Human beings were now a threat to the world given them to live in.

Bacon's paintings of that year reflected the menaces of his age. To his 'Figure in a Landscape', he added spouting machine-gun barrels or tubes of poison gas hissing in death chambers, while the orifices of the figure were wounds as much as mouths. And his 'Painting, 1946', which was bought by Erica Brausen of the Redfern Gallery for a hundred pounds and sold on to the Museum of Modern Art for a mere fifty pounds profit, was redolent of decay and bleeding meat under a mushroom cloud, here represented by a black open umbrella, covering a ghoulish dictator in a red plush amphitheatre, approached by the tubular railings of Bacon's Bauhaus furniture. Bacon called the carcass at the back of the painting 'the armchair of meat': it was a gruesome replacement of the ornate throne of the traditional state portrait. In his blithe way, as always, the spokesman of chance, Bacon said to John Rothenstein that his picture did *not* represent a relation between an aspect of spirituality and of carnality. He had begun that particular picture with the intention of showing a bird of prey alighting on a ploughed field. 'The carcass? Well, when I was a boy, I used to be fascinated by butchers' shops.' Actually, he had used chance to put together three of the major themes of his time, which also preoccupied him – war and the dictator and dead meat. He had achieved, first of all, the synthesis of the European grand manner with contemporary Surrealist art.

Comparing this picture to the triptych of the previous year, Rothenstein discerned contrary procedures in Bacon. Set against the retention in his mind over a long period of a particular, defined image were the happenings of chance and automation. 'He is capable of giving effect to a most precisely formulated intention or of abandoning such an intention – he does not begin a picture without one – in order to follow blind inspiration, when he becomes a sort of figurative action-painter working under the spell of the subconscious.' Bacon himself rejected any influence from action painting, particularly that of Jackson Pollock, saying, 'Starting from an image I want to be formal *and* vivid and yet to be vivid you have to be by chance. If I throw a lump of paint on the floor, it has vitality but no control. Pollock is not formal enough for me.' When he was asked if the wings of the bird of prey had perhaps become the umbrella or the forelegs of the background carcass, he replied the bird disappeared early in the process of coaxing out the image of the dictator taken from his war photographs of Goëbbels or Himmler or Mussolini, or even Roosevelt in his cape at Yalta and T. S. Eliot's Apeneck Sweeney, 'with the oval O cropped out with teeth' of his murderer's mouth.

Bacon's formative years as a furniture designer, and the Cubist influence of Picasso, led him to impose a curious discipline on his paintings. Often within the gilt frame, there are other painted frames. In the case of 'Painting, 1946', the railings seem to enclose steps that lead up to the ribcage of the hanging carcass as well as to the rostrum, where the carnivorous dictator grimaces and devours. Tassels hang ready to pull crimson curtains across the altar of immolation, where Sweeney waits for his victims. The shock lies in the incongruity, the black umbrella above the bestial monster, the plush surroundings to the bloody meat, as if a genteel ritual enclosed the massacre of every day. Later, he called the picture one of the 'most unconscious paintings' he had ever done. As for the meat, he had always thought how extraordinary carcasses were, hanging in great butchers' shops, 'how amazing their colour was, how beautiful they looked'.

Other paintings of the time were wrongly called 'Magdalenes' or 'Studies for Human Figures at the Cross'. They were associated with Bacon's 'Three Figures at the Base of the Crucifixion', but he said he never thought of any of these figures as the Magdalene and never associated them in any way with the Cross. All of these different three figures were crouching with their heads down. One, which was destroyed, showed a huddled creature behind a cluster of blue flowers and hidden by a herringbone overcoat and a grey hat. The second figure copied the mourning shape and enlarged the coat and the hat against an orange background. The third figure showed the long neck and arm and head of a woman screaming like the nurse in the film of *The Battleship Potemkin*, her head covered by an open umbrella, her buttocks and legs still draped in the herringbone coat. Its composition was reminiscent of the women in Grünewald's triptych at Isenheim and Giotto's 'Mourning the Dead Christ' at Padua. The umbrella represented the dark halo of the modern age, the poison cloud of the nuclear threat from the air, its ribs spread like the black lines of sound in Munch's 'The Cry' and complemented by the spiky fronds of the tropical plant in the foreground. The effects of spokes and leaves radiating from the hole and howl of the cavern of the mouth still make the picture cry out to the eyes. Bacon admitted that he never succeeded in painting the smile.

Yet Bacon could not stand the dreariness of London after the War. There was a draining of energy in the lacklustre and rationed peace. The writer Constantine Fitzgibbon agreed, describing the atmosphere among the demobilised and the Fitzrovians in 1945 'as one of exhaustion shot through with violence and hatred. We read about the concentration camps, and we wondered which pub would have beer tonight. We were horrified by Hiroshima, which seemed to make it all meaningless, and we wanted out.' Bacon already felt himself a European after his visits to Berlin and Paris, and he particularly wanted out to France, joining in the Gadarene rush of the piggish men of letters to their beloved land after its liberation. John Lehmann, despite help from the Publishers' Association and the British Council, found himself outdistanced on the run to Paris by Cyril Connolly and Raymond Mortimer 'and other literary lights of the London wartime firmament'. The artists of Fitzrovia were not far behind in their stampede towards good food and wine and Mediterranean light. The lanky, wild and gangling John Minton left the ravaged docklands of London to travel south with the poet and editor, Alan Ross. They went to Corsica to draw and write *Time Was Away* for John Lehmann. Michael Ayrton and John Craxton left for Italy and Greece. And taking the £100 from Erica Brausen for his 'Painting, 1946', Francis Bacon returned to the France that he loved, settling in the Hotel de Ré near the casino in Monte Carlo, where he became obsessed by gaming. He would enter the casino at ten o'clock in the morning and spend sixteen hours there, coming out at dawn. At one point, he won sixteen hundred pounds sterling, not subject to British foreign currency regulations, and took a villa and filled it with drink and food and 'an enormous number of friends'. He spent the lot in ten days, indulging in his commendable prodigality. What came flowing in was sent flying away from him. He felt of gambling as he felt of painting: he wanted to win even if he always lost. He loved living 'in gilded squalor'.

He gambled at roulette because it was impersonal. He disliked the relationships between players at *chemin-de-fer*. At Monte Carlo, he had a long patch of very good luck. He thought he could hear the croupier call out the winning number before the ball fell into the socket of the spinning wheel, and he would play three tables at a time, putting small stakes on the numbers on each of them. But he stressed that he was not like Dostoevsky's *The Gambler*, who played for the thrill of losing more than he had. 'I feel I want to win,' Bacon told David Sylvester, 'but then I feel exactly the same thing in painting. I feel I want to win even if I always lose.' Later, he would modify his words, saying that something happened in painting as well as gambling – 'greed caused him to take a risk beyond his powers'.

He confirmed that to Michael Wishart, who personally saw the pyramids and troughs of Bacon's bank account in Monte Carlo, anything from a low of five pounds to a peak of a thousand pounds. 'Nothing is more wonderful and refreshing than being completely cleaned out,' Bacon confessed to Wishart, who appreciated such a thrill of masochism. 'Losing is better than winning.' When back in England, Bacon went frequently to the greyhound racing tracks with Wishart, darting away from the champagne dinners in the White City to place his bets. His compulsion remained with him always, even when he was to make fortunes from Marlborough Fine Art. As Wishart said, Bacon might have more money than he knew what to do with, but 'he was winning and losing at the London casinos in ratio to what he was getting from the Marlborough.'

One morning, when he came back from the Casino de la Mediterranée, Bacon had a telephone call telling him that his old nanny had had a stroke. He left on the first Blue Train for England, and on his return, Wishart met him at the Gare de Lyon. Bacon was inconsolable and weeping. 'She was far and away the most important person in his life,' Wishart reported. 'His devotion was like that of a son.'

With this last attachment gone in England, Bacon stayed on mostly in Monte Carlo for the next four years. Eric Hall visited him there and continued to support him. Bacon was still searching for older men to love. 'I'm looking for a cruel father,' he told Wishart; he was still looking for his own father he had left. Yet Monte Carlo did his painting little good, although he learned a technique which was to change his art. The Mediterranean light was too strong for him after the greyness of England. It interfered with his vision. But after he had lost his money in the casino and wanted to paint, he turned round some used canvases and discovered that it was easier to work on the unprimed side. Instead of destroying his failures, he used their reverse and rough surfaces in France and continued to do so for the rest of his life. Poverty was the father of his invention. He found a villa on the heights above Monaco with a wonderful room to work in, or so he told Erica Brausen. It had windows all round and sensational views, and he even thought of decorating a club with murals when he was not trying to track down 'the movements of the fleet'. This project did not come to pass, but when Bryan Robertson, then the director of the Whitechapel Gallery, was to rent Bacon's villa on the foothills of the Alps, after having been drunk under the table at many dinners with the painter in the old Carlton Grill in London, he was to find a bedroom full of abandoned canvases of startling images and a cupboard stuffed with a comprehensive library on sexual perversions, 'which added a certain zing to hot afternoon siestas'.

Although he was to escape frequently to France and later to Tangier, Bacon was to remain a resident of London most of his life. One terrifying night, trapped in a hotel room near Cannes and surrounded by forest fires, made him remember the blitz. Even a refuge in France could be like being in London again. Yet he confessed to few English influences, mainly to European ones, such as Velázquez and Goya, Cimabue and Giotto and Titian, Grünewald and Rembrandt, Degas, and Picasso and Giacometti – who painted in 1946 a curiously Baconian picture of the French arts patron Marie-Laure de Noailles, looking like a blackened snail crawling out of its shell. Both of them were particular in working out their original combinations of philosophy and painting and experience – a synthesis between Existentialism as preached by Sartre and Camus, a legacy from Surrealism, and their personal bite on the bullet of living through world wars.

While Bacon became the major influence on English art, he took little from it, except an admiration for Matthew Smith and Constable's sketch of 'The Leaping Horse', depicted in agitated motion, in the Victoria and Albert Museum. Certainly, Bacon took nothing from his contemporary neo-Romantics, although his personal influence was immediately visible in getting Graham Sutherland and his wife to come over to the South of France. First, he persuaded Sutherland to show with him at the UNESCO exhibition in Paris along with Picasso and Braque. But he wrote back that he found all their work boring and lacking in reality and immediacy. Even with

Picasso, decoration was contaminating all. He felt he might be on the verge of doing something good and was working on three studies from photographs of the Velázquez portrait of Pope Innocent X. He returned to London for lunch with the Sutherlands at The White Tower, and Graham agreed to follow Francis's path to the sun in Monte Carlo, where Eric Hall had been lured to stay with his lover.

Once the Sutherlands had arrived, they were introduced to Hall and to gambling, which Graham called 'the painter's vice' and found a revelation of character. 'When one should be bold, for instance, one is timid,' he said. 'When one should be timid, one is bold.' Francis Bacon was always bold at the green table, and he took his friend painting not far from Vence, where the dried grasses and rocks of an arid river bed suggested the spines and thorns of some of their later pictures. On another trip, Graham travelled out with Lucian Freud, continuing the exodus from Fitzrovia, while Freud symbolically released caged birds from hotel windows all the way to the South.

Sutherland longed to meet the greater figures of Provence, something Bacon did not try to do. He met Matisse once and Picasso often. He was commissioned by Somerset Maugham to paint a portrait, which pleased the sitter although it made him look to others like a Shanghai brothel-keeper. Sutherland now deserted his British and neo-Romantic influences for the more brilliant colours and definitions of the Mediterranean sun. He abandoned landscapes for still lives and a new lightness and brilliance of colour, acid pink and mauve, orange and scarlet, emerald and chrome yellow. He used organic fragments, shells and roots and gourds and thorns, the ominous pieces of nature. Still praised by Douglas Cooper, who was then living with the art critic and biographer of Picasso, John Richardson, Sutherland began to lose the esteem which had put him second only to Henry Moore and far superior to Francis Bacon, whose desperate work was increasingly held to cast a malign presence over many of Sutherland's canvases.

John Richardson was the witness to the deterioration of the relationship between the two painters, which he held to be crucial for Sutherland, whose post-War success lay in his imitation of Bacon. In spite of his kind manner and early help to Bacon by introducing patrons to him, Sutherland seemed to Richardson deeply jealous of the rival painter and a sly man. 'I had every reason to despise Graham,' he said. 'He did what he could to keep Francis a secret from his friends.' It was useless as a tactic, for Francis was far more socially aware than Graham Sutherland ever could be. In fact, when Richardson fell out with Cooper and moved on and was blacklisted by him as the enemy everywhere, only Sutherland took the anathema seriously enough to run to the other side of Bond Street at the sight of him.

'My work is like a diary,' Picasso told Richardson. 'To understand it, you have to see how it mirrors my life.' Bacon's work was also like a diary and mirrored his life and loves, although it was transmuted by his particular retention of images and anguish of mind. He returned with Eric Hall from the south of France to a dismal London. There he met again the demobilised Patrick White, before he fled the depressed city back to Australia, selling his huge Bacon desk and the chairs and glass table, which he had bought from R. A. Butler. To White it seemed:

> Those who had spent the war in London did not appear so conscious of the graveyard it had become for a revenant like myself dropping in from another world. Sometimes the actual graves of those who had died in times of peace still surrounded the crater where a church had stood. I was less obsessed by the material particulars of death than by its infinity haunting the ruins of once stately houses or an expanse of street from which a comparatively humble terrace had vanished. Friends I failed to trace and my own memories of the blitz added to the feeling that death still hovered over the city I had known . . .
>
> Another determining factor was hunger. In London after the war it was almost impossible to feel fed, anyway for a gross character like myself. At the mercy of a ration book and a pair of scissors, you cast about in your mind for something to fill your belly. Even bread was on points, everything devoured long before the cheaper restaurants opened with their often nauseating offerings.

Fitzrovia had largely lost its charms, its regulars like Alan Ross finding it a dead and seedy place now, peopled by hangers-on and time-wasters. There was rationing, but no reconstruction. The vast bomb crater where St. Ann's Church had been opposite the French Pub was a stagnant pool, fringed with reeds and weeds, where used condoms floated like toy yachts. Yet wartime Fitzrovia was preserved artificially by the squalor of peace, even if the soldiers and the sailors and the airmen from far places no longer passed through in their transient lust and generosity. A central London of vice and crime had sprung up in the post-War years with prostitutes lining the streets more frequently than lamp-posts and a red-light district of a square mile in the back-streets, crowded with the illegal drinking-clubs that were a hangover from the War. London was full of the bored and the lonely, looking for purpose or jobs, and they congregated in the basement clubs to bemoan the cut of their demob suits – 'a sort of never-never land of clipped moustaches, army-style overcoats and old school ties. They were suffering a post-War weariness from which many never recovered.'

New elements thronged the pubs of Fitzrovia, also looking for business opportunities. To the demobilised were added the black marketeers and the 'spivs', who shaded into the criminal class in their striped suits with padded shoulders, Brylcreemed hair under fedora hats, and yellow shoes as pointed as daggers. They thrived on the inadequacy of the supply system. They could provide scarce goods at the right price from unknown sources, and they became the symbols, necessities and scapegoats of their age, just as a few notorious murders and murderers such as the con-man Neville Heath seemed to represent the suppressed violence of the peace. This was also particularly caught in the restless and seedy novels of the alcoholic genius, Patrick Hamilton, whose recording of the perverse gentility of the saloon bar appealed to the taste of Francis Bacon.

The real personalities of the post-War years, as Alan Ross knew, were those 'who in an age of rules, broke them'. Their names were a catalogue of deviance and crime: Max Intrator, Sidney Stanley, and the serial killer Neville Heath, who spoke of his murders almost as Bacon did of his paintings: 'I got excited and it went too far.' They echoed 'the shabby world of forged cheques, travelling restrictions and export permits; of pathological sexual obsessions and murder. The 'forties lived largely "under the counter": economically, sexually and histrionically. Overt sexual exhibitionism gave way to isolated acts of great violence.' The most sinister and inexplicable of the Soho murders was connected with the rise in vice and the beginning of the decline in the area. Freddie Mills had been a boxing champion and was found shot to death in his motor-car outside the Chinese restaurant which he owned in Soho. He was a member of a ring of practising homosexuals, and blackmail was thought to be the motive.

Homosexuality was still a crime in England. Even before the trial of Oscar Wilde, the area around Piccadilly had a long history of supplying youths for pederasts, some of whom were wealthy or prominent in society. The law compelled gay artists and aristocrats to consort with criminals to satisfy sexual needs. Legislation to allow homosexual acts between consenting adults was still twenty years away, but already the Fitzroy Tavern was becoming a gay rendezvous, while the Golden Lion near the French Pub was always of that persuasion, as was the Newman Arms. John Lehmann's *In the Purely Pagan Sense* disguised the names of the gay pubs and clubs, calling them the Broody Goose and the Alcibiades, but he attested to their prevalence after the War, filled with boxers, actors, businessmen and journalists. Eventually, the Fitzroy Tavern was to be raided in the 'fifties, and its proprietor, Charles Allchild, accused of running a disorderly house. Incredibly, he was acquitted in spite of accusations by the counsel for the prosecution that the pub was a meeting-place for obvious male homosexuals and sailors, soldiers and marines. 'There can be very little doubt that this house was conducted in a most disorderly and disgusting fashion,' the prosecutor said. 'These perverts were simply overrunning the place, behaving in a scandalous manner and attempting to seduce members of the Forces.'

The transition of the Fitzroy Tavern, however, from the beacon of bohemia in the 'thirties to a sexual encounter parlour in the post-War years, was a slow process. The regulars hardly noticed the changes over the years. Fitzrovia had always tolerated all sorts of behaviour. Prostitution and homosexuality were nothing new under the black-out or the lamp-light. What was new was their concentration in certain pubs and their overtness. In the War, open sexual behaviour had been permitted in the belief that the boys were having a good time before going back to camp or to die abroad. And there was the bombing. Danger allowed licence. But in what came to be called 'The Age of Austerity' after the War, the parade of sex in the pubs and the clubs and the streets seemed like flaunting it unnecessarily. Although London might have become the vice capital of Europe, performances were best left behind doors.

Such an atmosphere of clandestine perversity, a life of avoidance of the eye of authority, stimulated Francis Bacon into other painting portraits of protest and rage at the restrictions of existence within any society. From the last six years of the 'forties, only fifteen of Bacon's works survive because of his fierce self-criticism and destruction of his canvases. He was not yet bound by an obligation to a gallery to produce a set number of pictures each year, and he lived splendidly and squalidly on the margins of the metropolis for the rest of the decade. During the ten months before his first sole exhibition at the Hanover Gallery, which opened in the November of 1949, he produced seven paintings including five variations on 'Heads', a series or commentary on his progress and his life. He told John Russell that his break-through into his own vision came from 'the imperious character of the day-dreams' he had been having at the time. Russell commented on Bacon's split nature, his gregariousness contrasted to his solitary contemplation cut off from human contact, when he spent much of the day sprawling and dreaming, 'like a big cat in a cage'. When he sprang up, it was with an incisive light tread and quick glance beyond the trap of the studio walls, as if something would come in reach of his claws, so he could catch it. He lived in a 'state of animal readiness'.

The first of Bacon's 'Heads', painted in 1948, is jerked back as if ready for execution. The teeth are barren crops in the oval O of the mouth. The flesh seems diseased and the background melts and disintegrates. The second 'Head' has emerged from parted curtains: it is a man and beast, spouting a fall of slime. The paint is thick, layer encrusted on layer. It was one of the rare paintings that Bacon worked on and pulled through over many months. The fourth 'Head' shows a man's back dissolving into his ape reflection, while over the parted curtains, the thin lines of a cage or trap are faintly drawn. The image was taken from a safari photograph of a man looking at a small monkey, which Bacon transmuted into a version of the missing link. But by the sixth 'Head', a cube encloses the screaming papal figure, while the top of the head disappears into the curtains behind, and a tassel hangs where the brain should be. The shape is now dressed in white lace and a robe of purple and ultramarine, suggesting a caricature of Velázquez's portrait of Pope Innocent X, which Bacon had only seen in reproduction, not bothering to view the original on his one brief visit to Rome – a city he had loved although he had found Naples more exciting and better for work.

Captive and monster, the sixth 'Head' protests and devours: his holy office is snare and threat. He is held in a skeletal cube that is a dead loss, a boxed hell without escape. The picture assaults the power of the Church: it is blasphemous. It represents Bacon's heresy and protests against the rule of the organised religion which he had known in Ireland. He told a shocked reporter that his 'Heads' were 'an attempt to make a certain type of feeling visual'. The feeling was his own fear of mortality and rage against authority. 'Painting is the pattern of one's own nervous system being projected on the canvas.' Unlike Velázquez, however, he had used the unprimed surface of the cloth to make his 'Heads' harder and uglier. 'One of the problems', he said, 'is to paint like Velázquez, but with the texture of a hippopotamus skin.' The raw canvas was clogged with paint, almost soiled, and yet it was imprisoned behind plate glass and set in a heavy frame of burnished gold, the howling beast within the gilded gaol.

What Bacon had done was to transmute the state portrait into the unguarded snapshot. Each figure was isolated in claustrophobia in a sealed space, caught unawares and in crisis. 'While Velázquez portrayed the Pope *ex cathedra*, Bacon captured him *in camera*.' Talking to the perceptive critic Hugh Davies, Bacon expressed his admiration for Velázquez compared with Cézanne, whose 'apples are more intense than his people. His power of invention in forming an apple has never gone into his forming of human beings, he tends to make them inanimate objects, he doesn't extend his invention into the psyche of the human being. Yet if you look at Velázquez, his greatness is his interest in people . . . Velázquez came to the human situation and made it good and heroic and wasn't bombastic. He turned to a literal situation and made an image of it, both fact and image at the same time. The Pope is like Egyptian art; factual, powerfully formal and unlocks valves of sensation at all different levels.'

The exhibition of the 'Heads' at the Hanover Gallery provoked outrage and recognition. The Arts Council bought the sixth 'Head' and variations on it would become known as Bacon's style for the next eight years. 'His lacerated and tortured beings seem to be partly living on this earth and partly withdrawn into a shadowland of death,' the critic of *Studio* wrote, 'or is it just ghastly premonition?' It was not mere sensationalism. For those strong enough to stand the shock, the show was 'a mental and emotional experience'. In the last issue of *Horizon*, the critic Robert Melville gave Bacon his overdue accolade. He found that the 'Heads' recalled Dostoevsky and Kafka in literature; but in terms of visual association, the parallels came from the silent cinema, particularly that of Eisenstein and Buñuel's *Un Chien Andalou*, which 'has greater visual force and lucidity than anything achieved in the art of painting between the two wars, and only the recent paintings of Francis Bacon have discovered a comparable means of disclosing the human condition'. These had an air of extreme hazard. Bacon was probably the only important contemporary painter who was exclusively preoccupied with man.

> Bacon never makes a drawing. He starts a picture with a loaded one-inch brush of the kind that ironmongers stock, and almost the entire work is painted with such brushes. In these broad brush-strokes, modernism has found its skin: the 'works' no longer show.
>
> It isn't, of course, a simple matter of doing Cubism over again with thick brushes instead of thin ones. In releasing modern painting from the machinery of linear construction, Bacon makes a typically baroque statement: he gives reality to an illusion, and his pictures do not invite the spectator to investigate the means.
>
> The hole of a screaming mouth is sometimes the point of deepest recession in these pictures; or a little white arrow floats in front of the canvas and the rest of the picture starts at a depth which the eye judges to be *behind* the canvas; the canvas is thus rendered non-existent. But nothing can enter Bacon's pictures and remain abstract, and a small thing – an arrow or a safety pin – is anything but unassuming in a world of large, undetailed forms. It

> is like a fly in a prison cell. It assumes the proportions of a Visitor, or a Familiar, or even a Warder. The fact that nothing will be discovered about it increases its reality . . .
>
> Bacon is not making it any easier to paint pictures. His known works are few in number because he is compelled to destroy many canvases. When he works on a canvas, intellect, feeling, automatism and chance, in proportions which he will never be able to calculate in advance, sometimes come to an agreement. During the last twelve months these agreements have been more frequent; therein lies a hope for painting.

Until the success of his show at the Hanover Gallery, Bacon continued to lead his hazardous and bohemian existence. He used to quote two phrases in French, one from Madame du Deffand, '*Il n'y a qu'un malheur, celui d'être né*,' and the existentialist phrase, '*on joue perdant*'. He did not so much mean that the ill fortune of being born condemned him to misanthropy, but that life was a losing game, which one had to play at hazard. Gambling and running illegal games of chance were still Bacon's main source of income, but he was now given ten pounds a week and free champagne by Muriel Belcher to bring rich patrons and friends to her Colony Room, a drinking club upstairs in Dean Street in Soho with a licence to serve alcohol when the pubs were closed. 'It was possible to live on it, almost,' Bacon said later, 'before the pound went to confetti.' Muriel was a formidable lesbian, who claimed to be the heir in hospitality and repartee of the ancient Rosa Lewis of the Cavendish Hotel, where the rich paid the bills of the poor young men she fancied. Muriel referred to most men as 'Her' or 'Cunty' or 'Miss Hitler'; they were summoned to pay with the command, 'Open your bead bag, Lottie,' and closing time was announced with a reference to the gay slang for public pick-up urinals, 'Back to your lovely cottages.'

Muriel was a past mistress at the English art of making insults appear to be wit. Her clients enjoyed humiliation from her rough tongue. Along with Bacon, other painters and writers used the oasis of the Colony Room and left their impressions of that spiky watering-hole with its faded leopard-skin stools and bamboo bar. To Elizabeth Smart, its clientèle was composed of 'painters, writers, tinkers, tailors, sailors, editors, art editors, cartoonists, singers, African chiefs, burglars, strippers, composers, dress-designers, lords, land-owners, barrow-boys, advertising people, and unclassifiable people.' When Bacon ran into a young artist there, who asked him to come and see his own work because he so much admired Bacon's pictures, the older artist put him down, saying, 'I don't need to see yours – I've seen your tie.' To the chronicler of London street-life, Colin MacInnes, Muriel's was Mabel's in *England, Half-English*:

> And what of Mabel's place? Mabel's a character often met with in films and fiction, but oh! so rarely in reality: the platinum-tough girl with a heart of gold. Sharp, hard, ruthless and aggressive, she's generous, forgiving, considerate, and rather shy. Quite ignorant of the inner operations of the professional worlds of all her members, she can nevertheless assess, with uncanny accuracy, their intrinsic talents and current reputations. In appearance she's a *belle laide*, bulky and perpetually radiant. Her conversation's witty and salacious, her capacity for absorbing spirits without ill-effect apparently limitless. She's always glad to see you ('Sweetie! Come and kiss mother! You're a cup of tea'), and just as glad, when the time comes to tot the takings, to see you go.
>
> Of course, the spell of the drinking club is partly morbid. To sit in Mabel's place with the curtains drawn at 4 pm on a sunny afternoon, sipping expensive poison and gossiping one's life away, has the futile fascination of forbidden fruit: the heady intoxication of a bogus Baudelairian romantic evil. As the gins slip down your throat, and the dim electrics shine on the potted plants and on Mabel's lurid colour scheme of emerald green and gold, you feel like the fish in the tank above the cash-register – swimming aimlessly among artificial water-weeds, mindless in warm water. The pub, drear though it may be, is certainly more bracing – it offers none of the spurious comforts of this infantile hankering for the womb . . .

John Minton also left a sketch in words of the Colony Room: 'It was always night at Mabel's. Mabel stood an enormous matriarch behind the bar: you could get credit from her but it usually cost you a good deal one way and another: as the night went on her look would get a little more glazed, but she never faltered. "Purely medicinal" she would say, knocking back another double brandy which was chased up on your credit . . . Being at Mabel's was like being in an enormous bed, with drinks.' In the opinion of one of Minton's old friends, Minton was a liberation to Bacon. 'John, continually painting the sailors he had been to bed with the night before, released Francis from all sorts of reticences. It was a kind of sexual and artistic regeneration. Under Minton's wing in the 'forties, he managed to get rid of his inhibitions and behave quite freely.'

Late at night, the Soho artists met at David Tennant's night-club, the Gargoyle, where a lift no bigger than an upended coffin cranked and creaked with visitors up to the main room. The room had been suggested by Matisse himself, and eighteenth-century French mirrors had been cut into thousands of square wall tiles, which glittered, imperfect and awry, to entering eyes. Bacon did not go to the Gargoyle until the War was over, and would arrive, like most of the other guests, half drunk but admiring. 'But they looked for a moment like birds of paradise coming down this beautiful gold and silver staircase into what the multiplicity of mirrors made into a very beautiful room. I've never been a great admirer of Matisse, but this room really worked as a setting.'

John Minton first brought Bacon to the club in the days when his jealousy of Bacon's growing reputation had not yet driven them apart as it had in the case of Graham Sutherland. It was, in Bacon's opinion, the place for rows. 'They were nightly. They went on not only for hours, they went on for days. It was like one of those instalments where it says tomorrow you'll get such and such – well, you certainly did in the Gargoyle. It was great fun, really, in spite of the rows.' Bacon met Sartre there, with Simone de Beauvoir and Sonia Orwell, the poet George Barker and the painter Rodrigo Moynihan, later a close friend, and Henrietta Law, the wife of a film director whom Bacon used as a model, along with Muriel Belcher and Isabel Rawsthorne, twice married to leading British composers. Cyril Connolly went there a great deal, but Bacon found him profoundly unsympathetic. 'He approached you always as though he wanted to be wounded, which is a horrible way of approaching people. You only had to see his whole furtive look.' And Bacon never even found the ageing *enfant terrible*, Brian Howard, at all witty. Wit was a rare thing, 'a very acerbic commentary on behaviour'. There was more wit on one hair of Bacon's paintbrush than in all the saliva on Howard's loose tongue.

The Gargoyle housed the residue of post-War bohemia, where the aristocrats and the artists, the privileged and the patronised, would meet and drop the barriers of class, particularly if their homosexuality forced them into a clandestine security at a place that did not consider their preferences to be criminal acts. One night, Bacon and Minton and Lucian Freud offended James Pope-Hennessy, the Literary Editor of the *Spectator*, who had brought in a couple of his paratrooper 'rough trade' boys. When they emerged from the rickety lift, the paratroopers set on the artists. Freud jumped on the back of one of the bully boys, while Bacon kicked at his shins in a lady-like way. There were threats of legal action, which were dropped for fear of homosexual exposure. On another occasion, Bacon took John Rothenstein there and they were accosted by two fellow-guests with truculent demands for whisky. These were the Scottish homosexual painters, the two Roberts, MacBryde and Colquhoun, whose self-destruction through drink and destruction of his own art was deplored by Bacon. Colquhoun was doomed and damned by 'his gradual enslavement to a constrictive style', lacking the crucial part played by impulse and sheer chance.

The most intriguing description of Bacon's bohemian life at the time was given by Michael Wishart, a talented and beautiful and spoilt young artist. He had begun his sexual experiences early: he was, as he said, the precocious boy who never grew young. A German pilot knocked down in the blitz, now a prisoner of war, was his first encounter with the enemy, as Bacon had had in Berlin. 'I prefer not even to know my partner's name,' Wishart wrote, 'while sharing no language is a positive boon'. It had been the young German's mission to destroy him, but they made a private truce of the flesh. After the War, Wishart spent his adolescence on the floor of Lucian Freud's flat in London and in the Soho clubs, particularly the Gargoyle. Freud introduced him to Peter Watson, the patron of the arts with 'his haunted beauty'. Wishart went to Paris with Freud and fell in love with Peter Watson's dangerous and drug-addicted beloved, Denham Fouts, and ended by sharing his opium pipe-dreams and his bed. Escaping to London before he became an addict and before Fouts died in a lavatory in Rome, Wishart met, in a Soho pub a striking young man, who resembled David's self-portrait in the Louvre or pictures of the youthful Beethoven.

> I was struck by the intensity of his gaze: it was as though he had X-ray eyes. I succumbed at once to his romantic charm, which was allied to a caustic wit. This was actually a creative intelligence. A true visionary, he plunged the dagger of thought deep into the ridiculous sorrows of existence and twisted it. The funnier he became, the stronger was the sense of tears welling up behind his eyeballs. Within the same sentence he could pursue an idea into the darkest corners of human endurance and withdraw with an observation as hilarious as it was tragic. I had not met Francis Bacon before.

Bacon took the young painter back to his studio in Cromwell Place. He was very poor at the time, but he always managed to offer his guests enormous dry Martinis in Waterford tumblers under the dim glow of two huge glass chandeliers. The shabby chintz and velvet furnishings gave the old billiard room of the studio of Millais 'an air of diminished grandeur, a certain forlorn sense of Edwardian splendour in retreat'. It reflected Bacon's youth in the great houses of Ireland and his liking for Belle Epoque hotels in Monte Carlo, the seedy glamour of a fading casino. Then the nanny still sat in a rocking-chair at her knitting or slept on the kitchen table, looking forward to putting up a gibbet again at Marble Arch, where the Duchess of Windsor would be the first to be hanged, drawn and quartered. And the gaming parties continued, at which Bacon lived by chance and the spinning wheel. Wishart also met Bacon's lover and patron, Eric Hall. He appeared to be rather a philistine, plump and balding and not quite a gentleman, but obsessed with Bacon; a lover who bought the pictures to have the body.

Seated on the edge of the bath, Wishart used to watch Bacon make up his face before he went out. 'He applied the basic foundation with lightning dexterity born of long practice. He was more careful, even sparing, with the rouge. For his hair he had a selection of Kiwi boot polishes in various browns. He blended these on the back of his hand, selecting a tone appropriate for the particular evening, and brushed them through his abundant hair with a shoe brush. He polished his teeth with Vim. He looked remarkably young even before this alchemy.' He even used cosmetic on his face as if it were the canvas, while he was painting. John Richardson watched him in action in his studio. 'As he rehearsed his revolving brush strokes, he'd let his beard grow for three days, and he'd cover his stubble with sweeps of Max Factor pancake make-up as if duplicating on the bristle on his cheeks the brush-strokes on the rough side of the canvas. He acted out his pictures in skin pigment on his face.'

Bacon yielded his young friends and lovers with grace and generosity. He was asked to loan some money to another young painter, Anne Dunn, whose background was international café society. He sent the loan round to St. John's Wood in the hand of Michael Wishart. 'She opened the door like a spinster expecting a rapist: it was on the chain. I saw a tightly bandaged wrist. I fell in love with the bandage on sight, and very soon afterwards with the wearer, when we were dancing at the Gargoyle.' The wedding reception was held in Bacon's studio. Two hundred bottles of Bollinger were bought for two-hundred guests, but more cases had to be ordered because of the crush and the thirst of the gate-crashers. 'Francis astonished everyone by painting his two large chandeliers crimson, and his face a more delicate colour . . . For three nights and two days we danced.' David Tennant brought in the clientèle of the Gargoyle and Muriel Belcher all the members of the Colony Room. Tennant said that the prolonged ruby-lit bacchanale was the first real party since the War. It ended with a two-day regatta hosted by Bacon's good friends, Richard Chopping and Dennis Wirth-Miller, at Wivenhoe in Essex, where later Bacon would stay in the pub and paint and eventually himself buy a cottage. Bacon presented the young couple with all his family's collection of Waterford glass, although he kept a few china plates with the Bacon crest on them. And so the marriage celebrations and the 'forties were concluded through the commendable prodigality of Francis Bacon.

As Wishart told Lady Caroline Blackwood, Bacon had two major ambitions – to be one of the world's best painters as well as one of the world's leading alcoholics. While most people found these ambitions were contradictory and self-defeating, Bacon was to pull both off. At the age of eighteen, she had first seen the artist when he was committing one of his rare acts of outrageousness. It was at a party given by Ann Lady Rothermere, who was to become Mrs Ian Fleming. Princess Margaret was the guest of honour, wearing a crinoline with wooden hoops and singing Cole Porter songs accompanied by the band, while the amazed audience stopped dancing to listen to this impromptu royal performance. Suddenly at the back of the ballroom, the sound of a rumbling was heard which increased to a hullabaloo. Princess Margaret faltered in the middle of 'Let's Do It', turned scarlet and fled. Lady Caroline asked a gentleman in white tie and tails who had committed this act of loud treason. She heard that it was a dreadful man called Francis Bacon, who painted frightful pictures and should never have been allowed inside. Much later, when she was married to Lucian Freud, she asked Bacon how he had dared to cause that scandal. 'Her singing was really too awful,' he said. 'Someone had to stop her. I don't think people should perform if they can't do it properly.'

7
And Shew'd Us It

Bacon, like Moses, led us forth at last,
The barren wilderness he past,
Did on the very border stand
Of the blest promis'd land,
And from the mountain's top of his exalted wit
Saw it himself, and *shew'd us it* . . .
The work he did we ought to admire
And were unjust if we should more require . . .

From Cowley's 'Ode to the Royal Society', the preface to Thomas Sprat's *History of the Royal Society* (London, 1667)

Encountering Francis Bacon in a bar, the polymath Michael Ayrton found himself rebuked for accusing his fellow artist of not being able to draw. Ayrton stuck by his statement. Bacon looked at him and asked, 'Is drawing what you do?' pausing to add, 'I wouldn't want to do that.'

Ayrton felt that he was reduced to being a mere draughtsman. It was a palpable hit. Bacon's claim was legitimate. For him, the act of drawing was 'part of the act of painting and in no way separate'. He made a fierce and daring attack on form when he painted. He could not prepare for that by drawing. Even Bacon's inspiration for his series of popes in the early 'fifties, Velázquez, must have drawn directly in paint because so few of his sketches have survived.

> Bacon is extraordinarily intelligent but he is a gambler whose appetite for chance plays upon the insecurity of his sense of form. That a human hand is a structure totally incomparable to 'the

> lamprey, which hath no bone in it', concerns him very little compared to the sensation of a human presence. He seems to encounter flesh agglutinated haphazard on gristle rather than on bone. Unfortunately for me, I need the bones so that the flesh he thrusts and twists to such powerful effect is held in tension by some internal scaffolding and this requires a deep comprehension of structure which he disdains to establish below the neck. He understands and can gamble on the human head as no artist since Picasso has understood it. Indeed it is a measure of his mastery that he alone, since Picasso, can totally disorientate the formal elements which comprise a portrait head, without losing the likeness. By comparison he represents the human hand as if it were ectoplasm as incapable of holding a brush or a papal bull as his heads are capable of holding the character of the sitter and the attention of the spectator.

Ayrton went on to characterise Bacon as a formidable artist whose paraphrase could transfigure its source. The series of portraits of Velázquez's 'Pope Innocent X' introduced an element of dislocation from the primary image, which was to have great influence on modern art. Although Bacon claimed that he had never seen the original in Rome, Ayrton had. He had noticed that, when it was hung in the Palazzo Doria, the portrait was seen through open doors and mirrors, which distorted the brass rails that enclosed it. Bacon appeared to have seen a photograph of the Velázquez pope hanging in its proper place. 'The relationship between painted and photographed images has become a principal source of that ambiguity,' Ayrton commented, 'which is felt to provide the *frisson* in much contemporary art'. Bacon was involved with existing images, whether ephemeral or not. He wanted to capture the formal with its veil and mask down.

'I have always been interested in behaviour,' Bacon claimed, 'that is in life, rather than in art'. His view directly opposed that of Oscar Wilde, who put art before life. Bacon sought to capture in his art the split second of animals in motion, of men grappling in lust, of people in fright and politicians off their guard. That is why he was peculiarly attracted to the series of photographs taken by the Victorian Eadweard Muybridge. They were to Bacon, John Rothenstein wrote, 'what his breviary is to a priest'. These sequences of naked mammals in motion provoked Bacon to paint some series of related scenes or portraits that have the distorted immediacy of the string of snapshots that may be taken out-of-focus in a modern passport photograph machine or seen in strobe lighting on the live stage. As Francis Russell pointed out, Muybridge's photographs were uncontaminated by art. They were not shaped by consciousness or composition, as modern photographers shape their pictures and call them art. Bacon took from photography 'the initial stance: the readiness to accept a deformed or implausible image as true'. He gave back to photography 'its involuntary, uncalculated status'. One might say that Muybridge and Bacon were the King Lears of their various works. They showed unaccommodated man as the poor, bare, forked animal that he was. Yet finally Bacon was determined to excise the truth more than Muybridge might show. As Bacon said, he would 'make the paint speak louder than the story'.

Muybridge's series of pictures of naked men and women pursuing ordinary acts were extraordinary in their revelations of actual bodies in movement. Sometimes they were horrific as well as expository, as in 'Amputee Walking with Crutches'; 'Legless Boy Climbing in and out of Chair', which Bacon used in 1953 in his 'Study of Figure in a Room', capriciously restoring the missing legs; and in 'Paralytic Child Walking on All Fours (from Muybridge)' of 1961, the only work of his that Bacon identified from its photographic source and abnormal motion. Sometimes the mobile carcass was distorted by the force of the work as in 'Hod Carrier Climbing Ladder' and 'Man Performing Standing Broad Jump', again used by Bacon for depicting a naked man. Sometimes the limbs were blurred and awry in incredible effort as in 'Man Performing Forward Handspring' or 'Man Heaving 75-LB Boulder', once more Bacon's source in 1951 for his 'Study for Nude'. This last painting particularly illustrated Bacon's remark recorded in the catalogue of *The New Decade* exhibition of 1955, of how shapes were 'remade or put slightly out of focus to bring in their memory traces . . . as the snail leaves its slime'.

In the paintings derived from Muybridge's 'Men Wrestling', where one naked man pins another and falls on his protruding buttocks, Bacon saw the images of aggressive homosexuality and used them to produce paintings that mocked the moral codes and subverted the criminal law of the time. That he was not prosecuted for them as D. H. Lawrence had been thirty years before was a tribute to the changing climate of post-War London. But when Bacon was later accused of refusing to help the gay militance of the early 'nineties, with his usual disdain for explanation or justification, he never referred to his bold declaration of forty years back. Some of his more prurient critics, however, knew exactly what he was portraying. As Mark Roskill wrote in *Art International* on the use Bacon had made of Muybridge's 'Men Wrestling' in his version, named 'Two Figures', of men making love fiercely on a bed, 'Whereas the imagery of the source connoted athleticism and muscularity in their virtuous senses – man at the peak of his physical powers, exercising himself in sport for the sake of his physique – the connotations of Bacon's image involve nudity in the shameful sense, and homosexuality . . . The Bacon has the force of the comment: "This is what nudity and the locked posture really *are*."'

The 'Two Figures' of 1953 was given to or bought by Lucian Freud and was not exhibited until four years later, when it was put on loan to the Tate Gallery. It provoked no threat of legal action, although sexual intercourse between men would remain a crime until the 'sixties. When writing later about David Hockney's candour about his homosexuality, Robert Hughes declared that he was the first to do it in a garrulous, social way, as if it was the most natural thing in the world. He contrasted it to Francis Bacon using it as a pretext for reflection on the power of Eros to maim and dominate. He did not point out that Bacon grew up under a criminal law, which had the power to maim and dominate practising homosexuals, who had to rely on Eros to continue to love other men. After his student youth, Hockney did not have to fear prosecution for sodomy, although Bacon did until he was in his sixties. Thus his transmutations of Muybridge's 'Men Wrestling', which he called 'Two Figures' and 'Study from the Human Figure' and 'Two Figures in the Grass', were acts of defiance of the social system as well as expressions of his inner drives. They were painted in smudges so that the images of the copulating men seemed a fusion of the flesh rather than a sexual act; but all the same, they were a reckless defiance of convention that risked ostracism or even prosecution.

In this experimental period, Bacon was to make use of other photographs from Muybridge's *Animals in Motion* and snapshots of Africa, where he went in the winter of 1950 to visit his mother, who had gone out to stay with his elder sister Ianthe, now married to a farmer and a hunter. They were both to remain out there, and Bacon's mother would marry twice more, as her mother had – a Mr Montgomery and a Mr Mavor. Her son was carried by the Orient Line, on the first of three voyages that he would make to the southern continent during the decade, as he was not the most oblivious son in the world, and he represented the family trust in England. One of the directors of the Orient Line had become his patron, the wealthy and stingy Robert Heber-Percy, who travelled first-class while Bacon travelled steerage – 'far more fun', he later commented, 'among the stokers'. On his voyage, the white iron railings of the old liners with their polished wooden tops would have given, with their oblong definitions, a restraint and a cage to the violence of the living sea and the chaotic wake. His mother and sister had retired to escape the rigours of rationing in England and had left the youngest member of the family, Winifred, to live in a home for incurables in Putney, where Francis was to see her with his cousin, Pamela Firth, now married to the war hero Popski, who had once had his own Private Army.

On his visits to South Africa, Bacon always studied the wild life in the Kruger National Park: he was fascinated by the strength and camouflage of the animals in their natural environment, their merging and their ease through the harsh bush, their deception and elusiveness. 'I felt and memorized', he wrote to Erica Brausen, 'the excitement of seeing animals move through long grass.' He was even taken by the outrageous excess of post-colonial society on the farms, the drinking and the adultery, the riding and the cheap black help – a caricature of the Ireland he had known as a child. He became fascinated and friendly with Karen Blixen and found her unsparing view of Rhodesian life in *Out of Africa* as terminally honest as anything he tried to do in painting. Africa and its sights remained a concern of his, not only for his mother's sake, but for its merciless images. He took a great many photographs of wild animals himself. Their actual muscular movement had much to do with the structure of things he wanted to do. They were stronger than the things Muybridge had done on movement in humans and animals. What he wished to capture was 'the fact itself and nothing else'. He wanted his paintings to have 'the same immediate effect of an animal after the kill', as recorded in his photographs and those of others. As late as 1975, he would do portraits of Peter Beard, a young American traveller and photographer of Africa, who had repeatedly risked his life in his pursuit of capturing on film the beautiful abandon of animals leaping.

On his first voyage to Africa, however, Bacon travelled back to England without his protector and patron. He abandoned Robert Heber-Percy in a bar in Salisbury in Southern Rhodesia, now Zimbabwe, leaving with a transient and friendlier black man. 'I have left Robert and have practically no money,' he wrote back to Erica Brausen, asking her for an advance of fifty pounds. He found the countryside 'too marvellous . . . a continuous Renoir landscape', while the Rhodesian police were 'too sexy' with their 'well-starched shorts and highly polished leggings.' He felt twenty years younger and wanted to take a cargo boat at Beira in Mozambique for the Suez Canal to see the antiquities of the ancient Pharaohs and then to sail on to Marseilles on his way home. In Cairo the painter discovered a passion for the heads of early Egyptian art, particularly that of the Pharaoh Akhnaton, from which he later made a study. Returning to London, where he soon had to leave his Kensington studio because he could not bear to stay there after the death of his beloved nanny, he continued to develop his series of popes from the screaming and mutilated head – topped like an egg – of the first one he had painted in a cage.

Bacon once said to David Sylvester that he could not separate what he derived from Muybridge from what he owed to Michelangelo, or indeed Velázquez. 'Actually, Michelangelo and Muybridge are mixed up in my mind together.' He learned about positions from Muybridge, about the grandeur of form from Michelangelo and the voluptuous male nude. This combination can be seen in his 'Study of a Nude', finished in 1953, which is amplified from a Muybridge of a man preparing to make a standing jump. For his popes, Bacon used photographs not only of the Velázquez portrait, but also of Pope Pius XII being carried through the Vatican in his *sedia gestatoria*, a-flutter with white peacock feathers. A cross between mockery and reverence, between satire and tradition, these popes still flaunt and howl and gibber at us in their robes on the outlines of their yellow papal thrones.

Bacon used to deny that the apparent agony of his figures was meaningful. 'Rembrandt unlocks the values of feeling, but he doesn't necessarily say anything specific.' His open mouths were no more particular in their aspect than those described by William Gerhardi, who said that, seen at a distance, the hole of the mouth might be screaming or yawning, laughing or begging for water, talking or sneezing. Yet to the critics of the pope series, Bacon had invented a new form of painting experience, that of a man in increasing pain, as if under torture. 'Bacon places the Pope in a chair that has been wired to the mains,' one observer wrote, 'in the second picture the current has come on, and in the third His Holiness is in the last extremes of agonized galvanization.' Another critic saw Bacon as audacious enough to try for a continuous cinematic impression. 'He combines the monumentality of the great art of the past with the "modernity" of a film strip,' an experiment not to be repeated until ten years later by Andy Warhol in his 'Edith Scull, 36 Times'. Bacon was using the stills of human motion to comment on the processes of the human condition.

Bacon thought that what man wanted from generation to generation was 'to reinvent the ways that appearance can be made and brought back into his nervous system more violently, more immediately'. What had been made before had 'already become *an absorbed solution*. So every generation needs to reinvent appearance.' That is what Bacon was succeeding in doing in his experiments with paint and transmutations from photographs in the 'fifties, especially in his series of popes. Later, he would regret the impudence and disdain of his all-out attack on papal infallibility. He would say that he never got the scream vibrant enough. It was not really what he wanted at all. In the human mouth, he had wished to paint the beautiful colours of a Turner as well as a Monet, but all he had achieved was a black scream.

In a way, the great pope of Velázquez was such a masterpiece that there was nothing to be done. He had tried to do something about it, something even further, but it was impossible. Yet at the time, he was obsessed by his subject, and he admitted that he was expressing his revolt from the authority of his dead father and constricted childhood. 'He was the dandy of existentialism,' as the art critic Lawrence Gowing called him, and there was no question that his locking of his figures in isolated, enclosed, windowless space reflected Camus in *L'Étranger* and Sartre in *Huis Clos*. Hell was in this black vacuum, and it was human.

Bacon could accept the most dangerous alliance of all, that of novelty with history. The difficult thing, he said, was 'to keep open the line to ancestral European painting while producing something that comes across as entirely new'. Yet he would force fresh oils into old bottles. He had joined the painterly formula which Velázquez had inherited from Titian and Raphael to the creation of photography in the nineteenth century. Yet twenty years on, Bacon would declare his paintings of the Pope 'a great failure. I was hypnotized at the time by the sheer beauty of it.' His paintings 'were overstatements, too obvious and too cheap'.

In spite of such denials, these images of the howling or leering Pope remained as ikons of the protest against authority that was to emerge in Britain during the Suez crisis of 1956 and lead to the youth rebellion of the following decade. Apolitical and working from his subconscious in his transfiguration of images that his consciousness sought out, Bacon was expressing by intuition the social feelings of his time. He always maintained that he painted only for himself, but his serial themes represented the pictures locked within the minds of millions that were screaming to be let out. In his portraits of homosexual encounters and popes under assault of the early 'fifties, Bacon was the unwitting prophet of impending revolt. Another series of executives dressed in business suits, making useless speeches and gesturing within solitary glass cages and imprisoning darkness, demonstrated that Bacon's painting reflected the futility of the politics that would soon lead to an attack on the Establishment of his country.

Out of Muybridge's *Animals in Motion*, particularly his sequence of his dog 'Dread Trotting', and out of photographs of African animals from Marius Maxwell's book of 1924, *Stalking Big Game with a Camera in Equatorial Africa*, Bacon now constructed an unusual sequence of wild life. He looked at animal pictures all the time, he said, because the movements of the species were continually linked – also their appearances, as his head of a man merging into a baboon had already showed. His interest in monkeys stemmed from the fact that like humans they were fascinated with their own image. 'Their interest in themselves is displayed with an abandon and a relish rarely equalled by that of man.' On one occasion, when his friendly and proprietorial critic David Sylvester was sitting for him for his series of popes, Bacon ignored his subject and preferred to paint the head of a rhinoceros from a photograph. He never explained to Sylvester whether this was a direct reference to the critic's character, a joke or an act of imperious immediacy. He said merely that the animal's texture engaged his interest.

Certainly, Bacon mixed the human with the animal kingdom as much as he did Michelangelo with Muybridge. He might have quoted William Blake whom he was shortly to paint in a series of portraits.

> And am I not,
> A fly like thee?
> And art thou not
> A man like me?

Bacon's 'Study of a Dog' of 1952 and 'Landscape', showing a rhinoceros in outline in long grass by a coastal road with cars like the one near Monte Carlo, were characterised by a picture of an elephant fording a stream, painted after a second trip to Africa that same year, and two more of dogs. The British Council had put pressure on him for further canine pictures for his exhibition in the British Pavilion at the Venice Biennale of 1954, where he understudied Ben Nicholson and partnered Lucian Freud. There were other pictures of a baboon howling with bared teeth, and paintings of a chimpanzee and owls. Yet the most intriguing was his portrayal of 'Man with Dog', which was surprisingly inscribed on the back of the stretcher, 'Bacon – the Elephant'. A drain-cover and a kerb now replaced the strong grille pattern that had trapped his previous dog studies. This picture did not wholly derive from Muybridge's mastiff, but also from Balla's Futurist painting, 'Leash in Motion', which had recently been exhibited at the Tate Gallery. John Rothenstein has described how Bacon would go to exhibitions and concentrate fiercely on a few paintings, ignoring all the rest of them. In this case, Bacon took away Balla's idea of only showing the legs of a man taking his dog for a walk, but he did not suggest the movement of the dog in a succession of serial images, as if Muybridge's mastiff were superimposed upon itself severally. This is what Balla had done, based on Marey's chronophotographs, while Bacon chose to slur and smear the single image of the dog, so that it resembled the blurred early pictures of beasts in motion. As in his comments on Duchamp's famous 'Nude Descending a Staircase', Bacon tried to make his beings more dramatic in their stepping out, while Duchamp wanted to keep movement central. He did not want to make something mechanistic, a mere motor moving down stairs. He tried to cancel out all implications. 'He was the first of this century to attempt that. Seurat did the same thing – as they say in America, to keep it cool.'

It was not in Bacon's nature to keep anything cool, particularly not the live animal. He explored the dynamics of the moving picture to break the static work of art. When his exhibition of his African pictures caused a sensation at the Hanover Gallery, he told a *Time* magazine reporter that real imagination was technical. He was searching for the technique 'to trap the object at a given moment. Then the technique and the object became inseparable. The object is the technique and the technique is the object.' Out of Africa as well, he brought back the image of the Sphinx, which he set like his popes and dogs, on a grid or within a glass cage. These were his only four representations of a recognisable statue of a mythological creature of mystery within his paintings, although he was later to resurrect that cat-like and sibylline shape to illustrate Muriel Belcher of the Colony Room as the Oracle of Soho. By that time, his wit had overcome his reverence for antiquity, and he showed us it.

Also experimental in his work in the 'fifties were Bacon's tributes to two artists and writers that he admired, William Blake and Vincent Van Gogh. J. S. Deville had done a plaster cast of Blake's face in 1823, and a young German composer, Gerard Schürmann, took Bacon to see it in the National Portrait Gallery so that he could use it to design a cover for a song cycle of Blake's poems. Working intermittently at the Imperial Hotel at Henley-on-Thames on an allowance of fifteen pounds a month from the Hanover Gallery, Bacon was to execute seven variations of the mask, two of which he destroyed. While he did not admire Blake's painting, he was inspired by his poems. As with Aeschylus and Shakespeare, the words were translated into images. The five Blake portraits are cerebral, not bestial, as if the mind of the poet had refined all the fat and flesh from beneath his skin to leave only a rendering of intellect, as blubber is rendered into lamp oil to give light. Against their dark background, the features are as detached and aloof as a pale kite in a night sky. Later, Schürmann was to write a work called *Seven Studies of Francis Bacon*, which was first to be performed at the Dublin Festival of Twentieth Century Music and pay homage to Bacon's youth in Ireland.

The distance was not kept by Bacon in his treatment of Van Gogh. He saw the artist on the road to the sun in the South of France. For Bacon loved the force and immediacy of Van Gogh's letters as much as the whirling incandescence of his art. A series of eight paintings was based on a photograph of a self-portrait by Van Gogh and on his 'The Painter on the Road to Tarascon', unfortunately destroyed by fire in Germany during the Second World War. Van Gogh becomes a wraith and a shadow on the blazing road under his straw hat, a canvas on his back and a stick in his hand, the irreducible minimum of the artist on a quest for the source of light. This subject restored prime colours and richness back to Bacon's brush, which depicts the traveller on the road in smooth and glowing strokes like the spokes of brightness that can break through sombre evening clouds. Again the influence of Edvard Munch is seen in Bacon's work in a greater resonance of hue and the sweep of landscape, although Bacon still searches for the reality behind Van Gogh's vision, not for the vision itself.

To his critics, Bacon's splash into agitated Fauve colours was a revelation. His work began to be compared to de Kooning's 'Women' and Nicolas de Staël's landscapes. 'In the Van Gogh series', Lawrence Alloway wrote, 'the paint got out of control as it flooded the surface which previously it had only grazed, like an outburst from a gypsy violin after messages in Morse Code.' The restricted colours of Bacon's palette were forever altered into more startling and primary hues. Alloway made another shrewd point when he noticed in 1963 that Bacon's new paintings had the look not of black and white but of colour photography, as if he had moved with the times as magazines went over to colour. This view supplemented another observer's opinion that same year on the influence of the actual photograph on Bacon. 'He is the first artist really to have looked at photographs and to have accepted them on their own terms rather as mechanized sketches or immutable chunks of the outside world.' And not all the critics approved of his switch from the monochrome to the full range of the spectrum. Denys Sutton referred to Bacon's love of roulette when he wrote that the artist was evidently aware of many of the limitations which marked his earlier paintings. 'To use an analogy culled from the tables, he has staked so much on the *noir* that the *rouge* has been left to take care of itself; as a result the *rouge* has rarely, if ever, turned up. What is more, the significance of the *noir* (the image) has been lessened through familiarity: once the initial impact is digested, one begins to question and even to challenge the means with which it has been secured.'

Bacon was now painting over fifteen pictures annually, compared with two a year in the previous decade. In 1953, he painted twenty-four to supply his first American solo exhibition at the Durlacher Brothers Gallery, also another one at the Beaux Arts Gallery in London. He was selling his pictures, and galleries were making demands on him, which deterred him from destroying what he had done. He was also accepting commissions for private portraits or series of paintings from his leading patrons, especially from the wealthy Mr and Mrs R. J. Sainsbury. She sat for him as a model sporadically over a period of two-and-a-half years and was painted by him in eight studies, three of which still survive in the Sainsbury collection. He was initially forced on the Sainsburys by Erica Brausen at the Hanover Gallery, who would not allow them to buy a Giacometti without buying as well three Bacons at two-hundred pounds apiece. 'You must encourage young artists,' she said, 'even if you put them in the basement.' The Sainsburys, however, became converts and Bacon's foremost collectors.

The first named portrait by Francis Bacon was of Lucian Freud in 1951, a good likeness although the ambiguous pose of the figure in a doorway was taken from a snapshot of Kafka as a young man, reproduced in Max Brod's biography of him. Bacon's other portraits bore anonymous titles such as 'Man Eating a Leg of Chicken', although it was taken from another press photograph of the Marquis de Cuevas. The centrepiece of 'Three Studies of the Human Head' resembled a contemporary photograph in *Time* magazine of the Canadian Prime Minister Louis St. Laurent. It had not been planned as a triptych: in fact, David Sylvester tried to sell what would become the right-hand canvas to three dealers for sixty pounds only – and failed. Seven studies of a 'Man in Blue' met in the Imperial Hotel at Henley depicted him as an interrogator of the style of Senator McCarthy; and 'Two Americans' looked like executives on trial in the dock. His portrait of his second cousin and early supporter, 'Miss Diana Watson', was again mainly derived from a snapshot he had taken of her nineteen years before at Byland Abbey in Yorkshire, although she did sit two or three times for him while he completed it. His 'Study for the Human Body' had also been painted from a photograph of his cousin Pamela's husband Popski, who tragically died of a brain tumour in 1951, but was preserved for ever in his characteristic hunched post caused by his loss of half of his arm. Bacon also began to work on self-portraits, as if he wished at last to analyse himself in paint, a show of introspection. He naturally would not confess to the truth of his motive, airily telling John Russell, 'I couldn't think what on earth to do next, so I thought, "Why not try and do myself?"'

This period of experimentation confirmed Bacon's use of the moving picture and the press reporter's action camera as the sources for his inspiration. In 1957, he actually painted a 'Study for the

Nurse in the film Battleship Potemkin', in which she was stripped naked in the smeared motion of trembling fright and seated within the jaws of the outline of a high-backed chair. Only her scream and her pince-nez suggested Eisenstein's original image during the massacre on the Odessa Steps, while Bacon's transmutation of the film still recalled many of his nude and spread and howling figures trapped within a frame of gold rather than silver nitrate. He based her body on another Muybridge study of a 'Woman Sitting Down in Chair and Drinking Tea'. But a more compelling influence lay in one of his valued clippings of a shot of a crowd scattering in panic across a square in St. Petersburg during the Russian Revolution. 'Not one of these hundreds of figures looks remotely like a conventional figure,' he said to John Rothenstein. 'Each one, caught in violent motion, is stranger and at first sight less intelligible than one could possibly have imagined it.' He then indicated the shape of a fugitive, off-balance and extended and angular. 'Could anything', he asked, 'be more utterly unlike the conventional concept of a man running?'

The concentration on the form of the living creature, caught off-guard and unaware, undermined the tradition of representation in painting. To understand the animal in movement, Bacon did not study anatomy as Stubbs did, dissecting a horse to see how its muscles worked. He might haunt butchers' shops to scrutinise the flayed carcasses of sheep and cattle; he might even see the tortured creatures in the waxwork show of the atrocities of the concentration camps on Oxford Street at the end of the Second World War; he might examine the exhibits of murders and forensic science in the Black Museum at Scotland Yard; he might add arrows to point out the grisly details in his paintings as Fabian of the Yard did to show vital clues left behind by villains. But these excursions into the entrails and agonies of living beings were not as essential as capturing them in the gesture of private revelation, in the confession of the solitary act. The very nature of the press photograph or the grainy film influenced his portrayals so much that he sometimes used sand in his paint. 'The predominance of grey, the blurred texture of the surface, the transitional postures of the figures, and the avoidance of forms which would give his pictures a monumental, static character,' Rothenstein wrote, 'all derive from the photograph.'

Deluged with images as we are in the modern age of electronics, we must organise the information we record in order to understand and use it. But Bacon loved to live in a random form to contain his intention. The rubbish dump of the studios which he changed so frequently now, after selling his refuge in Cromwell Place in 1951, reflected the role of the fortunate glimpse in his choice of shapes in his creations. Clippings from newspapers, reproductions of old masters torn from art books, stained cloths and clothes and spattered tins of paint, thumbed copies of Aeschylus and Euripides, Shakespeare and Pascal, Montaigne and Baudelaire, Nietzsche and Dostoevsky, Van Gogh's Letters and Frazer's *The Golden Bough*, Yeats and Ezra Pound, added to the litter of happenstance. As he would say disarmingly of his clutter, 'These are my models and my subject matter.' Bacon preferred reading poetry to novels 'because everything is said so quickly'. Jean Cocteau was another of Bacon's literary influences, but only in his highly selective way: he called Cocteau 'a window-dresser who said something of genius, "Look all your life in a mirror and you will see Death working like bees in a glass hive."' He told Michael Wishart that he wanted to paint himself thus. When he moved, from brief stays at Carlyle Studios and 6 Beaufort Gardens in South Kensington, to live for a few weeks in the same houses as David Sylvester, at 9 Apollo Place and then at 19 Cromwell Road, he took only a few books and photographs and paints with him. He also was moving from drapes and darkness and abstract landscapes to the shock of contemporary designs set against the melt-down of the naked human figure. With an odd precision, he began to include in his art electric light-bulbs and switches, safety-razors and umbrellas, telephones and cameras, wash-basins and lavatory bowls, ash-trays and half-smoked cigarettes: the trivia of the everyday, the shock of the ordinary object. There is no attempt as in Léger or Man Ray or the Surrealists to turn the *objet trouvé* into part of a work of art. It is the thing itself. That is its effect. And when Bacon added arrows as if on road signs to indicate movement, this was a practical direction to the viewer's eyes, not a witty comment on the impossibility of painting flow on a still surface. The 'props' in his pictures, as he said, 'act as visual rivets'. Bacon sought to trap the odd truths of place and man, out of step.

And now he began to snare the strange truths of his own condition. He had fallen seriously in love and it became obvious in his paintings of copulating men. 'I can't paint for other people,' he said, 'I can only paint to excite myself.' It was only chance if it worked for someone else. Yet it was 'true of all painters that their work is very much autobiographical'. He painted 'Two Figures' in the summer of 1953, when he was living in a rented cottage at Hurst near Henley-on-Thames, next door to one occupied by his new grand passion, Peter Lacey. A public-schoolboy from the middle classes, a fighter pilot and a country gentleman with a slight endearing stammer, an alcoholic and a bar pianist, Lacey represented those self-destructive and dangerous characters of Patrick Hamilton, who appealed to Bacon's love of damaged respectability and distorted façades. John Richardson characterised Lacey as sadistic and bad for Bacon, a demon lover and destroyer. But to the artist, he represented a dynamic of masculinity, 'the raw statement of movement' he found in Muybridge and now in his own life, so powerful that he could paint it.

That was, however, on the occasions that he could paint at all while living near Lacey. At one time he wrote to Erica Brausen, from the Imperial Hotel at Henley, that he had given up any new work and did not wish to show the old. 'I am not able to finish any paintings at the moment so will you please *put off* the exhibition. I am terribly sorry about this but as you know these things happen with work.' He would let her have some paintings soon, 'but please do not have a show of the things you have got in the gallery of mine. I think it would be a great mistake to show them both for you and for me. As you know I want to replace most of them when I can, also there have been too many shows of mine – I am desperate and completely broke and am going to try and get a job for a time.'

For Lacey, Bacon had painted his most uncharacteristic picture of all, 'House in Barbados' of 1952, a mere copy of a photograph executed under his new lover's instructions, although Eric Hall also wintered in the West Indies. It was genius in thrall to the conventional. 'Two Figures', however, was followed by the more explicit 'Two Figures in the Grass' of 1954, in which the lower male figure has turned back his head to kiss the man thrusting down above him, and the dry blades rear their spikes, and a surrounding fence impales repeatedly. Bacon was then living in a block of flats off Sloane Street and working in a studio at 28 Mallord Street in Chelsea, which had been lent to him by the wealthy Honourable Michael Astor. More and more, he was changing places. He could not work well at Mallord Street because there was too much brightness, and trees waved in the wind through the skylight, creating ripples of shadows. He created two of his surviving portraits of Lacey at the end of 1957. In one of them, the naked man hunched in a foetal position lies asleep, his head on a pillow, in the womb of an enveloping sofa. In the other, he stares out in arrested motion from the corner of a seat, framed by Bacon's usual linear perspectives, ready to spring forward.

Bacon likened his device for sealing his figures within the outline of cubes to being in love. The suggestion of a cage made the viewer see the image more clearly, reducing the space of the canvas and giving the figure a greater impact. Bacon was not necessarily enclosing the shape in its own loneliness, 'But people go to bars to be closer to each other,' he said. 'The frustration is that people can never be close enough to each other. If you're in love you can't break down the barriers of the skin.' Yet that is what he was trying to do in the fused flesh of his depictions of homosexual love, although his extraordinary 'Man with Head Wound' of 1955 suggested that the barriers of the skull and of inhibition would only be broken open by the exposure of the meat within.

A year later, Peter Lacey took Bacon away from the South of France to Tangier in Morocco. There the painter rented an apartment for the next three years and lived a louche existence with hardly any painting done, except on his return visits to London, where he now had a small and cluttered studio on Prince of Wales Drive in Battersea, in 9 Overstrand Mansions. He was now sharing a flat with his friends Paul Danquah and Peter Pollock, also habitués of Tangier. As Truman Capote wrote of the place, 'Virtually every Tangerine is ensconced there for at least one, if not all, of four reasons: the easy availability of drugs, lustful adolescent prostitutes, tax loopholes, or because he is so undesirable no place north of Port Said would let him out of the airport or off the ship.'

At that time, Paul and Janet Bowles were the catalysts and scribes of the port city while William Burroughs was its manic and destructive genius and was writing of its inferno in *The Naked Lunch*. Bacon regularly visited Bowles, who admired the painter and his pictures. 'He was a man about to burst from internal pressures. Even with the articulate description he gave me of his method of work, I was unable to imagine for myself exactly what happened as he painted.' Bowles had as a protégé a young Moroccan artist, Ahmed Yacoubi, and he passed him on to Bacon who allowed him to sit and learn in his studio in the Casbah. There he watched like a cat. 'Ahmed and I had no common language,' Bacon remembered, 'but between my limited Spanish and French and his very good Spanish, we were able to talk a lot.' Bacon taught Yacoubi a viable technique and brought him back a good quantity of Windsor and Newton oils from London, as there were none in Tangier. Yacoubi progressed fast enough for Bacon to arrange a show for him in the Hanover Gallery. When Yacoubi was thrown into a Moroccan jail, in 1958, on the charge of seducing a fourteen-year-old German boy, causing an exodus of the Bowleses and many of the foreign homosexual community, Bacon stayed on in Tangier with Lacey and supplied Yacoubi, in prison, with canvases and food. He advised Bowles not to return until the crack-down was over, writing that he should be careful for Yacoubi's sake as well as his own. Burroughs was even more gloomy, writing to his former lover, the Beat poet Allen Ginsberg, that Tangier was finished. 'The Arab dogs are upon us. Many a queen has been dragged shrieking from the Parade, the Socco Chico, and lodged in the local box where sixty sons of Sodom now languish.' The prostitute boys, 'many beaten to a pulp, have spelled a list of hundreds'.

So homophobia had come even to Tangier, although it was sporadic and dependent on scandal. Yacoubi was soon released, the old ways resumed. Bacon was living in an empty apartment beside the Villa Muniria, a well-kept place run by a Vietnamese woman, said to have been a brothel madam in Saigon and certainly used to the proclivities of her guest and neighbours. Bacon went gambling at the casino, particularly with the Beat poets like Gregory Corso on their visits to Burroughs. They found that he looked young for his age, with a spoiled tragic face. He told Ginsberg that he had 'once been offered a gambling stake for allowing himself to be whipped, with a bonus for every stroke that drew blood. Bacon's painting technique was what he called psychic representation, the face formed as if by accident in a whirl of feathery brush strokes.' He said De Kooning was the greatest artist in the United States, for bursting through the abstract and planting an image on canvas.

Ginsberg thought that Bacon painted the way that Burroughs wrote. 'It was a sort of dangerous bullfight of the mind, where he placed himself in acute psychic danger of uncovering some secret that would destroy him. Burroughs had these unpublishable mad routines about talking assholes, with the recurring image of the spurting hard-on as the hanged man's neck snaps, and vast paranoiac theories of agents and psychic senders taking over the world in bureaucratic conspiracies. But Burroughs, although fond of Bacon, denied that there was any connection, and said, "Bacon and I are at opposite ends of the spectrum. He likes middle-aged truck drivers and I like young boys. He sneers at immortality and I think it's the one thing of importance. Of course we're associated because of our morbid subject matter."'

The two men also differed on drugs. Bacon could not smoke *kif* because of his asthma. He also disliked its effect. Burroughs and Bowles 'would smoke grass and just stop talking to each other'. At least, drink 'up to a point gets you closer to people. You loosen up.' Bowles 'liked marijuana and I liked alcohol, and they create very different worlds', so they never made much contact with each other. Actually, Bacon did experiment with Paul Danquah with *kif*, but Bacon's face blew up like a balloon because of his asthma, and he never tried it again.

Although Ginsberg once offended Bacon at Burroughs's room in the Villa Muniria by offering him liquor in a tin can from the rubbish bin – the artist was afraid of getting typhoid – the poet wrote an evocative description of him to Jack Kerouac, then on the road again in America. He described Bacon as having the aspect of an English schoolboy and the soul of a satyr. He 'wears sneakers & tight dungarees and black silk shirts & always looks like going [to] tennis . . . & paints mad gorillas in grey hotel rooms drest in evening dress with deathly black umbrellas – said he would paint big pornographic picture of me . . .' Ginsberg was then trying to edit *The Naked Lunch* into some form of final order, so he asked Bacon how he finished a painting. The answer satisfied Ginsberg. 'He said he did it with a chance brush-stroke that locked in the magic – a fortuitous thing that he couldn't predict or orchestrate.'

The English poet Michael Horovitz also saw the affinities between Burroughs and Bacon – 'the savage, sometimes morbidly horrendous vision, cross-cut and scorched under lightning-flashes of caustic humour; flailing homoeroticism; ruthless destruction of failed experiments as of clichéd successes; the welcoming – and later nurturing – of chance operations'. But Bacon was hardly able to paint in Tangier in the same way that he had been incapable in Monte Carlo. The light seemed to be too strong or the way of life was too exhausting. 'Such upsets! Rows and getting thrown out of the window!' So he told Cecil Beaton of his life with Lacey there, when he was trying to paint the portrait of the society photographer in London. He had a tooth knocked out and his face was in an appalling mess.

Bacon wrote confidently to Erica Brausen that he could paint in Morocco, since he had installed himself in a sixth-floor apartment on the Boulevard Mohammed V. 'I feel full of work and believe I may do a few really good paintings now.' But he really wanted two-hundred pounds to keep going with Lacey, and though he wrote that he would come back with more than twenty pictures, only three appear to survive – one of a hooded Moroccan man carrying a child, and another of a papal figure in glasses with folded hands and two owls perched on the back of his throne, and a third of the 'Landscape near Malabata', in which shapes seem to melt off harsh grass into a streaked saucer and a round night. That same stark barrenness contained in a bowl is the background of Bacon's third powerful picture of copulating men of that decade, 'Figures in a Landscape' of 1956 and 1957, surely the truth of his violent and erotic relationship with Lacey running into a desert of despair in Morocco.

'Eroticism for Bacon', the perceptive critic Lorenza Trucchi has written, 'is a total act, the extreme moment of truth.' It was not Bacon's task to alter or pervert reality by passing judgement. 'Utterly genuine in their sensual, often secret, and solitary rage . . . Bacon's figures in any case perform a rite of exorcism, one of the last rites granted to a man in his attempt to forestall death and assert life.' Bacon knew that Lacey was destroying both of them by his alcoholic excesses. The year of 1958 was fallow in the artist's life. Only six surviving paintings were completed. The quarrels and scenes with Lacey continued. It was the same when the two of them left Tangier for summer holidays in England at a boarding-house in St. Ives, a painting community in its own right, but conveniently near the sailors who visited from Devonport. The young painter Patrick Procktor had himself been a sailor there, and when he visited the Cornish boarding-house with Bryan Robertson, they found that naval mayhem had preceded them, the aftermath of a visit by Lacey and Bacon. 'Oh,' the manager said, 'it was awful. There were so many sailors falling off the roof. We can't go on with this.' The painter Karl Weschke also saw Bacon hurrying away down a Cornish street. He caught up and saw Bacon's face was badly bruised. As if he were talking about his flogging by the Irish grooms in front of his father when he was a lad, Bacon said of Lacey, 'When he's standing over me with a whip, what else can I do?'

Yet Bacon had to go on painting and he would not give up Lacey. He even completed from memory, in his room at 3 Porthmeor Studios at St. Ives, one portrait of a head of Muriel Belcher at the Colony Room. Yet he found that he was still able to work in London as long as he left Lacey to play the piano at Dean's Bar in Tangier. His life was changed in one way. He had inherited a position at the Royal College of Art through the good graces of John Minton, who had gone for several months to the West Indies in the September of 1950. He had given his professor's salary for a term to Bacon, who replaced him less as a tutor than as an honorary visitor. All he could do was to go there for two days a week, he said, 'and if the students wanted somebody to talk to, I was there'. He thought those who taught people at art schools were failures and taught their students to be failures too. But he continued to use the painter Rodrigo Moynihan's studio at the Royal College of Art until 1953, when he painted his last picture there, 'Study for a Portrait', of a businessman sitting in the cube of a leather chair within an oblong box and frame. This seemed to Bacon to represent the constrictions of formal academic life, and he only returned occasionally to the Common Room of the Royal College, where his relationship with Minton steadily deteriorated. Minton could not abide losing the supremacy of his British reputation as an artist, particularly as leading critics such as David Sylvester championed Bacon and Giacometti at the expense of their rivals. At one lecture by Sylvester on modern art at the Victoria and Albert Museum, Minton rose to his feet in an outburst against Bacon, whom he accused of leading certain European traditions into a cul-de-sac, not of extending them.

Bacon's other champion was John Rothenstein, the Director of the Tate Gallery, who had also been betrayed by the envious Graham Sutherland, who resigned as a Trustee of the Tate as a public protest against Rothenstein's alleged maladministration of the gallery. Rothenstein was also friendly with the shy and aged painter Matthew Smith, and he recalled in 1952, what happened after they ate a sedate dinner at the Athenaeum:

> We wandered along the streets of Soho, he lamenting the drabness of English cafés and places of amusement, when we suddenly caught sight, framed in a tall window, sitting on a high stool, of Francis Bacon. We joined him and he presently swept us along from bar to bar and club to club, eventually from the Colony to the Gargoyle. The more Francis drank, the more physically helpless his condition, the more marked his imperious dignity . . .
>
> It was a delight to be in the company of Matthew and Francis together. I never heard one praise – to his face – the painting of the other, but their tacit assumption of mutual regard and affection was manifest. Matthew used to say of the work of Francis that even at its least successful it never lacked absorbing interest, and Francis, who admires the work of few of his contemporaries, admires Matthew's with little qualification.

As a result of this mutual admiration, Rothenstein took his courage in his hands and asked Bacon to write a tribute for the catalogue of Matthew Smith's retrospective exhibition at the Tate. Bacon had never written a word for publication: his wit and knowledge of art lay in his conversation. Yet he accepted, as did the alcoholic and retiring Henry Green, perhaps the greatest living English novelist of that period. Green praised Smith for the sense of humour in his work, the lushness of his nudes and the lyrical poetry of his landscapes, above all 'for this torrent of beauty with which he has endowed mankind'. On the other hand, Bacon praised Smith's technique with paint and his use of chance:

> He seems to me to be one of the very few English painters since Constable and Turner to be concerned with painting – that is, with attempting to make idea and technique inseparable. Painting in this sense tends towards a complete interlocking of image and paint, so that the image is the paint and vice versa. Here the brush-stroke creates the form and does not merely fill it in. Consequently, every movement of the brush on the canvas alters the shape and implications of the image. That is why real painting is a mysterious and continuous struggle with chance – mysterious because the very substance of the paint, when used in this way, can make such a direct assault upon the nervous system; continuous because the medium is so fluid and subtle that every change that is made loses what is already there in the hope of making a fresh gain.
>
> I think that painting today is pure intuition and luck and taking advantage of what happens when you splash the stuff down, and in this game of chance Matthew Smith seems to have the gods on his side.

John Rothenstein also brought Bacon together with Henry Moore, who thought of Bacon as the best of living dramatic or romantic figurative painters – hardly what Bacon thought of his own work. Moore had doubts, however, of the possibility of creating enduring art out of such ephemera as press photographs and film stills. They would lose their force in time. Yet Rothenstein persisted in going out with them *à trois*:

> Henry and Francis, in spite of their mutual liking and respect, sometimes treated each other with the aggressive caution of heavyweight boxers. The three of us went together one night to a big reception at the Savoy, and Francis, attracted by some galaxy

> or other which held no attraction for Henry, said, 'Let's go over there.' 'I think', said Henry, 'that for a few minutes I'll stay where I am,' and Francis, whether in allusion to the sobriety of our friend's life or the consistency of his attitude as an artist I do not know, replied, 'Where you are is where you usually stay, isn't it, Henry?' and he strode off into the crowd.

Rothenstein had met Bacon at a fashionable dance, where he was very drunk and the only man not wearing evening dress. Yet his command of every social situation could not have been easier or more complete. He made clear, with courtesy and authority, that his interests lay in different worlds. In his early forties, 'he looked taller than he was; his hair had the springy look of a boy's; his face was full and rounded, slightly narrowing towards the forehead; his stride was long and a little undulant, his voice caressing with just a perceptible undertone of menace'.

Rothenstein and Bacon then made a habit of spending an evening together every few months. Bacon was a better host than a guest. As a guest, he could not indulge his sudden cravings for the expensive food or wine that he did not wish to demand, if invited. Hospitality played a very important role in his life. He would talk about painting in a way that riveted the attention, as a hazardous adventure, far more likely to end in disaster or a 'near-miss' than in success. He admired other painters, such as Velázquez and Rembrandt and Picasso, for their rare masterpieces. 'I hope the painter friends whom I respect', he said to Rothenstein, 'will never know on how *few* of their pictures my respect depends'.

Bacon's life was as original and audacious as his painting. He could only reach his desires when his strong sense of purpose was favoured by chance. He once told Rothenstein that no day passed without his thinking of death – and he was preoccupied by chance. In his company, anything might happen, but as a host, he was ready for it. At an evening party in the Hanover Gallery in March, 1957, to celebrate the opening of one of his exhibitions there, Rothenstein noticed:

> The small rooms were densely crowded with artists, collectors, students, and the teddy-boys with exotic haircuts and leather

> jackets (many of them very drunk), who mysteriously arrive as a matter of course, and in considerable numbers, at any quasi-public function of which Francis is the occasion. Above the noise a cry of pain was suddenly thought faintly to be heard. Before anybody else had even seen what caused it, Francis had appeared, instantly, from the far side of the turbulent room and was staunching a wound. Some object from the balcony had fallen upon a man below and laid open his scalp.
>
> Because of his authority as a host people who might otherwise have been apprehensive at the presence of a number of drunk toughs, moved among them without the slightest sign of disquiet.

What Rothenstein chiefly valued in Bacon as in Lucian Freud was their complete sense of classlessness. They would as easily talk to barrow boys as to the baronets, who sought their company – and Rothenstein was himself given a knighthood, while Henry Moore was made a Companion of Honour by the Queen and showered with honorary degrees. Bacon had no time for that sort of recognition and would refuse to be a Companion of Honour and a knight himself in due time. 'It might be fine for other people,' he used to say, 'but I want to stress I don't want anything for myself.' His chosen honours were to be with the few painters that he admired. He introduced himself to Giacometti in a café in Paris and found a soulmate in method and philosophy. Giacometti was never satisfied with his work. He also smashed or discarded most of what he did. He was full of self-criticism and bleak humour. 'I have always failed,' he once said. 'But I am sure no one can realise what he strives for! Oh, to be able to say, "That's it, I cannot do more."' Visiting him in his studio in Montparnasse to buy works for the Tate Gallery, Rothenstein found a clutter almost as messy as in Bacon's studio and an artist ready to destroy anything that was admired. The only time that his friends ever saw Giacometti smile was when he broke a leg and fell into the gutter in Rome. 'At last,' he said, 'something has happened to me.'

The influence of Giacometti can be seen in one of Bacon's more unusual paintings, 'Fragment of a Crucifixion' of 1950. He grew to dislike it later, calling it 'traditional story-telling'. It showed a Cross shaped like a T with a bestial shape crucified upon it, imprisoned within a spatial cage. Another ravening dog-like beast hung over the crossbar, raging and slavering to rend the crucified being. Yet in the background, figures as stick-like as those of Giacometti and cars in outline passed along a boulevard, indifferent to the crucifixion. Its restricted colours of blue and white and black suggested photographic prints, while the movement lay in the figures and the cars being rendered in slight blurring. Bacon declared later that he used the crucifixion, not because he believed in it, but as a myth which made him feel many things. 'It was always dried up for me,' he said, but in the end it was to become 'impractical to even use it.' Yet as Bryan Robertson noticed, Giacometti's pivotal 'Hands Holding the Void' and 'The Nose', through which the long phallic shape extrudes, were crucial influences in Bacon's use of the abstract space-frame. And curiously enough, beside Bacon's huge 'Painting, 1946' of the grinning shape under an open black umbrella in front of a crucified hanging carcass, the curator of the Museum of Modern Art in New York has set a bronze of a slinking skeletal dog by Giacometti, as abject and sinister as any Bacon.

Daniel Farson, the Soho photographer and author, watched the rift as it grew between Francis Bacon and Graham Sutherland and did his best to heal it. After falling out with Bacon, Douglas Cooper also bickered with Sutherland in the South of France. When Sutherland made the mistake of painting Cooper's portrait, his subject was too vain and mean-spirited to appreciate the result. But it was the increasing influence of Bacon which inadvertently and inescapably proved devastating to Sutherland, particularly his 'Christ Carrying the Cross', where the Saviour was kicked forward by a bloated and grinning soldier – a last-minute addition to his retrospective in the Tate Gallery in the May of 1953. Bacon was not to have his first retrospective until two years later, and then only at the avant-garde Institute of Contemporary Arts. Daniel Farson saw another Sutherland in a friend's house, commented that it was an odd Bacon, and was told that it was a Sutherland. Art critics began to point out that Sutherland's debt to Bacon was too blatant and heavy. And as Bacon's international reputation soared above his own, Sutherland added to his imitation in order to recapture his former glory. Although Sutherland's biographer stated that he seemed to be painting Bacon-like works on a given theme *before* Bacon himself tackled it, the evidence of existing paintings and contemporary critics is that Sutherland followed where Bacon's originality led – and became jealous of him.

The close relationship and mutual admiration between Bacon and Lucian Freud continued in Soho and elsewhere. They were both reckless gamblers. In each case, they found deep satisfaction in being beggared. It drove them back to brush and paint. Both of them found a sense of fulfilment in losing heavily. But Freud's painting, so Bacon told Cecil Beaton, was losing some of its intensity in his effort to paint quicker. It was no longer a complete expression of himself, and he was in the predicament of having to rediscover himself. Yet his intellectual brilliance, his complete independence and strength as someone who knew exactly what he wanted from life made him deeply attractive to Bacon, who shared these same qualities with his friend.

Keith Vaughan was a mannered painter who recognised Bacon's influence and power against the grain. In his journals, he attacked Bacon's 'lack of permanent formal, classical values, a sort of deliberate spiv-existentialist outlook on painting'. The portraits of Lucian Freud 'hit a new low in banality'. Yet even this disapproval could not stop Vaughan from recognising the imperious authority which Rothenstein had noted in Bacon. A close friend of Vaughan's, Dennis Williams, lived and worked in a small room near Bacon and became so besotted that he was incapable of any independent action. He admired Bacon's impressive dignity, his ardour and natural grace, his physical beauty that was supple and gentle and sensuous, and his view of people as mountains of flesh. Bacon was obsessed 'by this extraordinary capacity for flesh to breathe, walk, talk'. And Williams was obsessed by his own enslavement:

> There was nothing I could do. He would lie in bed in the morning, purple in the face, looking ill – terrible – unable to move until he had taken enough pills, but talking all the time about the paintings he had dreamed of. If I offered him a cup of tea he wouldn't drink it. He just didn't see me. I could have been anyone else and he wouldn't have noticed. I was in his studio one day and he came in with a suit which had just come from the cleaners. He laid it down

> on a large table in the middle of the room which was thick with paint, cotton wool, bits of dirty paper. He laid the suit down on top and said he had to go out for a moment. As the suit had just come from the cleaners I picked it up and put it on a hanger and hung it out of the way by the wall. My only reason for doing this was that I thought it would be helpful – a small thing – but something he was incapable of doing for himself. Directly he came back into the room, without saying a word, he went over to the wall, took the suit down and laid it again in the paint on the table. I felt absolutely shattered, as though my personality had been wiped out.

In his recent biography of Jeffrey Bernard, Graham Lord recalled that Bacon took over from John Minton in his occasional support of Bernard by slipping him the odd ten-pound note to support his gambling habit, but Bernard always denied that the artist had tried to seduce him. 'He preferred rough trade or very smart businessmen.' He advised Bernard on his philosophy of life, which wonderfully impressed the elegant scrounger. 'The only way you can possibly survive is to regard everything as being totally unimportant.' During a brief visit to New York for one of his exhibitions, Bacon was to save Bernard from freezing by purchasing an overcoat for him, and giving him hundred-dollar bills and champagne breakfasts at the Algonquin Hotel. And as age came upon them both, Bacon was to show concern for his younger friend, saying, 'Now that you've lost your looks, Jeffrey, what are you going to do?'

Bacon moved in all circles. In October, 1953, he went to Lady Ann Fleming's party for the fiftieth birthday of Cyril Connolly. He had met Cecil Beaton and Lucian Freud at Wheeler's fish restaurant in Soho, and they proceeded to the Fleming party, where the other guests included various peeresses and Maurice Bowra and Clarissa Eden, the wife of the Foreign Secretary, Stephen Spender and the philosopher Frederick Ayer, Sonia Orwell and Connolly himself. Bacon presented Connolly, whom he disliked, with a pot of caviar, while Beaton fell into conversation with a lad of twenty-three and asked him why Bacon had such an influence on the younger generation. The reply was that Picasso was old-fashioned, while Bacon had both aesthetics and sensitivity. Never before had any artist succeeded in breaking down 'all the rules and associations, a revolution in accepted creeds and standards of painting'. Bacon was the harbinger of the youth revolt to come.

It was also at Wheeler's that Bacon had shown his disdain for his health to Lucian Freud and his wife, Lady Caroline Blackwood. He came into the restaurant declaring that he had heard from his doctor that his heart was in tatters and was hardly functioning. Rarely had such a diseased organ ever been examined. If he touched another drink, his useless heart would fail. He then ordered a bottle of champagne, and then another bottle and another. As he became drunker, he was also more ebullient, while the Freuds grew more depressed. They took the diagnosis seriously and believed that Bacon would soon be dead, but then he went on drinking prodigiously until his eighties and seemed not much the worse for it. Although he was afraid of death, he could not treat it seriously enough to stop himself drinking. At the last glass, living well was better even if it meant dying soon.

On his visits to London, Patrick White renewed his friendship with Francis Bacon through Roy de Maistre, who introduced them to the Director of the Whitehall Gallery, Bryan Robertson. He saw 'Roy acting as a kind of father figure to the much younger Francis, often troubled by one or other of the three usual problems: health, love, or money'. He would sit on the vast couch designed by Bacon, still backed by one of the screens he had painted in the 'thirties. Patrick White always regretted leaving in England the large desk created by Bacon. So he had a copy of it rebuilt for his Australian home, Dogwoods. 'Had something of a reunion with Francis Bacon, who has matured as a person,' White wrote in a letter in 1958, 'and of course Roy de Maistre. I have bought a crucifixion by Roy, quite small, very beautiful . . .' He also took back to Australia the memory of Bacon's character, which he would flesh out in his later novel, *The Vivisector*.

Bacon did not appeal to all writers and poets, especially the young and the inhibited. Michael Hamburger was taken off to the Colony Room by him, and there they met John Minton, Lucian Freud and a variety of club members. Francis Bacon ordered champagne and expounded why 'artists have to become crooks'. In spite of the many martinis Hamburger had drunk at the party, 'my immediate response was to freeze up. From that moment I was a wet blanket.' He was not surprised when Bacon, Minton and the Freuds decided to move on to another haunt, leaving him to reflect on the tedium of the setting – 'the elderly barmaid with whom the guests exchanged endearments and insults, the jazz being strummed in the background by a Negro, the young artists trying to be younger than they are.'

John Minton was moving towards self-destruction as well as a rift with Francis Bacon. At a party at his house in Allen Street he insulted Bacon's paintings and Bacon poured the bottle of champagne he had brought over Minton's head and massaged it into his hair and said, 'I give champagne to my real friends, and real pain to my sham friends.' When Minton threw out one of his minions, Bacon met the young man on the streets, gave him five pounds and told him to get a meal at Wheeler's. Minton came into the restaurant later with some sailors, followed by Bacon, who walked up to Minton and asked him why he did not look after his back numbers. But before taking his life from alcohol and sleeping-pills in the January of 1957, Minton saw much of Bacon, whose generosity to his friends surpassed any love-hatred he may have felt for them.

Gerald Wilde was another Soho painter whom Bacon supported. Also an alcoholic, Wilde, in the 'forties, was considered by critics such as David Sylvester to be Britain's leading abstract expressionist. He once claimed that Bacon 'had ripped off his colours in the early days', but Bacon treated him with the largesse he always bestowed. Wilde's glass would be filled with champagne by Bacon in the French Pub or the Colony Room, and Bacon would give Wilde five pounds when his fellow artist banged on his studio door after midnight demanding money for drink.

Bacon met his women models in his Soho life. His evil genius was the malicious photographer John Deakin, who would record the subjects which Bacon wished to paint – Muriel Belcher and Isabel Rawsthorne and Henrietta Moraes. Bacon commissioned Deakin to photograph Moraes naked, and he took her in erotic poses with spread legs. But when Bacon painted her many years later from the photographs, he turned her upside down and added a hypodermic needle with bloodspots on the bedsheets. It was before she took to drugs, and she thought him a prophet. He promised her a painting, 'but he didn't give me one, did he?' What Deakin did was to peddle the nude photographs to sailors in bars for ten shillings a shot. Moraes never forgave him.

The Colony (or Calumny) Room was the afternoon drinking club where Bacon went to meet his friends. When Farson asked him what its appeal was, he replied: 'It was a place where we went to dissolve our inhibitions.' Nobody felt guilty there. They were protected from the law and the criminal code within. The jazz singer and art critic George Melly declared that Bacon's portraits of Muriel Belcher had ensured her immortality. 'She was a natural procurer,' the Soho poet Paul Potts wrote of her, 'whether it be a Bacon for the eggs or a date for the girl friend.' She also presides forever from her high stool in an evocative early picture by the young painter Michael Andrews. And another young painter, Michael Clarke, remembered gatecrashing the club in order to meet Francis Bacon, who greeted him warmly and offered him a drink, before he was thrown out. Yet he noted as he descended the stairs, 'this curious box outside, which had several left shoes in it: it reminded me of those early Giotto paintings with kind of space frame buildings, and Giacometti's space frames, and, of course, the space frames that Francis uses in his paintings.' He became a habitué and was to paint the death-bed portrait of Muriel Belcher.

'Wheeler's had particular panache in the 'fifties,' Farson wrote of the restaurant at the time when he would lunch weekly there with Bacon and other leading painters. They provided a sort of cabaret and were tolerated. Bacon could run up a bill, which he always settled in the end, although Farson once had to sell one of Bacon's screaming popes to a college friend for one-hundred-and-fifty pounds in cash so that the artist could settle his account. But in post-War and rationed Britain, eating and drinking in Wheeler's was a luxury. Farson described Bacon as talking in Mayfair cockney, in a whine with a touch of self-mockery. 'I'm not the fool I seem – *Pas du tout, chérie.*' He was always the host, signing for the oysters and Dover sole and Chablis. His penury never prevented his hospitality.

Bacon did not join in the diaspora of many artists from Soho in the 'fifties, because those who wished to survive had to flee or die of drink and waste of talent. He met Dylan Thomas in a Soho bar before the poet's death of alcoholism, but the encounter was a deadly failure to the listeners. 'They both wanted to do the same thing – talk.' Even Dylan fled to country life at Laugharne in Wales in order to put off the slow Soho death by ten-thousand drinks. But Bacon's flights to Tangier with Peter Lacey, who ended by playing the piano and running Dean's Bar there, were even more self-destructive than his existence in Soho. Yet his constitution was so strong that he was able to rise again after any nocturnal excess. And he was the antithesis of the Fitzrovian creed, a painter who survived success in a society which preferred failure. Even George Melly agreed that flight was the only solution to Fitzrovian life. 'In the end there comes a time when you must fight free or go under.' Most of the Fitzrovians followed the artists and dispersed after the War or worked for the state. If they wanted to live long, they went away and returned infrequently.

As if to prove its possibilities, from that ravaged ambience in the 'fifties emerged one radical genius, whose images have changed the perception of this time. Francis Bacon was to triumph over decades of a bohemian existence in London. It helped him to achieve the 'reality' which he sought in his art. For Bacon, the message of the artist was necessarily subversive, also his way of life. 'Artists are always disruptive,' he said, 'by their sense of reality they undermine the whole structure around them. It's the look of reality – they break the chain.' In his caged Velázquez popes entrapped in terror, he prophesied the plate-glass prison put around Eichmann at his trial in Israel, but he said he had done it only to cut down the scale of the canvas and concentrate the image by drawing in the rectangles. In fact, he did later see and cut out a photograph of the entrapped Eichmann, which confirmed his previous vision. In his flayed carcasses of men and meat of flesh, he has shown the face of our time, its torture and its violence, its horror and its waste of being. An admirer of Ezra Pound, Bacon has supplied what the poet asked,

> The age demands an image,
> Of its accelerated grimace.

And he knew profoundly what he was trying to do. As he told a reporter from the *Sunday Times*, in 1957, before leaving to spend the summer in Tangier, his object was nothing less than to paint, in his own terms, 'the history of the last thirty years' – something he did not always say about his work.

So radical, disruptive, seminal and real were Bacon's images, that he would achieve what the Auden Communist group of the 'thirties dreamed of: a major exhibition of pictures in Moscow, seen there as revolutionary protests against religious authority and the destruction of humankind. 'I was very much helped towards painting,' Bacon was to write to the Soviet Government, 'after I saw Eisenstein's films *Strike* and *The Battleship Potemkin* by their remarkable visual imagery.' Eisenstein's pictures gave Bacon a form for his 'reality', which had nothing to do with the dialectical materialism of scientific Marxism. He also was to quote to the Soviets a definition of painting by Vincent Van Gogh: 'How to achieve such anomalies, such alterations and refashionings of reality that what comes out of it are lies if you like but lies that are more truth than literal truth.' 'Reality', to Bacon, was created by technique and by the capture of chance. He searched for concentration on certain human situations. 'Somewhere there's a very hard rock, an instinct.' 'Reality' was 'the tough roughness of being. The painter's job is to make the images which return to reality more violently, if you're lucky.'

Bacon refused to recognise that his paintings had achieved a Greek 'reality' that was the essence of the spirit of his age, although he knew that he had achieved a communication to the people of his era. This could not result only from technique and caught luck and the violence of Bacon's own experience in Berlin in the 'twenties, in Paris in the 'thirties, and in bohemian London during the War and thereafter. His brutal way of living, amoral and disruptive, made him an unlikely recipient for the gift of conveying a universal message. But Rimbaud and, indeed, Shakespeare had also received that improbable gift, when neither had the vocabulary nor the background to compose their imperishable verses, which are still resonant for any age or country. Bacon demonstrated that a Fitzrovian life might provoke an artist into fifty years of supreme creativity, while Dylan Thomas remained the testimony to its morose fatality.

'The compelling power of Bacon's vision,' John Rothenstein wrote, 'once ridiculed as schoolboy obscenity, derogated as an affront to decent people, and so forth, has imposed itself on the public imagination, not only of Britain but of the western world. In the awkward strangeness of his figures we recognize ourselves; in his "affronts to decent people" we recognize understatements about our own age, the age of Auschwitz, Stalin, Hiroshima, Bangladesh, and about much that goes on beneath – though not far beneath – the surface of our own society. So completely, in fact, has it imposed itself that to some among the younger generation it has become almost commonplace. This untaught painter has become, by the audacity of his vision, by his dedication, his rare understanding of paint and its mysterious potentialities, a master.'

The recognition of Bacon's work internationally and his financial security were arranged by a new contract with Marlborough Fine Art Limited, to which he switched on 17 October 1958. That afternoon, he called at the Hanover Gallery and asked to see Erica Brausen. To her secretary, he appeared agitated and disappointed to hear that she was abroad. He wished to tell her that his debts had obliged him to leave the gallery. The situation was irrevocable. 'He knows that you will be distressed, as he is himself,' the secretary wrote to Miss Brausen, 'but he says his position was desperate and that he had no alternative. [He was] obviously upset and in some trepidation, bringing with him a cheque to clear his account . . . He said he would never have taken this step without consulting you but was up to the neck in personal debt to the extent of about £5,000 for gambling etcetera.'

Erica Brausen was equally upset. 'I've looked after Mr Bacon's interests for more than ten years,' she declared to the press. 'I bought his first picture. Now he leaves a message with my secretary that he is taking his business elsewhere. I intend to sue him. Admittedly, there has been only a verbal contract between us. But I have organized exhibitions for him in Paris and Milan.' The one at the Galerie Rive Droite in the February of the previous year had, indeed, launched Bacon's reputation in France. He had also been commissioned through his cousin Diana Watson to paint the famous cabaret director and *diseuse*, Suzy Solidor, herself the pupil of Yvette Guilbert – so often painted by Toulouse-Lautrec.

With pretended indifference, Bacon refused to discuss his desertion of Erica Brausen and the Hanover Gallery, saying that the matter had been taken out of his hands. Marlborough Fine Art declared that it had signed an agreement with Bacon in good faith, and that its solicitors would deal with the claims of the Hanover. The origins of the rival London gallery lay in the Second World War, when two refugees from Vienna, Frank Lloyd and Harry Fischer, met in the Pioneer Corps and decided to trade together, when peace came, in art and antiques and rare books. They reached Bond Street in 1950 and broke into the international art market with the acquisition and sale of the last complete set of Degas bronzes, one of which went to the Tate Gallery. Joined as a partner by David Somerset, the present Duke of Beaufort, they gained access to the major art collections stored in English stately homes, which often had to be sold to pay income tax and death duties. They also began to represent contemporary artists, Henry Moore and Graham Sutherland and now Francis Bacon. As Rothenstein wrote in the introduction to a Bacon show in Paris, 'The artist paints and lives his highly independent life; the Marlborough with no more than minimal consultation with him pursues, on his behalf, a brilliantly successful career.'

His deal with Mammon at the Marlborough made Bacon preserve more of his canvases for sale: there are fifty surviving paintings of his from the period of three years after 1959. His promotion by the Marlborough even secured him a showing at the Kassel Documenta that same year. And his powerful new allies increased the range of his patrons. The Marlborough paid him in rolls of ten-pound notes, with which he climbed through every stratum of society, playing the wilful host. 'He was ruthlessly upwardly and downwardly socially mobile,' his friend Bruce Bernard said of him. 'He wanted control after all those early years of rejection. He wanted to dominate. It had to be *his* choice. He had to show his power.'

Bacon appeared classless. He moved effortlessly through society without any discrimination except his own caprice. He treated Stephen Spender and a sailor on the same terms, although young sailors were often treated better. He was all things to all men, up and down the river. He went to dinner with Spender when the poet gave a party for his old friend W. H. Auden, who had returned to England from the United States of America to take up the Chair of Poetry at Oxford. At the party were Lady Glenconner and Osbert Sitwell, now dying of advanced Parkinson's disease, Sonia Orwell and David Jones and Bacon. Unfortunately, Auden annoyed Bacon by declaring that a friend of his, X, was a crook. 'He just isn't straight about money, and I don't approve.' Spender knew that Auden was right, but his dogmatic manner showed no realisation of the feelings of Francis. In his journals, Spender commented that after an argument, Auden 'admitted that he liked X but the admission had the same quality of filing X into some category of approval or disapproval as the criticism. It was really one of those strangely unsatisfactory controversies between the prigs and the anti-prigs, in which both sides are both in the right and in the wrong, one through being very moralistic, the other amoralistic – and both being so on principle.'

Bacon certainly cultivated a wealthy and artistic international set of patrons, although he dealt with them with aristocratic disdain. Nothing illustrated his flirtation with the *beau monde* and his contempt of it more than the episode of Cecil Beaton's portrait. Beaton had met Bacon in Tangier, which he called the 'oriental Cheltenham', while he wrote that Bacon went there for 'a close intimacy with the Arab world, with the brothel life, and the freedom that can be found only in certain Mediterranean countries where access to women is difficult'. In spite of Bacon's reputation for destroying his paintings, Beaton took Bacon's photograph and commissioned a portrait from the younger artist. He eagerly anticipated the sittings in his studio. 'Francis is one of the most interesting, refreshing and utterly beguiling people. He is wise and effervescent and an inspired conversationalist.' Actually, according to Patrick Procktor, who also did a sketch of Beaton and was ordered immediately to remove it from sight, there were long silences at the sessions with Bacon, only interrupted by the painter saying, 'Well, don't you *like* coming out of a black background?'

Beaton admired Bacon's manner at work. The artist had just

returned from a winter in Tangier, where he had been too harassed and ill to paint, but now he was full of the joy of London life. Unfortunately in the early months of 1958 he had a new and messy studio in the red-brick Overstrand Mansions in Battersea. The ancient curtains were livid and crusty from his habit of wiping his paint-spattered hands on them. There he set to work among a Dostoevsky shambles of discarded tins and rags and newspapers on an enormous rough canvas, covered with black paint, which he said he would cut down to size, if necessary, when the portrait was finished. He told the apprehensive Beaton, 'Your face is pink and blue. I can't make out if it is pink on top of blue or blue on top of pink.'

> Francis started to work with great zest, excitedly running backwards and forwards to the canvas with gazelle-springing leaps – much toe bouncing . . . Smiling and painting simultaneously, he seemed to be having such a good time. He appeared extraordinarily healthy and cherubic, apple-shiny cheeks and the protruding lips were lubricated with an unusual amount of saliva. His hair was bleached by sun and other aids. His figure was incredibly lithe for a person of his age and occupation, wonderfully muscular and solid. I was impressed with his 'principal boy' legs, tightly encased in black jeans with high boots. Not a pound of extra flesh anywhere . . .
>
> Of his many qualities I admired most his independence. I envied his being able to live in exactly the way he wished, and I was impressed by his aloofness from the opinions of others. We went out 'on the town', but I am not good at pubs, drinking clubs and late hours and would fade away just when Francis was about to enjoy himself.

Bacon called a halt to the enterprise for two years, and when Beaton asked him to go on with it, he showed his sitter an enormous black canvas, depicting a monster nude cripple with four legs and no head. Bacon said he would try again to get a likeness, but this time on a background of emerald green dye-paint. He worked fluently and talked incessantly. Beaton noticed, among the rubbish of old cloths and paint tins on the floor, two costly books on Crete and Egyptian art, which Bacon profoundly admired for the beauty of the heads.

> Occasionally Francis would sit down on an old chair from which the entrails were hanging and which had been temporarily covered with a few French magazines and newspapers. His pose reminded me of a portrait of Degas. He curved his head sideways and looked at his canvas with a beautiful expression in his eyes. His plump, marble-like hands were covered with blue-green paint. He said he thought that painting portraits was the most interesting thing he could ever hope to do: 'If only I can do them! The important thing is to put a person down as he appears to your mind's eye. The person must be there so that you can check up on reality – but not be led by it, not be its slave. To get the essence without being positive about the factual shapes – that's the difficulty. It's so difficult that it's almost impossible!'

When the portrait was finished, Bacon declared that it was one of the best things he had ever done. He invited Beaton to view it. Always vain about his appearance, Beaton saw a coloured cartoon of a bald and senile businessman.

> The face was hardly recognizable as a face for it was disintegrating before your eyes, suffering from a severe case of elephantiasis: a swollen mass of raw meat and fatty tissues. The nose spread in many directions like a polyp but sagged finally over one cheek. The mouth looked like a painful boil about to burst. He wore a very sketchily dabbed-in suit of lavender blue. The hands were clasped and consisted of emerald green scratches that resembled claws. The dry painting of the body and hands was completely different from that of the wet, soggy head. The white background was thickly painted with a house painter's brush. It was dragged round the outer surfaces without any intention of cleaning up the shapes. The head and shoulders were outlined in a streaky wet slime.

Beaton could not hide his sense of shock and pain at this caricature of him, so different from the flattering photographic portraits that he took with his camera. Bacon offered him the picture for only three-hundred pounds, while Beaton haggled for half the price. He simply did not know where he could hang it among the beautiful decorations of his home. It would give him 'a turn for the worse' every time he saw it. But it might be a good investment, and he could always sell it for more to the Marlborough Gallery. He gulped and said he would take it and staggered away with a great sense of loss. He had thought that Bacon's theories of life and art and beauty would be incorporated in the portrait, but the artist had seen him with a different eye, the essence within.

Soon afterwards, Beaton had a telephone call from the ecstatic Bacon, who told him that he had destroyed the portrait and most of the other pictures with an emerald-green background that were scheduled for his next exhibition at the Marlborough. He did not like his friends taking work that they did not like. He wanted no money from Beaton and did not mind wasting his time. 'He seemed jubilant at not getting paid, at *not* finishing a picture.' When Beaton told Augustus John of how Bacon had made him look like a piece of raw offal, John replied that he deserved it for sitting for Bacon and added sarcastically, 'These idiosyncrasies are the prerogative of genius.'

Actually, the prerogative of Bacon's genius were his dissections. He took out of Beaton what he saw in him, and set that on canvas. Beaton was the last man to see the flaws in his own nature, the vanity that denied growing aged, the greed and commercial instinct that he hid beneath his urbane wit, and the skull that certainly lay under the last of his hair. Bacon was as ruthless in his depiction of his patrons as he was in cultivating their presence. With all the charm and wit in the world, he wielded a brush like a scalpel and pursued a visceral truth. When Michael Wishart wanted him to paint Jean Cocteau and arranged an introduction, Bacon would not do it. 'Too much like Cecil Beaton,' he said.

8
The Blood of a British Man

> Child Rowland to the dark tower came:
> His word was still 'Fie, foh, and fum,
> I smell the blood of a British man.'
>
> Edgar in *King Lear*
> by William Shakespeare

Like the wise Edgar pretending to play the Fool – Fie, Foh, and Fum – Bacon was to smell the blood of two of his beloved British men within ten years of their deaths. These tragedies both were to occur at the moments of his triumphs, as though Edgar's father, the old and faithful and blinded Gloucester in *King Lear*, knew of the black truth of living:

> As flies to wanton boys, are we to the gods;
> They kill us for their sport.

Bacon often used to quote these lines and admired Shakespeare for his ability to enliven life, however futile it was. He was full of deep despair and pessimism as well as humour and an absolutely diabolical cynicism.

Rich enough now to afford a permanent studio in London, Bacon moved into 7 Reece Mews in Kensington, where he would live in the main for the rest of his life. From the outside, the house has the look of a bunker, undistinguished and enclosed above the locked double-doors of its garage. Yet Bacon was always influenced by places and sensitive to the atmosphere of rooms. The cloistered mews enabled him to work inside, and he knew that from the very moment that the house agent brought him there. The bell was kept out of order so that Bacon did not have to answer the door to salesmen or importunate friends, but loud knocks from expected visitors enabled them to climb up a steep flight of wooden steps holding on to a rope banister, which only allowed his large canvases to inch up. Then the guests would discover an elementary kitchen with a bath-tub by the cooker, a small studio on the right, and a bed with a spread of a dazzling Moroccan tent cover in a cabin of a sitting-room on the left. 'It's rather like a ship, isn't it?' Bacon would say.

The floor and the walls were bare; naked light-bulbs hung from the ceilings, while heavy curtains of dark green blocked off the windows, which Bacon eventually painted black. He had pulled down the studio ceiling to expose the joists and the rafters and had installed a grimy skylight to let some brightness falling from the air into the room, parked with the clutter of the artist. In the living space, a huge wall-mirror webbed with cracks recalled Duchamp's disturbing Large Glass, which Bacon thought took the problem of abstraction and realism as far as it could go. Beside an electric fan, a cast of the death-mask of William Blake rested pale on the top of a desk, littered with books on art, which were usually bought at Zwemmer's in the Charing Cross Road – Bacon's favourite Eisenstein had also ordered his art books from there. No pictures by other painters were hung, although Bacon had once owned a very early Frank Auerbach and had bought a Sickert of a woman lying on a bed with a man seated next to her. 'But, like a fool, I gave it to Lucian Freud.'

Bacon was also to feel this instant recognition of a place where he might be himself when he found a single room in Paris which he bought a few years later. He knew he could work in it, although he admitted to David Sylvester that his intentions in Paris were greater than his practice. Because he knew London better, he said that he was able to work there more easily 'than in a city which I don't know so well'. Yet France was to be his refuge from the limitations of England. He was always to feel more appreciated over there.

He continued to work in spite of Peter Lacey's increasing illnesses from alcoholism. Marlborough Fine Art was arranging more and more exhibitions for him – a one-man show at the São Paolo Bienal, a retrospective at the Richard Feigen Gallery in Chicago, and group shows in Amsterdam, Glasgow, Leningrad, Milan, Moscow, New York, Nottingham, Paris, Pittsburgh, Turin and Wakefield. His work was also on continuous offer at the Bond Street gallery itself. But his major goal was the offer by John Rothenstein to give him a retrospective at the Tate Gallery, a recognition of the value of his work to the image of his country. In the opinion of the Director of the Tate, only a small minority of painters were not aware that anything unusual was being done for them. Bacon was one of these. 'Had he never been offered a retrospective he would not have noticed the omission; had it been cancelled he would not have demurred, yet no one could have responded to it more warmly.'

Whatever Bacon said to his drinking companions about his contempt for being honoured, he co-operated fully with Rothenstein over the introduction to the catalogue for the exhibition and the show itself. When he heard that Rothenstein was giving Lucian Freud dinner at the Athenaeum to pump him for information, Bacon invited himself to supervise the interrogation. Before he arrived, Freud said, 'Don't overlook the influence of Nietzsche on Francis', and as Rothenstein ushered in his two guests, he was met with the mild disapproval of the aged anarchist critic Herbert Read at bringing two such bohemians into that august place. When the introduction was finished, Rothenstein read it to Bacon with some trepidation. He knew of his subject's fickleness and whims of anger. As paragraph after paragraph was heard, Bacon said nothing. Rothenstein looked up to find him in tears, saying, 'I *feel* like the painter you've described. It's an experience I've never had before, partly, I think, because you've treated my art in such a matter-of-fact way.'

That previous night, Bacon had been up late, gambling at Charlie Chester's Casino in Soho, the usual unglamorous place where he went to lose his shirt. During his absence, somebody had broken into his studio through a skylight and had stolen two pictures – he suspected that it was an acquaintance just out of prison. It was to be a prelude to his own future of choosing dangerous lovers. He and

Rothenstein talked of Lucian Freud, whom Francis thought one of his more intelligent and entertaining friends. He even admired Freud's life-style, which was as extreme as his own, but with girls – 'to bed, or rather to sleep, at three, then up again at seven, she posing as his model'.

Bacon had appreciated Rothenstein's introduction to the Tate catalogue because it had depicted his past life without frills and had related his paintings to their mundane sources and to the everyday. Two paragraphs particularly struck home and made him weep, because they appeared to prove that he had achieved what he wanted:

> Bacon's contemporaries belong to generations that have seen the destruction of cities by bomb, the flight of whole peoples under the lash of fear, the concentration camps, the death camps and the rest. His power of making human anguish dramatically significant to our generation is due in part to the dignity and the sobriety of his treatment of all his subjects, however horrible, and to the extent to which he draws his imagery from the most characteristic and the most widespread art-form prevalent today: the photograph reproduced in the newspaper and on the cinema screen. However extraordinary the imagery of Bacon, it speaks to us intimately because it speaks a language familiar to us all; a language which, more than any other factor, has formed our way of seeing . . .
>
> If artists are once again to concern themselves with external reality – and surely man's interest in external reality and his urge to communicate ideas are too deep-rooted to allow us to doubt that eventually they will – it is unlikely to be by returning to the conventions of the past. By the arresting originality and dynamism of his view of the external world, an originality which owes much to his reliance on automatism and chance, to the audacity of his forays across the borders of rationality, Bacon may well portend the revival of an art that makes no claim to be self-sufficient but seeks instead to communicate some truths believed to transcend it.

Rothenstein also commented on Bacon's originality and independence as a man as well as a painter. He took Lucian Freud's advice and wrote of Bacon having 'something of the dynamic amoralism that Nietschze justified; few people live lives more detached from organized society and none has less thought of making of his art a vehicle of success, of acquiring either recognition or possessions; he is indifferent to both'. This was the public acclaim that Bacon sought, the statement that he did not want public acclaim. He would smash the ladder of success rung by rung. And yet his very relationship with Rothenstein and his acceptance of a retrospective exhibition at a state gallery proved that the accolade was not a foreign gesture.

The Tate show of the works of Francis Bacon between 24 May and 1 July 1962 also proved that Rothenstein was right. He had recorded the familiar past of his time, he had achieved what he had told the *Sunday Times* before leaving to see Peter Lacey in Tangier, 'painting, in his own terms, "the history of the last thirty years".' To examine the Tate catalogue is to travel through time and view the images that haunted each generation in each decade, an examination of the waking dream and nightmare of those passing years. Starting with his odd pock-marked portrait of 1930; ranging through his early Christs on the Cross in their confined passion to his definitive 'Three Studies for Figures at the Base of a Crucifixion' of 1944, the howling Furies of the Second World War; viewing 'Figure in a Landscape', all wound and meat by the hissing orifice of a machine-gun; progressing past howling 'Magdalenes' under trilby hats and umbrellas on to salivating heads and screaming popes within a vacuum and an empty cube; the animal and the bestial protruding into power and executive privilege; the decomposition and melting of the figure in agony and lechery; the serial and newsreel studies of the congealing actions of mankind; the sombre ghost of William Blake and the lurid 'phantom of the road' of Van Gogh and the encapsulated howl of the nurse from *The Battleship Potemkin*; the contorted portraits that appeared to wring the real from the flesh as if wax from a floor mop; the abandon and mutation of man and woman in lure and motion.

These are the images that I saw at the retrospective that summer in London. And I thought I had discerned the history of our time. If I intrude into the text, it is because I have met and talked to Francis Bacon several times, and he has always treated me as the social historian I am, and not the art critic I am not. He has acknowledged my trade and its due place in his work. Most of the art critics appreciated the retrospective as well. As Director of the Tate, John Rothenstein asserted that the exhibition was a resounding success, attracting more praise than any exhibition by a British painter within his memory. John Russell saw in the show a grand, ordered, coherent look – 'a renewal of the European tradition, with very little about it that could be called bizarre or gratuitous'. Bacon was seen in his rightful place.

Particularly praised was Bacon's new version of 'Three Studies for a Crucifixion'. It reeked of blood and wet paint, for he had executed it rapidly for the show, mainly inebriated because he knew Peter Lacey was seriously ill in Tangier. To begin with, he had worked on the three canvases of the triptych separately, 'but later, as he brought them near completion, he worked on the three together. It is a picture that he painted in about a fortnight, when he was in a bad mood of drinking, and he did it under tremendous hangover and drink; he sometimes hardly knew what he was doing. "It's one of the only pictures that I've ever been able to do under drink. I believe that the drink helped me to be a bit freer."' To Lawrence Gowing, this triptych was 'the masterly evocation of bodily fate that explored unshrinkingly' the latent themes in Bacon's earlier works. The four figures in the three canvases were joined in the theme of the violence that men did to one another by the power of sex or hatred. The body on the right, lying head down, suggested an inverted crucifixion by Cimabue, which Bacon thought was like 'a worm crawling . . . just moving, undulating down the cross'.

The sudden death of Peter Lacey in Tangier was announced to Francis Bacon after the opening of his exhibition at the Tate. He had even spoken amiably to the press critics in the morning to Rothenstein's surprise – 'the kind of occasion he usually avoids as though plague-infested'. At the evening party after the private view, a very formal occasion –

> He appeared in clothes he had worn since morning: black and white check shirt and blue jeans, but instead of wearing his black leather coat he swung it about as a toreador his cloak. At a few paces distant he was followed by a few youths similarly dressed.

> He was very drunk, but his condition did not in the least diminish his dignity or the charm he so powerfully exerts. When he left he again thanked me for my part in the exhibition, embraced me, and kissed me on both cheeks, making me feel like a French officer receiving a decoration.'

A telegram reached Bacon at Reece Mews on his return from the party at the Tate. Peter Lacey was dead. It confirmed what he had been painting and telling John Rothenstein for the catalogue of his retrospective. He thought of death every day; he believed that there was no life after death; but he did believe in Hell – 'Hell is here and now.' Death had come for his lover, not for him. Yet it did not mean changing his existentialist routine. He went to the Colony Room the following night, seeking solace at a wake being held for his friend. Daniel Farson returned from Paris to find Bedlam in the Soho Club. He presumed all the members were celebrating the success of the Tate exhibition, and when Rodrigo Moynihan's wife asked him if he had heard the news, he replied that he had. 'Francis must be overjoyed.' She slapped his face, Bacon heard the sound. With his usual delicacy and courtesy, he steered Farson to the lavatory and told him that Lacey was gone.

This tragedy changed Bacon's subject matter in the 'sixties. It had more to do with intimacy than history. When the suggestion was made to him that he might allay his grief through his art, he did a 'Study for Three Heads' with a portrait of Lacey on the left and right canvas and a self-portrait at the centre. There were to be more portraits of Lacey from photographs and memory, and then a series of studies of his companions from the Colony Room, who had consoled him, particularly Henrietta Moraes, the wife of the poet Dom, and Isabel Rawsthorne, now married to a second composer, Alan, after the death of Constant Lambert. Bacon was also to paint his artist friends, particularly Lucian Freud, and his next beloved George Dyer, another burglar who may well have been the acquaintance who stole the two paintings on the eve of his Tate exhibition.

After lunching with Dom Moraes, Stephen Spender had also gone to the retrospective. He observed, rather censoriously, in his journal:

> Saw Francis Bacon exhibition at the Tate. The paintings make horrifying statements with very great force. They are by an observer so profoundly affected by the kind of life he observes that, although protesting, they seem corrupted by the corruption. After Bacon most other contemporary painting seems decoration, doodling, aestheticism or stupidity. His work extremely devoid of pleasure, perhaps this is partly due to the life of disillusionment he leads, which he faces in its implications; perhaps it is the old English puritanism and dislike of pleasure cropping up again.

Six days later at a dinner party, Spender met Bacon, who told him of the death of Peter Lacey. He was offended that the critics had said his pictures were full of hatred and without love. He had loved his dead friend. Spender said that it struck him that Bacon did not express that feeling in his art. Bacon replied that he could not do that at present, 'that certain friends were far too beautiful for him to distort – and he had always distorted'. Another week later, Bacon had Spender to dinner and continued to talk about Lacey, but cheered up when the conversation shifted to Raphael and Michelangelo. He declared that his ambition was 'to do something really beautiful and not ugly as all my paintings are, before I die'.

In his loneliness, Francis Bacon spent much time with a circle of old and new friends, who grouped around Sonia Orwell in her Kensington home. They saw the intellectual side of him rather than the hand on the champagne glass. He was always in control of his drinking: when he had a gall-bladder operation, he followed his doctor's orders for a year and foreswore alcohol, only to resume his evening carouses when his liver could support the damage. With Sonia Orwell, Bacon would meet Jeanetta Jackson, Shusha Guppy, Patrick Kinross, Joan and Patrick Leigh-Fermor, and the French cultural *attaché*, Jean-Marie Benoit. They ate chiefly in the upper room of the Etoile: Bacon would entertain his boon companions at Wheeler's. With his usual generosity, Bacon paid for everybody, and he would support Sonia Orwell through her long illness and final weeks at Blake's Hotel. Few artists were ever more giving to those friends who rescued them from the desperate isolation of the trade.

Bacon talked to literary figures in their terms, of hatred and love, of beauty and ugliness. He did not talk to his friends in the Colony

Room like that. The language there was honest and practical, jokey and unpretentious. It was hardly a question of the newspeak of George Orwell or the double logic of the Jesuits, but of the intelligence and taste of the artist, who could suit his sentences to the company he kept. A week before his Tate retrospective, Rothenstein had introduced him to Lord Cottesloe, who was the Chairman of the Arts Council. Bacon was, as always, determined to encounter the Establishment on his own terms. His first words were, 'I've such a hangover that I can hardly stand up', but after making his point, 'he carried on the conversation with the utmost suavity'. Bacon ever managed to be himself, yet all things to all men. He maintained the delicate balance of the tightrope walker swaying above the abysses of London society without a safety net. He would listen to anyone with courteous attention, then answer in his lilting and patrician cockney, wisely or waspishly, but always well.

The question was, whether *any* writer could describe him or his paintings. Patrick White came to London the year after the retrospective at the Tate and saw Bacon's exhibition at Marlborough Fine Art. He was celebrating with his British publishers the success of his novel *Voss* and also revisiting his old lover and mentor, Roy de Maistre, who was losing his sight and his health and trying to conceal the ravages of age with ochre pancake make-up, which stopped at his ears, leaving a pale white ring round his neck. De Maistre offered to leave to White in his will his studio with its screen and sofa designed by Bacon, but the novelist refused. He had in his mind to write about an obsessive artist, not to inherit the early and discarded works of one. The setting would be Sydney in Australia, not London. For one of White's frustrations was that he was destined not to become a painter himself. As he admitted: 'I had imagined that if I could acquire the technique I might give visual expression to what I have inside me, and that the physical act of painting would exhilarate me far more than grinding away at grey, bronchial prose. This could be the delusion of a writer who has always resented having to write.'

Instead, White set down in words *The Vivisector*. It was to be the most illuminating novel on the visions of a modern painter since Joyce Cary's *The Horse's Mouth*, which had been written during the Second World War. Yet White's protagonist, Hurtle Duffield, had a different mind and eye to Cary's Gulley Jimson. In his search for the truth in Sydney and the outback, Hurtle eviscerated his subjects as Bacon did, as a child drawing a tutor with a bestial and diseased appearance, and representing, when a man, an adopted and beloved hunchback sister as an octopus beside a bidet with a sponge on one sucker. In Chelsea in London, however, Gulley had been modelled on Augustus John and Matthew Smith, and his perception was filled with lush nudes and the divine glory of the light on the River Thames. But to Hurtle, creation was cruel. The motto he scrawled on the wall was:

GOD THE VIVISECTOR
GOD THE ARTIST
GOD

When White was writing his novel in Sydney, Bacon was already so influential that a school of young Australian artists was trying to imitate his inimitable style. Many of Hurtle Duffield's characteristics were those of the young London artist, whom White had first encountered with Roy de Maistre in the 'thirties – his love of paint, his urge to destroy his canvases, and his delight in the 'random arabesques' to be found on boards and walls. Like Bacon, Hurtle Duffield had an aristocratic descent and no early education except from one rector's wife. Adopted by a wealthy couple, Hurtle was reared in a big house like Straffan Lodge or Jesmond Towers, where he first saw some Victorian paintings of naked ladies and thought that they looked like 'old cold pudding'. Even writing of himself at the age of six, Hurtle declared he felt older than that. 'I don't think age has always to do with what you feel because my father and mother who are old never have the same feelings or thoughts as me. They do not understand what I tell them so I have just about had to give up telling.' The incomprehension that Hurtle suffered from his parents was also the early fate of Francis Bacon.

In one telling episode, Hurtle's adopted mother pushed the child's head among her dresses hanging in a wardrobe. 'The sensation was at first one of blinding, then of a delicious suffocation as his face was swallowed by the scented silky darkness.' Loving ladies' clothes as his

28 Painting, 1946.

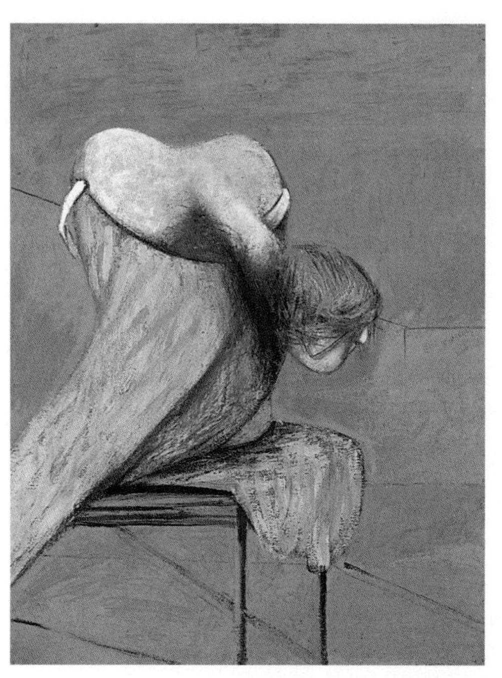

30 Crucifixion, 1965.

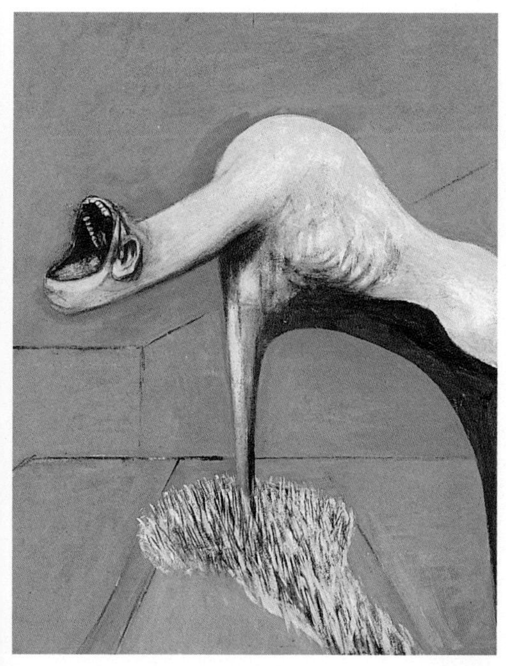

29 Three Studies for
Figures at the Base of a Crucifixion,
1944.

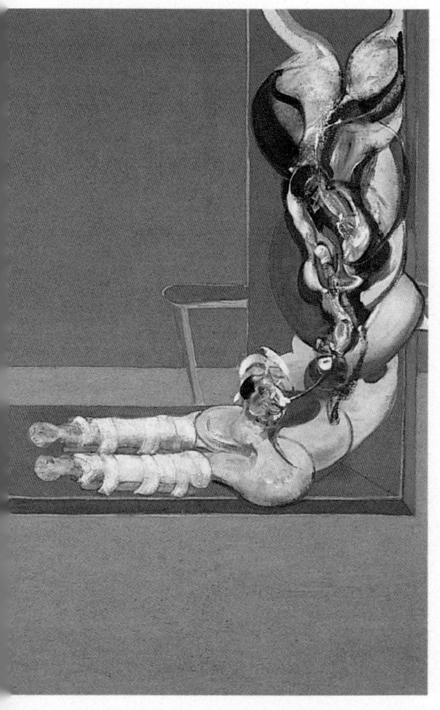

31 Study after Velázquez's
Portrait of Pope Innocent X, 1953.

32 Study for
Portrait of Van Gogh IV,
1957

33 Portrait of Isabel Rawsthorne
Standing in a Street in Soho, 1967.

35 Triptych Inspired by T. S. Eliot's Poem 'Sweeney Agonistes', 1967.

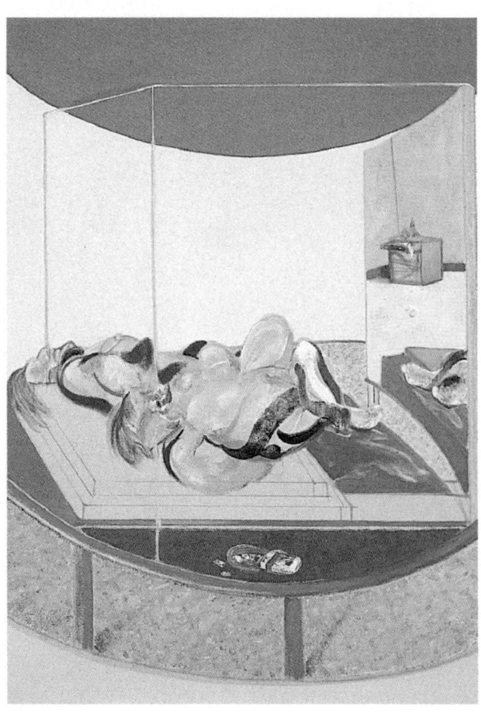

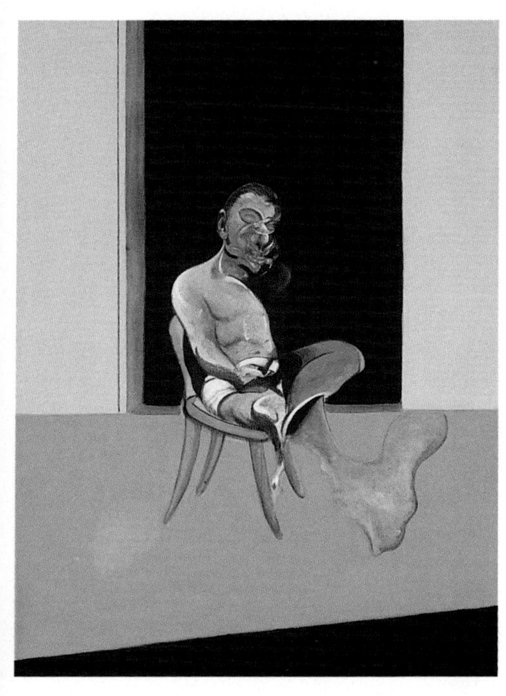

34 Triptych, August, 1972.

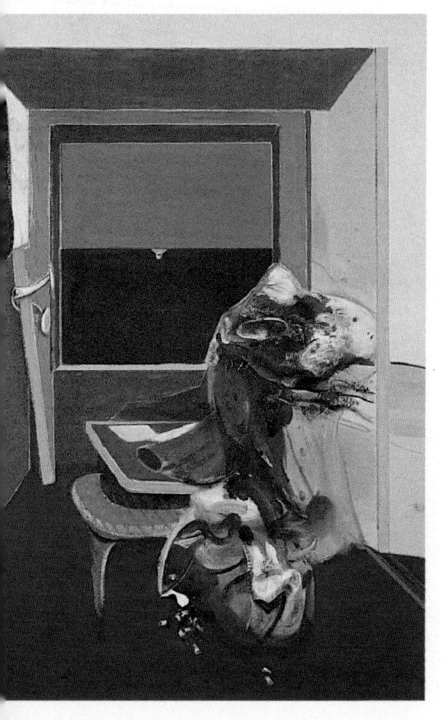

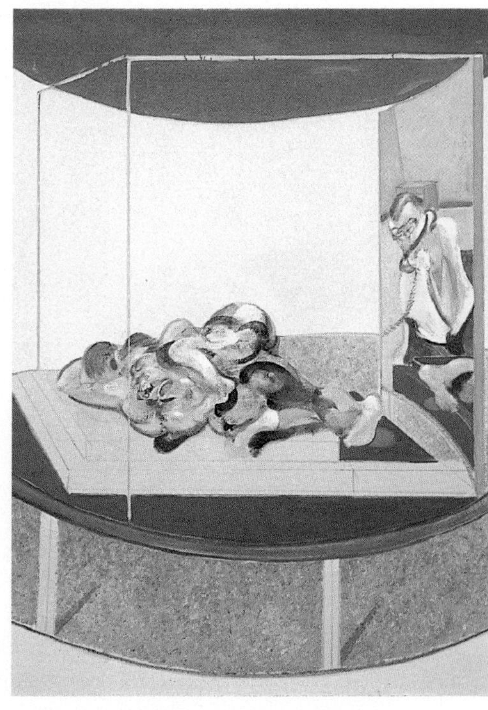

36 Study of a
Man Talking, 1981.

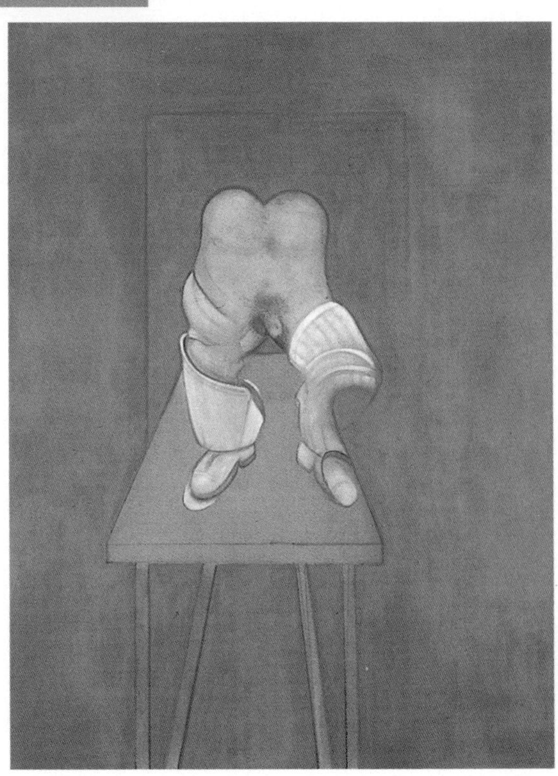

37 Study of
the Human Body, 1982.

prototype did, Hurtle also ran away from his grand house at the age of sixteen, but to enlist in the Australian Army during the First World War. He never returned home again, existing in Paris for a while as a dishwasher like George Orwell rather than as a boyfriend like Francis Bacon. Hurtle was heterosexual, although odd in his view of the act of intercourse, comparing his adopted mother and father making love to two plucked chickens. His first passion was for a blowsy Sydney tart called Nance Lightfoot – curiously enough, the surname taken as an alias by Bacon when a manservant in the 'thirties. Hurtle wondered how far art was dependent on sexuality, had a vision of his beloved as Goya's Saturn, and saw her as 'Nance Spreadeagle', just as Bacon depicted Henrietta Moraes for his Marlborough show.

Monomaniac and driven, Hurtle allowed Nance to prostitute herself to pay for his art, and also took cheques from his homosexual gallery dealer, who was consumed by an unanswered love for him. 'He guessed each was perverse enough to enjoy the voluptuousness of any suffering involved. Whatever the moral climate, the painter continued perving on and painting . . .' Nance herself accused Hurtle of being a secret homosexual, because all men were in love with themselves. Only when a man felt good about himself, he had to have a woman and call it love. 'At least the poofs are honest. They look around for another poof. To be on the right track, you oughter be, all of you, one big set of poofs!' Later, when Nance had fallen to her death down a ravine, leaving Hurtle to feel guilty about murdering her, he almost agreed with her remarks, while talking to a gay grocer on a park bench in The Gash in Sydney. 'Human beings aren't allowed to choose what they shall love: woman, man, cat – or God.'

Bacon was also destined to what he loved and to the loss of it, for Peter Lacey was now dead. Hurtle accepted that even the suicide of a loved one was a form of murder. Who knew what drove the self-destroyer to the act? His next passion, a Greek woman named Hero, specifically identified his art with that of Bacon, saying, 'The painter is cruel. Why do painters have to deform everything they see?' Later, she loathed his series of paintings of kittens being taken away by her husband to be drowned. Man was cruel, God was cruel. 'We are his bagful of cats, aren't we?' This was why Hurtle Duffield was a sort of Francis Bacon, to envision God as a Vivisector, and to see the pursuit of the image of truth to be the insertion of the flaying-knife beneath the appearance into the essence of things. As Hurtle's adopted sister told him, she might always be vivisected afresh, 'in the name of truth – or art'.

At the end of the novel, Patrick White invented a last love affair between the elderly Hurtle and an adolescent painter, Kathy Volkov. He was writing of his own introduction to the truth of being an artist, which was given to him by the older Roy de Maistre. At first Kathy would not let Hurtle paint her, because her mother said that she would be at the mercy of the painter, worse than the mercy of a husband. 'A husband goes away. But the painter has painted the painting.' Later she and Hurtle made love, and he did paint her. Although she ran off and became as egoistic a concert pianist as he was a painter, she did acknowledge in the end that he had shown her how to be an artist, as Roy de Maistre had shown the young Patrick White, too, in Eccleston Street and the young Francis Bacon before him. As she said to Hurtle:

> 'If I've learnt anything of importance, it was you who taught me, and I thank you for it . . . It was you who taught me how to see, to be, to know instinctively. When I used to come to your house in Flint Street, melting with excitement and terror, wondering whether I would dare go through with it again, or whether I would turn to wood, or dough, or say something so stupid and tactless you would chuck me out into the street, it wasn't simply thought of the delicious kisses and all the other lovely play which forced the courage into me. It was the paintings I used to look at sideways whenever I got a chance. I wouldn't have let on, because I was afraid you might have been amused, and made me talk about them, and been even more amused when I couldn't discuss them at your level. But I was drinking them in through the pores of my skin . . .
>
> 'I can't call you "lover", although I suppose that, technically, is what you have been – or "dirty seducer"! if I hadn't wanted, *had to be seduced* – still I prefer to think of you as the father of anything praiseworthy that will ever come out of me.

Hurtle Duffield also started to speak of the reason why Bacon chose to be a vivisector in his pictures. His adopted sister said that from his last exhibitions, she was now beginning to understand. 'The horrors are less horrible if you've created them yourself. Is that it?' He replied, 'No, I'm *still* trying to arrive at the truth.' She said that perhaps she did not understand, the truth could look so dishonest. But it was not, Hurtle insisted. 'If it were only a question of paint – but is it dishonest to pour out one's life-blood?' Although Bacon stressed that his pictures were only a question of paint, he was never dishonest and poured out his life-blood, too. And he was to refuse a knighthood as Duffield did, and he had been given a retrospective at the Tate Gallery just as Hurtle was in his State Gallery, only to comment that it was 'a bit of a give-away, though . . . To see your life hung out – your whole life of dirty washing.'

The Vivisector was dedicated by the author to his friends, Cynthia and Sidney Nolan, the best Australian painter of his time. Nolan also had a retrospective exhibition at the Art Gallery of New South Wales in 1967 in honour of his fiftieth birthday and came to believe that he was the only model for Hurtle Duffield, although his background and domestic life could not have been more dissimilar. White told him that he was not in the least the inspiration for the book, but Nolan preferred to think that he was and basked in White's praise of his retrospective show, that 'it was staggering to see all the imaginative and painting genius that has poured out of one man'. It was to end badly between the two Australians, with White accusing Nolan of marrying again too soon after the suicide of his first wife, 'throwing himself on another woman's breast before the ashes were barely cold'. Nolan retaliated by painting caricatures of White in his pictures and by saying of him on television, 'I'm fit, heterosexual, I produce the goods and he couldn't.'

The minor prototype of the aged Hurtle Duffield, the lover and teacher of both White and Bacon, was dying as Hurtle did at the end of *The Vivisector*. Roy de Maistre had been the only man, other than John Rothenstein, who had been allowed to view and criticise Bacon's works in progress in his studio before his Tate exhibition. Hearing how ill his old tutor in life and art had come to be, Bacon offered with his habitual generosity to send him and his young companion to convalesce in a Mediterranean resort; but the declining artist had a stroke and never recovered from the ensuing coma. 'He was a master of lucid, expressive composition,' John Rothenstein wrote of his valued friend, 'but also of colour achieved through scientific knowledge as well as sensibility. The brilliant light of a summer afternoon and winter twilight revealed different but equally moving ranges of his colour harmonies.' As he was associated with no fashionable tendency and had no dealers, he was neglected by private and public collectors. His art was in the teaching of it to the young artist.

Perhaps no painter may ever wholly be described by any writer, even those of genius such as Joyce Cary and Patrick White. The word can never be what the picture is. In this surly and egocentric age of deconstruction, each viewer is king and queen and judge. The art critic is said to be abolished. Yet the biographer and the social historian are not. Their job is to explain the interaction between the individual and his times, and whether as an artist, he expressed what he intended to those times. Talking to Bacon's friend, David Sylvester, J. R. Ackerley demanded to know how Bacon actually painted. When he was told, he found it analogous to his own methods and feelings at work. 'I think writers (and it certainly applies to me) live often in a state of emotional overflow as they work, tears (perhaps maudlin), self-hugs of delight, grins of satisfied hatred: these pleasures are partly psychological, partly artistic – the extant phrase or word, the inalterably perfect passage – ' He might have been describing Bacon's pleasure when he achieved the inalterably perfect brush-stroke by chance and design.

The paintings of Bacon, however, could deeply offend those qualified critics of art, who also had a moral point of view as major novelists. Anita Brookner was one. Originally, she welcomed his exhibition at the Tate Gallery because it contained a human drama which involved the spectator as much as it did the artist. 'It is like the last communication of a man forgotten at the bottom of a light shaft, and slowly degenerating from fear, hunger, and inertia.' Whereas artists had painted flowers and landscapes, Bacon did something only possible after the first generation of Freudians – he painted traumas. 'His slimly, slithering, purblind images' had been linked with Hiroshima and Eichmann; but these were modish reasons for that despair. The impact of a Bacon portrait was to induce sheer panic as in anyone 'who has fled in terror from a sickroom or experienced the motionless turmoil of Sunday solitude. Such painful weaknesses, breeding greater disgust on each recollection, are here captured in visual rather than literary form. I do not think that this has been done before. On purely quantitative grounds, therefore, Francis Bacon is a unique artist.'

Brookner agreed that Bacon was untaught and uncorrupted by art school training. Yet she considered that, whether he liked it or not, he was the legatee of the nineteenth-century Expressionists – Van Gogh, Munch, Ensor, Soutine and Kokoschka – as well as of his obvious references to Velázquez and Rembrandt, Muybridge and Eisenstein. She ended by admitting against her better judgement:

> Of Bacon's importance there can surely be little doubt, although cautious voices have been heard to dismiss him as 'fashionable'. (He is fashionable only in the sense that in certain moods we shall find his pictures irrelevant and repulsive.) Here at last is a contemporary painter of true stature, whose endless communion with the realm beyond our understanding marks a definite breach in the polite tyranny of formal conventions. Bacon is committed to his nervous system just as Van Gogh was once committed to his desire to love all men. The emotional rage has shrunk: the relevance for the rest of us is the same. We are not called upon to admire or applaud these works, and we are certainly not meant to enjoy them. But if we can acknowledge the fact that painting can still be a mirror to certain states of being, we may find that the standards we apply to the greater part of contemporary art have undergone a radical shift.

Fellow artists were his chosen company rather than the writers who saw him through the lenses of the sentences they heaped upon him. He painted Lucian Freud many times, finding in him another free spirit, who owned nothing and lived anywhere. He was as tough as Bacon with a constitution of titanium that hardly showed in his slight body and pale features. He shared Bacon's hatred of the law and made his own rules each day, reacting to every circumstance as Bacon always did. With no code or clock, he lived by steel whim at any hour of the day and night, and rejoiced at meeting his friends.

Frank Auerbach was another painter of extraordinary talent and acute mind, who had been inspired by Bacon's example and technique, saying his best portraits seemed 'like risen spirits'. He had been born in Berlin in 1931, and sometimes spoke of his art as if he were Bacon himself, saying, 'The paint itself seems to breed images. I try to take the picture to the point where it seems to make itself.' He also said that great paintings were done 'by people who were prepared to take a risk – when they've got something that is almost a success, they are prepared to destroy it, or chuck it away for something grander'. But Bacon found that Auerbach always contradicted him and said what he called accident was not at all accidental. Anyway, Bacon painted him along with Lucian Freud in a double portrait in 1964, each artist sprawling on a red divan, wearing white singlets and nothing else, their calves and thighs pink and voluptuous, their quick intelligences contorting their faces into the mobile essence of being that Bacon sought to show in those he knew. He insisted that he did not wish to make freaks out of them, he would like them to look as attractive as they really were. He was describing their behaviour by the methods of his art. He could not do it in conversation.

As a painter, though, Bacon's style had nothing to do with his artist friends, particularly not with a third companion, Richard Hamilton, said to be the founder of Pop Art. While Freud built up his studies of the human body by meticulous detail and hair by exact hair, Bacon charged at his subject in a whirl of brushes. Auerbach also was far more deliberate, and if there were traces of Bacon to be discerned in his early works, they found less and less in common outside the pleasure of their mutual company and the testing of their differences at Wheeler's over the Chablis and the sole. Bacon even owned a painting by Auerbach at one time, but he gave it away to a friend 'who just got drunk on it and that was that.'

With Richard Hamilton, however, the contrasts were fundamental and marked the times. Pop Art became more fashionable in the 'sixties than even Bacon was, and they both used contemporary magazine pictures. But while Bacon looked to the newsreel image, history in the making as in the shot of the crowd running in panic through the square in St. Petersburg, Hamilton chose the advertising image, the commercial aspect of reality. While Bacon searched for the moment of crisis in human action, Hamilton caricatured the motive and the cash of human acquisition. In his notorious definition of Pop Art of 1957, Hamilton set down every single thing that Bacon avoided like the plague in his art:

> Popular (designed for a mass audience)
> Transient (short-term solution)
> Expendable (easily forgotten)
> Low cost
> Mass-produced
> Young (aimed at youth)
> Witty
> Sexy
> Gimmicky
> Glamorous
> Big business

While Bacon was looking for a visceral Truth Art, Hamilton was defining Pop Art in gross and commercial terms, as if the condition of the people could be defined less by their pain than by their greed. Human desire was translated by Bacon into sexual terms. His sofas and beds were the battlegrounds of his tortured lovers and friends, Lacey and Freud. They were not the derisive objects of man's cupidity and comfort, bought from a furniture store. Actually, Bacon did trawl the Tottenham Court Road above Soho and stare balefully at the settees and three-piece suites and lurid carpets in the shop windows. He had crafted better objects in his youth. And he liked seeing himself reflected in the plate glass of Heal's as his viewers were in the picture glass that covered his own paintings. But he never guyed the bad taste of his time as Hamilton did. He wanted its guts, pure and simple. He was a surgeon, not a sceptic. At a high level, he went for the offal, while Hamilton was cerebral. At a lower one, he had the vision of a butcher, when Hamilton considered the eye of the consumer. Their messages were markets and cash registers apart. For at the end, Hamilton used the images of mass appeal not only to mock them, but to say, 'Buy my pictures, too.' As Michael Wishart said to Bacon, 'Pop is to painting as chewing-gum is to gastronomy. I prefer nourishment.' Bacon liked that. If he did admire Hamilton's technique, he could not digest its content.

David Hockney was another young artist, who escaped the influence of Bacon to become as financially successful, but at the price of transmuting the images of consumerism to appeal to his audience. He even used a series of colour Polaroid shots to make an expensive collage of a sunny swimming-pool in California, which cocked a commercial snook at Bacon's use of photographs merely as scalpels to penetrate the byways of behaviour. Hockney was impressed when he saw the Bacon exhibition of 1960 at Marlborough Fine Art, particularly by the male nudes. 'One of the things I liked about them', he said, 'was that you could smell the balls'. He thought that Bacon had resuscitated the importance of the human figure in modern art, and he liked the rough canvas – he was then painting on hessian. He also appreciated Bacon's use of magazine illustrations as sources for his work, because of their flatness. Still confined by the drawing methods learned at art school, Hockney further admired Bacon's technique of painting without sketching. These images had 'a crudity and vigour which help the impact of the pictures'.

Hockney himself was to follow Bacon's pioneering depictions of homosexuality and came out in 1963 with a painting, *Two Men in a Shower*. In a subsequent series also featuring curtains, he used Muybridge explicitly in his painting of two naked women, entitled as the Victorian photograph was, 'Seated Woman Drinking Tea, Being Served by Standing Companion', although it also had undertones of lesbianism as had Courbet's 'Le Sommeil' – a picture that had always influenced Bacon when he was showing two men entwined on twisted bedclothes. Overt homosexual art was becoming acceptable in the period before the repeal of the laws against sexual intercourse between men. It was a banner, faintly waving, for the advance guard of the long gay crusade to come.

A particular catalyst of the male artistic scene was Alfred Hecht, the picture framer in the King's Road in Chelsea. He was used by Francis Bacon to frame all his paintings, and his shop, as John Rothenstein averred, had become 'a sort of club which had many influential "members" and where issues for the art world were discussed and even resolved'. Bacon insisted that Hecht set his paintings in heavy gold frames under thick glass. This was not only to protect them, but to set them apart from their environment, also to contrast the elegant gilt surround with the human rage and passion contained within the picture. An amateur of chance, Bacon also appreciated the play of light on the glass in the form of reflections. His paintings could include the viewer and the background, a total immersion. Of his dark blue series, Bacon said that he wanted the spectator to see himself in the glass and join in the proceedings.

Hecht moved in the grandest of circles, knowing members of the Royal Family, as well as in the artistic milieu that was his livelihood. In putting together artists with rich patrons, he excelled even Roy de Maistre and most gallery owners outside Marlborough Fine Art. He collected paintings himself and gave the most interesting dinner parties in all Chelsea, mixing actors and artists, aristocrats and politicians, particularly with his good friends Aneurin Bevan and his wife Jennie Lee, and Arnold Goodman, the lawyer who would become Chairman of the Arts Council. He had great charm and wit, but a streak of melancholy, often complaining about having to hide his past and his preferences in public, as popular prejudice and the law were what they were. 'How can I say I am a German-Jewish homosexual?' he would moan, only to hear the reply from friends such as the interior dectorator, Kenneth Partridge, 'As if everyone didn't know, dear.'

With his political connections, Hecht was enough of a crusader to start a homosexual film society, run from offices in Shaftesbury Avenue. He also campaigned for the repeal of the laws against homosexuality, cadging pictures from sympathetic artists which were sold at Sotheby's through the benevolence of its head, Peter Wilson. Bacon himself would never give any of his paintings to any cause, and certainly not to political reform. Yet he pressed his art on those he loved: they were, after all, often the subject of his pictures. 'He gave money', Partridge said, 'where he felt it was personally deserved'. And he contributed anonymously to the acquisition by the nation of the masters whom he admired. 'You'll never get any money out of homosexuals,' Hecht would complain to Jennie Lee, 'even though it's for their cause'.

Because of his sexual preferences Bacon had been obliged to

break the law for forty years since the 'twenties. Although he could not profess his inclinations in public any more than Hecht felt that he could, he was well-known for them and had declared his passions in his paintings. Speaking to the liberal Sunday newspaper, the *Observer*, shortly before his retrospective at the Tate, he did say that he found the world of criminals more interesting than the world of normal people. He did not say that he was drawn to consort with criminals because of his homosexuality. He was outside the law, as they were. He was merely not driven to militance or to public protest, as some of his persuasion were. It is easy to forget how threatened homosexuals felt at the time. 'Jews, Quakers, Jehovah's Witnesses, homosexuals, and many others went to Dachau and other camps, and there they died,' Douglas Plummer wrote in *Queer People* in 1963. 'There are no concentration camps in Britain, but there are jails for homosexuals.' Although Bacon never fell foul of the statute book and would have rather gone to gaol than pay blackmail, he did what he wanted and avoided the law.

The profile of Bacon in the *Observer* stressed that if he did not fit into ordinary society, he was by no means a rebel or an activist. 'On his best behaviour, he would give no hostess anxiety about his performance at her dinner table. His manner is unformidable, gentle and unaffected. He is a good talker, bubbling, funny, friendly, gesticulating elegantly with strong, plump forearms.' He was an articulate, sophisticated character, who did not think there was much point in talking about his work, on the principle enunciated by Pavlova that 'if I knew why I danced I wouldn't dance'. He did say, however, that his starting point was always his own nervous system: 'I always want to *record* a face or body, and I want to do it as near my own feelings as possible. It's the exact opposite of abstract painting.'

The recording of faces and bodies chiefly in the portraits of his friends would be Bacon's war of nerves on the 'sixties. He had given up painting the sensational and the shocking. 'When I was younger, I needed extreme subject matter,' he told John Russell. 'Now I don't.' He wanted to paint the behaviour of those he knew intimately. Yet it was a business at risk, in a way more of a hazard than gambling at roulette at Charlie Chester's casino. 'To be *and* not to be,' he declared the problem of the portrait painter; what to put in of the known *and* the unknown, in order to reinforce each other. The task was not made easier by portraiture having a bad name at that time: either the painter was thought to be too servile to the vanity of the sitter or too merciless, as when the portrait of Winston Churchill by Graham Sutherland was destroyed by his family rather than shown for the nation.

The moving picture as the still work of art, the *aperçu* of unguarded action, these were to be Bacon's contribution to the art of the portrait. The desperate and despairing look of the faces caught in flinching and avoiding some unseen blow were explained by Bacon as nothing to do with the human condition. It was a question of his quick method of brushing paint directly onto rough canvas. If his people looked as if they were in a dreadful fix, he said that it was because he could not get them out of the technical dilemma. 'As I see it, there's nothing, today, between a documentary painting and a very great work in which the documentary element is transcended.'

To him, the production of that very great work depended on the chance of the paint. He continued to destroy more than he kept. He took to smaller spaces for his heads and serial images, the two sides of a triptych looking in at the staring centrepiece. In the 'Three Studies for a Portrait of Henrietta Moraes' of 1963, the edge of the frame slices off the body as figures are cut by the edges of Japanese porcelain saucers or as dominant profiles are inset against a background in Flemish or Italian Renaissance small heads. Yet Bacon's subjects seem to writhe within the oils. The three mouths of the loose-lipped Moraes pout and sulk and stammer, while her sets of eyes wink and hold and glance. To look at the triptych from left to right is to watch mobile features making a comment that says in silence: 'See – I – Live.'

Although the faces in the portraits were inevitably contorted, they appeared as the blur of a movement, an action caught in a glimpse from the corner of the eye. He did put in ears and eyes on faces, but he liked to put them in as irrationally as possible. He always changed a resemblance. 'One thing I'd like to have', he once said, 'is an enormous room lined with distorting mirrors from floor to ceiling.' He had a cracked and webbed mirror covering his bedroom wall in Reece Mews, but it shivered the reflections of bodies into fragments rather than making them bulge. 'Every so often', he went on, 'there'd be a normal mirror inset among the distorting ones.' He had mixed mirror glass with opaque and clear glass in his oval table-tops of the 'thirties, the angled reflection with the obscure and the transparent. 'People would look so beautiful', he ended, 'when they passed in front of the normal mirror.' As Russell pointed out, in Bacon's portraits of the 'sixties the normal image was laid on top of the distorted one. They were both simultaneously present in an arrested motion, the superimposition and the dissolve of the cinema.

As he had once studied in Paris an illustrated text on diseases of the mouth, now Bacon was reading a book called *Positioning in Radiography*. He was fascinated not only by the X-ray photographs of the bones and sinews and nerves beneath the skin, but also by the angles used by the medical photographer to view the body to the best effect. The vivisector had to approach his victim from the right stance. He had to penetrate to the recesses of human behaviour, the very motives of the instinct for violence. As John Russell perceived as deeply as Bacon, the portraits of the period progressed:

> To the point, in fact, at which the face as we know it would disappear altogether in the jewelled slime of the paint, leaving behind it an eye-socket, or the deep cave of a nostril, or an irreducible patch of hair, as tokens that somewhere among the strong-willed chromatic smearing a named individual was commemorated. No question, here, of setting the scene: we are at a dentist's distance from eyes, nose, mouth and teeth, and the rest of the world is blocked out.

Bacon used to patronise a medical bookshop in Gower Street to pick up textbooks, such as *A Colour Atlas of Nursing Procedures in Accidents and Emergencies*. He was fascinated by the illustrations of syphilitic sores and other wounds and tumours, which he used in his paintings. He did not shudder at them, but thought himself fortunate. 'My God,' he would say, 'I'm lucky I don't have *that*.'

After meeting Bacon in the street in the summer of 1962 and hearing him say uncharacteristically that sometimes it was good to take a very long time over things, Stephen Spender visited the painter in Reece Mews and wrote down what he said about his art.

It should not be a record, but an exploration of reality which gave it a new twist. What he was thinking all the time was how in painting he could slightly complicate the game. 'I can do very little but I think when I am optimistic that I might still live to make the game a bit more complicated.'

By the new twist, Bacon meant some little thing, which gave the image added depth and poignancy. Spender said that with the whole weight of past painting behind him, even that little thing might be too much. Bacon considered that the current New York school was wrong, because it simply ignored the past. If painting was treated as though it had never happened before, the result would be mere decoration. 'Picasso, he thought, often went too far and simply produced decoration.'

So had the models and giants of his youth been overtaken by his solitary pursuit of his own genius. In a way, he personified the creed of the young artists of his time, who had rediscovered Nietzsche's philosophy and called it self-fulfilment. The artist was the expression of his own ego. His message was only himself. He was an outlaw, and society, if anything, owed him a living. The artist was, above all, self-declared. 'I am an artist because I *say* I am,' was the statement. There were two fundamental differences, however, between Bacon and the young painters of the 'sixties. Although self-taught, he had trained and worked at his trade with dedication for forty years, while they put protest above their short practice. And he had genius, while the less their talent, the louder they howled. In a decade when there were hundreds of thousands of young artists who achieved their position by stating they were what they said they were, there was only one Francis Bacon, unparalleled, unmatched and unrepentant.

His fame grew without his help. A modified version of his retrospective at the Tate Gallery, which included nearly half of his surviving pictures, travelled across Europe, to the Kunsthalle in Mannheim, to the Galleria Civica d'Arte Moderne in Turin, to the Kunsthaus in Zurich, and to the Stedelijk Museum in Amsterdam. In Switzerland, one of America's greater poets, John Ashbery, reviewed the show, acting as the art critic of the international edition of the *New York Herald Tribune*. Although he knew of Bacon's loathing of American abstract art, Ashbery thought that Bacon's statement on painting published in the catalogue was reminiscent of Jackson Pollock, De Kooning or Kline:

> Real painting is a mysterious and continuous struggle with chance – mysterious because the very substance of the paint, when used in this way, can make such a direct assault on the nervous system: continuous because the medium is so fluid and subtle that every change that is made loses what is already there in the hope of making a fresh gain. I think that painting today is pure intuition and luck and taking advantage of what happens when you splash the bits down.

Ashbery also saw in the Zurich Museum the large collection of Romantic and Gothic paintings by the Swiss-born Fuseli, the friend of Byron and Shelley. He commented that nothing made him uneasier than Fuseli's scenes from Shakespeare, unless it were Bacon's portraits of Van Gogh. 'The work of both painters suggests high-speed snapshots of a nightmare. Out of vague and terrifying spaces, figures suddenly congeal with the incontrovertible reality of characters in a dream.' The essential difference was the concentration of Bacon:

> His subject matter is still man in the horror of his isolation – naked and obscene on a studio couch, or grinning baboonlike from behind a desk. Yet, strangely enough, Bacon's work is neither horrible nor depressing. His tremendous gifts crowd out all feelings but admiration, and after the initial shock one begins to feel almost on friendly terms with the creatures in his zoo. It may be an ugly, obscene and terrifying world, but it is also a deeply human one.

The following year in the October of 1963, another retrospective of Bacon was mounted in the Guggenheim Museum designed by Frank Lloyd Wright in New York. Even the startling and gutting images of his aggressive century seemed as postage stamps or slogans of hate floating like graffiti within the curving spaces of that immense spiral of concrete. What were his howls and vacua and black cages to this luminous and grandiose conch-shell? For once, Bacon's art was overwhelmed by the architecture, which reduced its force. To view it was to spy on anguish through peepholes. And no silent scream from an imprisoned pope could release the painter's genius from this vast, bright snare.

It is hard to know whether a great painter reflects the image of his age or creates a recognisable one. Both are probably true, in a process of unconscious interaction. Yet by painting his personal obsessions, Bacon appeared to represent dominant visions of the 'sixties. 'Violence is the natural artistic language of the times,' Peter Brook declared '. . . it's our reality, there's no way round it.' He was currently directing in London a play of outrage, Peter Weiss's *The Persecution and Assassination of Marat as Performed by the Inmates of the Asylum of Charenton under the direction of the Marquis de Sade*. Asked to comment on Brook's assertion, David Hockney supposed that the theatre director was thinking of Francis Bacon when considering violence in art. 'But a painter using violence as an activity, as Bacon does, is rare.' The theatre dealt constantly with human activity, but the range was wider in painting. Although many religious pictures had violent themes – and the Crucifixion was an act of supreme violence – a successful painting of violence had to have human connotations.

> Violent action alone becomes *placid* in time. Destructive painters, creating pieces of plastic to be destroyed by acid, or sculpture which blows itself up, are not violent in the way that Bacon's screaming Pope is. A picture painted in a violent way, an action painting where the artist slashes away, throwing paint about, has nothing directly violent about it. It can never leave you with the taste of violence in your mouth as Bacon can, even if the guy killed himself painting it. It is merely decorative.

Hockney understood the violence within Bacon's paintings which was, perhaps, 'the natural artistic language of the times'. But he did not comprehend how Bacon used even the violence, which put Christ on the Cross, to examine human behaviour. To him, aggression was part of the truth of man: it could not be ignored. When speaking of his Munich 'Crucifixion' of 1965, Bacon said he knew religious people gave a different significance to the nailing of Jesus on the tree. 'But as a non-believer, it was just an act of man's behaviour, a way of behaviour to another.' All Bacon's paintings of violence had human connotations.

Other artists in their genre were to use the grammar of the mundane to create an atmosphere of tension and terror, as Bacon did more and more, even congealing his model to a lavatory bowl in one triptych of 1964 which was eventually bought by the French Government. Harold Pinter was such a one in *The Birthday Party* and *The Caretaker*; he heightened and deformed the clichés of speech and the banalities of home life into suggestions of the unspeakable. The ordinary in his words became the menace, the trivial was translated into the threat. As in Bacon's portraits, it was the perception of the horror of the hotel and the wash-basin, the razor and the safety-pin, the dumb-waiter and the newspaper, slowly torn into strips. 'Just as Bacon used the conventions of the room, the portrait, even of the Crucifixion, as the starting point for his repertoire of distortions', Bryan Appleyard once observed, 'so Pinter used the conventions of the language of a dramatic "reality" for his. In his work the shabby, gloomy, iconography of the nineteen-fifties takes on the status of a myth of futility and of alienation within the net of words.' In fact, Pinter and Bacon eventually encountered each other at a party. They got on and exchanged telephone numbers. But when Bacon rang the playwright, he was writing and would not take the call. There was a perfect pause which led to no further communication. In the future, Bacon denied that he had ever liked Pinter's work.

Within the whirl of paints, Bacon's descriptions of his private world were seen as an iconography of modern times, an all-out assault on most conventions. When Keith Vaughan saw John Osborne's play, *A Patriot for Me*, at the Royal Court Theatre, which had to become a club to bypass censorship by the Lord Chamberlain, he dismissed it for its 'polymorphous aggressiveness. He attacks law, society, Catholicism, homosexuality, people, his audience, anything – so long as he does not have to commit himself to taking sides. He is like Bacon as a painter.'

Vaughan's dislike of Bacon made him wrongly impute a similarity to Osborne. The hero of *A Patriot for Me* was a member of three despised groups in the last years of the Habsburg Empire. Redl was lower-class, a Jew and a homosexual. But it was his homosexuality which led to his treachery in Austria. In a climatic ball scene, the gays of Vienna dressed up as drag queens and mocked women and high society. The Baron, who was their host, declared, 'This is the celebration of the individual against the rest.' It was not. It had nothing to do with the liberation of the self from the closet. It recalled the ostentatious parades of transvestites which the young Bacon had seen in Berlin and Paris, and which the old Bacon avoided and never painted. His lunge at society was through its pain, not its ostentation. His images of homosexuality were those of potency and despair, not of weakness and betrayal. Osborne had openly attacked the dominance of homosexuals in all the fields of the theatre, while Bacon never protested except in paint. His art was his crusade, while Osborne's polemics often marred his plays.

Joe Orton in *Entertaining Mr Sloane* was quite another matter. Here was somebody who rejected the prevailing opinion of British society that homosexuality was a form of sickness or a clinical condition, something like kleptomania or alcoholism. The British Medical Association had diagnosed it as something of a malady in 1955. Outside a gay 'marriage' of long-standing and faithful partners, which might be acceptable in liberal circles, the practice of the love between men was a deviance. They were maladjusted. Above all, they should not flaunt it. 'The behaviour and appearance of homosexuals congregating blatantly in public houses, streets, and restaurants are an outrage to public decency. Effeminate men wearing make-up and using scent are objectionable to everyone.' This sexual disorder was somehow linked with social disorder, as it was in *A Patriot for Me*. It did no good that some of the traitors to their country of the 'fifties, particularly Burgess and Maclean, had been blatant homosexuals.

For Orton and for his hero Mr Sloane, sex was enjoyable. It was natural, whether with a man or with a woman. There was no crisis or problem about homosexual desire. Although he had a 'marriage' with Kenneth Halliwell, who was to become his murderer, Orton remained promiscuous, living in the enjoyment of the cottage or the public lavatory of the day. Cruising with anonymous men was sexual liberation to him. Above all, he was without guilt, as was Mr Sloane.

And that was the progression of Francis Bacon slowly throughout the 'sixties. He emerged from a catharsis of grief and even guilt about the death of Peter Lacey in Tangier into a certain relaxation in his casual relationships with other men, more and more acceptable in metropolitan society, which was soon to earn the name of 'permissive'. If homosexuality had been 'the love that dares not speak its name' to Lord Alfred Douglas and Oscar Wilde, in a London of increasing tolerance it was named openly, by Orton especially, after the paintings of Bacon had already done so.

The law had not changed yet. It followed the revolt of the blacks and the young and the minorities during the decade. Legislation follows opinion just as trade follows the flag. It was ironic that Bacon's pictures of personal protest seemed to have become the banners of the masses, rebelling against their universal maltreatment. Certainly, Bacon avoided this interpretation of his work. His features were never worn on T-shirts like those of Che Guevara. His revolt was as withdrawn and significant as that of his friend Giacometti; both of them were merely trying to alter the way the world saw the human form in its struggle to exist. Bacon would become even gloomier about his efforts than the pessimistic Giacometti. At one dinner arranged by their mutual drinking companion and model, Isabel Rawsthorne, in 1962, Bacon became progressively drunker and more rambling on the subject of death and accident and futility. When he asked what his guest thought, Giacometti said, 'Who knows?' It was too much for Bacon, who tipped up the side of the table until all the plates and glasses crashed onto the floor. Giacometti shouted with glee. Instant action had solved the meaning of existence.

More and more, Bacon clung to his friends. He was looking for another Lacey in his life, and he was to find him by the time Giacometti had his own retrospective at the Tate Gallery in London, three years after Bacon had. When riding around in a taxi with Bacon and his new love, Giacometti patted the regular boyfriend on the knee and said, 'When in London, I feel homosexual.' Bacon had such sympathy with Giacometti that he thought homosexuality might suit his friend well, but it had hardly made Bacon particularly happy. He once expressed his doubts enough to ask Giacometti, 'Do you think it's possible for a homosexual to be a great artist?' There was no answer given to that.

Bacon continued to paint portraits of his close circle. As Andrew Forge wrote, he was not looking behind the social mask, nor was he creating a caricature. His scandal was that he claimed to be reproducing a likeness, while affronting every taboo and convention of what a portrait really was. 'Sometimes his people seem to be all appearance, nothing else. Sometimes they seem to be made of nothing but their own expression: faces dominate heads, features dominate faces. Sometimes the features themselves seem to be nothing but shine, sheen, surface, there in a flickering instant, not to be grasped. Sometimes they are holes.'

To those critics like the late Peter Fuller, who took a moral stance on Bacon's work just as Anita Brookner had, Bacon did not idealise, but he denigrated in a universal way. 'It really does not matter whose likeness he exploits: their face will emerge as that of "a gross and cruel monster" – *and nothing else*. For Bacon, an individual's face is no more than an injured cypher for his own sense of the irredeemable baseness of man.' Robert Hughes, however, praised Bacon's feats of aesthetic self-removal, which enabled him to inspect the gums and saliva of a screaming mouth as Monet did a lilypad. 'This distancing has enabled Bacon to master his gruesome and convulsive subject-matter . . . the paint has a dreadful materiality, as though the grainy cellular structure of the pigment, swiped with a loaded brush across the canvas, were a smear of tissue.'

Yet the Holocaust, in Hughes's opinion, had made it impossible for painting to deal with modern horrors. Even De Kooning's 'Women' and Bacon's male nudes looked isolated in their time. 'After Auschwitz, Expressionist distortion of the human body in art seemed to many sensitive minds to have no future – in fact, to be little more than an impertinence or an intrusion, a gloss on what the Nazis had done, on a vast industrial scale, to real bodies. Reality had so far outstripped art that painting was speechless. What could rival the testimony of the photograph?'

Bacon transfigured the testimony of the photograph through his personal pain and sense of loss. He had a sensitive mind, and he knew that his paintings could never match the terminal degradations of the Holocaust; and so he usually stressed that they were his own obsessions, a diary of his life, although he had also declared in the 'fifties that he was trying to paint the history of the past thirty years. Yet his figures and portraits do appear to be those of people caught in a glimpse of agony, and as in pictures of the Crucifixion, they came to represent in the suffering of one creature the suffering of all creatures.

Bacon insisted that he was always interested in *behaviour*. That was why his portraits had their shine and dreadful materiality of paint and illusion of movement. They were the bare fact of flesh seen at a desperate moment. Bacon did not denigrate his subjects. He caught them off-guard, in shock, at risk. He did not think the human condition was irredeemably base, but that the individual was in danger at each second. He was the translator to his age of the revulsion from the Holocaust and the 'fear in a handful of dust' of the atom bomb, through the contorted features and tormented figures of his friends. He wrought more than he said. His portrayal of his sense of loss and hurt made millions of people see it as their own.

9
Freedom and Gaol Bait

> It cannot be denied but outward accidents conduce much to fortune: favour, opportunity, death of others, occasion fitting virtue. But chiefly the mould of a man's fortune is in his own hands . . . And that this should be, no doubt it is much in a man's self.
>
> 'Of Fortune'
> by Francis Bacon, Lord Verulam,
> Viscount St. Albans

Bacon once said that he only had two regrets in life – two more than Edith Piaf, who sang that she regretted nothing. He was sad about giving up a couple of places: Millais' old studio in Cromwell Place in Kensington and a renovated Georgian terrace house on the Thames River in Narrow Street, Limehouse. That was when I was his neighbour, for I had initiated the rebuilding of the six bombed and derelict houses on the waterfront, where the iron barges at their moorings bumped against the back doors at high tide and made the old brick walls tremble on their clay foundations. In wooden ships hardly larger than these lighters, Sir Walter Raleigh had sailed to found his lost colony at Roanoke in Virginia and to search for Eldorado in Guiana. There had been dockyards at Narrow Street since Tudor times, and the setting sun turned the river bend into the burning golden bow of William Blake, pulled towards the west between the cranes and warehouses of the imperial waterway.

Bacon found the light too bright for him to paint there, as he had also found at Monte Carlo and at Tangier. 'When the tide was in and the sun was out', he told David Sylvester, 'there was a continual glitter inside the place'. It was too difficult for him to work: he needed a flat light. He made of his studio in Limehouse 'an almost bare show-piece used only very occasionally for entertaining'. It was nearly as minimal as his first garage studio of the early 'thirties, but arranged with modern functional wooden furniture. The steel tubes of the Bauhaus designs of his youth, however, were now brushed rather than plated in chromium, and they served as the handrails on the staircases. Oblong mirrors, rather than oval ones, were attached to the pine or plaster walls. But there were no abstract or geonometric carpets to be seen, just the stripped boards, even in the bedroom. It was Bacon's return to a tidy and ascetic ambience, a place of pleasure, not of labour.

His Soho friend, Daniel Farson, had first begun the colonisation of Narrow Street from the West End of London in 1958. Trawling up and down the Thames to find a place of his own on the river among the docks, which were still working then, Farson discovered, as Raleigh had, that there was a large population of native East Enders already living there. Between 90 and 96 Narrow Street, the remarkable Mrs Dolly Fisher, who wore a monocle and dressed in men's suits and smoked cheroots, ran a repairing yard for her fleet of two-hundred barges, which still supplied the wharves of the inner city with goods taken from the merchant ships up-river at Tilbury and Gravesend. Coal was unloaded by old cranes at the dockside beyond The Bunch of Grapes, which was alleged to be the pub called The Six Jolly Fellowship Porters by Charles Dickens in his novel, *Our Mutual Friend*, and which was patronised by Rogue Riderhood when he was not patrolling the river banks for drowned corpses to plunder. A little further downstream was the entrance to the Regent's Canal Dock. At the height of the industrial revolution, it had connected by horse-drawn barge the factories built beside the interior waterways with the salt-caked smoke-stacks of the steamers, which carried British goods from the Thames across the English Channel to the seven seas.

Limehouse was still a community of dockers and street traders, immigrants and sailors. Its location, on a muddy bend of the eastern river within the metropolis, made it a special village in London with a fierce sense of continuity and family and local pride. The Jews had settled round Hessel Street in the next parish of Stepney and sold the best food in the neighbourhood. The Chinese, who had arrived in dockland after the Jews, had remained in Limehouse and had even inter-married with the daughters of the dockers. After generations of strife that verged on a racial war, the descendants of the Chinese were respected and ran the best of the local restaurants, the Old Friends and its allied eating-places.

What Limehouse had to endure was not so much from the settlers or the passing seamen, but from the neglect of the Government after the blitz had burned most of it during the Second World War. For a quarter of a century, no administration had addressed the problem of thousands of acres of bomb-sites and decaying small industries, because Limehouse was a safe Labour seat – even the Prime Minister Clement Attlee had represented it and there was no need to buy the vote. Some appalling concrete towers were built to accommodate the citizens in new vertical slums; but these had to be destroyed within thirty years because they were uninhabitable and dangerously flawed in their construction. Actually, the blitz had spared the walls of the few Georgian houses in Narrow Street, just as they had survived the Ratcliff blaze of 1794, the most widespread in dockland between the Great Fire of 1666 and the Nazi bombings of the early 'forties.

At a time when the dockers were being laid off and their frequent strikes were being broken by forced redundancies and the use of casual labour at other provincial ports, the men of Limehouse could only escape the dole by becoming street traders or fish porters up the Hill of Despair at Billingsgate, boxers or petty criminals. It was this economic situation which led to the rise of the Kray Brothers to the status of local heroes as well as the most notorious villains in the East End since Jack the Ripper and the opium barons of Thomas Burke's novel, *Limehouse Nights*. The way out of social security was to join the neighbourhood gangs, as it has always been in the deprived quarters of major cities. But for the young women of Limehouse, there was always work to be found in the shops or hairdressing salons, followed by marriage and bringing up children in a society that still put the matriarchal family on the level that the Italians did.

The culture of dockland was centred on flowers and birds and dogs and Victorian antiques. All traded illegally on Sunday, the day of rest elsewhere in the country: the flower-market on Columbia Street, with its boxes of potted petunias and marigolds auctioned off for a few shillings after comic chaffering; the spaniel puppies and budgies, goldfish and tortoises sold in Sclater Street by the Bethnal Green Road, where the strong men flogged sets of china – fallen off a truck on the way to Buckingham Palace, what else? – or aphrodisiacs like Spanish germanica to stop your woman leaving you because you didn't feel up to it; and the antique vendors, bartering from the backs of lorries or hand-carts in Bermondsey and Bethnal Green, with their mementoes of past voyages carved or embroidered by seamen and chaise-longues and settees and aspidistra-pots and hatstands – the souvenirs and remnants of Victorian respectability. The docks had once been the focus of empire, busy and rich. And in their going down, there was memory abiding. Some families of dockers looked up their pedigree in Somerset House and could trace it back to the ten generations that had worked on the waterside. And there was still a pride and circumstance in dressing-up for the big occasion, the rare show in declining times. This was usually after pay day on Friday and Saturday nights in the corner pubs, where the costumes and the hairstyles surpassed those in many a West End club or watering-hole.

There was also the attraction of the privacy of the area, an antagonism to the law that had lured Verlaine when he had fled to London with Rimbaud. They had found themselves least persecuted in Soho and the East End, where most forms of human behaviour were practised and tolerated. By their trade and lack of alternative choice at sea, sailors were used to homosexuality and to providing favours to gentlemen when they ran out of money on their shore leaves. Nobody talked to the police, because the lethal sin of the community was to nark or grass, to rat or tell tales. Even the Kray brothers never descended to homosexual blackmail, as Daniel Farson testified in his evocative but impersonal *Limehouse Days*, perhaps because one of the twins preferred boys, saying, 'Little angel faces, less evil-minded than girls.' The point was that no sexual inclination was taboo in Limehouse, unless the police got an ill wind of it; but the breeze rarely blew that way.

To his outpost in Limehouse, Farson invited his Soho friends, especially Francis Bacon and the fellow members of the Colony Room. I lived next door for a while, hiring another converted sail-making loft from Mrs Fisher while I was beginning to renovate the six bombed shells of houses towards The Bunch of Grapes. Eventually, my house was ready enough to enter and I became the resident of 88 Narrow Street. I could walk across two terraces facing the river and hop over a low wall to find myself outside the back of Farson's home. Alone and immersed in writing a bardic novel called *Gog*, I was invited by him to a party one night. When I arrived rather late, there were only men there, Farson and his Soho friends, a few East Enders and more sailors. Rather shy and heterosexual, I was embarrassed, but pleased to talk to Francis Bacon for the first time. I had previously lived in Soho Square and had often seen him in Wheeler's and the French Pub without daring to approach him. We talked a little of our mutual love of the Greek dramatists. On a second approach from another man, I ran away. It was not quite my scene.

A month later, there was more of a drama. Early in the morning, a banging at my terrace window woke me. A bleeding and naked sailor from the Regent's Canal Docks was demanding to get in. I opened the terrace door, patched up his cuts, gave him some old clothes and a little money, and sent him back to his ship through the Limehouse dark. I never said a word, but obviously there was some rough business down among the ships. A month later, I was woken by thumping and running on the higher terrace above my head. This time I did telephone the police, who rushed round immediately to catch some burglars already reported by Farson for breaking into his premises. The police surrounded the terrace from street and foreshore, believing that the thieves could not escape. Then they conferred with me. The noises off that I had heard were the boots of the coppers themselves. They had disturbed me. They had come to put the handcuffs on their own wrists.

Life at Narrow Street was never without the incident and accident and chance that Bacon loved. Daniel Farson solved his problems of theft by importing a minder recommended by the Krays to live in his attic with a ferocious Doberman. Such a remedy appeared to me to be worse than the malady. I went to the landlord of another local community pub, The Black Horse, and made it known that I would sign job references for any Limehouse criminal on his release from gaol on the condition and his oath that he would not steal from his honest job, whatever he stole elsewhere. I would also represent the neighbourhood to the local Council in its just demands for better schooling and lighting and pedestrian crossings, though not policing. In return, I expected total protection from burglary and arson for the six houses in Narrow Street, which were being occupied by me and my friends. We both kept our side of the bargain for a decade, until I left my home. There is a deal of honour among East Enders. Farson recalled that. Francis Bacon found it out, when he was talking to a young friend of Ronnie Kray's, who listed the charity and benevolence of his patron. In the end, Bacon could not bear the litany of praise, and exclaimed: '"Fair touches the heart!"'

'It does, doesn't it!' said the delighted wide-eyed boy. In fact, the actor Stanley Baker had already introduced Bacon to the Kray twins in Tangier, and Ronnie Kray and two of his henchmen visited Bacon one Sunday morning in his studio to deter him from suing a friend of theirs for paintings that had not been paid for. Bacon was persuaded.

The seductive privacy and lawlessness of Narrow Street could not survive its colonisation from the West End. Particularly, politics crossed crabwise from Westminster. David Owen bought his house next door to The Bunch of Grapes for three-thousand pounds, as a poor doctor from St. Thomas's Hospital. By the time he had become Foreign Secretary under the brief Callaghan Government, he had swallowed up the adjoining ground area for a price ten times more than he had paid for his original place, and he would pay a small fortune to Francis Bacon, who had become his improbable neighbour in the studio built above the derelict ruins of the old houses. Daniel Farson, who had brought Bacon there, had left by this time, as I had. We no longer found at Narrow Street the rough and isolated culture of the East End, but the beginning of a property explosion extending to the Isle of Dogs, which would destroy the area by valuing it beyond the means of the local people in the name of reviving its industry through newspaper presses and office blocks, relocated from Fleet Street and the City. It was another blitz by boom that gave good homes to few East Enders.

True to the culture of his place in London before he left for the countryside, Farson ran a singing pub on the Isle of Dogs, which he renamed The Waterman's Arms. He revived a version of the Music Hall there with occasional turns by George Melly and Annie Ross. Francis Bacon brought along his Tangier friend, William Burroughs, and the Beat English writer Alexander Trocchi. Many in film and show business came, Jacques Tati and Claudette Colbert, Groucho Marx and Trevor Howard, Lord Delfont and David Merrick, Tony Bennet and Shirley Bassey, Joan Littlewood and even Judy Garland and Clint Eastwood. In a way, Farson was like Owen, destroying the culture which he loved by introducing into it the glamour and power of other parts of other cities. Finally, The Waterman's Arms was killed by its own success. The more crowded it became, the more Farson lost the money, which ended in his opinion in the pockets of his employees and his associates. Running a profitable club or a pub in the East End needed the techniques of the Kray brothers, not of an excellent photographer and a good writer, whom even the acerbic Colin MacInnes recognised as 'realizing his own dream'.

As the last survivor of the authors and artists in Narrow Street, until the film director David Lean was to move to an old banana wharf further down the road, Bacon used his studio occasionally as a place to receive and entertain. In a hilarious story he used to tell to his friends such as John Richardson, he even claimed to have encountered the next love of his life there. He said that he was asleep and alone one night, when he woke to the noise of a burglar in his bedroom. He did not behave like the Edwardian lady in her mansion in the same situation, who announced, 'I am the only thing of value in this room, and I am removing it immediately' – which she did. Bacon's tactics were contrary. 'Take all your clothes off,' he said to the burglar, 'and get into bed with me. Then you can have *all* you want.'

That is how Francis Bacon used to tease George Dyer about their first encounter in 1964. The story may have been just a funny one;

but Dyer had served time for breaking and entering in Borstal and in Pentonville – a fact which emerged in court when Dyer committed the ultimate sin of his background and set up Bacon on drugs charges at the end of the decade. However they did meet in reality, the choice of Dyer as a habitual lover marked Bacon's descent from the older educated mentor to the younger rough trader. And at the end of his life, he was to repeat his choice of a young East Ender to see out his fortune and his days. No more the raffish genteel for Bacon, but the lawless prole. In a way, it was back to the grooms and the stable-lads of his adolescence and Oscar Wilde's downfall.

Yet there was to be a sea-change in the law and in the attitude to homosexuality during the 'sixties. With the Sexual Offences Act of 1967, homosexual acts between consenting adults ceased to be criminal. The Obscenity and Theatre Acts were reformed the following year, leaving the only weapon of attack against works of art or public performances, deemed by some to be offensive, to be private prosecutions for blasphemy or for procuring acts of gross indecency. Bacon's paintings of men coupling like dogs had never been prosecuted nor his Crucifixions of gruesome reptilian mangled shapes. But his private sexual life had made him vulnerable to a gaol sentence for the more than forty years of his adult life. It was almost perverse of him to be liberated from the threat of the law and enter of his own will into the daily menace of the criminal mind. Yet, forced to act as a potential outlaw for so long, he had come to find, as Oscar Wilde had, the company of wide boys and grafters more interesting than of social climbers and scholars. He could not kick the habit of his low life.

Even more, the personal was the practice of his painting. George Dyer became his chief model as well as bedfellow, and Bacon's representations of that man's lusty, fleshy, evasive nature would dominate his work, even after the final tragedy in their relationship. The 'Three Studies of George Dyer (on light ground)' of 1964 concentrated on the loose mouth and glancing look with his strong jaw and quiff of hair. Two years later, 'Portrait of George Dyer on a Bicycle' is almost joyous, the trick of motion taken from Duchamp and Balla seen in the series of bicycle wheels, so that Dyer seems to be riding a penticycle from a single fixed handbar, although his profile is contradicted by a full face and single eye staring backwards, and the force of his pedalling is shown in the voluptuous curve of calf and rump. But the despair of portions of the love affair are already evident in 'Portrait of George Dyer Staring at Blind Cord', of that same year. There Dyer's body congeals into his cross-legged thighs as he squats on a curving sofa looking both ways like Janus, and a tasselled cord hangs into the cage of isolation that surrounds him. A spurt of white paint that may be spent semen gushes from the buttocks of a shape kneeling in the worship of the flesh before him beside an empty folding chair with a red seat, and a lying dog is the voyeur, pointing his muzzle towards his master.

Two other portraits of 'George Dyer Crouching' and 'George Dyer Talking' of 1966 show the corporeal challenge of the man. In the first, the curving sofa has changed to a pool with a void as its water. Sitting on his heels at the end of a springboard, with a handkerchief knotted over his scalp, the naked Dyer waits to pounce with a peering elongated face and a glittering animal eye on some discarded underclothes on the sofa seat. His arched and parted thighs emphasise his carnality, while his hanging arms and hunched head are accentuated by the swipes of his lover's brush. He is 'Sweeney Among the Nightingales':

> Apeneck Sweeney spreads his knees
> Letting his arms hang down to laugh,
> The zebra stripes along his jaw
> Swelling to maculate giraffe . . .
>
> The silent vertebrate in brown
> Contracts and concentrates, withdrawn . . .

In the 'Portrait of George Dyer Talking', the naked lover is squirming in the pleasures of confession. The blind cord swings in double image above, while a naked light bulb hangs over his penitential stool of interrogation. Bacon liked to say that 'jealousy is the greatest aphrodisiac there is', and the loving strokes of paint that illustrate the body language of Dyer's embarrassment and equivocation are proof of his sexual power over his artist lover, while the pages of his transgression stream out of him over the carpet.

Bacon's other portraits of his close friends demonstrated his growing supremacy in that branch of his art. In particular, 'Portrait of Isabel Rawsthorne Standing in a Street in Soho' is a masterpiece. The road is a sandy arena with smeared touring cars and people, black windows and blue restaurant awnings beyond, contained within the metal poles that might construct a tent for a reception. A black dress hides a bulky and commanding figure, swirling forward, while the same jets of white paint blobbed onto her hip indicate her sexuality. The dark wipes of Prussian blue similar to the dress material seem to shadow and disfigure the proud and adventurous face, which is described around a mouth as wide as a gash that runs into the neck and a surprised glance from eyes with dead black pupils. White streaks on brow and nose and chin make the bone come through the skin so that the wild hair flying behind appears as a fright wig mounted on a skull. The whole figure is monumental and subversive, sensual and condemned by her context. It is as if Isabel Rawsthorne was incarnated by Bacon as the Lady Life-in-Death of Coleridge's poem of *The Ancient Mariner*.

Henrietta Moraes was also painted frequently at this time by Bacon from the nude photographs of her commissioned a decade previously from John Deakin. Her face is almost simian with sunken eye-sockets and jabbering mouth, while the pink flesh of breast and belly and buttock is given the full lush brush-stroke of a Rembrandt or the finer outline of Ingres. Black splodges at knee and top of thigh indicate flaw or maltreatment, while in the version taken from her photographs of the 'Study of Nude with Figure in a Mirror of 1969', she has drawn up her legs while lying on an oval glass table-top, her ape-like face oblivious to the man in a trilby hat staring at her as in one of the Soho peep-shows, where naked women pose behind one-way mirrors for voyeurs, at a pound a time. She also served as the model in a series of portrait heads of her painted at the same time with similar monkey-like surrounds of black hair and eyebrows and enclosing blinded sockets or closed lids and teeth chattering inside an orange or dark smear.

Lucian Freud was another favourite subject of Bacon in their mutual appreciation of each other's disparate art. In the first of two triptychs, Freud sprawls with one shoe pulled up, on a kitchen chair placed upon a crimson rostrum with an armchair back. The extreme mobility of his features in conversation and of his arms emphasising his points appear in the smudged outlines of skin and blurs of flesh and repetition of features that was becoming Bacon's signature. The second triptych of 1969 left Freud on a kitchen chair, but in front of the rails of a brass bedhead and confined within the framework of one of Bacon's sentry boxes. The nose was more prominent and bulging with flaring nostrils, the mouth was loosened from the cheeks and lost beneath the chin, the intimacy gone within the devices of distance. Yet two years before, in the 'Portrait of George Dyer and Lucian Freud', the lover is transfixed by the brilliant chat of the fellow artist, as they raise or draw up their feet under themselves on a purple banquette, and a cat on a dark-green square table watches with interest the two-faced Freud talking so animatedly that his face swerves to right and left simultaneously.

Although Bacon was accused of exploiting or denigrating his close friends in his portraits of them, John Russell believed that he turned them into heroes and heroines. In the ancient Greek stories of the Gods, so treasured by Bacon, the scoundrel and the hero were the same. The cunning tricks of Jove trying to bed Danäe in a shower of gold or of Ulysses trapping Cyclops to get his crew alive out of the giant's cave under the bellies of sheep – so often the themes of previous painters – were devices as wily and desperate as any con game perpetrated by a Soho survivor or an East End burglar. Bacon's portraits of Isabel Rawsthorne and Henrietta Moraes, of Lucian Freud and George Dyer, set them in the frame in the grand manner of Velázquez or David, even if their shapes were contorted to reveal an inner imbalance and knavery. Bacon metamorphosed his women into Furies or Amazons, his men into a Priapus and a Janus, arrogant and potent, devious and finally doomed. There was some myth in his intentions. Outside his studies of the Sphinx, he saw in those he loved a classical significance.

Although he now maintained that he had given up story-telling in his pictures along with horror and exaggeration, his Munich 'Crucifixion' of 1965 and a painting after Muybridge and studies for a series on bullfighting all showed that he had not wholly abandoned the drama of history in his art. In his previous Crucifixions, Bacon had not centralised the action, but in this case, the appalling butchery of a genetic experiment in the middle is watched by two grinning men in blue suits and floppy white straw hats on the right, while a naked girl on the left gives a cursory glance at the scene of massacre on the bed which she has just quit, and of mutilation in the middle. On the bed gibbers a slavering and spattered beast with abounding human arms crossed behind a Ku Klux Klan hood, perched above a face that is all blood and teeth and skull. In the centre, two trotters in splints run up to an eviscerated human belly, and from it, tripes and innards ascend to a vague carcass sitting on the red throne of power. Beyond the businessmen watching such a spectator sport on the night, a Nazi ghoul skips forward on green pin legs, his face a void of hurried blackness, his peaked cap in a shroud that leads to an armband of the swastika, which complements a curious rosette of a blue cross within white-and-red petals, also worn by the beast on the bed. When Bacon was accused of making historical points by inserting the Nazi armband, he would not answer any more than the jesting Pilate. He merely said, 'I wanted to put an armband to break the continuity of the arm and to add that particular red round the arm.'

Even though the figures on his triptychs were carefully arranged to indicate each other, Bacon insisted that they were locked in their own solitude. He hoped not to tell a narrative, but to portray a great number of figures without linking them. He admitted that the Nazi armband in the Munich 'Crucifixion' was taken from photographs of Hitler standing with his entourage, but he asserted that it was included 'as part of trying to make the figure work'. The problem was that if a story were being told between one figure and another, it would begin 'to cancel out the possibilities of what can be done with paint on its own'. The art of painting was in such a state in the present day that it was difficult enough to do one figure on its own. In his triptychs, the images played off one against the other without leaving their own space. He chose threes because the balance was better. Fours seemed too many and more was like Mickey Mouse: he might go on for ever.

Yet Bacon had added the symbolism of the swastika and of the red, white and blue rosettes to his Munich 'Crucifixion'. These were explicit statements about what he thought of Nazism and the patriotic fervour of waving the flag during the Second World War. He was telling a story and making a moral judgement. And in his 'After Muybridge – Woman Emptying Bowl of Water and Paralytic Child on All Fours' of the same year, he placed his contorted and crouched figures on the raised bar of a circus ring, set against lurid purple and orange and red panels, appearing to be the endless and futile human action of running like a trapped dog to move a turnspit and roast the meat on the fire. The throwing of the water by the woman in the picture was as useless as pouring a full glass over Etna.

The studies on bullfighting, however, were a major departure, which signalled Bacon's first attraction to the Spain of the mainland in 1969, where he saw the sport a little as Hemingway had done, 'like boxing, a marvellous aperitif to sex'. His two versions of 'Study for a Bullfight', the first of which used to hang in the Senior Common Room of the Royal College of Art, used his current iconography – the circular arena containing the rounded and lunging bull, spewing out the white spurts of its potency; the shadowy matador evading with face and cloak the onset; the crowd as voyeurs contained in one segment like a mirror of the orange billboards around; and a brown pool of disappointed lust trickling off the base of the canvas. And yet, as Bacon had really tried to abandon drama in his work, he felt the weights of history and association were too heavy for him to complete his proposed triptych on the bull ring, and he called the project off.

He was mainly engaged during 1965 on a proposed exhibition in Paris that excited him still more than his retrospective at the Tate. It was to be at the Galerie Maeght in the following year. To him it was the verdict on his career: he wanted acceptance or acclaim in the city where he had lingered and been excluded as a young man, but which he had always admired as the centre of art in all the world. As John Russell wrote after talking to him:

> Bacon still holds the view, now incomprehensible to most people under fifty, that if a work of art looks well in Paris, it has passed the supreme test. In believing this, he is concerned not so much with today's judgements as with the unsmiling tribunal of the past.

> Paris is the place where the great things were done – or, if not done, nurtured – over the last hundred-and-fifty years. Relations between the painter and society in Paris had been almost uniquely harmonious, in that to be a painter at all in Paris was to pursue a valued activity. Bacon has a small private treasury of French insights . . . and I suspect that he prefers good French conversation to almost any kind of formal entertainment. He loves the radical, unsparing character of French talk; and he loves the prodigality of imagination which has been shown by the best French painters, the vaulting ambition, the total seriousness, the readiness to dare anything, the instinctive knowledge of how to pace a career.

In Paris, Bacon was to meet an art critic, who was later to become a close friend, Michel Leiris. He was struck by a passage in a book, which Leiris had written, about Baudelaire and his concept of beauty. It was an idea that dated back to the Christian heresies and the concept that Lucifer or sin was a creative force, and that Saint Judas enabled the Crucifixion to happen by his betrayal of Christ. There could be no beauty without the wound or the ugliness. There could be no perfection without the spoiled work, the flaw in the mirror, the fly in amber. A work of art had to bear within itself 'the drop of poison, the rogue element of incoherence, the grain of sand that will foul up the entire system'.

That is what Leiris saw in Bacon's sinister paintings. These had a counter-purpose and contained an anti-image. Paradoxically, the more brutal and depraved they appeared to be, the more the painter was trying to rehabilitate the strange beauty of modern times. Bacon was vulnerable to that argument. He had never believed that he hurt his friends by their distortion in his portraits: he was trying to describe their true behaviour. He once asked David Sylvester to tell him 'who today has been able to record everything that comes across to us as a fact without causing deep injury to the image?' When the critic answered that Bacon might be expressing both love and hostility towards the sitter, he said that it reminded him of Oscar Wilde's remark: 'You kill the things you love.' It might be that. He did not know.

In refusing to admit that his triptychs told a story or that his portraits passed a message about the human condition, Bacon took more and more to maintaining that life for the artist had become a game. It was a version of Huizinga's masterpiece, *Homo Ludens*, in which man's capacity to play is the art of his life. 'The public now looks on painting as a means of distraction,' Bacon told the readers of the popular *Sun* newspaper, 'and therefore the artist must make it more and more distracting by painting life as he sees it in different facets. What makes it even more fascinating, and incidentally more difficult, for the artist is that if he is to stay a good artist, he must deepen the game, stay ahead of the field and find a variety of new ways in which to describe life and emotion round him.' But the game of painting was not cricket. There were no rules. 'You should steal from anybody and anything that will help you.'

The fact that Bacon often destroyed more paintings than he kept was the result of his persistent experiments and efforts. 'Like most artists, he frequently takes a picture too far and past the point of no return,' the *Sun* reported. 'Unlike most artists, he has the courage to destroy these. He says that this frequently happens to his best paintings, as they start with inspiration and then he takes them too far in his enthusiasm.' He even agreed with David Sylvester that if people from the Marlborough or his friends did not come to his studio and remove paintings he would go on working on them and mar their quality and destroy them all. If painting were a game, at the moment of his victory through chance and skill, the result had to be snatched away, because he would certainly lose the match in extra time. As he said in 1963, what he was always hoping to do was 'to permit the one picture which will annihilate all the other ones and concentrate everything into the painting'.

Marlborough Fine Art was more and more successful with the portraits which were being snatched from Bacon before their annihilation. In his exhibition during the summer of 1965, seven of the nine paintings on display were sold for about five-thousand pounds each along with other pictures from the gallery's storeroom. The total value of works sold during the exhibition was sixty-thousand pounds. But Bacon continued to show his generosity by donating his art to his friends. He even gave a portrait of Lucian Freud to Bernard Walsh, the proprietor of Wheeler's, in memory of hundreds of splendid lunches there, at which John Deakin and

Freud and he would deliver acid remarks about the distinguished members of the Thursday Club, coming down the narrow stairs from their lunch above – the Duke of Edinburgh and Peter Ustinov, Larry Adler and James Robertson Justice and the Court photographer Baron Nahum. 'You have to look at it three ways to see it's Lucian,' Walsh said of the portrait, 'but it is recognizable.' He did not hang it in his restaurant, however, where it might deter the clients from appreciating their sole *à la meunière*, but in his London home.

At the exhibition at the Galerie Maeght, Bacon did receive the recognition that he desired in Paris. 'If the French like my work,' he had said in a rare admission, 'then I shall feel that I have, to some extent, succeeded'. His reception was greater than his hope. He had painted sixteen portraits or studies expressly for the Paris show, and he had included his controversial triptych, 'Three Figures in a Room' of 1964, which depicted a man with meaty, concupiscent curves on his shoulder blades and buttocks astride a lavatory bowl, a sprawled male nude on a blue armchair, and a twisted one scratching his hair and perched on a bar stool, reminiscent of the later 'George Dyer Talking'. The general praise included one acute observation on Bacon; 'His work carries the mark of his life rather like a person whose flesh has retained the scars of an accident.' There was also a truth on his current influence. There was no country in the world where young artists were not imitating him. 'Francis Bacon is certainly the artist who has cast the strongest spell over a whole generation.'

After this seal of approval in France, Bacon began to win international prizes. He particularly appreciated the Rubens Prize in 1967, presented to him in June in the master's birthplace in Siegen in Germany, because the inspiration for his voluptuous flesh tones had come partly from that source, although more from Courbet. He donated the prize money to help the restoration of art works in Florence. He was also one of three British artists to win a prize at the Pittsburgh International Exhibition at the Carnegie Institute in that city in the same year, and he then exhibited another twenty works at Marlborough Fine Art in London. There he received the kind of criticism of his pictures that he deserved, but did not accept.

'Paint is handled, sometimes slashed, with a kind of sophisticated fury. Yet there is no reassuring sophistication about the overall effect of these latest works of Bacon. Nor is there about the napalm bomb, a massacre in the Congo, or the empty heart of the tortured city dweller. This is the art of a moment in history when many have lost their bearings. It is not pleasant, but it will live for it says much about the human dilemma.' Another critic, Nigel Gosling, thought that the input of his painting was like being hit in the crotch, but found the painter personally generous, charming, fanatically sincere and incorruptible by any temptation yet invented.

> He will go on and on compulsively probing an image, like a child exploring the site of an extracted tooth . . .
>
> He explains that he is 'trying to create formal traps which will close suddenly at the right moment, recording this fact of a man as accurately as I can'. The right moment chosen by this psychological impressionist is the one which reveals 'this fact of a man' exposed to these two forces.
>
> The sense of duality and tension between contradictory forces is always strong . . . His own work is always rich in opposing associations. His macabre, grotesque imagination is Gothic but expressed in full, rhythmic Renaissance forms. A dog slipping across the corner of the retina is pinned down into permanence. A figure turning as it crosses the room is transformed, like Lot's wife, into a pillar of paint. The random flailing of copulation is composed into a single complex . . .
>
> Tension breeds violence, and violence is everywhere in Bacon's work. You feel the presence of a sensibility so delicate that the gentlest stimulus is an assault. 'I believe that anything that exists is a violent thing. The existence of a rose is a violence' . . .
>
> As usual the big unclothed figures dominate the show. In spite of their careful, balanced placing – sometims inside a kind of containing frame – Bacon's subjects always retain a voyeurist element. They are not nude but naked, caught in a moment of unaware privacy like some secret snapshot taken for evidence at the final judgement.
>
> They are deeply sensual. Their curves swell passionately or split under the attack of devouring intimacy. The cell, the grass, the carpet become an arena for a combat stained with homosexual eroticism. The figure which sprawls on its back, one leg up, on the

> ugly modern couch seems to be waiting with an abandon which has nothing admirable or enviable about it for another helping of what has already flattened it – pleasure or pain, vision or debasement. It all seems one . . .
>
> Bacon has dredged deeply and agonizingly into the spring of existence. What he brings up is murky, rich, even rank, but it is certainly one aspect of truth. I believe that future generations will continue to be moved by it, and even, which might alarm Bacon, find it totally beautiful.

The Tate Gallery held, also, in 1967, a retrospective of one of the painters most admired by Bacon – Marcel Duchamp. As Russell said of him, Bacon might not be displeased if he ended as the last man in the world playing the last hand that would put the other players out of the game for ever. Duchamp had already cleared the table by his rigorous attitude of mind, by his logic and his historic sense, his decisiveness and his disdain for self-promotion and making a career. Bacon thought that Duchamp had successfully changed the technique of art by *not* being avant-garde and trying to create a new art. He made symbols of the figurative, 'a sort of myth of the twentieth century'. Although Bacon preferred Duchamp's philosophy to his individual works, I saw him at that retrospective exhibition studying each picture with the intensity of a kestrel hovering over a field mouse. He had always had the power of ruthless and selective choice, discarding the whole of Matisse, for instance, except for 'Bathers by a River', painted during the First World War. He swooped on what he could use, concentrating on this or that, excluding the whole show. In this case, he moved about with his spring-heeled, cocky walking in pursuit of Duchamp in general rather than in particular. When it was pointed out to him that strange affinities appeared in his work with painters he was known to dislike, he would snap back in defence of his magpie instinct of stealing the best and the brightest from all the other artists' nests, 'Remember that I go to see *everything*.'

One old literary theme that had long haunted him made him place his lover George Dyer in a special painting in 1967, 'Triptych Inspired by T. S. Eliot's poem "Sweeney Agonistes"'. The Sweeney poems had always been favoured by Bacon, and his relationship with

Dyer had increased his involvement with him in that world of drifting and drinking, casual acquaintances that might lead to crime, bought sexual favours and incursions from the night. The central panel bears witness to a murder and robbery in a Pullman sleeping-car on a train; a tangle of bloodstained clothes suggest unspeakable violence and Sweeney's line, 'I knew a man once did a girl in.' To the left, two human shapes lie back in exhausted billows on a rostrum within a circular cage, while the head and shoulders of a third watcher or sexual participant is sketched below an open gas cooker and beside a pack of cigarettes. On the right, a detective on a telephone reports on a howling humping of male bodies in their rutting. This was the year when sexual intercourse between consenting adults became legal in Britain. It was a last outcry against the blackmailer and the informer.

Bacon went on painting his lover obsessively. Three pictures of him in 1968 were variously called 'Two Studies of George Dyer with Dog', 'Portrait of George Dyer in a Mirror', and 'Two Studies for a Portrait of George Dyer'. In the first, the naked man slouches, leg on thigh, on a kitchen chair within Bacon's usual circular arena and cube of cage, but his other face, the right cheek and frontal lobe eaten away, stares at us as if a formal bust on a mount at the front, while a dog flops in a doormat at his feet. Later Bacon said he liked the dog best in the painting. It looked as though it had had a really good run. It was exhausted with its tongue out, just lying there. The second study sets all on a circular purplish carpet and splits Dyer twice in two; his real body, turning on a chair towards a mirror, squelches halfway into a mess of warped movement, while the mirror image of sky blue divorces his profile in an azure tear, neck and ear separate from eye and mouth and thrusting neck and nose. The third shows a bored Dyer looking away on his chair from an ashtray and oblong carpet scattered with cigarette stubs, while a portrait of him as a carnivorous ape-like Sweeney devours a bloody morsel, asquat and betailed and nailed five times to the canvas within a canvas to point his bestial behaviour and condition.

Yet perhaps Bacon's most penetrating description of his personal feelings for Dyer was contained within another triptych, 'Two Figures Lying on a Bed with Attendants'. The nude male figure moves behind the back of another hunched on a bed under a slatted Venetian blind and dangling knob. Both raise their arms to strike or plead. On the left, Dyer of the rounded hips and shoulder-blades sits on his kitchen chair, watching his sexual action with a web-footed wading bird breaking from its glass case to plunge its beak in. On the right, a distorted face leers from crumpled clothing on a transparent table, while a dark-suited man with a watch peers and gibbers at the central event. Above him, a painting on a canvas of a man lurching forward into his own shadow, counterpointed on the left by a second canvas of another shadow striding upright, casting only a small dark semblance on the ground.

Bacon was now painting his personal life. He stressed that fact on every occasion. He claimed his triptychs told no story, and that the three panels were unrelated, and that each figure was intended to be solitary – yet these examiners of the sad, fierce coupling on the bed, this scrutiny from the edges did speak of Bacon's nervous state of mind. He feared Dyer's detachment from their love-making, his performance without involvement. He was also frightened of the intrusion of his intelligent and artistic friends such as Lucian Freud on the intensity of his private life. Dyer had a rough charm and an easy social manner; but he was no intellectual and subject to mockery, even by Bacon. The strains in this affair of four years began to show in New York City, where both the men went in the November of 1968 for an exhibition of twenty of Bacon's works including two triptychs, one of which was 'Two Figures Lying on a Bed with Attendants', at the Marlborough-Gerson Gallery. They were to stay for ten days at the Algonquin Hotel of literary fame. They had recently been separated for several weeks, because Bacon had just returned from visiting his remarried mother and ill sister Ianthe in South Africa.

Bryan Robertson had made the selection of Bacon's painting for the show, and other friends were in New York, particularly Rodrigo Moynihan and his wife, and John Richardson. The gala opening was even attended by Princess Margaret and Lord Snowdon, who had photographed Bacon. He was becoming an unwilling darling of society; but he could bite back. In one hilarious story told by George Melly, Bacon accepted against his instinct an invitation to a lunch given for him by a woman of power and influence. He was carefully placed next to a beautiful, but inarticulate young man. Told that this American Adonis was the nephew of Jackson Pollock, he fixed him with his green and lizard gaze, and said: 'So you're the old lacemaker's *niece*, are you?'

Like Muriel Belcher, Bacon used to refer to younger men as 'she' in his waspish moods. His deteriorating relationship with Dyer reached a climax at a club restaurant called Charade where they were dining with Richardson and the Moynihans. Dyer tried to buy the drinks with the few dollars Bacon had given him. 'Don't listen to *her*,' Bacon said. 'Not a penny in her pocket. *She* can't buy a drink for us.' Dyer had suffered enough from being baited by his lover in front of his smart friends. He felt ill at ease off his own territory. So he stormed back to the Algonquin Hotel and found the bottle of strong sleeping-pills which Bacon always used. Dyer removed from his lover's suit the roll of dollar bills provided by the owners of Marlborough Fine Art for the painter's American expenses – ten-thousand dollars in all – pocketed the money, found a bottle of scotch, drank it to swill down the barbiturates and left for the Charade. He was making the plea for love and help that adolescents make when they attempt suicide, wanting in reality to be rescued. Dyer only reached the door of the hotel room before collapsing across the threshold. Bacon found him two hours later. He was unconscious, but still breathing. So Bacon telephoned the Moynihans and Richardson, hiding his horror under his levity. 'Guess what?' he said. 'She's committed Susancide.'

What was to be done was more the question. Scandal had to be avoided. Dyer recovered enough to make his way to the window of the hotel and threaten to jump out. Bacon told him to do so, adding with some exaggeration: 'It's the twenty-fifth storey so you won't feel a thing.' Dyer backed into the bedroom and was taken off by limousine to the airport, where the owners of the Marlborough had bought air-tickets in a section of the First Class to transport their prize artist and his wayward friend home.

The quarrels and the reconciliations of the lovers continued. Some friends of Bacon like Daniel Farson found Dyer a charming and hopeless man with impeccable manners, far more of the gentleman than the minor villain. But most of them put him down and tried to exclude him, jealous of their own relationship with an artist, now receiving the wealth and recognition that he had long deserved. A clique of close friends surrounded him at the Colony Room, almost throttling him with their concern and wounding the intruder Dyer with their barbed conversation. The Cockney playwright Frank Norman even tried to write on Bacon's Soho life at the time, but all he could record on bits of lavatory paper were epigrams from the master, saying that he had never had any love in his life and wanted none. 'All I do is cast my rod into the sewers of despair and see what I come up with this time.'

To distance himself from Dyer, Bacon bought his lover a cottage in Kent, but Dyer could not live there without him and sold the place at a profit. He became more and more disorientated. One morning Farson was woken at his house in Devon by Dyer and a party of friends who had driven down all night from a Soho club called the Apollo. Farson thought that Dyer usually looked half-asleep, but now he excelled himself, stumbling out of the car and blinking with surprise at the empty sands below. 'I thought', he said, 'we were going to Brighton'.

The worsening situation led to the denunciation and first arrest of Bacon in his studio. On 2 September 1970, the police took him to Chelsea Police Station and charged him with possessing cannabis. Released on bail the next day, his trial took place at the beginning of June the following year. Detectives with sniffer dogs had investigated the artist's place at Reece Mews after receiving information from George Dyer. The report of the evidence at the trial read:

> At Inner London Session yesterday, Francis Bacon, 61, of Reece Mews, Chelsea, whose works hang in the Tate Gallery and throughout the world, was found not guilty on two charges of possessing cannabis.
>
> The jury heard that the police found a 12-inch pipe stem among underclothing in a chest of drawers.
>
> And in the studio under a pile of clothes, a police dog, 'Colonel', sniffed out 2.1 grammes of cannabis wrapped in silver paper in the bottom of a paintbox.
>
> The police tip-off had come from Mr George Dyer, who had

been employed by Bacon as a model and general handyman for eight years.

Miss Ann Curnow, prosecuting, said police led by Woman Det. Sgt. Carol Bristow raided Bacon's studio at 8.25 a.m.

Sgt. Bristow said that Bacon answered the door and when shown a search warrant, said: 'May I ring Lord Goodman?'

Miss Curnow asked: 'Who is he?'

Sgt. Bristow: 'I understand he is a solicitor.'

She continued that when shown the pipe stem Bacon said: 'Look, I have various people here and it must belong to them. It must have been here for years. It is not mine. What is it used for?'

When the cannabis was found in his studio, Bacon said: 'I do not smoke cannabis. I do not smoke at all. I am an asthmatic . . .'

Bacon in evidence, said he did not smoke because of his asthmatic condition. In 1956 in Tangier he made two attempts to smoke cannabis but suffered from violent asthmatic attacks and had never smoked it since.

He added: 'I would not allow people to smoke it in my premises if I knew what they were smoking, with the law as it stands.'

Writers, artists, students and people of the art world were frequent callers at his studio.

He said he had employed Dyer for eight years. Dyer, ill through alcoholism, often made allegations against him when drunk. Dyer had told him he had been to Borstal and jail.

Twice Dyer had attempted suicide.

Bacon continued: 'When he is drunk he feels I don't pay him enough. Sometimes he has broken down my front door and broken into my flat.

'I pay him a regular wage but that doesn't suffice because of his drinking and he comes and asks for more. Sometimes I give him some, sometimes I don't.'

On Aug. 27 last he declined to give Dyer any more money and he learned later that he had gone to the police.

Bacon said the pipe stem belonged to a man who had visited his flat five years ago and was now living abroad. He found the stem on the floor after the visit and put it away and forgot all about it.

He said he had no idea where the cannabis in his studio had come from.

Bacon had pleaded not guilty of unlawfully possessing 2.1 grammes of cannabis resin on Sept. 2 last; and having unlawful possession of an unknown quantity of the drug on or before that date.

> After his discharge Bacon said: 'I bear no animosity towards Mr Dyer.
>
> 'He is a very sick man. I still employ him and I have kept contact with him while he was in hospital.
>
> 'I shall continue to employ him. Naturally I am relieved this whole business has cleared my name. It has been a great strain.'

Even after the denunciation and the trial, Bacon had gone on paying and loving the importunate Dyer. Their relationship appeared to be bound to end in tragedy, as had the one between Joe Orton and Kenneth Halliwell, which had many of the same characteristics. Halliwell had tried to commit suicide five years before he murdered Orton in 1967: their relationship together had lasted for fifteen years. Halliwell used anti-depressants such as Valium and barbiturates, which he mixed together in a large jar. As Orton's fame and earnings grew through *Loot* and his other plays, Halliwell felt snubbed by his lover's new friends from the theatre and the social world, and he would rage against the way they made him feel inferior. Pathetic attempts to put his collages on display ended in the cellar of an antique dealer at the wrong end of the King's Road, with two of the pieces withdrawn for fear of prosecution and described by Joe Orton as 'a nude Venus and a picture called "Cosy Couples" – several sections of young men cut from physical culture magazines juxtaposed with large flowers and distant views of horses'. Halliwell was jealous and possessive and wanted to play the housewife in a permanent relationship, while Orton was promiscuous and sociable and seductive, content to cruise and guiltless over any casual pick-up – as was shown by his holiday in Tangier of that very lethal year in the apartment where Tennessee Williams wrote *Suddenly Last Summer*. Bacon had enjoyed the same delights with Peter Lacey there, the easy venal Arab boys and the conversations with the European queens in the cafés: but Bacon had come back to London battered and bruised by his lover, who had died alone in Tangier, where Halliwell had become violently angry and had attacked Orton for the first time, hitting him about the head. Finally that hot and oppressive summer of Orton's success and Halliwell's despair at his own failure, he exploded at his lover picking at his sulking with comments such as, 'You're getting to be a fucking Mater Doloroso, aren't you?'

It had been too much to bear. Their bed-sitting room might have been modelled on a Bacon painting or an early studio of his. Austere and arid and comfortless, it had Venetian blinds and an electric heater and a scrubbed linoleum floor, while the walls were covered with huge collages of Renaissance and Egyptian art and Greek and Roman gods and headlines from the gutter press – the *mélange* of reproductions of masterpieces and myths and clippings that inspired Bacon. And the final frenzy of hammer blows to Orton's head had flung spots of gore all over the artwork and had converted his skull to shattered brain and meat, while his killer's nude body, drugged to death with Nembutals, was lying bald and blood-spattered on the linoleum.

As their love became self-destructive, Bacon continued to paint Dyer: a head dark and shadowed under nose and chin peering at Isabel Rawsthorne, also doomed by black outlining and a spot beneath her jawbone. 'Three Studies of the Male Back' of 1970 showed the strong curves of Dyer's torso and upper arms turned away from the artist; twice to shave his own cream-flecked face seen in a bathroom mirror while he considers or sharpens the razor; once to read the newspaper, his naked shape central and dominant and indifferent, as a black shadow seems to run down the single support of the swivel chair into a pool of black matter. But the last 'Study of George Dyer', painted before Bacon's mammoth retrospective of one hundred-and-eight works including eleven large triptychs that opened at the Grand Palais in the October of 1972, was another examination of indifference and of sex divorced from feeling. A large foot treads down the discarded pages of a newspaper with headlines of gibberish – the capital letters of non-communication. Dyer's sitting body is thicker now, like an ageing middleweight boxer, and his lip flaps loosely beyond his nose in complaint. But in a mirror, a calf and thigh can be seen, echoing Michelangelo's Adam on the roof of the Sistine Chapel in Rome.

Before leaving for the Paris exhibition with Dyer and John Deakin and Muriel Belcher of the Colony Room, Bacon confirmed to the art critic Richard Cork that he was picturing his personal experience and intended to paint an autobiography. He had been offered a great deal of money to write one, but he had refused. 'What's the point, unless you are Proust?' He hoped to crystallise time through his series in the way that Proust did with his novels: he did not say that he had already done so with his portraits of the 'sixties, particularly those about his relationship with Dyer. This intended autobiography would probably absorb his energy until his death. Although grateful, in the mornings, to wake up at all and find himself still alive, 'even when one is in a strong sun, casting a black shadow, death is always with you'.

Cork was aware of the physical passion behind Bacon's words and gestures, the arms shooting out to stretch up and clutch the meaning of what he was trying to say, the fists clenching when he declared that he wanted 'to paint a nose with all the violence of a real nose' and to 'make things as *raw* as possible'. He disclaimed the anger in his work and stated that, while he did not consciously look for violence, he had less veils than most people to screen him from life, so that every time he entered a butcher's shop, he was 'made aware of the violence which custom protects us from'. There was great beauty in the colour of meat to a painter, and the large stores such as Harrod's were great halls of death with all the meat and fish and birds lying dead there.

Interestingly, as Bacon usually discounted all but the most discerning critics close to the aims of his work, he confessed to reading the reviews of his past shows at the Marlborough and realising that nearly all of them were bad. It did not concern him; he knew he was outside the mainstream of modern art. What did concern him were current influences and trends, particularly among the avant-garde:

> Young artists today think that choosing a new medium is the answer, but it usually turns out to be a *substitute* for creation rather than the thing itself. Everyone wants something new, including me, but of course it won't be new unless you have the compost of the past as well. The past nourishes you, and denying that source of nourishment is like cutting off one arm to make the other better. I've never felt the need to reject the past. I feel I relate to tradition very strongly.
>
> But I won't ever know whether I'm really any good because it

> takes such a long time for things to fall into place. And there's no point in worrying about what you feel you *ought* to be doing in terms of the historical evolution of art, either. You can only do what your impulses demand, and that doesn't mean I see myself as the last of a line. The possibilities of oil painting are only just beginning to be exploited: the potential is enormous.

Dyer's death on a lavatory bowl in Paris, with blood pouring from his nose and mouth, was to cheat Bacon of his triumph there. He committed suicide at the third attempt in the posture of the man in 'Three Figures in a Room' of 1964, painted by the artist shortly after the beginning of their long affair. Denham Fouts, once loved by Michael Wishart, had died from an overdose of drugs also on a lavatory in Rome; as Wishart told me, taking drugs is constipating and overloads the heart. When he had tried to turn Bacon on to the psychedelic drug LSD, Bacon would not take it, agreeing that he 'did not want to break the cellophane between oneself and insanity'. Yet Dyer had now broken the cellophane between himself and mortality.

The self-destruction of Denham Fouts had once almost killed the emotions in his adorer, Peter Watson, one of the first patrons of Bacon as a young artist. Now Bacon was stricken too. He had not heard this last scream for assistance, he had not seen this act of defiance against him on the eve of his elegant opening in Paris, the first British painter in history to be so honoured in France. Apocryphally, he was said to have heard the news on the ceremonial steps of the Grand Palais, where he showed no emotion. Actually, he heard of the suicide when he returned to the hotel in the evening where the *concierge* said to him, 'I have something terrible to tell you, your friend's committed suicide.' '*Eh bien*,' Bacon said, 'where is he?' '*Eh bien*,' the *concierge* said, 'he's in the mortuary now.' He had taken an overdose of sleeping-pills, vomited in the basin and died on the lavatory seat. That night, Bacon screamed at La Coupole, where David Hockney told him how sorry he was about Dyer's sudden end. 'He took out a large handkerchief and let out a big scream. He said all he could do was laugh or cry.'

Kierkegaard stated that suicide was an act of courage and of affirmation. Certainly, Dyer's act was a rebuttal of Bacon's own intense fear of death. And in striking out against his lover's glory and his increasing indifference and a personal sense of inferiority, George Dyer, like Kenneth Halliwell, did kill the thing he loved. Although Bacon lived on for twenty years, the wound from this self-murder never healed. It bled inside him; it could not be staunched. If he did not admit to guilt, he did to fate and the Furies. 'Fact is a ghost,' he used to say, and he would always be haunted by this deed of love gone awry.

A poem had been written the previous year by Lawrence Raab, inspired by one of Bacon's paintings and called 'Figure with Hypodermic Syringe'. It showed how the artist's private grief and particular world cried out to much of the world.

The man at the door has something to sell.
The prowling cars have someone to find.
Room's closing in, nothing left to take.
It's all the same, go in, go out, get on.

– I had a friend once but he died.

After a while even bleeding
begins to soften and goes away.
The man at the door is promising nothing.
I only sell the stuff; you take it from there.

– I had a woman once but she left.

The face on the wall is no face at all.
Any moment the real thing may arrive.
We do what we can with what we have at hand.
Who can say where it all begins.

– If I wasn't here I'd be somewhere else.

The window goes in, the window goes out.
The striped cloth creeps across the bed.
Cracks open in the wall. Needle's
in the arm, knocking's on the door.

– If only the hurt would keep the pain away.

10

Fact Leaves its Ghost

> Fact leaves its ghost.
>
> A frequent remark of Francis Bacon, the painter

Bacon told David Sylvester that he had a very unfortunate life, because all the people he had been really fond of had died. He did not stop thinking about them. Time did not heal. 'But you concentrate on something which was an obsession, and what you would have put into your obsession with the physical act you put into your work. Because one of the terrible things about so-called love, certainly for the artist, I think, is the destruction.'

After the international success of his exhibition at the Grand Palais – the magazine *Connaissance des Arts* published the results of a European poll which placed Bacon at the head of the ten 'most important living artists' – Bacon returned to London and tried to exorcise Dyer's ghost in the fact of his work, to bypass his obsession in the physical act in paint. His first picture was a triptych called 'In Memory of George Dyer'. It was a return to the past, the colours more subdued, the composition less startling. 'It would seem that under the tempestuous and agonizing pressure of his memories', wrote one of his leading critics, Lorenza Trucchi, 'Bacon sought to set down some of the more oppressive images, so that while in the two side panels – one with a figure crouched in an acrobatic pose, and the other with the image of Dyer reflected mirror-fashion, like on a playing-card – the style is still concise. In the central panel it is decidedly realistic and detailed, adding up to a sort of poignant inventory of "things": the stairs with the threadbare runner and shiny handrail, the light bulb, the bell, and the newspaper on the floor – almost a grasping at "things" in order to prolong in more concrete terms a memory still painfully alive, an anguish still rooted in flesh and blood.' In this physical need to call back the dead, Bacon appeared to record his own arm behind the figure of Dyer, repeating the familiar gesture of putting the key in the latch and opening the door of the house together. 'This is one of the most moving details in all of Bacon's work' – perhaps his only howl from the heart. When Bacon was asked whether he derived the turning of the key in the front door from Picasso's Dinard bathing figures opening their beach-huts, he said it was more the influence of T. S. Eliot in *The Waste Land*, 'I have heard the key turn in the door once and turn once only.'

Another painting dedicated to Dyer, 'Portrait of a Man Walking Down Steps', showed the buried lover coming downstairs at Reece Mews like an undulant feline, holding onto an edge of the black square rail beyond. It is a cold and black and formal farewell. Death has separated the lovers. Bacon recognises the fact. 'From this point on in many works – and especially in the stricken "Self-Portrait" of 1972, where the painter depicts himself in an empty room, dazed and trapped in a hopeless hope, and in that gloomy requiem, "Triptych, August 1972" – a true *meditatio mortis* is revealed.' Trucchi linked Bacon with Heidegger and Sartre, asserting with them that beyond the body was silence, nothing. She quoted him in saying 'death is the shadow of life, and the more one is obsessed with life, the more one is obsessed with death.' Yet the most efficient exorcism was eroticism. The art of inevitable death yielded again to the urge to live. In the three years after Dyer's death, Bacon also painted 'Three Studies of Figures on Beds', 'Triptych, August 1972' 'Two Figures with a Monkey' and 'Triptych, March 1974', all of which showed the sexual battle at full force. As Bacon had remarked to Sylvester about an orange triptych painted the year before Dyer's suicide, 'I wanted to put two figures together on a bed, and I knew that I wanted them in a sense either to be copulating or buggering.' But he did not know how to do it so that it would have the strength of the sensation which he felt about it. Now his homage to Dyer and his memory of his lover gave him the strength of the sensation he had once had.

The brutal facts of Dyer's ending were met directly in 'Triptych, May-June 1973'. Against black backgrounds set up like screens with a white arrow pointing to the action, Dyer is seen vomiting into a basin on the right, staggering with head and shoulders across the central panel – his shadow a bat-like angel of death on the carpet and slumped in an animal crouch on the lavatory bowl on the left, abased in his final spasm. It is the suicide caught in reverse, three action stills read from right to left, as if a police surveillance camera had replaced the tragic happening to the jury of our eyes. Bacon later admitted that this triptych was the nearest he had ever done to something which had a story, and that was how his lover was found dead.

Yet Bacon's most poignant tribute to Dyer was a triptych of his lover and himself and Lucian Freud. As the painter said of his triple studies of single figures or heads, he usually did them 'like police records, looking side face, front face, and then side face from the other side'. In this case, Dyer in his characteristic nude pose with a foot balanced on one knee, does move his head sideways to look at Bacon in the centre, but a frontal mug shot of him is pinned to the wall behind his body. Bacon sits alone in the middle, his face loose with grief, staring forwards as does Freud in the right panel. But Freud's mug shot is side face, drawing the viewer's attention to Bacon's isolation. The divisions of the triptych give the effect of Dyer looking hopelessly across the abyss at the two living artists, who look forward at the living eye, while behind them, the simulated photographs recall the terrible memory of the past that snapshots can provoke.

When he made a selection of his work for a book on his art written by his friend from Paris, Michel Leiris, published in 1987, Bacon devoted four full pages to three triptychs and four individual self-portraits, all painted in 1972, and intercut with the furious circular arrowed motion of the copulating male 'Figures on Beds', also painted in that year. These introspective studies showed a man shocked by grief and pain with a blubbering mouth and black eyes lowered in despair. The jaunty curl of the forelock is ragged and matted on the forehead. And in one self-criticism, the artist is seen with an injured eye, as pink and swollen as a third cheek on his face. As he told Sylvester, he had been doing a lot of self-portraits 'because people have been dying around me like flies and I've had nobody else left to paint but myself'. It was a little mad to paint portraits of dead people. Their flesh had rotted away. 'Once they're dead you have your memory of them but you haven't got them.'

The self-portraits revealed the inner reality of Bacon's mourning for his friend. He was not an expressionist painter, as he said. He was not trying to express sorrow about somebody committing suicide; but he did admit that perhaps his grief came through without his knowledge. His outward manner showed nothing. Leiris found him as he always seemed to be, with a clean-shaven and chubby and tormented face, as roseate as that of a Georgian empirical philosopher, that seemed to reflect a 'wide-eyed astonishment as well as an intelligent stubbornness and – allied to a hidden fury – the sensitive distress of a man who has not forgotten that he was once a child whom almost anything could move to wonder'. His manner indicated that everything might be called into question, his light walk seemed almost on the point of breaking into a dance, while his casual and irreproachable clothes denied his late nights and spattered studio life. In sorrow or in anger at death, Bacon faced life in the studied manner of English good breeding, however much life itself had let him down.

At the Bacon exhibition at the Grand Palais, Léger's work had also been on show. For one English critic, Guy Brett, it was hard to imagine two more dissimilar spirits. While Léger's paintings expanded, Bacon's fearfully contracted. 'Bacon's world seems to contract inwards from the walls of the room into the crushed faces. His desperate imagery is combined with complete respect for the traditional limits of European painting. Bacon has said that the subject of his painting is "the History of Europe in my Lifetime". He has made of it a cramped, violent stage, which reflects Europe's obsession with itself and refusal to look outside.'

Yet the leading French critics such as Pierre Schneider had found that Bacon had radically changed modern art, which had destroyed the postulate that pictorial signs could signify reality. Now there was a painful divorce between the literal image and the subtle curtain of paint. Bacon's aggressively tried to bridge that void, but the violence did not belong to the artist nor to his subjects. 'It is the violence of representation. Modern paint is the ghoul, not Bacon.' When the artist said there was no torture in his paintings, he was right. As Schneider wrote:

> Since the 'sixties, the painting is the torture. The scale is often epic, but portraiture is always at the centre, because it states, in its most radical terms, the contradiction between the autonomy of paint and the identity of the subject, corralled, attacked from several sides at once. The light is switched on suddenly, to catch reality by surprise. It tolerates no protective shadows; it is relentless, uniform, lidless – the light of cross-examination. The curious affinity of certain recent triptychs with Toulouse-Lautrec (and, through him, with Japanese screens) stems from Bacon's interesting reliance on the sharpshooter's passionate precision. Nothing in the setting is left to chance . . .
>
> The contortion characteristic of Bacon's forms is a hanging on to a quarry that tries frantically to escape. There ensues a seesaw struggle in which writhing pigment achieves a succession of brief and partial triumphs: those moments when we forget it because it has suddenly become, with a kind of savage presence, a foot, an ashtray, a cheekbone, a knee clasped in that inimitable British way. And at once the image dissolves into brush-strokes. Thus painting can be said, in Bacon's words, 'to be and not to be'.
>
> What makes Bacon frightening is not his subject-matter but the fact that, in his practice, he shows art and actual living to be 'unmixable and inseparable'. The council of Chalcedon, in AD 456, thus defined the nature of Christ: I can think of no more apt definition for Bacon's paintings.
>
> Indeed, his fascination with the Crucifixion may well be attributed to the fact that Christianity's central mystery provides the pattern for the mystery of painting: reality must allow itself to be put to death by paint in order to be resurrected as image. Hence perhaps Bacon's jubilation at the disappearance of painting in our time: it proves that 'painting is just beginning'. The image will have reality only as long as we do not mistake it for reality; and when we do (when we want to touch it), the image relapses into paint. And so on indefinitely, within each picture . . .

> Tertullian called this period (those glacial three days before the Resurrection), *'refrigerium interim'*. No artist has given us a grander version of this ghastly moment of suspension, which is the Christian legacy to our post-Christian age. The great areas of colour, stilled by nocturnal brilliance, should clash, but do not. They are petrified while the dice are rolling.

Such important and incisive criticism persuaded the Metropolitan Museum in New York also to offer Bacon an exhibition there. Less than a week after his opening at the Grand Palais, Bacon was delighted to tell the press that he had been asked to show his work of the past five years at the Metropolitan, even without the Museum Director travelling to Paris to see what was on show there. It was an even more remarkable honour than the French exhibition, 'for the Metropolitan is essentially an Old Master Collection – the National Gallery and the British Museum rolled into one – and living artists are only shown there under very special circumstances.' *The Times* further stated that Bacon's success in Paris reflected credit on his mother country. French intellectuals were likely to think rather better of Britain after a disturbing visit to the Grand Palais, than they did before – not that Bacon cared a fig leaf for what *The Times* or his mother country thought.

Bacon's refusal to allow Dyer's suicide to prevent his inaugural success in Paris, and his insistence on continuing to see the Soho friends he had brought out with him, provoked a mistaken reaction to his apparent callousness. The concern and perhaps guilt, which were wrenched from his brush in his memorial pictures to George Dyer, would never have been displayed in his life, which was for living. His grief was private; he lived for the contradiction of it. Daniel Farson was shocked by John Deakin, also dying himself of lung cancer, writing in a letter of the celebrations of Bacon's success in Paris as 'a blur of brandy, illness and purple hearts', and merely ending a post-postscript with the words, 'How's about George's demise?' But such apparent brittle indifferences were merely a brave face to death, such as Bacon adopted to mask his admitted fear of it. This casualness that concealed commitment deceived some of the painter's more rigorous friends, particularly the extraordinary Vera

Russell, an *emigré* actress from St. Petersburg, who had married Bacon's leading critic John Russell. The artist did not live up to her exacting standards over Dyer's death. He seemed to be enjoying his fame and friends too much, and he would not exhibit in her Artists' Market in Covent Garden. She was also becoming estranged from her husband, and when she had a serious accident to her leg, Bacon was suspected of having used that mishap and their ill-feeling to produce a group of paintings involving a bloody and injured limb.

Such misunderstanding of Bacon's feelings for the death of his lovers and friends was proved untrue by the demise of John Deakin after an operation at the Westminster Hospital. Bacon had agreed to subsidise his convalescence, first in the Ship Hotel at Brighton, then on the Greek island of Poros. Deakin died in Brighton, but named Bacon as his next of kin. This seemed a dirty trick to the artist, who could not stand all the formalities. Deakin had enough money for a decent funeral, for Bacon had already given him the proceeds of the sale of one of his pictures. But characteristically, he told Daniel Farson a joke about identifying the corpse of the Soho photographer. When the sheet was lifted from the body, 'his trap was shut for the first time in his life'. It was most certainly him. Farson did not misinterpret such a bleak jest, but printed in his memories of Soho a glowing and rare tribute by Bacon to Deakin's art at a posthumous exhibition at the Victoria and Albert Museum: 'his portraits to me are the best since Nadar and Julia Margaret Cameron'.

Bacon spent more and more time at his studio in Paris at 3 Rue de Biraque in the Marais. It was not only because of the acclaim from his exhibition there, but a mark of his increasing friendship with Michel Leiris. It was a continual pleasure to Bacon, as John Russell wrote, 'to have that great lord of language only a short walk away'. The artist had already had five previous mentors in his life: Roy de Maistre who had taught him control in painting; Eric Hall who had contributed an appreciation of the finer arts and tastes of life; John Rothenstein with his imaginative sympathy and broad analysis of European painting; David Sylvester with his rigorous scrutiny of the artist's intention and execution; and John Russell himself, who was leaving the *Sunday Times* in England to work as the art critic for the *New York Times*. In his book on Bacon's work, so rich in its historical analysis, he paid tribute to the artist for being a good neighbour in Kensington for thirty years. Francis Bacon 'has never finished a bad book, he has never entertained a dull thought and he has never made a commonplace remark. Of how many of us can that be said? In life, he has set his own standards; and neither as a beginner nor as the most sought-after of living European painters has he fallen below them.'

Michel Leiris set Bacon very much in the mode of French Existentialism, while praising his originality. The *raison d'être* of an artist was not to entertain, but to make his personal statement in the chaos of existence. Although Bacon insisted that he was only a painter playing games and conveying no messages, there was a *real presence* in his figures, which had nothing to do with theology. The spectator had direct entrance into his pictures not unlike the experience of making physical love. This presence was ambiguous and alluring, wild and shining, an intense and sensuous delight that could repel by the force of its impact.

Bacon's aim was not to produce a decorative painting, but to use the canvas as an experimental assertion of certain realities. He differed from the Surrealists, who were obsessed with dreams and the imagination, by seeking an immediate method to describe his sensations, although he did admit that Sigmund Freud's work and Surrealism had changed his own sense of realism, 'because we've been made more conscious of how realism can draw on the unconscious'. He was also removed from the Impressionists, with their open windows or keyholes of pictures, flattering the eye with some luminous detail of the ordinary world, and from the Cubists with their structured compositions of what they held to be the true shape of things. Bacon now denied any influence from Expressionism, eschewing dramatic lighting and theatrical or satirical effects. He painted his subjects in the harsh flatness of naked electric bulbs or the glare of the sun at noon. For Leiris, Bacon insisted on putting all his cards on the table and paid cash down.

'The space in which we breathe and the time in which we live here and now: this is what we find, almost without exception, in Bacon's pictures, which seem to aim at the immediate expression of something immediate . . . They make the spectator feel as if he *were there*, or even *is actually there* (inside the picture, not simply in front of it).' In this total participation, the viewer entered into the state of Roland Barthes's phrase, *that is*, where the past is replaced by the present. Bacon's mature paintings were close and life-size and seemed to rest on a floor that extended over the bottom edge of the picture onto the floor of the gallery itself. Bacon changed the museum visitor into the voyeur of an autobiographical moment of crisis, in which he was trapped and enclosed in the small room or confining cage of the central figure. Bacon's art represented the space in which we actually live.

Moreover, it represented 'our time as well'. Bacon used personal objects to point out topicality and the passage of the hours. Like T. S. Eliot's people, whose lives were marked out in coffee-spoons, Bacon's were measured in cigarette-ends and shaving cream, the instant scatter of the everyday. The clothes were always common-place and crumpled, the naked figures stripped in casual or sexual action. It was painting devoid of distancing. It was a paring down like the quick choice between numbers before the rapid spin of the roulette wheel. Yet although Bacon claimed to have removed from art its religious and moral dimension in order to play a game of chance, there was a ritual in his pictures, as there was with croupiers in a casino, a form of 'blank liturgy' without any transcendental reference. Bacon and Giacometti's games consisted of trying to become the most accurate and effective figurative artists by risking the interplay between the theme and the artist's image produced by his sensations. This created the necessary tension in a picture, which suddenly seemed complete.

To Leiris, Bacon's most characteristic canvases suggested the rhythm of life. There were incandescent parts in them which seethed with energy in contrast to neutral parts where nothing happened. As there were solo breaks in jazz rhythms, as Stéphane Mallarmé counterpointed Dionysian frenzy with Apollonian calm, so Bacon threw the dice like a hurricane into the neutrality of the abyss. His figures had to have the personal mark of his throw, his cast of the paint, to make the spectator believe in them. In using distortion to translate the reality of the sitter to the viewer, Bacon never risked it for dramatic or even aesthetic reasons. He saw his models in their inner turmoil, already attacked by stress and decay, somewhat as in the process of the magic portrait of Dorian Gray in Oscar Wilde's tale, where the flesh remained perfect and the portrait of the real man showed the ravages of time.

The most alive of Bacon's pictures seemed to Leiris to result from a paradox: distorted figures were combined with a fairly naturalistic background. 'Such a marriage of hot and cold cannot fail to arouse attention and heighten the sensation of presence.' The geometry and pattern of the setting put in place the whirling energy of the figures, which seemed to lose their bone structures in swoops and turns. This was the art of immediate sensation, and even when the subject was called a Crucifixion, it used the myth no more than James Joyce used the ancient *Odyssey* in his modern *Ulysses* – Bacon was shortly to paint two pictures of Joyce's hero, Leopold Bloom, sitting side by side in felt hats, each talking to a duplicate of himself. Bacon even told Leiris that his use of the triptych was no longer inspired by Grunëwald or Cimabue, but by the panoramic screens of certain cinemas. He was determined as an ageing man to divorce himself from his early religious beliefs and influences.

Yet the distortion in Bacon's painting approached disruption and André Breton's definition of beauty for the Surrealists: 'Beauty will be convulsive or not exist at all.' Even so, the flesh of Bacon's models was so warm and elastic and voluptuous, his paint was swept on so directly from the sensitive brush, that the artist not only remodelled the forms, but kneaded the very matter of life itself. As a loaf rises from dough, the reality of his forms emerges from his bold manipulation and gambles with paint and sensation. 'His chief driving-force is a vehement desire to grasp reality . . . This frantic, almost panic, urge produces an emotional breaching of boundaries which introduces, into the texture of the canvas, the disturbance felt by the artist himself.'

Bacon tried to define what he meant by realism in a letter to Leiris, which he wrote in French with the help of a friend – he spoke excellent French, but wanted a precise language in his missive. Realism was 'an attempt to capture the appearance together with the cluster of sensations which this particular appearance excites in me'. He also stated that the most profound expression of realism was always subjective. There were inner realities to be revealed. Realism in art must not be confused with the simple wish to translate things which objectively existed. It had to be creative. It had continually to be re-invented. It did not represent; it might establish a truth beyond what might necessarily be seen. Leiris particularly admired two pictures which were to be painted in 1982; a male torso with a thrusting penis and buttocks as shoulders, the legs clad in cricket pads, and a female trunk crowned by two breasts after a drawing by Ingres. These were not slices of life, they were disturbing presences.

Bacon's devices for creating a real presence were by oblique intensification – a shadow becoming a dark pool emanating from the figure, a mirror reflection denser than the original, the omission of heads or limbs, the emphasis on splints or hypodermic needles to rivet attention, the unbalance of the position of the body as in a man using his foot to turn a door-key. These tensions through the interplay of contrasting energies and objects achieved 'the brutality of fact', which Bacon stressed in his interviews with Sylvester, and also as he often said to Russell – 'fact leaving its ghost'.

He wanted the help of accident and chance in his painting – by the use of drips or slips of the brush; by wiping with rags or by throwing on paint or sand or dust for texture; by adding circles and blots, arrows or whiplashes of white paint; by inserting the incongruous object or throwaway detail that marked the arbitrary and haphazard nature of modern living. It was the rebellion of caprice and disorder against the containment of chaos. And there was an element of myth in some of his paintings, taken from his reading or his Jungian unconscious – particularly in a 'Triptych' of 1976, where the centrepiece is of a Prometheus ripped apart by a bird of prey, his guts flowing down into a bowl, with other bestial shapes feeding on the innards, and a chalice dripping a veil of blood off the foreground in the suggestion of a communion cup. This and another picture painted four years later, 'Carcase of Meat and Bird of Prey', seemed to Leiris to achieve the tragic resonance of a sacrificial scene through the majestic quality of the structure and of the colour of the meat.

Although Bacon declared that he had no message to deliver, Leiris found, from personal experience, 'that his pictures help us, most powerfully, to feel the sheer fact of existence as it is sensed by a man without illusions'. The dazzling nakedness of the very moment of the paintings seemed to be 'images in keeping with the inanity of our situation in the world as ephemeral beings, more capable than any other living creatures of brilliant and pointless ecstasies'. They corresponded to that modern state of mind that used to be call *mal du siècle* – and in that way, the personal painting of the private artist did correspond to a universal perception.

In the same way as Samuel Beckett, whose plain sentences were like 'the discreet emanations from a mouldering peat fire', Francis Bacon expressed 'the human condition as it truly and peculiarly is today'. Consequently, he could be called a realist, however strong the tragic and mythological element was in occasional paintings and in references to the Sphinx or Prometheus or the Furies, to the *Oresteia* or 'Sweeney Agonistes'. 'As an authentic expression of Western man in our time, Francis Bacon's work conveys, in the admirably Nietzschean formula he himself has coined to explain the sort of man and artist he is, an "exhilarated despair".' Indeed, when Hugh Davies had commented that Bacon's figures in isolation were like those trapped people of Camus in *L'Etranger*, or of Sartre in *Huis Clos*, the painter had said, 'I have nothing to express about the human condition, but everyone reacts to their times.' It was impossible to work in an ivory tower. 'I look at everything from cave paintings to contemporary art and I'm influenced by them all.'

The especial importance of the opinions of Michel Leiris was that they related the French analytical approach to a personal awareness and knowledge of Francis Bacon, who approved this interpretation of his intentions. In his continuing autobiographical frame of mind, Bacon painted two portraits of Leiris, which were to be included in the book about him. They show a lean-faced man with generous and sensitive lips and eyes that express sympathy and inquiry. Talking of the two paintings to Sylvester, Bacon said that the one less literally like Leiris was more poignantly like him. His head was rather globular, but in one portrait it was long and narrow and seemed more real to Bacon, who intended that the pictures should look like the subject. 'There's no point in doing a portrait of somebody if you're not going to make it look like him.' But by making the features artificially narrow, Bacon seemed to capture the Frenchman's acute sense of logic and fine power of reasoning. And in the second portrait, the deconstruction of the features bore tribute to the current French thinking of Barthes and Derrida as well as to Bacon's love of the X-Ray images in *Positioning in Radiography*.

In his portraits, Bacon tried to trap the energy, mental or physical, within the appearance. He even occasionally talked of emanations from people, of fact leaving its ghost, which he tried to hunt down. He was not now painting so many self-portraits, as two very good-looking people he had known in the past had turned up in his life again. One was the American explorer and photographer in Africa, Peter Beard, and the other was a tall young Canadian from Montreal, Barry Joule, who served as the model for the male torso in the cricket pads, along with a news photograph of David Gower at the crease. In 1975, Bacon twice painted 'Three Studies for a portrait of Peter Beard', and for once, the physical beauty of the features transcended the added white circles and blobs and furrow marks of orange and pink and white. Bacon admired the bone structure behind the face and did not dissolve it, as he had so often before in his portraits of Isabel Rawsthorne or himself. He talked to Beard of death as the only absolute certainty. Artists knew they could not defeat it and were very aware of their own annihilation. 'It follows them around like their shadow, and I think this is one of the reasons why artists are so conscious of the vulnerability and nothingness of life.'

Barry Joule had first met Bacon while washing his car in Reece Mews. He had left his English-Canadian father and Irish mother in Canada and had settled as a neighbour to Bacon, who leaned out of his kitchen window to ask a question. It led to a close and lasting friendship between the two men, which was only to end with the painter's death in Spain – Joule heard the news on his farm in Normandy, while waiting for Bacon to join him from Madrid. He particularly admired Bacon's rigorous pattern of work from six to twelve in the morning, rather like that of Graham Greene. Then anything went. But when Bacon was possessed by a concept, the work did not stop for nights and days on end. This excess of dedication was always followed by a binge of play with Francis consuming huge quantities of champagne and food with a few old friends and sometimes with bevies of young admirers. 'Age was a curse,' he always said to Joule, but he looked and behaved as if preternaturally young. 'He always wanted to be one of the boys,' Joule said, and Bacon was generous to those he loved, helping Joule with advice on how to add to his art collection and on how to paint the figure. He once gave Joule five-thousand pounds in cash to use for food and drink for one week when Peter Beard was staying in London, and he spent eight-hundred pounds on a dinner for the two of them – the port cost two-hundred pounds alone. All the presents he was sent in the 'seventies, the pictures by other artists and the inscribed art books, he gave to Joule to keep as his historian and archivist – a role later played by John Edwards, the last long companion of the artist.

Bacon himself wanted nothing which he could not consume, and he held onto few possessions. What did concern him more and more was his reputation. Greatly interested in the history of photography, Joule tried to persuade Bacon to mount an exhibition of the photographs which had most influenced him. Such a demonstration of the connection between photography and a modern painter would have been of seminal significance. But Bacon demurred. He wanted 'to be pure about his art and not muddy the waters about his work'. According to Joule, 'Francis Bacon always saw himself beside Picasso – he was very aware of the paintings Picasso had discarded in his eighties. He was very tight about what he let out of the studio in his old age. When he could, he bought back and destroyed his early works or exchanged them for like paintings on a similar theme.' Actually, these earlier paintings had very little value on the market. 'Yet Francis was very aware of his place in history and where he stood.'

'I'm greedy for life,' Bacon said to Sylvester, 'and I'm greedy as an artist.' He wished for chance to give him in painting far more than he could calculate, he wanted the excitement of things happening and being with the people he liked. Yet he did not dice with death, carefully looking both ways before he bounced cockily across the road. Only occasionally did he use drink or pills to help him finish a picture. They were not good for him: they dulled his final judgement. Fatigue could help him if he could lose his will and feel free to go anywhere with his creation. Even a bout of despair about the impossibility of completing something might lead him to do anything. 'And out of this anything, one sees what happens.'

Stephen Spender found Bacon's feelings of frustration and despair when painting the same as if he were writing poetry or even reviews for the *Times Literary Supplement*. Often mentally and quite convincingly, he abandoned something which he would pick up again, or he felt overrun by a rush of ideas that he could not organise. In the case of Bacon:

> Despair occurs when the artist does not work with a pre-prepared or a preconceived structure, such as a drawing, a model or object before him, in other words when he has not predecided his ideas and efforts. Everything – ideas and means – the paint itself – surrounds him with its swarm of potentialities threatening to engulf him. Creativity is a struggle to control this rush of ideas and means. Despair is almost a necessary condition in such circumstances. It is the measurable point in time and place at which the force he is trying to control almost overwhelms him, the point at which victory and defeat are in balance. It is either the moment of defeat, or of breakthrough.

Such a reckless charge at painting and living was a potent example for young artists who wanted to walk on the wilder side of existence. The extraordinary Australian painter, Brett Whiteley, the youngest artist ever to be bought by the Tate Gallery, took as his role models Baudelaire and Van Gogh and Rimbaud and Cocteau, but especially Bacon, all of whom he turned into portraits with his energetic and flowing brush, fuelled by heroin and marijuana and alcohol. Jeffrey Bernard was also stimulated in his career as the Boswell of low life in Soho by weekly lunches at Wheeler's with Isabel Rawsthorne and Bacon. 'We would gossip generally and always talk about sex and death,' Bernard wrote. 'He seemed amused by both subjects and he used to quiz me about my being heterosexual as though I was a creature from outer space.' He once caused a walk-out of American tourists from the next table by asserting that he would like to be buggered by his favourite pin-up, Colonel Gaddafi. Bacon considered Bernard 'an honorary poof', while Bernard felt honoured to be a friend. They had a shared love of gambling, and Bacon would stake Bernard to his bets and would anyway stuff a fifty-pound note into his jacket pocket if he did not place it on a horse. 'He was never flashy with his generosity, but he had a healthy contempt for money. "Bits of paper," he called it after a good night at the roulette table.'

Although Bacon had little interest in politics, he did know some politicians, particularly the remarkable Tom Driberg, who was also an habitué of the Colony Room and of the company of young men. On one occasion, Driberg was with a *Sunday Times* interviewer, when they bumped into Bacon at the foot of the stairs of Muriel Belcher's bar, and there the politician and the artist embraced effusively. While Bacon went up on his spring heels in search of an afternoon's fun, Driberg had to return to the House of Commons in his sober dark blue suit, collar and tie. The report of the meeting showed the abyss between Westminster and Fleet Street on one side and the liberty of the painter on the other:

> He [Driberg] would have been as happy as a poet and has always enjoyed Bohemian company, finding many friends among the strange community who have made their spiritual home in Soho. Instead, journalism and politics imposed on him the need to preserve some vestige of respectability and it is a mantle which has always been uncomfortable round his shoulders.
>
> When we were walking away from the Colony Room late that sunny afternoon, our brief encounter with Francis Bacon obviously triggered off a familiar sequence of thoughts in Driberg's mind because he was silent for some time, then, looking around at the flickering neon signs of the strip clubs and restaurants and pubs and delicatessens, he said, quite softly, as if to himself: 'You know, I've always wished in a way that I could have lived this kind of life.'

Living in many worlds under the camouflage of his respectability, Driberg did live at times the kind of life of the artist Bacon, who was himself a pioneer in the demonstration of his preferences. Although, with the Sexual Offences Act of 1967, homosexual acts between consenting adults had ceased to be criminal, while overt contact magazines and specialist papers such as *Gay News* appeared, a backlash of the moral majority led by Lady Birdwood and Mrs

Whitehouse had begun. The blasphemy of Bacon's various triptychs of Crucifixions had never been prosecuted, but blessed by the state and hung in the Tate Gallery. Yet the publication of a poem by James Kirkup, a young friend of E. M. Forster and J. R. Ackerley, under the title of 'The Love that Dares to Speak its Name', led to a charge of blasphemy against *Gay News*. The poem told of a centurion left alone with Christ's body before burial. He entered orifices and wounds and revived the corpse for a last time to sodomise himself. The message was that homosexuality now dared to speak its name. It was out of the closet as Christ was out of the Tomb. Kirkup admitted that he knew his poem would dismay and shock some people – but had he not himself 'been deeply offended, dismayed and shocked by *their* version of the Crucifixion'. His sentiments were similar to Bacon's, who knew that his versions of the Crucifixion with their orifices and bleeding meat would shock some people, and who saw no religious significance in the Cross, only human violence and torture and sexual connotations, as in the left panel of the Munich 'Crucifixion' with its glancing nude leaving a slavering bestial creature on the twisted bed.

The difference was that Kirkup's poem was trite and arch with puns such as Christ being 'well hung' on the Cross, while Bacon's 'Crucifixions' were born in personal anguish and executed by a genius. Kirkup's effort was judged in court for its 'quite appalling and most scurrilous profanity' with its 'reckless disregard for the feelings of Christians and non-Christian sympathisers'. Fines were levied against *Gay News* and its publisher, who also received a suspended prison sentence. The victory for the moral majority, however, did not deter the publication of two important homosexual memoirs, Christopher Isherwood's *Christopher and His Kind*, dealing with many of the same sexual encounters that the young Bacon had experienced during his early visit to Berlin, and Tom Driberg's *Ruling Passions*, which brought him out of the closet and the cloacal cottages with a vengeance. Published posthumously in 1977, the book recounted in full detail, including posture and Vaseline, the young Driberg's liaisons with hungry, unemployed men in the 'thirties or cruising in male lavatories off Piccadilly in the 'fifties. Homosexual culture had reached the page.

In his undemonstrative way and only through his art, Bacon had long since dared to depict, as Oscar Wilde said in his defence, 'the love that dare not speak its name in this century'. In declaring that he was painting his autobiography, in showing frequent pictures at international exhibitions of male nudes coupling or tearing at one another or performing bodily acts in their bathrooms, Bacon put the actual names of his masculine lovers on the works, particularly that of George Dyer. He was not denouncing them as in an American trial by Senator McCarthy. He was commemorating his passion and obsession for one man at a time across the world, an act of homage and defiance that the ten-thousand banners waving for Gay Liberation could never have achieved.

Yet his philosophy prevented Bacon from being interested in any form of politics. Sexual or economic or social matters were excluded from his thoughts, if they did not personally affect him. He was rather on the right wing and certainly against the welfare state that the Labour Government was promoting in Britain. He thought that being nursed from the cradle to the grave would bring boredom to life. He felt no moral case against theft. He had often stolen as a young man. He did not need to steal now and would no longer risk the nuisance of being caught and put in gaol. But he did accept that most of society was against theft and people now expected welfare and the nanny state. Too much security, however, curtailed the creative instinct, which fed on despair about existence. Although all life was artificial, social justice and egalitarianism made it pointlessly so. The suffering of people and their differences had made great art. 'Who remembers or cares about a happy society? After hundreds of years or so, all they think about is what a society has left.'

This attitude to individual achievement and the leaving of monuments to future generations made Bacon a prophet of British government in the 'eighties, when the Conservative Party would turn away from the welfare state as far as it could towards initiative. He was not really a do-gooder, as he said. He supposed he should want to improve life and did not like to think of people suffering; but it was their problem. They bred at such a rate, they were bound to suffer. Bacon did not value the opinion of the masses or the mob. His pessimism and concentration on the personal had increased with his years. Born before the First World War, he had seen the failure of the socialist experiments in Europe over the past four decades, and he would pursue his own road as Van Gogh had in Provence. Alexander Pope might have declared that the proper study of mankind was man. But for himself, the proper study of Bacon was Bacon.

During 1974, Bacon worked at pictures for his successive exhibitions at Marlborough Fine Art in Bond Street and for the show of his recent work at the Metropolitan Museum in New York. In a sense, it was an autobiography of his last years with Dyer and the process of the cleansing of his bereavement. The two earliest triptychs among the thirty-five pictures in the American showing dated from 1970, 'Three Studies of the Male Back' and 'Studies from the Human Body'. They showed Dyer in his voluptuous and gravid use of the bathroom, and then in his violent coupling, with Bacon as an onlooker with a camera on a tripod or as a watcher of animal lust in split-screen indecision. The various tributes to Dyer after his death including the factual 'Triptych, May-June, 1973' were concluded by another black-backed triple painting of March the following year. Dyer's body has been transmuted to grace in movement, the blur of an athlete in competition, the Greek sculptor Myron's 'Discobulus' contorting his mighty body in a last heave under a naked light bulb. This time the viewer on the right has his face hidden by his hand camera with its spouting orifice, while a butcher in his apron on the left turns away in his heavy boots from his pinkish and carnal shadow to shut up shop. The fact of still death is transformed into the mercy of moving memory, duly recorded, but the episode closed.

Among the series of self-portraits at the Metropolitan exhibition, mounted in Hecht's identical strongly-moulded and heavy-glassed gold frames with an exact spacing between the panels of the five inches specified by the painter, one revealing study showed the seated Bacon slumped at a washbasin, time ticking on the wrist of the arm he has thrown over his grieving head. Behind him, his image sits in reverse, held in the open door against blue sky of happier days. In addition there was a 'Seated Figure', which ringed the repeated knees in the shape of pairs of buttocks with a black circle.

A dark noose was also thrown around the private parts of a 'Sleeping Figure', asprawl on a camp-bed.

Two other major works of 1975, 'Studies from the Human Body' and 'Three Figures and a Portrait', took Bacon back to Muybridge. Although the distorted small portrait is still of George Dyer, the convoluted and twisted creatures, spiny and creased, recall the deformed subjects of some of the Victorian photographer's work, as do the sprawling hermaphrodites of the body studies. An uncharacteristic 'Portrait of a Dwarf', done in that same year, showed him bifurcated in his perch on his high stool and trapped in a corrugated corner. It further signalled a return to the photographs of the people once called freaks in the previous century.

The later works in the last of the three galleries devoted to Bacon in the Metropolitan Museum were realised with a palette almost reduced to black and white and red and yellow. It was the four-colour system of the Greek painter Apelles and his classical contemporaries, as Pliny had noted. The effect was one of dramatic gravity, compared with the bright decorator-colours of the backgrounds of the earlier pieces in the other two galleries. Both the influence of Greek sculpture and Renaissance art was evident in the works of the previous three years, Dürer's 'Melancholia' in the central panel of 'Triptych, May-June 1973' as well as Myron's discus-thrower, that quintessence of human motion.

Bacon had recently been talking to David Sylvester about taking up sculpture, putting his figures on rails or armatures as in his paintings. These interviews with Bacon were published in New York to coincide with his exhibition there. He had expressed a heightened admiration for antique and Renaissance sculpture and art, saying that they constituted for him the greatest images men had made. These feelings, in the words of the critic of the *Burlington Magazine*, 'underlie the kind of classical clarification and sculptural-like force of concept evident in the late paintings', which had 'elevated the basic, later-twentieth-century substance of Bacon's art, without at all sacrificing its personal, elemental force, to a more universal level of expression'.

Bacon's critical triumph in New York put the laurel wreath on his international reputation. He seemed to have won his Olympic games with chance. He was adept now at one-line remarks for mass publicity, talking of a life divided between 'the gutter and the Ritz' and of surviving on 'a diet of oysters and despair'. The prices of his work were climbing and exploding like *feux d'artifice*. A Sotheby's sale of a painting realised more than £70,000 in Rome in 1973; two years later in London, Sotheby's received £65,000 for a screaming pope. Already, he was highly prized and priced throughout the world. But his success could not wholly fill the void in his life in pursuit of extreme sensation, which had been checked by Dyer's death. Although he declared that he would give up painting self-portraits, he went on with these exercises in self-analysis, picking at the scabs forming on his grief. And more and more, he restricted himself to the company of old friends, looking for a stability in affection that he had never had.

In search of some sort of permanence, Bacon bought a terraced house in the country, at Wivenhoe, near Colchester in Essex. Dennis Wirth-Miller lived in the village with his friend Richard Chopping at the Store House on the Quay. They had given the *fête champêtre* there after Michael Wishart's three-day wedding reception in Bacon's former studio. The writer and illustrator Chopping taught at the Royal College of Art. Wirth-Miller was something of a painter until Bacon told him that he did not have the right to touch a canvas and discouraged him completely. The two men at Wivenhoe had the stable relationship that Bacon was again seeking, even though Chopping was famous for his performances at the Royal College's pantomimes, particularly as the Good Fairy, which prompted Bacon to say, 'Well, that's the best Cinderella I have *ever* seen.' Chopping's performance in drag as Marlene Dietrich was also a tour-de-force, particularly his 'Falling in Love Again' from *The Blue Angel*:

> 'Men cluster to me
> Like moths around a flame . . .'

At Wivenhoe, Bacon was immensely popular in the local pubs because of his lavish hospitality and unbuttoned conversation. What surprised another neighbour, the newspaper editor Sir Peregrine Worsthorne, was Bacon's 'interest in, and knowledge of, history and politics; also his *reactionary* views . . . he was an ardent supporter of the Vietnam War. Equally surprising was the toleration demonstrated by the Wivenhoe residents to Francis's endless chasing of all the pretty boys. The village view was that he was harmless, in spite of his devilish pictures.' Bacon appreciated not only his tolerant neighbours, but also the flat countryside and the Essex marshes. He had spoken to John Russell about how sensitive he was to every kind of enclosed indoor space as well as to level ground:

> 'I'd rather have a carpeted aircraft hangar, any day, than an ugly house. The huge space with a bathroom and lavatory in one corner could look very grand. Even the pipes could look so beautiful. I'd like it to be in flat, treeless country . . . Essex or Norfolk . . . because very intimate country, "rolling country", is not for me. I was brought up for much of my childhood on the edge of very flat marshlands full of snipe and plover. That's the kind of country I find exciting.'

These flat expanses of favourite countryside were the spaces that Bacon tried to reproduce in his paintings, a blank immensity in a little room. A rare 'Landscape' of 1978 showed a sandy beach with rough-brushed grass in the shape of a plunging human creature with two red arrows pointing to the whirl of earth and sky, yet all enclosed with the night in a transparent box. Even nature to Bacon was in a trap. And he felt that he was, too. His autobiography of the 'seventies placed himself with his single figures on the level of an infinite plain within a definite enclosure. If the viewer were to enter such a painting, he would meet the painter inside his captured distances.

The studies for his self-portraits now showed a reflective face or one with a wine glass flying to its lips. His 'Two Studies for Portrait of Richard Chopping' continued his making of his private life into a public art. They are full of insight and sensibility, the eyes of the subject caught in a glance of concern in full face, while a side view demonstrates the same interest in a turn of the head, exposing a fine cheek-bone and jawline. These were loving pictures, as were those of Michel Leiris, the counterpart of Chopping in Paris.

Such portraits of understanding friends marked Bacon's refuge from his passion for the semi-criminal Dyer into a haven of sympathetic intellectuals, who understood the tension and sensation of his character and style of life, the ferocity of the commitment, the desperate pursuit of chance, the seizing of form and figure out of chaos, the wilful excitement of ducking and delving into the base and the best, the despair of the true artist in the chase after a love that might destroy his art. Bacon transcended his obsession with the ghost of Dyer, but he did not recover from it in the society of like minds. He had had an anarchic *nostalgie de la boue* ever since his adventures with the stable lads in his father's racing establishment. He would look again for that satisfaction and not feel the sensation of exhilarated despair until he found the fact of it.

II

So Many Eyes, So Many Ears

> The poets made Fame a monster. They describe her in part finely and elegantly; and in part gravely and sententiously. They say, look how many feathers she hath, so many eyes she hath underneath; so many tongues; so many voices; she pricks up so many ears.
>
> 'Of Fame'
> by Francis Bacon, Lord Verulam,
> Viscount St. Albans

The self-portraits by Bacon in the late 'seventies show the painter coming to terms with his grief. In one of 1978, muted greens and blues give a rural feel to the artist sitting on his stool with folded hands and calm face in profile. There is no distortion of the features, only a luminous shadow behind the side of the face to emphasise the contemplation of the figure. Although entrapped in a hoop of white, Bacon shows himself mentally at ease. And the 'Three Studies for Self-Portraits' of the succeeding year, chosen by Bacon himself to illustrate Michel Leiris's book about him, accentuate the artist's round cheeks and blond forelock. His eyes and mouth no longer mourn, but inquire and open into the sensation of living. Almost for the last time, George Dyer appears in 'Seated Figure, 1978', but only as a handsome profile on a plinth, excluded from the transparent cage, in which the mysterious figure in cricket pads sits under an umbrella. A black arrow points the way to a red ring round his obscure sexual organs. Another lover is removing Dyer onto the pedestal of the past.

Bacon always related what he felt about death to what he felt about life and about gambling. He had strong feelings about them all, and dying to him was only another turn of the coin. His attraction to casinos was reflected in his pictures, as death was. There was the excitement of people winning or not winning, the despair of the players losing everything. And all went on in a very concentrated place, the confine in which he set the figures in his paintings. He played roulette because the odds were most against him, but if he hit the right numbers, the rewards were quicker and greater. It was instant gratification. But in the end, not even he could beat the odds. He was the perfect compost for casinos, because he was nearly always losing. At Aspinall's in Curzon Street, on one occasion he was allowed to run up a bill and pay by cheque. Everything went wrong and he found himself owing nearly forty-thousand pounds. Even with the money he was earning from his growing fame, it took him months and months to repay. On another occasion at Crockford's, he entered with £6,000 in banknotes carefully divided into two jacket pockets. This was his form of caution. To have to dig into a second pocket should be an obstacle to losing it all. It was not.

Yet gambling to Bacon was hardly a real risk, such as risking one's life. Nor was painting a real risk, more like an accident within his power to alter. In gambling, once the wheel was spinning, there was nothing he could do about it. With a brush in one hand, he diced with chance, he was still in the game. And he played it with full commitment in deadly earnest. His concern over the survival of his best work lay not only in his efforts to destroy or deny his earlier or inferior works, but also in trying to stop a lucrative trade in fake Bacons that was started in Milan in Italy.

The problem was that Bacon rarely signed his paintings, and the fakes bore no forged signatures, so that their artists could not be prosecuted for fraud. What the false pictures had attached were doctored provenances or attributions by small dealers. Two Italian forgeries of portraits of Isabel Rawsthorne were authenticated by a Chelsea bookseller and a London art dealer. The bookseller admitted that the portraits came to him from the 'gay network of dealers', and he should have put in his Letter of Provenance, 'in the Francis Bacon style [although] it was a strong Bacon and did speak so well'. The art dealer explained his Letter of Provenance by stating that when he wrote that he had acquired the 'Rawsthorne' portrait, it did not mean he had bought it. In the trade, 'acquired' did not imply ownership, as it might to ordinary people. He had not bought it for himself, so he was not responsible for verifying a forgery.

There was also the problem of Bacon's abandoned paintings. He had left one incomplete canvas in a coal-cellar which was sold in Sotheby's for £71,000. 'Before the sale', he said, 'Sotheby's, on my behalf, made it clear that it was discarded, but it sold. I can't tell you why people are fools.' He had to cut up all the paintings he had discarded in order to prevent them reaching the art market, but he forgot about some of them when he moved and others had been stolen from him. He did, however, take steps to deny the forgeries from Italy. 'I have even signed the backs of photographs of fakes, "This is a fake and not by me." But forgers have then cut out the genuine signature to accompany one of their latest fakes.'

The Milan forgers, however, were making one basic mistake. They were painting on the front of the canvas, while Bacon painted on the umprimed back. But as his fame and his prices soared, the forgeries multiplied. There were many abandoned canvases knocking around from his various old studios, and as he loathed the unsigned early works and incomplete versions, Bacon was not past denying his hand in anything he disliked, even if he had done it. The London art dealer who had sold on the 'Rawsthorne' fake had to admit finally that 'if the living authority, the artist himself, challenges a work, he must have the final word'. Indeed, and Bacon only authenticated the works of which he now approved, and he tried to cut up the rest.

He was in no way a doctor of his past, but he wished to preserve solely what he considered the best of his paintings for posterity. The worth of anything done by him was so valuable that he himself had become vulnerable to exploitation. However much he tried to restrict his circle to old friends, his penchant for younger men led to approaches by those looking for a killing from his fabled generosity or from burglary. It was the price of his fame. He was perfectly aware of the danger, but naturally gregarious when he went to the Colony Room or other favourite haunts. And he was a canny man about his pictures, fearful that they would get into the wrong hands. Even when he was arguing about the aspect of something, and a close friend asked him to sketch it on the tablecloth, he was no Toulouse-Lautrec or Picasso to do it and enrich the friend or the waiter with the scrawl he left behind him.

The film director Derek Jarman often told a story which Bacon had told him about one morning when his caution about the company he kept backfired badly. He felt in the money and indulged himself with a rent-boy for the night in the era before AIDS was a known plague. He hid his gold Swiss watch under the bedside rug so that the rent-boy did not take it with him as he departed. But rising to go, the rent-boy put the heel of his boot on the watchface and shattered it below the rug, totally destroying it. The best-laid plans of vice and men ganga a-gley.

Bacon's nocturnal adventures could even affect his pictures, given his love of the chance element in painting. As he told Kenneth Partridge, if a passing bedfellow did not know where to go and looked for a window to relieve himself and the golden shower fell on a wet painting, so it stayed, if Bacon liked the effect of the incident on his work in the morning. It was the same if a visitor brushed against a wet canvas and smudged it. It was also the same if rain fell through the old roof or the skylight of Reece Mews and spattered the drying oils on a painting, or if Bacon had to move his bed out of the deluge and the end of the sheets smeared his art. He once outlined the round rim of his dust-bin lid with black paint to paint a ring round the genitals in one picture. Any of these actions might provide that happy accident which made the picture: that moment of fact where luck met design.

As Farson wrote of Bacon, most of the young men he encountered in the Soho bars became his friends, not his boyfriends. And he could pass them on to other friends, as he did to Joan Wyndham's lodger, called Sal in the third volume of her autobiography. She had finished an affair with Lucian Freud and had introduced Sal to Bacon in the French Pub and through him to a successful West End art dealer who became his lover. Sal was later to commit suicide, but his diary reflected the feelings of so many of the young men who clustered around Bacon, now in his sixties, and his circle and became close to them. To Sal, the art dealer was 'hot, a pure boy's peril, the ultimate corruptor of young acolytes'. He did not know why he found himself in bed with the older man.

> What am I doing in this homosexual mayhem, stretched out like a beast in four-posted splendour lit by the maverick flame of our penultimate candle?
>
> What am I doing with this man of forty-five? When he drinks his cheeks flush and the wine dribbles from the corner of his mouth. When I sleep with him I emerge parched, barren and dizzy from his clutches. This is not love, not truth, just rotting physicality.
>
> I try to pretend I am doing it for experience and edification – I offer you my sweetness, you offer me your culture. But I suppose I am just what they call an Art Tart. Afterwards I cry and wash manically, trying to expiate, to purify myself.

A great friend of Bacon and part of the circle of his framer Alfred Hecht was Geoffrey Bennison, probably the best interior decorator in Britain. He had darting eyes, which dissected the onlooker and often undid him. He lived in Golden Square with three male acolytes to serve him, Babs and Carlotta and Scotch Agnes. They had been frequent visitors to Tangier, where they would stay at the Riff Hotel. They had met Bacon in his days there with Peter Lacey, and Bennison put up William Burroughs in his guest house in Kensington. They were particularly adept at picking up for the price of a packet of cigarettes the young male offenders after they were released from Brixton prison. Bacon found Bennison's group a little *outré* for his plainer tastes, particularly at a drag ball given with young actors hired to be waiters in ruffles and wigs and knee-britches. 'Far too camp,' he said and left.

Yet he had a level of sophistication which surprised even the urbane Alfred Hecht. When Bacon invited him to Claridge's or the Connaught for lunch, Hecht was startled to hear the maître d'hôtel say, 'Mr Bacon, your usual table in the corner there?' Hecht had some very good early Bacon paintings, a triptych of George Dyer, a distorted 'Pink-faced Baby', and a 'Man with a Watch', who was bending down with a measuring-tape, said to commemorate the coming of the Metric System to Britain. All of these pictures had to be sold to private collectors in the last years of Hecht's life to pay for his medical bills. Hecht finally induced Bacon not to paint on any old size of canvas because of the high insurance costs, while he was framing them. In that way, he uniquely cut Bacon's pictures down to size. Both men also ruined their art books and sliced them apart to see and read them the better. And like Bacon, Hecht liked to give, never to receive; to have the power of the host, not the obligation of the guest.

During these indeterminate years without a single special attachment, Bacon spent more and more time in the Colony Room. But Muriel Belcher was ill and dying. Bacon paid for her and her friend to go to recuperate in the West Indies but she did not really recover. He painted her again as a Sphinx in 1979, which was to prove the year of her death. In it, the almost bald Belcher with a beaked nose sits with a black open tunic over her shoulders exposing her breasts, while her clawed thin shanks are thrust forward on two large wooden joists or splints. Slabs of purple and orange surround her, and a simple black trapezoid turns these into spaces. A jumble of newsprint lies on the floor, perhaps to suggest the jargon of any obituary.

When Belcher died, Bacon had lost another dear friend. But he went on visiting the Colony Room, now run by the ex-barman, Ian Board, who imitated Muriel in her style and foul language, though not in her sex or warmth. The drinking laws were still in place, and there was nowhere more convenient to go in Soho during the afternoons when the pubs were closed. 'These ghastly English laws, you can't have a drink, can't do anything,' Bacon complained to one interviewer. 'Do you think they'll ever change them? I don't think so – the Church will stop them, you can be certain. I can take you up to that awful Colony Room if you like.'

He went on taking people up to that afternoon drinking club. It suited his hours and his style of life. He even liked seeing strangers there, watching the formation of their faces and their movements, and he would introduce himself to any young man who caught his fancy, as he had to the artist Michael Clarke on his first visit there – Clarke also painted a death-bed portrait of Muriel Belcher. Bacon found that people were very free in the club. It was like a pool in which they forgot their inhibitions, most lively and amusing. And it gave him the material for his portraits. As he now said, 'All the people that I've painted I've either met in pubs or have known very well.'

Except when he took a brat pack of tough young acolytes to one of his exhibitions at Marlborough Fine Art, Bacon kept his private life extremely discreet outside the places in Soho, where he knew that his reputation was protected. Because of this sense of privacy and discretion, Bacon was invited to become a Companion of Honour in 1977, although he had previously declined a knighthood. Previous recipients had included Henry Moore and Graham Sutherland and Graham Greene and would include Lucian Freud, who was to fall out with Bacon over his acceptance of the award. Bacon firmly stuck to his principles of detachment from established society and refused this second accolade from his country. 'I always decline these honours,' he said. 'I never want them. I have no opinions on the honours system. It might be fine for other people but I want to stress I don't want anything for myself.'

Bacon's apparent disdain for convention and morality turned some of the art critics against him. They saw a contempt in his works for his viewers and for society. At his triumph in Paris, a critic who had once thought Bacon a hero for the vital tension in his painting had lambasted his fondness for Grand Guignol symbolism and glory. Richard Cork thought that Bacon's bitter-sweet amalgam of tenderness and brutality, sliding from an area of sensuous splendour into a mass of brutalised slashes, had degenerated into boorish caricature, outright sensationalism and a bullying despair at the 'inability to turn unruly ambition into the discipline of great art'. Bacon protested too loudly in his determination to pitch the tenor of his statements as high as he possibly could. 'The result is a fatal recoiling on the part of the spectator, who feels he is *expected* to be stirred and so withholds a wholehearted reaction.' And at an exhibition of Bacon's recent paintings at Marlborough Fine Art in January, 1978, Edward Lucie-Smith had to admit that Bacon was the most celebrated and prestigious of British painters, but disliked his restricted imaginative world and obsessive themes of horror, anxiety and fear. The linkage of the grandeur of the past, as in his pictures derived from Velázquez and Ingres, with the muck of the present, was unacceptable. The grand manner should not be put at the service of deliberate squalor. 'What emerges from Bacon's late paintings is a contempt for the audience which is also, perhaps, the painter's contempt for himself. Can art as great as Bacon's is supposed to be, base itself upon a sneer?'

Such misunderstandings, by some critics, of the intentions and the commitment of Bacon's works were based on a confusion of the artist's way of life with his work. He had declared that he was trying to paint the history of the past thirty years; he now insisted that he was painting an autobiography without any message. Yet many people in his audience disliked the style of living and were shocked at his portrayal of it. The paradox was that, as his art became acclaimed internationally – he had exhibitions in Mexico City and Caracas and Madrid and Barcelona at this time – it seemed to lose its universal concept for a personal statement.

Bacon did not appear to care what his critics thought outside the few mentors that he valued. Michel Leiris had already described how Bacon's private depictions of his small world had public significance and another French critic, Gilles DeLeuze, was to complete the definition of Bacon's work in a general logic of sensation, an emotive scale of colours, and a theme in the history of painting. Such rational analyses from France would resolve in words the painter's daily battle in his studio between chance and intent, luck and design, and they certainly would absolve him from the accusation that he deliberately pursued squalor rather than the truth and the fact of things.

Bacon used to say that he liked his paintings being called ugly. Van Gogh had said of 'The Night Café' that it was one of the ugliest paintings he had ever done. But Bacon found it extremely beautiful. Of course the people in the café were ruining themselves by drinking, but why should they not? By swirling the light round the bulbs, Van Gogh had given his painting an extraordinary intensity, something which Bacon strove to achieve. This intensity might be called ugly, but those who thought it was condemned their own vision. Bacon was much more pleased when some people really hated his paintings than when they liked them. There might, after all, in that case, be something there.

What he disliked was American abstract art. He thought that Jackson Pollock's pictures appeared to be bits of old lace, while Mark Rothko's looked like yards of dirty maroon cloth rolled out for the eye. The room given to Rothko in the Museum of Modern Art in New York had depressed him for a whole day after he had seen it. They were the dreariest paintings ever made. He had thought that there might be lovely vibrant colours in abstract art, but actually the back of his studio door and the walls in Reece Mews were his abstract paintings, because he used them to test out his colours and they were much brighter than Rothko's were.

'Any painting that *works* today is linked to the past,' he once explained. 'In a way it was better when there wasn't so much individuality. But because today there is no tradition and no myths, people are thrown back on their own sensibility. Abstract art was perhaps one attempt at getting away from this, but it never worked because the artists made their own patterns in their own ways. That is why American art is, on the whole, boring. They want to start from nothing. I understand their position: they are trying to create a new culture and identity. But why try to be so limited?'

Even though Bacon loved to work in chaos, his *métier* was to put an order on the disorder in his work. He had tried occasionally to clean up Reece Mews, but it was impossible for him. 'I live in squalor,' he chose to explain. 'The woman who cleans is not allowed to touch the studio. Besides I *use* the dust – I set it like pastel.' Chaos bred the images and textures he sought, although inspiration only came from regular work, and he painted nearly all the time. He did try to have a beautifully tidy studio in Roland Gardens nearby, but it was a disaster. Although it had the most perfect light and he fitted it with curtains and carpets, he made it too grand. He felt 'absolutely castrated in the place', and he had to give it away to a friend and only make occasional visits there. There was no hope of ever painting in such eunuch splendour.

His paintings at the end of the 'seventies were heralded by a rare triptych, painted over four years between 1974 and 1977, not executed in his usual frenzy. Two large heads, similar to those on either side of his Promethean painting of the same period, bracket a naked kneeling figure, turning away in a pool of purple shadow. A great arc of beach seems to reach across all three panels while on the right and left, two men are raised on wooden ironing-boards and entwine themselves around dark umbrellas rather than sunbathe on deck chairs. Two distant riders on the strand, inspired by Degas, were added as an afterthought. The whole composition appears as the artist's memory of holidays in the South of France, and as a tribute to Degas and Picasso in his sequence of Dinard bathers.

That homage was continued in 'Painting, 1978', in which a naked figure again uses a foot to turn a key in the latch, although the contorted shape with a seeming weight on its shoulder also derives as much from Muybridge's studies as from those at Dinard. The straining toes appear to unlock the door to a stairway, for two red arrows point to the head and shoulders of a man descending and to a discarded and illegible newspaper, announcing something he has left behind him. 'Study for Portrait' and 'Seated Figure' of the previous year repeat the message that there is no message. Beneath pale male shapes slouched with legs akimbo in high chairs, discarded paperbacks and newsprint float ignored in puddles of shadows. 'Figure Writing Reflected in a Mirror' of 1976 had already shown the mirror image turning its back on the blobs of letters that the man seated at the desk was scrawling, while 'Figure in Movement' of that same year had expressed a rare disgust at homosexual love, a cow's head staring at a thrashing lonely figure caught in an orange circle within a cage, his buttocks duplicated and ringed in a hopeless passion for no one there.

Three years later, however, 'Triptych – Studies of the Human Body' showed that Bacon was very much back in the business of love. On either side of the violent coupling of two men in the centre, two masculine figures in underpants recline on raised boards. They are descended from the nude sculptures of Day and Evening that face each other on the tombs of Giuliano and Lorenzo de' Medici in the Florentine family chapel created by Michelangelo, whose male drawings were the greatest things in existence for Bacon. This is not grandeur borrowed to show squalor, it is a passion for the body enclosing the daemon of the sexual urge. A bloody gash opens a wound in the figure representing Day, while Evening is encircled as if trapped in hoops. The ferocity of the love-play in the centre is also ringed and smeared, and the teeth of the lower figure are bared in a howl of sensation. Discarded pages of books and papers again trail out of the picture, meaningless even in the Letraset print that Bacon sometimes used. The whole effect against the bright orange background is one of sensual pleasure and pain, regarded with Olympian detachment by time and an ideal of human beauty.

Passion for one man and for the act of love had revived in Bacon at the age of seventy. When he was asked why there were so many violent couplings of two men in his paintings, he replied that he was not really a conversational artist. There was very little conversation in sex, it cut out the words – rather as he represented the leftover newspaper and pages beneath the beds of his lovers. Most couplings were fairly violent. Ejaculation was violent. He painted what he felt about homosexual love, but he did not know how violent it looked to other people. If it looked like the act of animals, humans were animals, part of animal life. That is what he saw and sensed and showed. 'I just like men,' he once said. 'I like their brain. I like the quality of their flesh.'

His new and last protracted love was John Edwards, a young man from the East End, who replaced the fading image of George Dyer. As charming, but far more intelligent in the wisdom of the streets, Edwards was to become a dominant influence in the last decade of Bacon's life, along with his brothers and their friends. His father was a docker who lived in Cable Street, and Bacon found him working in a pub at the end of his Limehouse period. Rather dyslexic, Edwards was still made into the minder and photographer of Bacon's life and the main keeper of the treasures and gifts that the artist liked to shower on his friends. He satisfied Bacon's perennial instinct, which created the necessary tension in his life and his art – the raffish set against the genteel, the dealer opposed to the owner, the beginner versus the established, the outsider enraged at the system, the boy on the make depending on the generosity of the older man. As with Dyer, Bacon entered in his lengthy relationship with Edwards into the Pinteresque world of the play, *The Homecoming*, where a refined menace pervades throughout.

It was significant that in his paintings which he chose for Leiris's book on him, Bacon put in the 'Three Studies for a Portrait of John Edwards' of 1980 and 1984 soon after his carnal 'Triptych – Studies of the Human Body' and some self-portraits. With his crossed and lifted leg seated on a stool, his dark quiff of hair, his sweeping jawline and his heavily handsome face, Edwards bore a remarkable resemblance to his predecessor in Bacon's affections. Yet there was a strength of portrayal of Edwards that was rarely given to the shilly-shally of the Dyer portraits, a certain brooding stillness that bespoke a touch of respect and even fear in the painter.

The fleshiness of Bacon's idiom began to resurrect in his brush, and the fierceness, and the sense of rushing movement. 'Carcase of Meat and Bird of Prey' of 1980 revives the theme of the butcher's shop and the crucifixion of human meat suspended from a hook, while the divine vulture is equally forced by its cage to peck out the entrails. Another 'Triptych Inspired by the Oresteia of Aeschylus' of the following year recalled on the left panel the Eumenides at the base of the Cross in the early painting in the Tate Gallery. On it was a bat-like hanging beast with a gaping wound watching a trail of blood running beneath a door; in the centre, vertebrae and skull were bent back from a body into the gore of a bowl held above the buttocks below; on the right, a headless desirable male body with flesh-toned shadow was walking out into the void through a door. The whole triptych represented the furies and frenzies of the flesh. Bacon was depicting the private demons of his present passion. 'We are always hounding ourselves,' he told Hugh Davies in 1983. 'We have been made aware of this side of ourselves by Freud.' He had reverted to Greek myth to explain his human obsession.

The love of John Edwards threw up in Bacon's art even more violence and voluptuousness. He appeared twenty years younger than he was, although when this was pointed out to him, he used to reply, 'That means I am still *old*.' He painted uncharacteristic pictures of rushing motion in nature, a 'Jet of Water' and 'Water from a Running Tap', in one case throwing a bowl of grey wash over the picture to achieve the effect in his personal form of action painting. He seemed full of a terrible energy, a consuming sensation for living as well as for working. His pattern of reaction between hazard and order, painting and playing, circumstance and control, was eased by his concentrated affection. And this necessary tension within the artist was to be reduced to a philosophy that would satisfy him for the rest of his life.

12

To Define the Undefinable

> He commanded where he spoke, and had his judges angry and pleased at his devotion. No man had their affections more in his power. The fear of every man that heard him was lest he should make an end.
>
> Ben Jonson on Francis Bacon,
> Lord Verulam, Viscount St. Albans

As he aged, Francis Bacon became more like his great Jacobean ancestor and namesake, the philosopher and essayist. Cogently and clearly, he could tell his critics exactly what he was trying to do. He related his work and his life to his thought as well as his fortune. As the playwright Ben Jonson wrote of the original Francis Bacon, 'The fear of every man that heard him was lest he should make an end.' His descendant also achieved a command of language and of paint. In that definition of what he did, in 'the matter of fact' that he now called his pictures, he had been helped by the inquiring and sceptical interviews of English art critics, particularly David Sylvester and John Russell and Hugh Davies. But his articulate presentation of himself was refined by the rationalism and analysis of the culture he most admired. Michel Leiris, and now Gilles DeLeuze, gave him a French conceptual framework for his every intention, however far his reliance on luck and the unconscious affected his actual execution of a work of art.

Leiris had a personal sympathy for Bacon, while DeLeuze applied to the *oeuvre* of the painter only the full rigour of his methodology. His introduction to his book, published in Paris in 1985, stated that

Bacon's pictures would be considered in an order that led to a general logic of sensation. The conclusion of this logical process would be a theory of sensation through colours. Each aspect could also serve as a theme in a particular sequence in the history of painting. Starting with the circle and the track, DeLeuze referred to the circles and cubes and bars of rails and arches of sofas that enclosed each of Bacon's figures in isolation, to avoid narration or illustration. Yet there was a *rapport* between the figures in a triptych, what the artist called 'matters of fact'. Yet what facts surrounded each lonely shape? The answer was lively, uniform, and immobile blocks of colour with the function of creating structure and space. The very shadows were thin and hard and seized the Figure. As Bacon himself said, he tried even to make the shadows as *present* as the figures themselves. The three elements in his painting, the material structure and the circular contour and the set-up of the image were countered by the flow of the brush. As André Bazin had written of the art and movement of Jacques Tati, it consisted 'of destroying the precise by the precise'.

Modern painting had to seize the Figure from the figurative. For Bacon, even his hero Velázquez had been too close to figurative art because he had not had the benefit of photographs, and because painting was still linked somewhat to religious feeling. Now painting was an atheistic game. In a world clogged with instant images, the modern artist approaching the white canvas found it already full of clichés of the past that had to be erased. But the games which the artist had to play were not spectator sports. The voyeurs and photographers and passers-by in Bacon's triptychs were witnesses, as were the painted photographs on the walls or heads set on plinths. In that function, these silent witnesses were like those in Kafka and Beckett. To eliminate any sense of the spectator, the Figure adopted 'a singular athleticism' and was often enclosed in a cylinder to exclude any viewer. The Figure was the source of intense movement, to escape both from the trap of the background and from the flesh itself. That motion was a spasm as in 'Figure at a Washbasin' of 1976, when the male nude was stuck to the taps, abject, trying to escape through the plughole, pouring out newsprint. These spasms represented ejaculation and vomiting and shitting and screaming.

38 'Man in a Cap' by Francis Bacon, 1941–42. An unfinished picture painted in his cottage in Petersfield during the War.

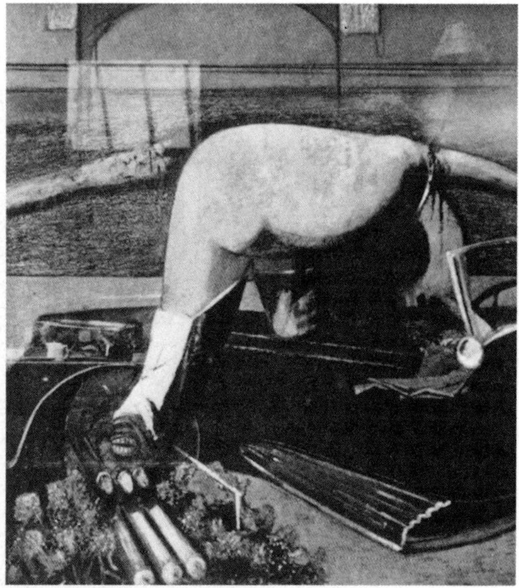

39 'Figure Getting Out of a Car' by Francis Bacon, 1939–40 and 1946. A rare case of the artist overpainting, also influenced by Hitler at Nuremberg and images of the War.

40 'Figure in Landscape' by Francis Bacon, 1945. Painting of Eric Hall asleep in the Park.

41 Francis Bacon at the age of fifty.

42 'Figure Study II' by Francis Bacon, 1945–46.

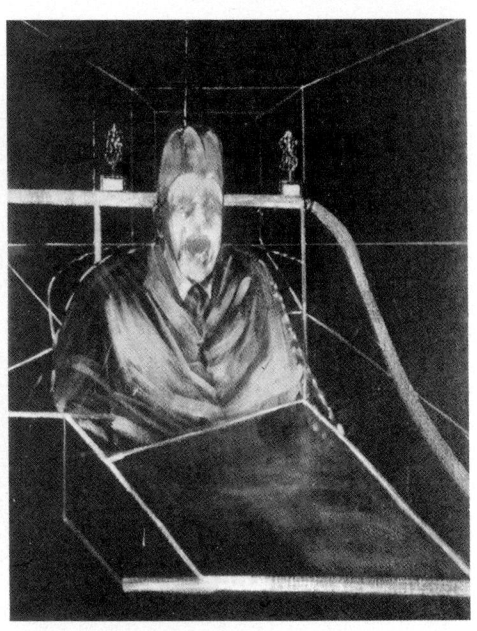

43 'Study for Portrait VII' by Francis Bacon, 1953.

44 'Paralytic Child Walking on All Fours (from Muybridge)' by Francis Bacon, 1961.

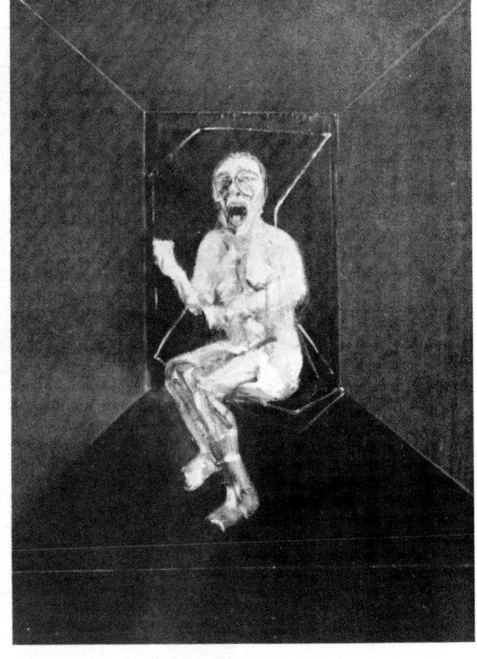

45 'Study for the Nurse in the Film *Battleship Potemkin*' by Francis Bacon, 1957.

46 'Man with Dog' by Francis Bacon, 1953.

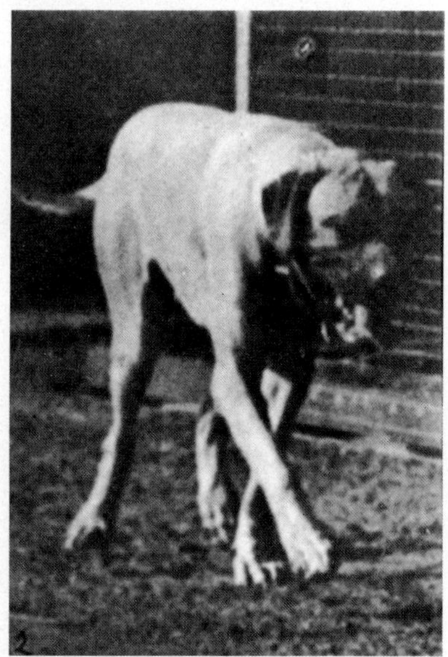

47 'Dread Trotting' from Eadweard Muybridge's *Animals in Motion*.

48 'Men Wrestling' by Eadweard Muybridge.

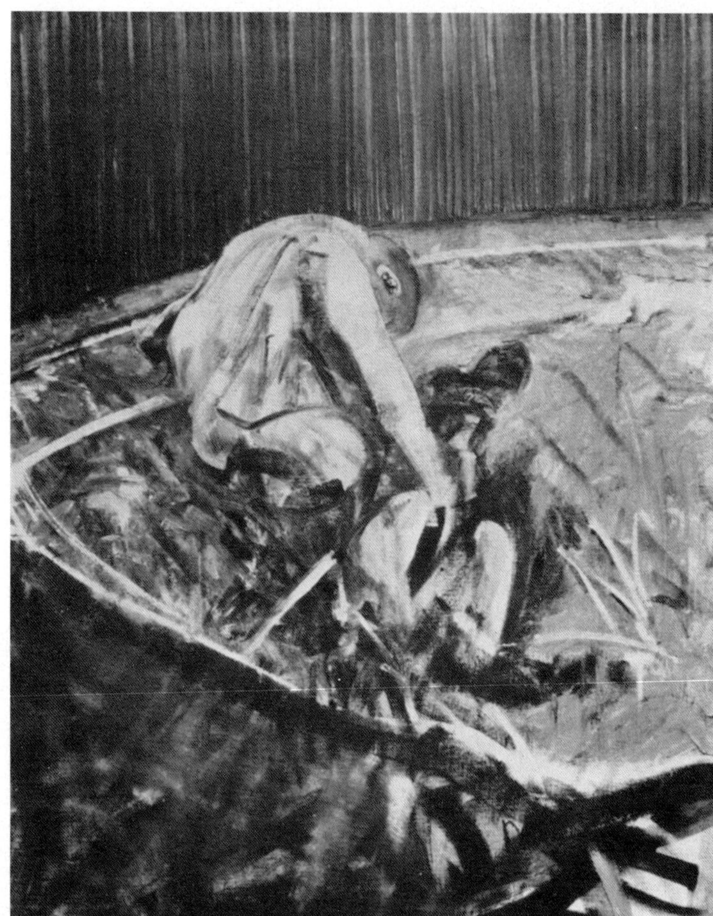

49 'Figures in a Landscape' by Francis Bacon, 1956–57.

50 Lunch at Wheeler's (from left): Timothy Behrens, a financier of the Hanover Gallery, Lucian Freud, Francis Bacon, Frank Auerbach and Michael Andrews.

51 Andrew Sinclair in the ruins of Francis Bacon's studio at 80 Narrow Street, Limehouse.

52 Francis Bacon's studio after rebuilding.
53 The view of the River Thames.

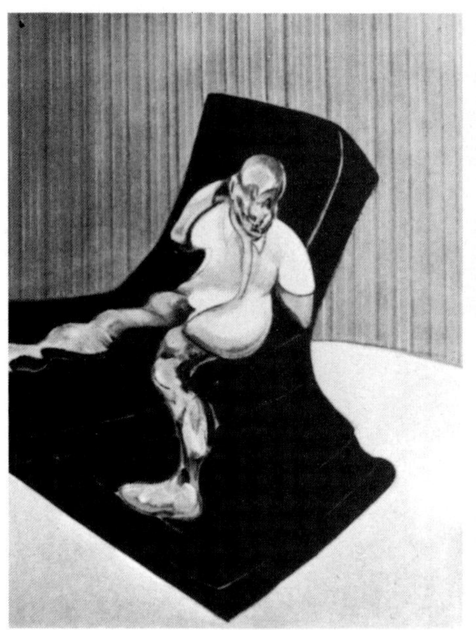

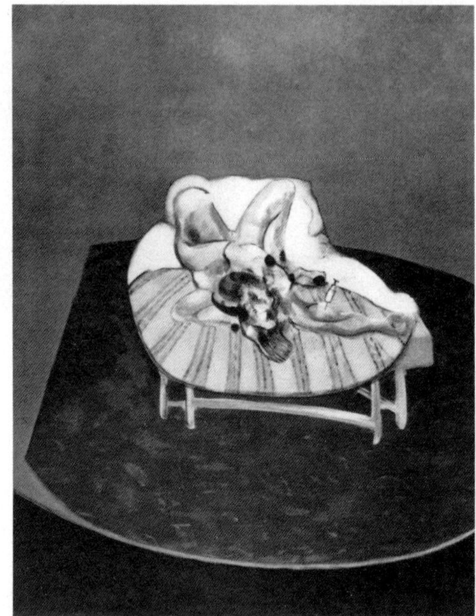

54 'Seated Figure on Couch' by Francis Bacon, 1963.

55 'Lying Figure with Hypodermic Syringe' by Francis Bacon, 1963.

56 Francis Bacon and William Burroughs.

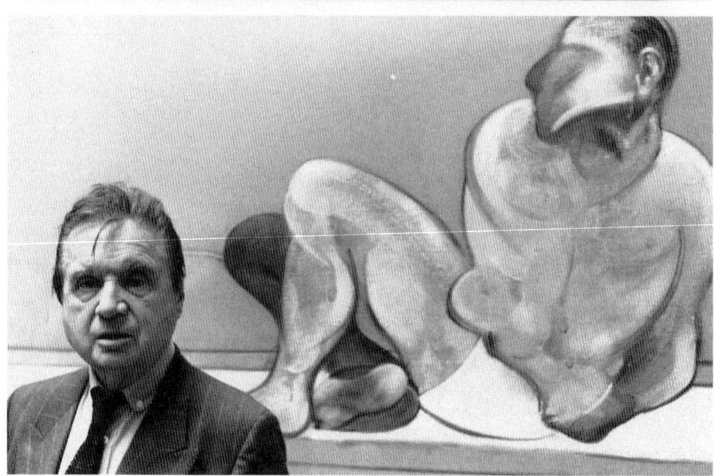

57 Francis Bacon in 1985.

58 & 59 Francis Bacon in his studio, Reece Mews, London.

60 Francis Bacon at Roald Dahl's house, Great Missenden, Buckinghamshire, 1984.

61 Francis Bacon and Barry Joule.

62 Francis Bacon on the London Underground shortly before his death.

The body was trying to escape through its organs, the mouth and other orifices.

As a portraitist, Bacon painted heads, not faces. The head was a dependency of the body, which represented the animal in man, a pig or dog or beast. Bacon unmade the face and sprang the head from the features, using the indeterminate zone between the human and the animal. He was more interested in the meat and the flesh of the body than the bones, which only served as a spatial structure. Meat for Bacon represented his pity for the long butchery between the English and the Irish as it represented for Soutine the sorrows of Jewish history. The animal carcasses were the colour of vulnerable living flesh and were imbued with suffering. The painter was certainly the butcher and his shop was the church, as the hanging meat was the body of Christ. Only in the butcher's shop was Bacon a religious painter. Generally, in treating the head as the body, he removed the skull and made the features rather boneless. He particularly admired the quality of Rembrandt's last self-portrait, now exhibited at Aix-en-Provence, which showed only the decaying flesh with black holes for eyes. In this bloody view of humanity, the body could but escape from the screaming mouth as from an artery.

The ways to avoid narrative or illustrative painting were by the abstract or by sensation, as Cézanne did. The Hegelian idea of sensing and feeling was translated by Cézanne into how to paint, how to use spontaneity and temperament and instinct and the nervous system and the vital moment to create a picture. He taught the Impressionists that sensation did not lie in the play of light and colour, but in the feeling for the form of an apple. Sensation was what was painted, not what was represented. It was what was lived while the sensation was experienced. Painting that sensation linked Cézanne to Bacon, and sensation was also the mistress of distortion. Every series of triptych by Bacon showed variants of sensation, which occasionally accumulated or coagulated.

And yet Bacon eliminated the sensational. He had finally to renounce in his pictures the violence of Ireland and Nazism and the Crucifixion. In fact, the greatest violence in his works was when the figure was seated or squatting alone, suffering no torture except from the power of the paint. This was pictorial violence in its proper sense; as Bacon himself said, there was nothing to be seen in the violence of painting which had anything to do with the violence of war. He sought the sensation that would best occupy the flesh. He found it in the sensation of movement, from figures seized at odd moments on strange journeys, as in his Van Gogh series. He tried to achieve a unity of all the senses, as in his portraits of Isabel Rawsthorne. Above all, he tried to capture a vital rhythm in his visual sensation, as Cézanne had. But he sought that reality by artifice, while Cézanne had sought it in nature.

Like Artaud, Bacon also looked for intense bodies without organs, transported from the flesh by nerves and feelings. Like Burroughs, he saw the organs as indeterminate and transferable. The mouth could become an anus or a wound. Like Gauguin with his 'insatiable eye', Bacon wanted to discover the material reality of the body with a system of lines and colours. To do that, he had to operate on Klee's formula, 'not to render the visible, but to make visible'. He had to show the invisible forces that affected the body such as pressure and inertia, weight and attraction, gravity and growth. Force was the condition of sensation. Cézanne's genius had shown the slippage of mountains, the growing of apples, the thermal push of landscape, while Van Gogh had pictured the turbulence of all living things. Bacon's genius lay in seeking out the forces oppressing his heads and figures, their agitation under stress and pressure, their dilation and contraction, their swelling and withdrawal, rather like the forces affecting a space traveller in a capsule. In painting a scream, Bacon showed all the energies that had expelled it, a cry at not being. Although mentally pessimistic, he was nervously optimistic, and so he painted the violence of the sensation of the scream, not the terror of it. With Beckett, he spoke for a very intense life, not for a belief in death or horror. Their human figures were unconquerable. They endured by their insistence and their presence, even when threatened by mutilation or failure or fall. Bacon was the detector of the forces that made life work.

Under the action of these forces, sensation passed through different levels and degrees. If two sensations confronted each other, they were treated differently, but both were matter of fact. 'What is painted is the sensation.' Yet the images of two men copulating could unify. Bodies could crush together under the vigour of the coupling. This did not contradict Bacon's principle of isolation, because there was a single sensation linking the two figures. In his triptychs, indeed, Bacon implied no progression and no story. They only incarnated at times a common fact for the separate figures. Bacon particularly admired Cézanne's 'Bathers' because the figures were united on the canvas, but it did not have a narrative. The ancient religious triptychs, indeed, had been mobile paintings, with shutters that opened for the viewers, and that is why Bacon inserted his witnesses in his triptychs and included forced movement and a circular organisation of space.

DeLeuze began to run into difficulties when trying to find an order in Bacon's triptychs. He first saw in them three rhythms and three figures, and then rhythms as witnesses, and finally active and passive rhythms. But he had to admit that Bacon had the freedom to combine these elements as he chose – if they existed, that is. He also saw in the triptychs forces of isolation and deformation and dissipation, held together by a unity of colours. This led DeLeuze to find principles in the triple paintings: the maximum unity of light and colour contrasted with the maximum division of the figures. That was a lesson from Rembrandt: light engendered rhythmic people – whoever these were.

DeLeuze was faced with the problem that Bacon had so often told his English critics how much his paintings depended on luck or accident. The Frenchman countered with the assertion that no painter ever stood before a white canvas. He had many things in his head, around him, within the studio. All were present potentially on the canvas. The artist did not fill the blank surface, he emptied it, uncluttered it, dusted it off. He did not reproduce a model, he had *données* or gifts of ideas. He had done his preparatory work well before he picked up a brush. He must rid himself of all the figurative clichés, such as photographs and cinema images, although he could transform them as Cézanne had transformed the apple into the essence of the apple. Had not D.H. Lawrence written that Cézanne's apple was more important than Plato's ideas? The painter must find the real form and content of things, he must discover a true look beyond photography. His battle was against the cliché with every painting that he started.

Although Bacon depended on photographs, he thought they had no aesthetic value. This is why he liked Muybridge's studies of motion and manuals on radiography. These captured the happening, the inner nerves, the fact. This radical hostility to the photograph stopped him from incorporating it in his paintings – as Hockney did with his Polaroids of swimming-pools. When Bacon painted a camera, he made it look like the head of a prehistoric beast or an elephant gun. DeLeuze ignored the painted mug shots, which Bacon sometimes stuck in his triptychs, and became even more troubled and rational in explaining Bacon's reliance on luck and accident. This seemed a sentimental attitude to DeLeuze, who considered that the artist must have precise rules of rejection of his failed pictures. He might talk of luck to his friends, but he did not seem able to understand its precise role. He had thought the picture through before he used some luck to paint it.

'On the canvas', DeLeuze wrote, 'is an order of equal or unequal probabilities'. Accidental strokes of the brush might liberate some of these possibilities, but they did not signify all of them. Anyway, they were only the result of the hand of the painter destroying the cliché. They were manual marks which made the Figure spring out into a visual image. In that sense, luck could be seen as a certain type of act or choice. For Bacon, luck was not separable from the possibility of using it. It was *manipulated luck* as distinct from conceived or seen possibilities.

Bacon had a concept before he began to paint a picture, even if the concept changed during the painting of it. The hazard of the brush-stroke did not create a picture, which was made by the whole act of painting. All the brush did was to 'extract the improbable Figure from the ensemble of all figurative probabilities'. There was even a science of probability, and Bacon had stacked up those probabilities before he began to paint. He used his choice of probabilities to extract one of them by manipulating his brush in the art of painting. And so he made a picture.

Through Bacon's obstinacy, DeLeuze wrote, and through the incomprehension of his English interviewers, he declared that luck and accident created his pictures. But he did really know what he wanted to do. He did not always know how to make it happen. He relied on the 'chance' of brush-strokes to achieve his intent. Yet that was not the problem of the modern painter, who did not have to enter the canvas so much as get out of the cliché. The 'chance' of the brush-stroke gave him that possibility. He had to use cunning and repetition and prudence to conquer the cliché and each painting was a new struggle. But it was the only way to the Figure.

This brilliant denial of Bacon's insistence on his use of luck in painting was immediately followed by DeLeuze stating that we did not listen enough to what painters said. They declared that the painter was already *in* the canvas, before he began work. Admittedly, Bacon did not do sketches as other painters did before starting on a picture. All the same, he must do invisible, silent, intense preparation, which led him on to hysterical action – actually Bacon himself spoke of this process as long periods of daydreaming. But to DeLeuze, Bacon's use of chance – putting dust on paintings, or using the magnified skin of a rhinoceros or a portrait, or throwing paint to suggest a jet of water – these were mental choices, although done by hand. The fingers might seem independent as they used Brillo pads and cashmere sweaters, scrubbing brushes and cotton wool, rags and sponges, paint-tube caps and slop buckets as well as artists' brushes, but they only worked under the direction and organisation of the sovereign eye. That was the act of painting. A picture could fail twice over visually or manually. But in creating a painting, the artist introduced 'possibilities of fact'.

The painter entered chaos and tried to leave it. Abstract art did so with codes, abstract expressionism with a geometry of the canvas, and Bacon with a diagram in his head and a logic of sensation, mainly of colours. He followed Cézanne in creating a sensation of endurance and clarity. Cézanne had told the Impressionists to 'treat nature by the cylinder, the sphere, the cone, all put in perspective': to this Bacon added the cube. It was an analogy with geometry, and painting was *the* art of analogy. Cézanne's chief work was to create a modulation of colour. By doing so, he 'realised' sensation. And so did Bacon, using a similar method to pass in a picture from the possibility of the fact to the fact of the final work.

There were huge differences between Bacon and Cézanne, but also correspondences. Bacon was the heir of the post-Cubism of Picasso and Braque, and this was evident in his use of the junctions between the vertical and the horizontal and of slabs of colour as space. He also employed the deformation of the naked body rather than Cézanne's emphasis on form in clothes. But he did push to the extreme the use of painting as a language of analogy, he did employ cylinders and geometrical shapes to suggest volume and distance, and above all, he relied on lines and colours to constitute the Figure.

DeLeuze now stated that each great painter in his manner resumed the history of painting. Bacon admired Egyptian art. He liked its flatness and its contours, the form and the background on the same plan, the *presence* of the Figure, and the precision of the work. He had even wanted to do sculpture himself, but he had discarded the idea. What he did was to expand Cézanne's systems of colour sequences and modulations – Lawrence Gowing had written on these as well as on Bacon. Bacon was not eclectic, but he stopped at points in the history of painting, at Egyptian art and Grünewald, at Rembrandt and Velázquez, at Van Gogh and Degas and Picasso, to recreate them in his own way. To Egyptian formalism, for instance, he added the fall, the accident, and catastrophe. He even added to his art the eye of the cyclone of Turner. And he particularly used colour to escape from the classical past. For him, light was time and colour was space. It was Cézanne who had put order back into colour by following the succession of the spectrum, while Van Gogh had vaunted himself to his brother Theo as an 'arbitrary colourist'. After him and Gauguin – much criticised by Cézanne – Bacon was one of the greatest of colourists. Indeed, he had left his sombre period with his paintings of Van Gogh on the road in the South of France.

The three elements in Bacon's painting, the structure and the Figure and the contour, all converged in a unity of colour. The space in his pictures was crossed by large washes of colour. The triptychs were held together by bright monochromes of orange, red, ochre, golden-yellow, green, violet and pink, also by curvilinear contours. These were the linking bands of colour and hue. Yet the counter-pointed figures were full of the broken tones of blue and red, the colours of the flesh. Often their shadows were black or lively, as real as the bodies. Colour and structure gave way to colour and force, which would subordinate the contour. But in the end, both the Figure and the contour communicated and converged in the colour.

It was not enough to say that the eye judged and the hand operated. There was a rich *rapport* between the two in every great artist. Yet in Bacon's case, even if there was occasional manual insubordination, the picture was prefabricated. It pre-existed in his mind. He only used the hand and the brush to take a shape out of nature, called the Figure. Rarely did he change from one concept to another, although in his early 'Figure in a Landscape' of 1945–46, he did begin to paint a bird alighting in a field and end with a man asleep under an umbrella. Even then, his mind released a more profound image than the senses could discern. His mental picture or diagram allowed him to pass from the bird to the umbrella. It was the agent of transformation, aided by the accident of the brush. The mind and reason controlled through a logic of sensation expressed in a convergence through colours. So Bacon passed from the possibility of fact to the pictorial fact.

DeLeuze had defined the undefinable. He had demonstrated how French logic could cage the hazard in Bacon's art rather as the artist himself put his cylinder and cubes round his figures to confine them inside the canvas. Both Leiris and DeLeuze categorised Bacon to himself. Largely, he accepted their rationalisations in terms of the French clarity of expression, which he so much admired. Their essays on his works were a *reductio ad mentem* of all other art criticism. But Bacon did not accept these French analyses when he was speaking to the English with their pragmatic values, nor did they apply to the facts of his own life, although they might to many of the facts of his art. Rather like King Lear in the play which he most valued by Shakespeare, Bacon both played the Philosopher to the French in the manner of his great Jacobean namesake, and the Fool to the English. Across the Channel, his art was more logical. In London, his art was more lucky.

The fact was that his art was logic and luck. As DeLeuze had written, the problem for the artist was to pluck order out of chaos. Each picture was a new battle every time it was started: as Heraclitus had stated, the sun was new every day. Bacon did actually allow accident to make up part of his paintings – the golden shower of a companion for the night, the dust from the studio floor, the rain-drops through the leaky skylight. But these contributions of chance had to pass the scrutiny of his waking eye. As he told David Sylvester, it was 'really a continuous question of the fight between accident and criticism'. But for DeLeuze, sight was sovereign, whatever the slip of the hand or natural causes. Through the optic nerves, the mind was the final judge of when a picture was complete, whatever happenstance affected its composition. Yet even so, in Bacon's ironic and impish cast of mind, some accidents and spatters were allowed to remain on the final works just because they seemed appropriate as the marks of that particular moment.

The French rationalists also discounted Bacon's statements as late as the 'sixties that he was trying to paint a history of the past thirty years and after that, an autobiography. Influenced by the fashionable theories of Structuralism and Deconstruction, the Parisians put little emphasis on the influence of social or personal history on an artist's work. The paintings existed as they were. It was the job of the critic to make them more real to the viewer. So DeLeuze talked of the logic of sensation, the intense feeling of the painter which he translated onto the canvas. But Bacon's most gripping sensations were in his personal life, and he was particularly affected by George Dyer's death in Paris, even painting a triptych of that tragedy which was totally an autobiographical narrative. There was no logic in that sensation of grief. There might be a logic in his use of colours and contours and spaces and figures, but he often said that the sensation of love for another man interfered with his painting and with the sensation he felt for his art. The personal feeling did not always translate into an emotion on the canvas.

Equally, Bacon's continual stress on the power of chance and instinct in his painting, his insistence that his original concept for a picture was mutated by accident or brush-stroke or sponge or rag, these assertions were substantiated by his way of work and life. The hodge-podge of photographs tacked up on boards on his wall, the pages ripped from art books, the clutter of paint-tubes and old clothes on the dirty studio floor, this chaos of facts was seized upon during the act of painting and changed the final work through whatever came to finger or eye, from the photograph of a man with a monkey to a handful of dust. While Bacon's mind was logical, his thought was affected not only by the débris of his surroundings, but by his health and nervous system. He had high blood-pressure as well as asthma, he suffered from bad hangovers after his drinking bouts, and he took too many barbiturates to make himself sleep, so that rising each morning made him feel like a daily Lazarus escaping a recent death. In the sensation and the act of painting, he did truly become alive, and in a way, he exorcised the excesses of his life through his work. But the night before and the drugs and his dodgy health entered into his paintings as well as his logic and his overall eye of judgement, which pronounced the final sentence – to preserve or to hack to bits.

Except for a brief reference to Proust and memory, DeLeuze also seemed to ignore the considerable influence on Bacon's painting of the visual storehouse of images, which the artist had amassed since his childhood in Ireland. Bacon admitted that he did paint from the unconscious and from the pictures retained in his mind's eye from his past life. He thought of the unconscious as a deep sea, which he knew nothing about; but he hoped the most wonderful images would emerge from it. In a sense, the sweep of the paint-brush was to him the taste of the *petite madeleine* that led Proust back to the scenes of his childhood. Bacon called the result of that unconscious recreation a matter of luck, although the final outcome was a matter of fact. It was similar to Samuel Taylor Coleridge's claim that 'Xanadu' was dashed off at the end of an opium dream and interrupted for ever by the arrival of the man from Porlock. The brilliant study of him, *The Road to Xanadu*, by John Livingstone Lowes, conclusively proved that he had been hoarding in his mind the phrases and visions of the poem for many years. It was the result of wide reading and deep experience. It was so with Bacon. His seventy years of personal wondering and wandering, of moving and staring, allied with his extraordinarily retentive memory for images, gave him a picture library that sprang out of the canvas with each sweep of his brush. As with a drowning man, his whole life was there before his eyes, standing every morning in front of a blank surface. He could call on the multitude of signs and figures that he had laid away to drive any cliché from his composition.

Furthermore, Bacon used Egyptian and Greek myths as well as narrative in some of his most powerful portraits and triptychs, and he made conscious allusions to drama and to poetry. Overtly, he brought up the cruelty of the Crucifixion and the power of the papacy and the spectre of Nazism. He might in later life say that there was no story or message in his paintings, but he knew that there had been, and he continued to paint recognisable symbols of myths into his triptychs into his old age. He preferred to discount what he had done in view of the brilliant analyses of his rational work given to him by his French critics.

The greatest gift of DeLeuze to Bacon was the illumination of his connection with Cézanne. Four years after the book was published, an exhibition of *Cézanne: The Early Years 1859–1872* was mounted at the Royal Academy in London, and these curiously obsessive early paintings riveted Bacon, who visited the show many times, scrutinising the pictures with his eagle-eyed vision. As Sam Hunter wrote, Bacon relished 'the strangely unfinished, touching images of Cézanne's family and intimate circle of friends and his violently erotic inventions, with their fresh, contemporary spirit and vital handling. The combination of evident gaucherie and expressive power within a once-derided system of figuration that is now recognised as clearly original particularly moved Bacon.' He had learned of Cézanne's system of colours, reminiscent of the therapeutic use of the spectrum invented for the Australian wounded soldiers in the First World War by his original mentor, Roy de Maistre. Although his use of his palette and particularly of acrylic paint to cover large areas did seem to emerge from his own imagination, Bacon also relished the link to the radical Cézanne, perceived by French logic.

What the Parisians did not understand was one of the few English conventions which Bacon had adopted. This most intelligent artist tried to escape from the pressures of his incessant mind in the company of the amiable and the criminal. With his raffish friends, he said what any Anglo-Irish gentleman would, particularly if he were an artist. He did not really work at it or think it out. It was all a matter of luck. When someone said in a Soho pub that Bacon was a painter, and then he was asked to paint somebody else's house, he merely said that he was busy and did not say he was an artist. Indeed, he compared the first marks on a canvas to painting a wall. The brush made the dash, it had the vitality. Unless that primal mark was right, the wall and the picture would be lost.

Conversely, to the international art Establishment, Bacon could be extremely rigid and precise about the intention and execution of his painting, particularly after his education from his French critics. He used to quote DeLeuze in order to present himself merely as a maker of images and to deny any relationship between the figures in his triptychs. He would talk in 1985 of creating images which were 'a concentration of reality and a shorthand of sensation'. He had 'to abbreviate into intensity'. Equally, to guard his refusal to explain his work, he might say that he did not try to read it. 'I only know what it means to me formally.' A painting was a visual shock without a story. There was nothing in it 'except what people want to read into it'.

Taught by the French to leave the message of a picture of his to the viewer's judgement, Bacon was not duplicitous when he told the English interviewers and his Soho friends that he threw paint on pictures, and how they turned out was a matter of luck. His triptychs just happened to join up, and his instinct told him when they were finished. This was his understated answer to British people, who hated the serious or the uppity, and who found logical analysis 'boring'. As he spoke and knew the idioms of both countries, he attuned his responses to his hearers. In England he did as he had been taught in Ireland. 'Speak as you're spoken to . . . Don't put on airs . . . Above all, don't be clever.' In France, he did the opposite, explaining the logic of his acts of painting. Both statements were true for a painter always hoping that his battle against the blank canvas, his endless skirmishes between concept and chance, would work out by design and instinct.

He had several languages – logical, dismissive, exact, witty, wise and camp. They were all different ways of expressing the same thing. He tried to make a game of his life as well as of his art, and he played it to the full, but always in pursuit of the fact. That was what he called the real or the truth. And the truth was that no logical analysis could remove the accident or the hazard from his living or his method of working. He knew that and said so in England; but it did not suit the acute reasoning powers of the French critics. Both their victim and their exploiter, Bacon redefined his intentions largely in their terms; but he could not deny the gambling streak in what he did.

Curiously enough, DeLeuze referred to Bacon betting on three roulette tables at once and added that he painted his triptychs in the same way, but he did not follow up on such a brilliant analogy. And on the back of his book on Bacon, he printed the strips of Photomat images, which Bacon knocked off to serve as the haphazard models for his self-portraits. It was an odd postscript to a thesis on *Francis Bacon: The Logic of Sensation*. The logic of Bacon's painting was intermittent: his life was wayward, but he loved those who would give it and him a convincing coherence. As he now said, admitting his contradictions, he believed in 'a deep ordered chaos' in his work, plucked out by luck.

13
A Deep Ordered Chaos

Costly followers are not to be liked; lest while a man maketh his train longer, he make his wings shorter. I reckon to be costly, not them alone which charge the purse, but which are wearisome and importune in suits.

'Of Followers and Friends'
by Francis Bacon, Lord Verulam,
Viscount St. Albans

In the 'eighties, the ageing Bacon, now in his seventies but looking twenty years younger, continued to defy time and chaos. He did achieve a deep order in his work and an 'ebullient despair' in his life. The reason for his curious happiness and unusual sense of security lay in his relationship with John Edwards. It was the role of an old master, who had finally defined his art to himself, teaching a pupil, whose animal strength and quick Cockney wit made him an admirable model and pupil. It was the reversal of the role which Bacon had once played with Roy de Maistre. With the death of John Deakin, Edwards took over the role of Bacon's photographer, and if he did not pose in the flesh for the artist, he provided the snapshots of the desired subject matter, man or beast.

The triptych of John Edwards which Bacon painted in 1984 already showed an increasing tenderness for him. It was one of the few portraits that the artist thought had really worked. In some of the previous ones, Edwards had been fairly deformed, even though Bacon thought that they all looked like him. Increasingly, in the 'Study for Portrait of John Edwards' of 1986 and 1988, the stocky and rounded muscle of the figure is described in its beauty, and the buccaneering face left undistorted in forceful profile or full-face. In his fresh-found certainty, Bacon was depicting the man most close to him without wavering or exaggeration. It was reality; it was the fact.

A new country life was set up for them, a looking for memories worthy of Proust. As a young man, Bacon had often stayed with his first cousin Pamela Firth, now Mrs Matthews, the wife of an American magazine editor, at Cavendish Hall in Suffolk. There he had dressed as a flapper for a fancy dress ball and had declared his preferences and intentions. Now he moved back, buying 'The Croft' outside Long Melford nearby, a gamekeeper's cottage that had been gentrified with mock-Tudor beams and a garage. Soon he was to purchase as a country studio the rear of the old village school, a Victorian redbrick copy of Melford Hall, the great house of the village, which now belonged to the National Trust. It was a curious reversion to time past for Bacon, trying to recover some happy moments of his adolescence at aristocratic Cavendish Hall, yet intruding on the close-knit Suffolk society with the Edwards family from the East End of London. For John's brothers and their friends would follow Bacon up to Long Melford, until they became the largest landowners in the village and wealthier than the Firths had ever been. On the proceeds of the sale of a Bacon painting or two, this rising Cockney family would outdo the heirs of the Anglo-Irish Ascendancy, who had fled the troubles back to their homeland.

For Bacon was becoming a millionaire. The prices of his paintings were soaring in the boom years of the 'eighties. The triptych of George Dyer, which he had painted after his lover's death in Paris in 1971, was sold ten years later at Christie's in New York for $350,000. Five years on, another memorial portrait of Dyer clasping a lavatory pedestal, 'Seated Figure' of 1978, was sold by Christie's in New York for $935,000, turning Bacon into Britain's most expensive living artist, outpricing even the works of the late Henry Moore. Although these huge sums of money might benefit some of Bacon's costly followers, who had received gifts of his work, the artist himself remained totally indifferent to the fortune that was coming his way. As long as Marlborough Fine Art looked after his business affairs and kept his pockets full of rolls of fifty-pound notes, he went on living in the same style as he had for the past thirty years. He hated the growing commercialism of art, and he thought those who bought modern pictures were more influenced by money than by good painting. He said he was surprised his paintings sold at all, as he painted them for himself, and they were about his personal life. He had always thought he would have to take some other kind of job to paint at all – but that was the luck of his life. He could live off his obsession, what he tried to do.

Luck played less of a part in his philosophy and his life in his old age. A certain definition was creeping upon him. Although he remained a nihilist, he said that his nature was optimistic. Something exciting was going to turn up. He remained greedy for life and as an artist. Anything he could not get by logic, he wanted chance to give him. He loved food and drink and the company of friends, the good things of the moment. All artists were greedy for themselves. 'I just take what I can find.' This was not uncommon among artists. 'I think all people who create are like that. Painting is about nothing more than what it does to me.'

Yet even if Bacon believed in nothing, that 'we are born and we die and that's it', he was profoundly optimistic about nothing. Existing each day made him optimistic. His impulse was his life, drifting from bar to bar, and working as if he would live for ever. He insisted now that he was not tormented. He did not worry about life and had no sense of sin. He was lucky in that way, but he had not been brought up to feel guilty. Only if he tried consciously to bring harm to somebody else would he feel he had committed a sin.

Bacon might be imposing some order on the chaos around him, but he still insisted that the images he created were more than the products of his intellect. Life itself was nothing but sensation, what he felt, what happened to him. In his day dreams, he could see 'masses of flesh out of which every so often images emerged.' Although art was artificial, the intense use of the brush or whatever happened to come to hand allowed some forms to form themselves. Although occasionally the work flowed out of him, usually he painted in despair of the result and found it more helpful, because it made him take greater risks in forming radical and final shapes. The rapid movement of the brush, the manipulation of the paint and the colours, these altered the implications of the image. It was difficult working in oils. He created an image and it was changing all the time. It had to do with his instinct and his sensibility, which also veered and wavered.

That was why he painted so fiercely and rapidly, assaulting the canvas. He liked the starkness of what he did. He wanted it to give him a visual shock like a sneak attack on the senses. Even his triptychs, which appeared to have a strong unity, were painted separately and quickly. First, he could only get one large canvas at a time into his small studio. Second, he had to paint them fast so that they would achieve the sort of togetherness that the panoramic screen had in the Soho cinema which had installed it. But finally, he claimed that, whatever his methods of working on his triptychs, they just happened to join up.

With the growing influence of the Edwards family on him, Bacon began to detach himself from his artistic friends, particularly Lucian Freud and Frank Auerbach. He had always said that he felt isolated as an artist. He envied the relationship of Yeats and Eliot and Pound, all working together and having a strong influence on each other. But he had to work alone and began to resist the criticism of his English circle, although not the appreciation of his friends in France. Auerbach told Stephen Spender in March, 1982, that he no longer saw much of Francis Bacon. He did not think that they had quarrelled, but 'friendships wear out'. Spender did not want to admit that, but he also was seeing less of Bacon, although the artist had visited him in 1980 when he was in hospital with both legs in plaster, and had presented him with a case of '71 Rothschild Lafite claret. With Lucian Freud, however, there was a definite falling-out, which was to culminate in Freud's refusal to loan Bacon's early picture of two men wrestling or coupling to his second retrospective exhibition at the Tate Gallery. When Michael Wishart saw the picture still hanging in Freud's Coombe Priory in Dorset, he was reminded of Mae West's question: 'If it's all in, why wrestle?' Bacon could never understand Freud's refusal, asking Wishart why Freud was so unfriendly. Had he sold the picture? When Wishart and he went to the Freud retrospective at the Hayward Gallery, Bacon riposted by saying, 'Well, Lucian's extremely gifted, but I've never been interested in Expressionism.' The rift remained. When Wishart reported to Bacon that Freud would not see him again 'because his conversation is so repetitious', Bacon retorted that he would not see Freud again 'because his work is so repetitious'.

The breach between Bacon and Graham Sutherland had also proved irreparable. Daniel Farson gave them a drink of reconciliation in Jules Bar in Jermyn Street. As he told the story in his book *Sacred Monsters*, the two artists at first rejoiced like long-lost brothers, and Bacon invited Sutherland and his wife and Farson to dinner at Wheeler's in Old Compton Street. Something went wrong there. The mood changed. When Sutherland said with the sweetest of smiles that he had been doing some portraits and had Bacon seen any of them, his old friend replied that he had. They were 'very nice if you like the covers of *Time* magazine'. And to Michael Wishart, Sutherland wrote that he did not regret the break with Bacon: 'The association was becoming too acid and boring to support and I had my own thoughts to try to expand in peace.'

Yet Bacon was courtesy itself to his favoured collectors, whom he treated with a firm delicacy. The American financier, Donald Hess, and his wife used to meet the artist at the Connaught, where they always found him charming and intelligent and critical – and never drunk. He spoke openly of his homosexuality and urge for self-destruction. 'We all have our problems and I am an artist. Painting is how I overcome them.' As his art developed, he grew stronger. His dedication enabled him to subdue his frailties. To the Hesses, he appeared always the Anglo-Irish gentleman of his birth. But when Donald Hess telephoned Bacon to ask him if he might remove the heavy frames and glass from his paintings because they distorted the images and showed the living-room in the pictures, Bacon replied, 'But I want you and your place inside my picture. It makes you *see* my picture. If you change that frame or glass, you will never buy another picture from me.'

Bacon was equally courteous to his East End friend John Edwards, who was introduced to the habitués of the Colony Room such as Daniel Farson and George Melly, although that club was not the same after Muriel Belcher's death. But when its new owner Ian

Board was told that Soho was not what it used to be, he always replied, 'It never was.' What the club needed was the agile and commanding presence of Francis Bacon, no longer hired as its tout, but become its big spender. 'When Francis arrives', one of the regulars said, 'it's as if the place has been in darkness, and everyone suddenly becomes alive and alert and full of vitality. I've seen him do that without even opening his mouth.' But his usual restaurants were being transformed. Wheeler's in Old Compton Street became part of a chain, and L'Escargot nearby had been refurbished. Bacon still visited these old haunts, but more rarely, telling the proprietors of the freshened L'Escargot that it looked like an ice-cream parlour. The French Pub had not altered and he still went there frequently. As its proprietor Gaston Berlemont said, the customers changed, but they stayed the same. 'The crowd we have now is just a carbon copy of the same crowd that was coming in forty or fifty years ago when I was a boy. They are the same type of people. Our type. People who like life, who like to drink wine and enjoy each other's company. They themselves create an atmosphere. It's no use putting up a couple of plastic onions and saying that you're creating a French atmosphere, it doesn't work like that.'

The fame of Bacon grew faster than his train of followers. Small or large exhibitions of his work went on show in Tours and at the Galerie Maeght as well as through the donation of the Kahnweiler-Leiris collection to the Musée National d'Art Moderne in Paris. Marlborough Fine Art continued to exhibit his recent works in London and New York, and he was also represented in shows at Yale in New Haven and Chicago, in Sheffield and Edinburgh, and in Amsterdam and Lausanne. He broke through to Japan, where an exhibition travelled from Tokyo to Kyoto and Osaka and Nagoya. But the culmination of this period of work would be a second retrospective at the Tate Gallery, twenty-five years after the first, and destined to transfer to Stuttgart and Berlin, after two previous small showings in Germany at Hanover and Cologne. It was sponsored by Global Assets, a company directed by Gilbert de Botton, a married Swiss financier and art collector who would be painted by Bacon in a hotel bedroom, as if he were shot unawares by Jean-Luc Godard, whose film images were a major influence on

Bacon's efforts to capture a fugitive reality. De Botton had to produce masses of photographs for the painting, some taken at a conference, others by his son in rear view. He never knew what the portrait would look like because of Bacon's 'enormous shyness'. Finally, it showed him speaking into a mirror while adjusting his tie before pushing his rumpled shirt into his trousers. He stares through round spectacles at himself, caught in the act of dressing. His face is vivid with the effort to communicate and is without distortion except for a blackish circle below his open mouth – the shape of a microphone taken from the conference photograph of him.

Bacon's most spectacular painting of the period was one based on that of Ingres in 'Oedipus and the Sphinx'. He had always admired Ingres as one of the greatest painters of female flesh, much as he might prefer male flesh himself. In his opinion, Ingres had created some of the most sexual bodies ever made in painting. He had to have loved women's flesh to have created the figures in his 'Turkish Bath'. But his nude male Oedipus addressing the female breasts of the Sphinx was voluptuous and muscular, and the shape suggested to Bacon the image of a bull-necked thug in vest and shorts, adjusting a bloody bandage round his right leg and left foot, stuck up on an empty book-case. As Andrew Forge described the painting in his perceptive book on Francis Bacon with Dawn Ades, published in 1985 to accompany the second Tate retrospective:

> His limbs are massive, but even more massive is his short neck, a stubby cylinder nearly twice as thick as his calf. The head sprouts out of it, a flattened half-transparent knob, the sheen on jaw and cheek floating over the rounded poll as though glassy axe blows had uncovered the movement of the face against the light. The tender pink orifice of the ear is low down, at the hinge of the jaw.
>
> Sphinx and man are at opposite sides of a room. The walls are of flat cyclamen pink, the floor beige. The Sphinx is half out of the left side of the frame. Its torso is like a light urn on slender footing, its breast and the root of its wings smoothly turned. This suggestion of symmetry seems to speak of an alternative anatomy, opposite to the man's virile maimed weight. The Sphinx's neck is thick like the man's but smoothly graded like the lid of an urn in contrast to Oedipus' brown heavily modelled stump. The Sphinx is an apparition outside time. Its head is turned towards Oedipus alertly, as if

to focus its glance upon him, but its face is veiled. It is as though the face – the face of a handsome, full-lipped man – was encapsulated within the head, screened by an opalescent covering. The stare we look for is withheld.

In Ingres' painting there is a witness to the encounter with the Sphinx, a companion of Oedipus' who turns with a fearful gesture before running off down the hillside. Bacon's witness is more central. Between the two pink walls there is a door open to the darkness of the night. Set into the door is a plate glass sheet covering three quarters of the opening. Hung at the top of the glass, smashed against it, crawling up it or looking at us through it, is one of those stumped-pawed, pod-bodied chimeras that Bacon has identified as Eumenides. The body ends in a long crest or tail and a round hole – eye or anus – cleanly drilled as if by Black and Decker or bullet.

This being, too, is bloody. One could picture it as a fragment of offal thrown and stuck, half dried, to the glass. But it is avidly alive too. A white arrow points to the centre of its bloodiness, and beyond to the marble-like breast of the Sphinx. An ellipse, like an enormous slide-frame, partially encloses the creature. Similar devices frame Oedipus, enclosing his torso and hanging over his broken foot like a halo.

In Ingres, Oedipus and Sphinx stare intently into each other's eyes, their hands almost touching. Oedipus has put his question and, his eye focused to a point, is listening intently to her reply. The Sphinx is speaking, her head arched like an angry swan, her wings erect. Her face has that look of flashing fury that opera singers take on at moments of greatest projection. In Bacon, it is doubtful whether the question has or ever will be put into words. It is implicit, not in Oedipus' gesture – his bandage absorbs his attention – but in the Sphinx's turned head, and in the memory of the earlier picture which haunts our reading.

Two extraordinary paintings of a 'Sand Dune' and one of 'A Piece of Waste Land' also signalled new departures for Bacon. The first sand dune enhanced his previous painting of a jet of water. There were overflow pipes and bathroom fittings and a sea horizon containing a misty, grassy, animal form of pinkish browns, nature in movement against the set traps of civilisation. The hazy effect was created, indeed, by using an aerosol spray. The second 'Sand Dune' was overtly a human torso gone to ground, sliced off by a panoramic screen of sky enclosed by the red walls of a room. It seemed alive, as did 'A Piece of Waste Land', a sprawling weedy shape, littered with crumpled newspaper, and reaching to the arc of the edge of the world. The effect of all of them was to find wild life in the earth, as if digging a badger from its set.

Bacon also developed his paintings of the naked torso in cricket pads, set against an orange background. 'Study from the Human Body – Figure in Movement' of 1982, had the male thighs whirling round with a push of penis and flailing arms in the attitude of a naked wicket-keeper stumping a reckless batsman. In the left-hand panel of the diptych of 1982–1984 of 'Studies from the Human Body', the wicket-keeper crouches on a trestle table, stretching out his huge gloves in his traditional position behind the stumps, his shoulders a pair of naked buttocks with two light cords hanging above them. But the right-hand panel is subtitled 'from a Drawing by Ingres' and shows a female torso sitting on a slab, newsprint and a red arrow veiling her calves and indicating her sex, while her headless shoulders swell into her two breasts. The ultimate of this series of images is depicted in 'Figure in a Movement' of 1985, where the wicket-keeper wears his white flannels and seems to have smashed the ball into the bails, for his head is shrieking in protest or more likely, 'How's that?', as Bacon might well ask himself on the completion of any painting.

Two curious works of the period were experiments that were not pursued. In 'Statue and Figures in a Street', a hunched male is caged in a trapezoid within other geonometrical snares, while along a track that looks like a plank, small blurs of strollers like Giacometti people walk by without concern. But more strange was Bacon's effort to paint the star of the Rolling Stones, 'Three Studies for Portrait (Mick Jagger)'. For the first time, Bacon appeared to be approaching Pop Art, a sort of smeared Andy Warhol or Roy Lichtenstein. There is hardly an effort 'to deform into reality', as the artist claimed of his intentions in portraits. The beauty of the rock singer's bone structure and the sensuality of his mouth are shown with love and care, while only maroon stripes over the eyes suggest the fury and the force of his performance. Some critics declared that the Jagger portraits were so bland because Bacon dissected the rubbery mask and could find nothing behind it.

In the increasing number of interviews that Bacon gave in the years before his second retrospective at the Tate Gallery, his own performance became more and more assured, culminating in two television appearances with David Sylvester and Melvyn Bragg. He conquered his slight lisp and knew precisely what he felt about his work. As the interviewer for Bacon's profile in *The Times* discovered, the painter frequently thought he was being incoherent, but that was never the case. He said after making statements with some self-admiration, 'Isn't that clearly put?' He spoke of unlocking the valves of sensation to bring his viewers nearer to a kind of reality, to make them more aware without it being a dictatorial awareness. If anguish came out in his painting, it was because life was packed with anguish, and this fact made his paintings the more realistic. He spoke of Yeats, saying, 'As an old man he worked on himself, made himself more remarkable.' Although old age was a bloody nuisance and put him nearer death, he did not mind 'so long as the brain goes on and one can move about!' To another interviewer, he said that only what one did between the two absolute points of birth and death counted. Anyway, painting was an old man's occupation. The accumulation of the years had made him more inventive. Some of the greatest artists had done their best work in old age: Titian and Picasso and others. 'So I hope I shall go on and drop dead while working. When all is said and done, what matters is instinct.'

The television appearance with Sylvester was the culmination of the art critic having recorded rich and rare interviews with Bacon over the past twenty-five years. The title of the programme, 'The Brutality of Fact', referred to the artist's dispraise of Matisse, who did not have the intention of Picasso and turned fact into lyricism. 'He doesn't have Picasso's brutality of fact.' Bacon himself tried to trap reality, using the subject as bait. And he like working on his own in a haze of sensations and ideas so that he could allow the paint to dictate to him. To Bragg, who filmed him in the clutter of his studio, Bacon was more open than he had ever been, confessing his sexual differences with his interlocutor and his love of male flesh, and allowing John Edwards and his friends at the Colony Room to take a bow. He stressed that he was not a conversational artist, he preferred to show violent male couplings, which was a way of cutting out all the talk in action. 'Reality', he said, 'is what exists'.

Bacon's methods of painting and his destruction of his failed works fascinated all who managed to approach him. He had never been to art school nor had he had to learn the techniques he did not want to know. He had taught himself by fifty years of trial and error. He sprang straight at the unprimed side of the stretched canvas and attacked it with paint. He blocked in a background in thin washes or even acrylic or house paint, then added his figures in oils in a rush of sweeping and swirling marks. If anything went wrong at this stage, he had to destroy the canvas. As he was painting on the absorbent and woven side of the cloth, he clogged the surface and could never overpaint it even if he wished to do so. It could not be cleaned, as the paint soaked into the texture of the canvas. An indelible mark was left behind, and anyway, he could never recapture the accidental sign made by his original brush-stroke. His very method as well as his dissatisfaction did imply the destruction of much of what he did.

The oil on his figures, however, remained malleable while it dried. And he did rework the figures, particularly in his triptychs, even though these were usually completed in a matter of weeks of intense energy and concentration. The composition was disturbed by hurling on paint and using his hands and any other available material to smudge or trouble what was already there. Thick impasto and sand and dust were added in great blobs over fine washes and the weave of the unprimed surface. After these extreme contrasts in his assaults on his painting, Bacon would suddenly stop with his sensations exhausted and his intellect satisfied that this time in the process was the end of it. Sometimes in the work, he lost the best moments in a painting by trying to take it further, rather as Picasso did in Chabrol's film about his multiple images of a goat in *Le Mystère Picasso*. Bacon would also have liked a camera running to record the figures he had lost while he was painting, Only rarely in his early years had he returned to an abandoned picture and had overpainted something quite satisfactory on it. The picture now must be immediate or nothing.

Bacon told his interviewers that he frequently destroyed his work and usually added that he should have scrapped a great many more, while others should be burned. He was glad when his paintings were sold, because he saw the last of them. His only satisfaction was the sensation and process of the work itself. His paintings, indeed, were generally the record of his sensations and his personal life, so that he had every right to destroy what displeased him. The problem was that, as his old friends such as Bruce Bernard were to discover, Bacon was also beginning to distort and destroy the evidence of his actual life, to try and control the recording of the past as he did painting on a canvas. Increasingly, he liked to dominate what he did and to select from what he had done.

These were the actions of an old man, who was gambling and playing young, but who wanted to impose his opinions on his world. He would not yet divide his domain among his followers, as King Lear had among his daughters. More and more, his imperious whim was the dictate of his actions and of those about him. He began to enjoy his fame and the power it gave him. 'Not since Turner and Constable has a British painter achieved such universal recognition,' Richard Francis said, the young curator who was helping him to select the best of his works for the second retrospective at the Tate Gallery. 'The interesting thing is that so many young artists acknowledge his importance and influence without trying to imitate him.'

In imposing his own will on the accidents in his life, Bacon counterpoised the growing influence of the Edwards family from the East End of London against his French connections; Michel Leiris and Gilles DeLeuze; the French-Canadian Barry Joule, who was buying a property in Normandy and spending more time there; and now Gilbert de Botton. In the end, Bacon did arrange for some of his new fortune to be banked in Switzerland. He would often joke to his companions that his English accountant had told him to move to the cantons and the snowy mountains for tax reasons, 'but he could not stand all those bloody views'. The truth was that Bacon would never become a tax exile and long wither out his earnings in a bitter nostalgia for where he wished to be. No millions saved from the Inland Revenue were worth the liberty of moving freely.

David Somerset, soon to become the Duke of Beaufort, and Valerie Beston were the two guardians of Bacon's fortunes and reputation at Marlborough Fine Art. His finances were never discussed, his expenses were always met on demand. Access to him was made difficult by his own request, but it was not impossible. As far as a major artist could be protected from the company he chose to keep, Marlborough Fine Art were admirable overseers of his genius. In particular, Miss Beston fulfilled the role of his lost nanny. She was fiercely protective and controlled all access to him, taking in the pens and the tape-recording machines at the door. She removed his paintings from his studio while they were still wet to be exhibited at the gallery in Bond Street, although he insisted that none should be sold for three months in case he changed his mind about them. Although sometimes there were half-a-dozen clients queuing up to take a picture at a million pounds a canvas, Bacon would appear after eighty days and reclaim all his paintings. He only wanted to retouch them, he would say. That was his usual code for destroying them; but some dozen were stored away in a warehouse in Victoria. This was to constitute the bulk of his estate and included another bull-fighting triptych, which featured a man with a bandaged leg in the ring. Yet in spite of all these efforts at control, there was no question of ruling such a fickle life that was now becoming imperial as well as remaining intermittent.

The big guns of British criticism were wheeled out to fire their salutes for the second retrospective at the Tate Gallery. One of the more waspish representatives of the art establishment and the good friend of Sir Anthony Blunt of the Courtauld Institute, Brian Sewell, argued the case for placing Bacon among the great painters of history.

> Hockney is a virtuoso playing to the gallery. Bacon works in the tradition of a Renaissance master, and is only a painter – no etchings, lithographs, finished drawings or designs for the theatre. His subjects are not pretty things for the drawing-room, and the scale of his work suggests that he makes no concessions to the private patron.
>
> He deals with Renaissance themes of religious and temporal power, authority, corruption, conflict and lust, and has compiled his own pantheon of superhuman images with which to demonstrate them. Titian turned to the great texts of classical mytholoy, the New Testament, and to portraiture to express the human

> predicaments of an age riven by Reformation, counter-Reformation, and political struggle. Bacon turns to popes, presidents, businessmen and the tormented nude to make comments on our day – astute, perceptive and horrifying.
>
> His figures are often caged; the effect can be as aloof and remote as the appearance of a bland politician on the television screen, but the same device can become a trap, with the occupant screaming for release. He defines small spaces within his canvases, setting a stage for the action as in a circus or a fashion photographer's studio, and what is beyond the bright light is irrelevant; the creatures performing are human, but they often have animal references in the way that they walk, or move, or squat, distorted far beyond our ape relatives and into the world of the butchered carcase.
>
> Paired figures on a bed are not seen in any affectionate contiguity, but in the attitudes of erotic violence; they stem from photographs of footballers, boxers and wrestlers, but Bacon brings them close to hardcore pornography and then elevates them with his vision and technique into an abstracted allegory on which he makes a savage, shuddering, visceral comment.
>
> He is the master of the moving multiple image, not by the intellectual and analytical methods of Cubism, nor the near caricatural distortions of Picasso – though he recognizes their power – nor by any obvious adaptation of the photography that he acknowledges as his source material. Within a generalized and recognisable silhouette that makes a bold and simple statement of the pose or action, there are subsidiary indications of movement that may complement or run counter to it . . . any man who has ever handled a brush, or has an empathic response to the action of painting, must find in Bacon's pictures an astonishing mastery. Among post-Renaissance artists he is a great painter; in the wilderness of post-war art he is the towering giant.

Lord Gowrie, who had been the Minister for the Arts as well as deriving from the same part of Ireland as Bacon, wrote a trenchant tribute to him. Since the death of Picasso and more than any other painter, Bacon had provided the age with the image of Ezra Pound's accelerated grimace. He did not record the past and was the least narcissistic of artists. He used a present preoccupation or recollection to prompt any act of painting. He was a man of great but narrow erudition, because he was impatient of anything less than masterpieces that he could use for his art. His bleak view of human life did not stop his joy in it. He was good company and generous with money, because he had been a hustler and now had more than he needed. 'Politically, he is an old-fashioned aristocratic liberal with a low threshold of boredom.' He thought the Right was the best of a bad job, because it interfered less than the idealism of the Left with individual liberty. The British did not know what to make of this 'elegant, wealthy, rather conservative gentleman who paints such scary pictures'.

Nevertheless, Bacon was the greatest living painter and the most important British one since Turner. He shared the aloof intuition of French romantics like Baudelaire. He had the nihilism and gaiety of certain eighteenth-century minds. Nature was threatening and monotonous; noctambular urban life was his territory. Like Beckett, Bacon was 'an artist of endgame'. He did not paint from life, except from his face in a mirror. His subjects were a few friends and himself, recorded from snapshots and memory. Yet 'Bacon himself looks very like a Francis Bacon'. In this respect, he was close to the contemporary he admired, Alberto Giacometti. He was 'unique in this century in his ability to render the indoor, overfed, alcohol-and-tobacco-lined flesh of the average urban male. His painting is how most of us look.'

By the artist's request, the catalogue contained no notes or previous critical responses to the one-hundred-and-twenty-six of his works that he chose for the retrospective to hang in thirteen galleries of the Tate. He wanted the visual shock on the viewer without preparation. 'Painting is its own language,' he told one interviewer, 'and when you talk about it, it's an inferior translation.' This long screening of his life's work did not win over all of his new critics. Waldemar Januszczak discovered the notorious sequence of Crucifixion triptychs that dominated the middle of the show to be the work of 'a significantly lesser artist, a melodramatic pseudovisionary prone, unfortunately, to sensationalism'. But the six or seven triptychs near the end of the show took the spectator quietly and honestly into the painter's domestic existence and introduced the close circle of his friends.

> As a social observer, Bacon, like Lucian Freud, has done much to turn the grim facts of everyday life into a convincing and heroic subject for high art. As a painter of loneliness – not the screaming, existential, theatrical variety, but the quiet, numbing, ordinary kind, that saps your faith in life and impresses you with the emptiness of the room you are sitting in – he is, I think, incomparable.

Bacon even agreed to take two representatives from *The Times* around the huge exhibition. To them, his ageless bearing was dwarfed by his remarkable owl's head – 'feathers puffed out chuffily, eyes hooded and with an uncanny ability to pursue and trap with their roving gaze'. He discounted some of his early pictures and commented on others. Of the centre panel of his 'Sweeney Agonistes', he said drily: 'This one warns you never to go into a sleeping car . . . Those two have been in Chicago but one of the people in the committee didn't like the idea of the penis showing. That was that.' The tenderness evident in the triptych of 1973 of George Dyer's death was banished by the factual tone of Bacon's voice, saying it was a picture of a great friend who had committed suicide in Paris. 'And I suppose in so far as my pictures are ever any kind of illustration, this comes as close as any to a kind of narrative.'

Referring to a painting of 'Sand Dune', he confirmed that it was sprayed on and covered with dust from his studio floor. He was surrounded with dust, which lasted for ever. 'Wherever I live becomes appalling disorder at once. For some reason I find I can work much easier with chaos around me.' The likeness of the self-portraits to the living painter was startling, and he also confirmed that he was usually his only human model. 'Shaving in the mirror every day, looking at oneself, doing one's hair or anything – you have a very good idea. I only do self-portraits when I have no one else to do.' He preferred to paint the nude, and he answered those who were offended by the feeling of dead meat in some of his works. 'People ask me why my pictures have this feeling of rawness and mortality. If you think of a nude, if you think of anything going on around you, think how raw it all is.'

As an inveterate gambler, Bacon must have known the risks attached to a second major retrospective at the Tate. He had taken the challenge, accepting that the chances were against him, and the gamble paid off magnificently. That was the opinion of John Russell Taylor, now the art critic of *The Times*. Although the viewer might be left like one of Pinter's heroes, asking, 'What have I seen, the scum or the essence?' the analogy with the playwright would not go away. 'Their imaginative worlds are similarly haunted, their artistic means as meticulous, the ultimate sources of their inspiration as obscure – even, one suspects, to themselves – and the climate of violence which pervades their work is created or recreated with the same total urbanity of expression, not a word or a brush-stroke too many, nothing anywhere which is slapdash or arbitrary.'

To the critic, the terms of Bacon's vision were buried deep inside the image. 'Out of them a terrible beauty is born.' He was not so much provocative or perverse as possessed. He had a species of telepathy with the spectator. His emotion dictated the quality of the feelings of the viewer. He was one of the supreme colourists of the century. He was the most painterly of painters. There was nothing he did not know about how to apply pigment to canvas for the greatest of effects. He enlarged sensibilities in a way that no other painter had been able to do since the first revolution of the Cubists. Those who saw the show might hate every moment, but they would not be quite the same again.

This second British retrospective was the apotheosis of Bacon's art. He had always said that he was more appreciated and sold better in France and in the United States of America; but now he had full recognition in his homeland. Perhaps more sweet to him was to be asked by the National Gallery to choose from its masterpieces an exhibition of fourteen works called *The Artist's Eye*. His choice cut through period and style. The works were assessed on their qualities as paintings. They were hung widely spaced to give the maximum visual impact and to emphasise their singularity. They told no stories, they were themselves.

On the first wall, there were two portraits by Rembrandt of Margaretha de Geer, the wife of Jacob Trip. The massive ruff severed the head from the body like a butcher's knife. Raphael's painting of the Pope Julius II, which had inspired Velázquez to paint Bacon's model, Innocent X, had been ignored in favour of that painter's 'Rokeby Venus' or 'Toilet of Venus'. Bacon thought it a most beautiful painting, although it was only a marvellous thing to look back on. Once it was there, he had to make more concentrations of images, to cut down the conveyance and deliver the sensation.

He contrasted, however, the Velázquez Venus with the pastel of Degas, 'Woman Drying Herself'. He prized Degas for returning to the observer 'the *fact* of the subject as if he had never before seen a woman's body as it really is'. He also was a great student of people caught out in their private acts inside their own spaces and rooms. He had taken from the past only and exactly what he could use in the present day. And his terrible and incisive artist's eye had remade not only how the watcher saw the counterpoint of the centuries, but the loneliness of the little doings and sensations of the billions of singular beings in their artificial confines on this planet.

14
Optimism about Nothing

> Riches are for spending, and spending for honour and good actions. Therefore extraordinary expense must be limited by the worth of the occasion.
>
> 'Of Expense'
> by Francis Bacon, Lord Verulam,
> Viscount St. Albans

For a living artist, if fame is the spur, price is the seal of success. In May 1987, one of Bacon's eight early popes from the collection of the Belgian banker, Baron Lambert, sold at Christie's in New York for more than a million pounds, while a portrait of 'George Dyer Talking' fetched only a little less. Two years later, Bacon's triptych of the death of Dyer on the lavatory in Paris was sold by the American cartoonist Saul Steinberg through Sotheby's in New York for nearly four million pounds, although a Jackson Pollock, 'Number 8, 1950' reached almost double that figure. And at Christie's again in November 1989, another one of Bacon's studies for a pope reached £3,600,000. Although these proceeds did not find the artist, they confirmed his reputation as the leading living British painter.

Indifferent to money itself, particularly now that it was available in such large quantities, Bacon let Marlborough Fine Art fix the price of his new paintings at about a million pounds apiece and went on living as he always had in the chaos of his London studio or at Long Melford with John Edwards or in Paris, where he frequently visited his friends. Unfortunately and inevitably, the huge sums of money now attached to his work and his name attracted both the greedy and the jealous. Peter Langan kept on prodding Bacon to decorate his Brasserie as Hockney had done, but Bacon would not, knowing very well that Langan got the capital back from his restaurant for the value of the paintings which he was given and hung in it. So Bacon became more exclusive and cautious, saying that he no longer respected the opinions of any critic of his work, particularly 'the critics in England who loathe everything I do'.

John Richardson now followed Douglas Cooper in turning against Bacon's art. Writing a definitive life of Picasso himself in several volumes, Richardson thought that the ageing Bacon did not retain the creativity and force that Picasso still had in his last years. Bacon's work seemed facile and tired, particularly the pictures with the newsprint on the bottom that seemed a confession of a failure to communicate. 'A lot of the time Francis was right to destroy his canvases.' And Peter Fuller found that Bacon restated his established themes: figures seated in front of crucified carcasses; disintegrative portraits of himself and his friends, and images of lonely and naked men at their private functions. His handling of forms, though not of paint materials, was growing looser. He could no longer unite figure and ground.

> The only development was a movement away from reliance on the photographic image towards a new element of mythic symbolism – but it often seemed arbitrary, even absurd. It was as if the Eumenides, in forms resembling pink elephants, had returned to haunt the sordid events in hotel rooms, or the sphinx had materialized amidst the used dressings of a casualty ward. Bacon drew less upon his day-to-day life in the 'sexual gymnasium' of the modern city; the references to the recognizable circle of friends diminished; those to Aeschylus and Ingres greatly increased. But, although Bacon's painting was greeted with increasing acclaim, nothing reduced his relentless sense of surgical, but increasingly meaningless, despair, of paint thinned not so much with turpentine, as formaldehyde.

Fuller's condemnation of Bacon's later work contained that streak of moralism which judged the subjects the artist painted as well as the style of his life. The critic had to share Bacon's view of humanity to accept him as a realist. He had used his expressive skills to denigrate and to degrade. He presented one aspect of the human condition as a necessary and universal truth. The fact that his works were more highly valued than those of Graham Sutherland merely exposed the values of those who made such a choice. 'Bacon's skills may justly command our admiration; but his tendentious vision demands a moral response, and I believe, a refusal.' If Bacon was possessed by genius, it was of a life-diminishing kind.

Such British censoriousness was anathema to Bacon's French and American critics, who saw in his work the very human condition and a necessary and universal truth, and even a terrible beauty. He could not be judged, only received. Acceptance was all. As Robert Hughes wrote, Bacon was perhaps 'the extreme voice of the *misère des hôtels*, the sense of being trapped within the city by unassuageable and once almost unnameable appetites ... In his work, the image of the classical nude body is simply dismissed; it becomes, instead, a two-legged animal with various addictions: to sex, the needle, security, or power. All moral relationships are erased from the world of his paintings. It is unified, instead, by the smeared documentary force of certain key images clipped, as it were, from the grainy stock of the twentieth century and then edited abruptly together.'

This return to his early wish to paint the history of his century along with his autobiography was revealed by Bacon in the most remarkable serial picture of his later years. In his 'Triptych, 1986–87', Woodrow Wilson in his top hat and overcoat and spats walks down a step from darkness. He has vainly brought peace in the world into being at the Versailles Conference by creating the League of Nations, that ineffectual instrument for preventing another world war. In the central panel, the circumcised figure in the cricket pads sits, this time with the heavy handsome features of George Dyer combined with John Edwards, and raw life leaks in a pink sensual shadow onto the black raised rostrum at his feet. But on the right panel, a bloodstained sheet with a hole in it covers a writing-desk, held down by a desk-lamp and meaningless newsprint. The president of the United States holding under his arm his useless treaty that leads only to violence, is poised against the murder of Trotsky at his desk by a Russian assassin with an ice-pick; these two wings contain the truth of the fact – animal love set against the nothing of death.

In another triptych of the previous two years, a 'Study for Self-Portrait', Bacon showed himself self-contained, but beleaguered. His hands clasp his knees or the top of his stool-chair. A red arrow points to his loose and suffering mouth. White circles ring his neck and lower jaw, while the left side of the skull spatters and smears away in doubt. He seems almost ready to pity himself as his feet move restlessly about. There is a quality of isolation and introspection that is absent from all of his other self-portraits. He had done a number of them, not because he liked his face. As he said, he hated it, but there was nobody else to do at the time. He was more lonely now and self-absorbed, and if, in his own words, the subject was the bait, he had swallowed his own hook and gaffed the fact of who he was.

Two other triptychs of the succeeding years proved his detractors wrong and demonstrated the old master at the height of his assurance and his powers. 'Triptych, 1987' shows on the left an orifice and a wound ringed by a blue circle within human loins and bandaged ribs on an operating table; centrally, great thrusting legs with plasters on walk through an open doorway, exposing a penis and a bleeding aperture; on the right, a bull's head strikes downwards with his horns, while a Fury imitates the beast below with flying prongs. This mythical and sexual dream sequence was followed in 1988 by a 'Second Version of Triptych, 1944', which the artist ended by presenting to the Tate Gallery. At six feet high and almost fifteen feet long, it was more than twice the size of the original. The significant word 'Crucifixion' was omitted from this explicit psycho-sexual sequel. In it, the left of the three Eumenides still sweeps on with double hunch-back, but placed against a murky crimson ground, not a blood-orange one; in the middle, the blindfolded screaming head, descending from a pregnant belly and buttocks on its stand, is isolated on its callipers above a dull red dais put against a sandy wall; and on the right, the howling head is shifted to the edge and set on a table top, as if the bestial protest against the bloodiness of it all were more marginal in the sensation of a life going down.

Certainly, the rawness and spewing of the younger triptych of forty-four years before this other version was denied in the spacing and the distance of an old man's feeling. The neon of the first became the damask of the second, as if the same glare of vision were now a closing of eyelids or a drawing down of blinds. The earlier picture was painted in oil and pastel with paint brushed and smeared and scratched on, while the background of the later one was dark maroon and black thinned with turpentine and sometimes sprayed, so that all attention was focused on the figures of the Furies. To one critic, these three pictures could no longer be viewed in a classical or Christian context. The creatures in them represented the state of mankind at birth when the new-born infant blindly experienced all sensation through the ears, mouth and anus. The blindfold, the gag and the woman's torn clothing turned them from timeless archetypes to sado-masochistic fantasies.

> They symbolize a state of being whereby, in order to feel anything at all, victims willingly offer their bodies to be violated, dismembered and killed. Every altered detail of the new canvas serves to stress physical suffering. Bacon eroticizes pain and seems to deny that such a thing as the human spirit exists. Life is physical suffering, fear and death . . . There is something here more deliberate, more chosen and more willed than despair. Something vicious and purely evil.

On hearing of this, Bacon merely said, 'Really, I thought they were rather nice, myself.'

Bacon did not admit to being so haunted by the Furies in his age as he was in his youth. Yes, all men had a sense of guilt at times, but in his late seventies, he was 'not very much haunted with guilt these days'. He remained fond of Aeschylus because reading the plays still brought up exciting images to his mind, the violence and the gore. When accused of painting merely to shock, he would reply that what was called Surrealism had gone through art at all times, and ask, 'What is more surreal than Aeschylus?' He even read aloud from the *Oresteia* on television:

> Over the wide rolling earth, we've ranged in flock,
> Hurdling the waves and wingless flight, and now we come

All hot pursuit, outracing ships astern.
And now he's here somewhere cowering like a hare.
The reek of human blood, it's laughter to my heart.

Of all the pictures of this late period, the simplest had the greatest effect, certainly in Paris. 'Blood on the Floor' of 1986 was the most arresting painting at Bacon's triumphant show of fourteen paintings at the Galerie Lelong in Paris the next year. Only three of them were not presold: a triptych was on offer for £2,400,000 and two single canvases for £850,000 each. The reviewer for the *Sunday Times* was struck by the pin-striped and jaunty Dorian Gray figure of the painter, surrounded by admirers and telling of his love of France, where he was truly appreciated. The sensation of viewing 'Blood on the Floor' was similar to receiving an electric shock. The blood spattered on the grey and orange cell looked as if it had burst from a wound with the barest of devices and no human figure. Bacon had created 'the most disturbing narrative of human anguish with masterful understatement and ambiguity'. Yet he would not explain his work, saying:

> I don't know how that painting came about. I think I just dropped some paint on the floor and thought I'd draw blood on the floor. It's just . . . well, it's just blood on the floor.
>
> I never think of my work except in terms of images and I have never thought of it as violent. I just think of myself as a realist. Painting is not a thing you talk about. It is its own language. I've just always painted to excite myself. There is no explanation.

Never complain, never explain. Increasingly, Bacon lived the old French adage. His Anglo-Irish upbringing as a gentleman prevented him from complaining, while his dedication to his own method and his unconscious vision as an artist stopped him from explaining. More gnomic and set in his utterances year by year, he watched his worth rise and his reputation spread. The same year as the Paris show, the Marlborough Gallery of New York also put on a successful exhibition in that metropolis while Galerie Beyeler at Basle mounted a retrospective of his works. Another eight of his paintings travelled in a show named 'British Art in the Twentieth Century' from the

Royal Academy in London to the Staatsgalerie of Stuttgart, while yet eight more of his pictures wandered in 'A School of London' from the Kunsternernes Hus of Oslo through Humblebak and Dusseldorf and on to Venice. Yet the apogee of this international fame – and almost a harbinger for the end of the Cold War and a proof that Gorbachev's policy of perestroika was meaningful – was his invitation to hold a restrospective in Moscow, a city that had never seen so personal and visceral an art.

If chance played a part in creating Bacon's work, so it did in putting on his show in Russia. The young James Birch, who ran the Birch and Conran Gallery up Dean Street from the Colony Room, went to Moscow to try to have his own artists represented there, only to find out how many Soviet artists appreciated the paintings of Bacon. He also made the acquaintance of a Soviet diplomat, Sergei Klokov, who had exceptional contacts in artistic circles and really wanted to meet Bacon. 'But I can't propose this or I'll end in Siberia,' he told the Soho gallery owner, 'so you must propose it to me. But if Mr Bacon comes to Moscow, I'm sure the queues will be bigger than those for Lenin's tomb.'

On his return to London, Birch approached Bacon in the Colony Room and asked him whether he would like a Russian exhibition. At dinner later that night, Bacon gave the art dealer his private telephone number and confirmed in the morning that he was still interested. So Birch telephoned Klokov and rounded off the negotiations by giving the Soviet diplomat oysters and champagne in Wilson's fish restaurant in Jermyn Street. After that, the details were passed over to Marlborough Fine Art and the British Council and the Union of Soviet Artists, which issued a formal invitation. Since Turner, no British artist had been so honoured, and except for Chagall, who had been born in Russia, Bacon had beaten all contemporary European and American painters to the New Tretyakov Building on Gorky Park. His selection caused a reported outcry from the Prime Minister, Margaret Thatcher, 'Not that dreadful man who paints those horrible pictures.'

The artist lost a little of his enthusiasm for the Moscow show because some of his more explicit paintings were excluded. 'His most important work in the permanent collection is his central panel of buggers,' David Sylvester told a reporter. 'They've censored it. I feel the British Council quite rightly toes the line because it's not like sending a cricket team to Russia, is it?' If Bacon's excitement waned with this censorship, he did not protest too much. He refused to go to Moscow and nominated John Edwards in his place, an ironic gesture of sending a proletarian to the home of socialist 'realism', especially as his nude of Edwards had been banned from the show as 'pornographic', although the poster was his portrait of Edwards. 'The main reason he's not going there', Sylvester continued, 'is because he's had terrible asthma recently. *Terrible.*' Bacon reiterated that his bloody asthma had stopped him leaving. He had been looking forward to it. 'Everything was closed up after 1917. It would have been fascinating to see the country now.'

Moscow's loss was my gain. Because he did not go, he sprang into my longest meeting with him to talk over the culture of the 'forties. He was not suffering from asthma at all, only the thirst for more champagne. He gave me the catalogue of the Moscow Exhibition, complaining of the censorship there and the refusal of Lucian Freud to lend his picture of two men copulating, even though it would have been banned. He read for me his letter to Russia, printed as the frontispiece of the catalogue:

> It is a great honour to be invited to have an exhibition of paintings in Moscow.
>
> When I was young, I feel I was very much helped towards my painting after I saw Eisenstein's films *Strike* and *The Battleship Potemkin* by their remarkable visual imagery.
>
> In one of Van Gogh's letters he makes this statement: 'How to achieve such anomalies such alterations and refashionings of reality that what comes out of it are lies if you like but lies that are more true than literal truth.'
>
> Francis Bacon
> London 4/6/88

There were long queues in Moscow to see the exhibition, and they began to form nine hours before the opening. Bacon had said that he did not know what the Russian reaction would be. 'All I know is that my pictures are some of the most disliked among modern paintings. I have no idea what the Russians will make of them.' At the ceremony before the event, considerable diplomatic finesse was displayed by Lord Gowrie and Comrade Salakhov of the Union of Artists. The issue of Bacon's homosexuality was raised by a couple of British journalists, who asked how it related to the Soviet criminal code, which made that male act punishable by five years in a labour camp. Gowrie replied that there had not been, nor could there have been, any discreet censorship of Bacon's pictures in Moscow, since homosexuality was never an *overt* subject in Bacon's painting. Salakhov followed this delicate mouthwork with the suggestion that times were changing in this area, as in so many areas of Russian life, and that certain laws were long due for review. Indeed, that was why the Bacon show was happening. It was important now to see the real thing. In Soviet art since the Revolution, much had been hidden or suppressed and now was being reassessed and put on show. It was the period when 'we must fill in the white spaces'.

In fact, Bacon's subversive message at his Moscow show was not for homosexual rights, but a political protest. The right-hand panel of his 'Triptych' of 1986–87 suggested the killing of Trotsky at his desk by an assassin sent by Stalin, and some of the Russian audience understood what they were seeing. It was taken from a photograph of the victim's study in Mexico City, but it was not mentioned in the title, thus foxing the authorities. 'The subject is still virtually taboo in the Soviet Union,' *The Times* correspondent noted:

> But Soviet gallery-goers who recognize this image may begin to see doors opening upon their country's deeply troubled past, as well. That Bacon's work can carry these potent significations is an added reward.
>
> To the Soviets, this exhibition comes at an extraordinarily significant moment. Deprived of the literature and art of Western European existentialism for some forty years, they are now, by all accounts, beginning to recognize feelings of alienation in themselves – from authority and from the state, particularly – and from the still excessive bureaucracy that dominates Soviet life for the majority. They may not go wholeheartedly for Bacon's elaborate fascination with wounded and crippled flesh, but the show is

> almost certain to spark off debate about the validity as well as the limitations of Bacon's isolationist posture.

One-hundred-and-fifty-thousand people visited the exhibition in six weeks, and they left the Visitors' Book peppered with their comments. An architect wrote that these were the work of the devil, a war veteran supposed that Bacon suffered from severe concussion of the brain, a doctor diagnosed him as psychologically traumatised. Other comrades called him a charlatan and an idiot, and they found his work disgusting and sick and repulsive. It was as if one were put through a mincer in a butcher's shop. Still others hailed a genius and an artist of the future and a feast of absurdity, while the more daring observers saw a warning against totalitarianism and Communism itself. The wisest and the saddest comment came from an actress: 'Excuse us, but throughout the period of Soviet power we have been fed with a different kind of art. We have been deprived of inner freedom, perception, thought and feelings. And a great deal of time will yet have to pass before we are capable of taking in Bacon's art.'

The English critic Brian Sewell was right about Russians under perestroika leaning over backwards not to condemn Bacon's pictures as further evidence of the decadence of Western society. 'The problem will be that they won't find anything they can attach to their own tradition. There's no painting in Russia which in any way resembles Bacon's work.' The truth is that there was no painting in the world which resembled Bacon's work, which might borrow from tradition, but transmuted it to inspiration. The less he explained, the more the viewers and critics read into him. And in the diversity of their opinions, his originality became more marked.

Something of the acclaim of Bacon could be deduced from the extraordinary theft of his portrait by Lucian Freud from the National Gallery in West Berlin while on loan from the Tate. The meticulous painting showing Bacon with lidded eyes and sour mouth was evidence of the long link between Britain's two leading living painters, and thieves demanded a ransom of one million pounds for it, after they were unable to fence it within the underworld of art because of its notoriety. Eventually, the ransom was not paid, and the picture was never recovered. The only consequence of the theft was the early closure of the travelling British Council exhibition in Germany.

Bacon's awareness of his own inevitable death extended to others. Sitting in Mario's in Chelsea with John Edwards, he saw a friend enter, the art dealer Robert Fraser who was dissected, the blotches on his face and his emaciation understood. 'It's AIDS,' Bacon told Barry Joule next morning, voicing the fear of the disease that scared the homosexual community of London. Four months later, Fraser was gone, and the three companions and prophets of his end held a quiet wake for him in the Colony Room. Most of Bacon's contemporaries were dead now, many of them of drink, and even Bacon admitted to part of the process of growing old. 'I mean', he said, 'life becomes more of a desert, in a sense, around you.' He had even failed to ask most of the Colony Room crowd to his second retrospective at the Tate, telling Joule, 'I'm not having too many of those crooks there.'

His way of life and continuous drinking of champagne could not deny age and time forever. Even Dorian Gray succumbed at the end of Oscar Wilde's tale. Just after his eightieth birthday, the artist was taken to hospital for a kidney operation. Few of his friends expected him to survive it. As it was, his strong body and his resilience saw him back in Soho and his studio within a few weeks. He celebrated the end of his eighth decade by having no celebrations and failing to turn out for a party in his honour at Marlborough Fine Art. Although Lucian Freud had accepted to become a Companion of Honour, Bacon still refused all awards, saying that he would then be 'cordoned off from existence'. He did not even know what to do with all the flowers sent round to Reece Mews. Among the pyramids of squeezed tubes and rags and paint tins on his floor, he had nothing to put the blooms in. 'I'm not the sort of person', he said 'who has *vases*'.

To his interviewers and well-wishers, Bacon's responses became more and more stock and predictable. His usual remark about the meaning of his pictures was the dismissive epigram, 'If you can talk about it, why paint it?' Or he would say of his work, 'You can't be more horrific than life itself.' One young reporter from *The Times*, who had just seen the film *Batman* before seeing Bacon in Reece Mews, noted that the only painting in Gotham City's Flugelheim Museum that the Joker prevented his henchmen from destroying was a Bacon; the reporter then visited the Constables in the Victoria and Albert Museum with Bacon, to hear him praise the older master's free style and tremendous spontaneity, and deliver a set piece about his methods:

> I know that in my own work the best things are the things that just happened – images that were suddenly caught and that I hadn't anticipated. We don't know what the unconscious is, but every so often something wells up in us. It sounds pompous nowadays to talk about the unconscious, so maybe it's better to say 'chance'. I believe in a deeply ordered chaos and in the rules of chance. I have to hope that my instincts will do the right thing because I can't erase what I have done. And if I drew something first, then my paintings would be illustrations of drawings.

The interview ended as others had over bottles of champagne in the Colony Room, where Bacon concluded it with his favourite *obiter dicta*, 'I am an optimist, but about nothing. It's just my nature to be optimistic. We live, we die and that's it, don't you think?' This careful show of bleak hedonism was exactly the last portrait that Bacon wished to speak of himself, when a painting would not do. He was constructing a consistent *persona*, irrespective of his wayward beginnings. And this desire to dictate the presentation of his past and to delete the inappropriate explained his strange treatment of an old friend's 'scrap book', *About Francis Bacon*.

Bruce Bernard had conceived an illustrated book on the painter, designed in a square format to show the triptychs across two pages, and illustrated by personal photographs as well as paintings, while the bulk of the text would be leading reviews of Bacon's works and some personal comments on them by Bernard himself. The painter and Marlborough Fine Art were enthusiastic about the project, and the many dinners with the artist were convivial. All went well until Bernard submitted his personal opinions on some of the pictures and Bacon asked for a few small changes, striking out words such as 'incarnation'. He even approved the lay-outs, but suddenly jibbed at the rough colour proofs, which were inaccurate and confirmed his misgivings for the project. Now he insisted on the removal of the personal photographs and Bernard's own comments and the reproduction of any of his paintings before his first Tate triptych. Bernard and his publishers would not accept the alterations and *About Francis Bacon* still has not appeared in print. 'Friendly agreements are', Bernard wrote ruefully, 'by their nature vulnerable'.

In private, Bernard was more bitter on the subject of the about-turn of the artist. He said that at the end of his life, Bacon could round on any friend and deny anything he had said which deviated from his public image. 'Never heard of him,' he would say. 'Never met him. What he says on me is lies.' He wanted all deleted from Bernard's book on his relationship with Eric Hall, and he declared that he had not painted a gouache of 1929 found by Bernard, although it was signed by him. Like many another genius come into their greatness and their glory, at the end of his days, Bacon wanted to dominate and destroy his past in the way that he still dominated paint by his rules of chance and destroyed his early canvases and his failed ones. The problem was that evidence and memory and history could not be hacked apart by a kitchen knife. He could not make up an autobiography from the lucid and brilliant philosophy of painting and living, which he had learned in part from his French friends and critics of late. He could not deeply order the chaos of yesteryear.

'He was a wicked man in his greatness,' Patrick Procktor said of him. 'He could not bear that other people could draw or paint. At the end of his life, he became so particular that he didn't think there was anyone of any talent in the world at all.' He was alone on his pinnacle. Nobody could challenge him in his old age. It was the final vanity of the soon-to-die, the revenge of a man who had been rejected and outlawed and poor until his late middle years. He used to ask Procktor who he thought was any good as a painter. To tease him, Procktor would think of obscure artists and reply, 'What about Francis Rose or Stephen Tennant?' And Bacon would answer, 'Oh, I don't like *her*.'

The past that Bacon wished to preserve he had put into photographs. In 1988, he went to an exhibition by William Burroughs in the October Gallery in London. There the two old friends from

Tangier were photographed by John Minihan, who had recorded Bacon wearing a shiny black mackintosh in Paris in 1977 during a show of his art at the Galerie Claude Bernard, and now caught him, holding up the frail Burroughs and looking with desperate concern at the desiccated writer lighting a cigarette and staggering forward. Neither of them was shown with Beckett, reclusive to the last, ascetic and alone in these rare pictures of which the photographer quoted George Bernard Shaw with approval, 'If you cannot see at a glance that the old game is up, that the camera has hopelessly beaten the pencil and paint brush as an instrument of artistic representation, then you will never make a true critic, you are only, like most critics, a picture fancier.'

Bacon was, of course, a photograph fancier, but he never thought it capable, more than paint, of artistic representation. He was also a fancier of the written word, and Beckett was one of the writers he particularly admired along with Pinter. As Sam Hunter wrote in his incisive essay for the catalogue of Bacon's major retrospective exhibition in Washington D.C. in late 1989:

> Like those severe but tonic writers, Bacon feels his art represents the simple unalloyed truth of existence as he perceives it, no matter how hard to bear that reality may be. For him, the philosophical Existentialists and their literary followers set the tone with their perception that the basic problems of existence were loneliness, the impenetrable mystery of the universe, and death. Basically, Bacon believes in a form of the philosopher Friedrich Nietzsche's nihilism and certainly, too, in the aspect of the Greek ideal that Nietzsche so enthusiastically endorsed, the Dionysian conquest of pessimism through art.

The Washington retrospective at the Hirschhorn Museum and Sculpture Garden at the Smithsonian Institute followed an exhibition at the Marlborough Gallery in Tokyo, which saw Bacon break into the Japanese market and begin to become exceedingly rich. In America, his reputation was at its height, and the retrospective travelled during 1990 to the County Museum of Los Angeles and then to the Museum of Modern Art in New York. His critics particularly praised his studies for self-portraits and of John Edwards. His triptych of himself of 1985–86 showed a new manner in him, an awkwardness in gratuitiously demeaning poses, somewhat derived from Muybridge's photograph, 'Man Performing Standing Broad Jump'. This humiliating view of himself contrasted with Edwards who was depicted as a heroic male nude in the tradition of the Elgin Marbles and the Italian Renaissance. The flesh appeared both ghoulish and strangely beautiful, swallowed by a vaguely sinister panel of black:

> Over the years Bacon has proved himself a voluptuary of the flesh, like Rubens, Watteau, or Soutine in their distinctly different ways, and in his later years, he seems most like the aging Rembrandt. Flesh is for him the essential material of being and things, life's basic substance. Paint becomes flesh in its colour, texture, material density, and fluidity – and a vehicle that serves desire and rekindles his historical and personal memory, allowing him to discover the physical and spiritual particularity of a specific person . . . In 'Study for Portrait of John Edwards' Bacon compresses his figure of Edwards into a kind of iridescent pigment skin where paint and depicted body gloriously fuse, pushing his warped figuration to a point near dissolution, not unlike the gorgeous sunsets of Monet that he tried to emulate in his disturbing early paintings of the papal scream.
>
> Ever the wily magician in his manipulation of paint, Bacon has lost none of his touch or invention with the years. In his recent work he continues to bait the 'trap' for capturing the distilled essence of reality, salvaging the mysterious living image of man from the ruins of time, as the great paintings of the past have done . . .

Although he had objected to the word 'incarnation' applied to one of his paintings, Bacon had achieved the incarnation of John Edwards and had salvaged that particular man from the ruins of time. Both during the rest of the artist's life and after it, Edwards would receive glory and riches, unlimited by the worth of the occasion.

15
A Homecoming

> Wisdom for a man's self is, in many branches thereof, a depraved thing. It is the wisdom of rats, that will be sure to leave a house somewhat before it fall. It is the wisdom of the fox, that thrusts out the badger, who digged and made room for him. It is the wisdom of crocodiles, that shed tears when they would devour.
>
> 'Of Wisdom for a Man's Self',
> by Francis Bacon, Lord Verulam,
> Viscount St. Albans

Bacon was not wise for himself. He was a passionate and reckless man, who declared that he painted and lived by sensation. But many of those who still remained close to him were wise for themselves and knew that they could rely on the legendary generosity of the aged artist, who hardly spent his millions on himself, but on his court of friends and those he loved. He was lavish with his suitors.

At one time he had admired the plays of Harold Pinter, and particularly *The Homecoming*. It tells of a brother who has left the East End of London, but who returns one night with a wife, Ruth. The East End family decide to include her with all the understated menace that also broods over the work of the artist. The hard one, Lenny, speaks to her of his past like Eliot's Sweeney or Bacon's 'Sweeney Agonistes': 'The facts being what they were, so I clumped her one. It was on my mind at the time to do away with her, you know, to kill her, and the fact is, that as killings go, it would have been a simple matter, nothing to it.' He quickly finds out that Ruth is of the same metal and temper as he is, and he sets her up as a tart to subsidise and service the whole male family. As the old father says, 'You're kin. You're kith. You belong here.'

Bacon's homecoming to Cavendish Hall and neighbouring Long Melford was with his freshly-acquired East End family through John Edwards, who was one of six children. The Edwards brothers had now bought a string of pubs in East London and more property and pubs in Suffolk. They had only gone in the first place to Long Melford to be near Bacon's first cousin, Pamela Firth Matthews, in her Georgian stately home with its lavish and beautiful gardens, so reminiscent of the great houses of the Ireland of the artist's youth. Whether Bacon wished for a meeting of minds between his old world and his new one, or whether his sense of irony demanded a confrontation were questions not to be solved by the time of his death. The Edwards clan with their near friend, the Irish dealer in antiques, John Tanner, acquired Westgate House, another Georgian mansion with extensive converted stables, and Dale's Farm, a barricaded house with many outbuildings, surrounded by gates and walls and signs of: GUARD DOGS – WARNING. Particularly assertive were a Rolls-Royce and Land Rover and a Bentley with the numberplate: BOY 1.

One banker, who went to dinner with the Edwards brothers and their friends in the village, found himself seated with eight men and two women at the table. Four of the men boasted of their prison sentences for burglary and demanding money with menaces; but the food and the wine were excellent. The rooms of the house were superbly decorated, but the banker was told that the old furniture and the pictures were changed every three months. They went in and out, a passing show. The constant factor was the numerous paintings by Francis Bacon, which were even hung in the lavatories. The untold worth of these pictures explained the need for tight security.

The old landowners and villagers in this part of Suffolk were alarmed by this incursion. There was little effort by the East Enders to fraternise, only to dominate. It culminated in the extreme mortification of Pamela Firth Matthews. Occasionally, during the summer, she opened the gardens of Cavendish Hall to the public. The last time that she met her cousin Francis Bacon before his death, the

Rolls-Royce and the Bentley cruised down the drive and disgorged the Edwards brothers and the artist. They supported him across the lawn and sat him down under an old tree, where he had played as a child with his cousin Pamela. When she left her other visitors to greet Francis, she found him paralytic with drink and incapable of speech. She looked at the smiling Edwards family and said, 'Drive him home.' His home was no longer hers at Cavendish Hall. In this encounter between the old and the new, she felt deeply wounded and ashamed and sad, particularly as she would never see him again.

It was rare for Bacon not to be in control of his life. Even in his eighties, he was not capable of being pressured or blackmailed. He simply walked elsewhere. But in this case, he had brought his fresh Cockney family to the scene of his youth. He might well have agreed with E.M. Forster's dictum: ONLY CONNECT. Yet he would have countered it with: ONLY REVERT. Between new connections and reversions, his life did lie. The disaster and the pleasure lay in trying to mix them. And finally, he could never revert, once he had gone away. He could not mix the elegant with the raffish and the formal with the unconventional, especially in Suffolk, where his homecoming turned out to be most unwise for himself.

The Edwards ascendancy at Long Melford, which had overtaken the Anglo-Irish one, could only be answered by flight to France and then to Spain. There Bacon discovered a last love in Madrid, the city which his master Velázquez had glorified in paint, and where he would die. His wish was that his lover, a Spanish banker, was to remain anonymous, and it should be respected. But although his recurrent illnesses brought him down again and again in the last two years of his life, he did achieve that final and transient passion, which he had pursued in his desperate search for the fact and the sensation. A week before his death, he said that he was becoming progressively happier, and that he wished to die while enjoying himself. He repeated his feelings in Soho to an old friend, Sandy Fawkes. 'He once told me the only cure for a hangover was suicide. When he died he was in love again.'

'My mother made me promise never to grow old,' Bacon used to say, 'and now I know what she means.' All his friends worried about him falling down the cabin stairs at Reece Mews and breaking a hip or his neck. Yet he never did, although he succumbed to hepatitis and three bouts of pneumonia in a year. Once his friend and neighbour, Barry Joule, found him as good as dead, while checking up on him in his studio. He was unable to breathe with aggravated asthma and had to be sent to hospital again. He was given heavy medication and despite his doctor's orders, he decided to travel to the mountains of Spain, where the air was meant to be better, although he had always thrived on London grime.

In an act of prodigality and after the example of Turner and Henry Moore, Bacon gave his 'Second Version of the Triptych of 1944' to the Tate Gallery, which had already been given the first version by Eric Hall. It was worth three million pounds, but Bacon wanted the two to hang side by side so that the comparison could be made. He had only painted the second one because the first had been too fragile to travel to his Washington retrospective, and he had always wanted to paint a larger version of the subject. 'I thought it might work,' he said, 'but I think the first one is the best.' The second version had been presented to the Tate at the instigation of Gilbert de Botton, then a Trustee of the Gallery. When Bacon had lent it to the institution, de Botton had told him that it would be a shame if the work ended in private hands abroad. 'Your rethinking on that theme was wonderful, and you would be giving that gift of comparison in perpetuity to the nation.' In his gentlemanly way, Bacon had replied, 'Oh, I don't think they'd be interested.' De Botton knew the artist's style and replied quite casually, 'Quite possibly. But if I probed this, would you be willing to give it?' Bacon said he would, but de Botton knew his habit of having second thoughts. And indeed, after a time, Bacon said that he could not do it. There was a problem with gift taxes. De Botton let more time pass and asked Bacon if that was the only problem. Bacon replied that it was. Meanwhile, the Director of the Tate Gallery sorted out the matter with the Treasury, and Bacon did make the gift a few months before he died. 'It was a remarkable exercise in generosity,' de Botton said, 'but I had no idea it was a race against time. I could have delayed more, and then it would have been lost.'

Bacon was doing little now, although he did plan a series of paintings about places where murder had been committed, 'one in a field, one on a pavement, and one in a room'. He abandoned the project and finished his last picture before the Christmas of 1991. He knew and did not want to know mortality was soon coming to pay a final call. He was such a legend that he was already thought to be dead. The *Observer Magazine* even called him at Reece Mews to ask if he had passed away. He answered the telephone to say that he was 'sorry not to be able to help on this occasion'. Given the fact of death, even life was a better alternative. In one of his last interviews with Richard Cork in his studio, he admitted that he had had his life-mask taken, although he bitterly regretted the experience once his face was smothered with plaster. 'I hate the thought of death,' he said. 'I hate the thought of it all coming to an end.' Then he cried out, 'Shall we have some champagne?'

He had daily been aware of death. It was just around the corner all the time. When it came, there was no escape. This was why he was so glad to wake at all each morning that he did. He had known many people die or commit suicide, but he had never thought they were anything but dead. 'I am certain there's nothing after that, and I like the finality of the American expression "drop dead"'. Although reality was pain and horror which was the daily bread of newspaper and television, death could be confronted by art, as the Egyptians had done. They had attempted to defeat it by leaving images, as he was trying to do.

Yet his images were immediate, for this life, now. He loathed the idea of a museum like the Tate giving a whole gallery to his past painting. In a swipe at Henry Moore, he said that he found 'the profound vanity of these old men who try to immortalize themselves through foundations very boring'. He would leave his money where he pleased, even if it were scattered to the winds. 'Nothing would give me greater horror than to allow a vain old man to perpetuate himself in dead art.'

He wanted no record of himself except what people chose to read into his surviving paintings. When Lord Gowrie pointed out that somebody would write his life anyway, he replied, 'Yes, but I shall be dead and I shan't have helped and I shan't care.' Only the second statement was wishful, because he talked extensively to possible biographers, and his interviews and his pictures were highly articulate. He had even made no secret of his homosexuality in the last decades of his life, actually signing a protest against Clause 28 of a Conservative bill to discourage homosexual propaganda despite his dislike of gay militance. 'I don't go about shouting that I'm gay,' he told Richard Cork, 'but AIDS has made it all much worse, you know.' People were very odd about it. When he had offered a telephone engineer a drink in his studio, he had received a strange look and the query, 'You're gay, aren't you?' before the man would touch the glass.

Certainly, he was a dandy in the manner of Baudelaire's 'cult of the self'. As John McEwan recalled of his meetings with Bacon:

> This Byronic aspect to his nature had something to do with a complete absence of sentimentality, a recklessness, a bleak rationality, an awareness that his lack of religious faith was in itself despair and also an intense animalism.
>
> The animalism was the first thing one felt on meeting him, a palpable magnetic field. It gave one some inkling of what he meant when he rather mystifyingly described his art as trying to record his feelings about things as closely to his 'own nervous system' as he could. He wanted to conduct this nervous energy into his painting, to vent its expressive power.
>
> On one occasion I was standing close behind him when an artist he disliked entered the room. Immediately he stiffened, bristled, became alert as a dog. It was the only time I have witnessed the hairs stand up on the back of a human neck. No fight ensued, or hostile conversation. It was more menacing than that. As a younger man he must have been capable of being quite terrifying . . .
>
> In older age he defiantly wore tight trousers, the better to show off his figure. He was dapper and had settled on a late nineteen-fifties 'mod' taste for leather jackets and pastel slip-on shoes. His face was soft and pink and he was shamelessly vain, admiring himself in the nearest mirror and combing his hair even when carrying on a conversation. He was made for an age of blades and beaux.

Bacon as the dandy and heir of Baudelaire was also stressed in the catalogue of his exhibition at the Tate Gallery in Liverpool in 1990. The French poet's essay on 'The Painter of Modern Life' was used to describe the artist as a *flâneur*, a passionate spectator. His work was to distil the eternal from the passing show. He must stand outside his society and be a modern aristocrat, a dandy who could transform the instant into the constant and become a hero. Even Bacon's attitude to money and to his growing fortune seemed to stem from Baudelaire, who had declared: 'The dandy does not aspire to money as to something essential. This crude passion he leaves to vulgar mortals; he would be perfectly content with a limitless credit at the bank.' Bacon's indifference and even isolence towards earning vast amounts of cash was, indeed, that of a dandy. He could be believed when he said he would be happy going back to the income he had once had when he worked as a cook and a general servant, although this would hardly have suited his followers in his late age.

In spite of his open hands and filled pockets, Bacon did intend to leave a fortune behind him to somebody. He was very pleased by the astuteness of Marlborough Fine Art in marketing his paintings. 'They just sell all my pictures abroad,' he said, 'and there's no VAT on exports.' Many millions of pounds were placed in Switzerland, although much of this money was spent on generosity to the surviving members of his family in South Africa and to some of his close friends in Europe. In fact, when I spoke at length to Bacon in 1988, he ended our session by leaping to his feet and saying, 'Can you think of a bad cause, Andrew?' I had the temerity to reply, 'What about yourself, Francis?' He laughed and said, 'That's *too* bad a cause. But if I don't get to my solicitors this afternoon, a few million is going to go to my something sister in South Africa.'

As it turned out, he reached his solicitors, and there would be a vast fortune to leave behind him. He was not in the position of Salvador Dali or de Kooning at the end of their lives, when their surviving relatives and batteries of lawyers surrounded them to manage the millions and try to exclude the galleries with their contracts. Dali had ended sick and besieged in his house, while thousands of his faked works flooded the art markets of the world. De Kooning had been set to paint to the bitter end, even though suffering from advanced Alzheimer's disease which was said only to affect his memory, not his brush-strokes or his vision. This moribund industry was too valuable to let the man idle, after one of his pictures reached a price of twenty-million dollars. But Bacon retained control of his faculties and his paintings and his estate until his death. The rule of chance may have been his ideal, but never the loss of the mastery of his choice.

Like Picasso, the painter he thought the greatest artist of the century, Bacon held on to the end. In the last interview he gave to the Director of the Picasso Museum in Paris, he said that he was very influenced by Picasso when he was young, although 'now you're so flooded with illustrations of everything, you hardly know what you're principally influenced by'. He said that he thought Picasso as a Spaniard was basically Surrealist. He particularly loved Picasso's pictures by the beach, the blue and the colour of the sand, and the quality of pathos in his heads of Marie-Thérèse Walter, pathos in the sense of a longing for something which could not happen. Pathos existed even for him, although he knew he was finished at death.

He travelled to Madrid in the spring of 1992, to be consoled by his Spanish banker. He felt unwell and was taken to a hospital in the city. There he had a heart attack and could not be revived. He died on the 28th of April at the age of eighty-two at the height of his renown. Yet his funeral was in keeping with his command over his life. There were few formalities and none of his close friends were present. As Ian Board, the inheritor of the Colony Club, declared: 'Francis said he came into the world with nothing and wanted to leave with nothing. He said the gutter or a ditch was good enough for him, so he settled on cremation. He was not a theatrical man and crowds gathering around a grave was the last thing he wanted.' Some journalists appeared at the final ceremony at the Almudena Cemetery and saw a solitary bouquet of yellow and white roses sent from his drinking companions at the French Pub in Soho. Just before three o'clock, a hearse disgorged a plain, dark wooden coffin with two copper handles and a cross on the lid – a final religious touch that Bacon would not have approved. Within eight minutes, the coffin was wheeled into the recess over the furnace to the taped music of Gregorian chants, and the body of the artist was reduced to ashes. The urn was consigned onto a flight back to Britain. That was all, an exit without sentiment. 'We can remember Francis without a service,' Ian Board said, holding a champagne wake in the club. 'He was not a religious person, so why bring in God after his death?' A last photograph of him in his coffin showed Bacon with slick hair instead of curls, and a bandana round his forehead with his name on it. 'He probably commissioned it himself,' Board said.

The tributes from his fellow artists were the most significant. 'Bacon achieved Flaubert's wish to be as unlike his neighbours as possible,' R. B. Kitaj said. 'I think he realized some of the most unexpected stylistic insights since the War, the best painter in a barren time,' Peter Blake concurred, although he was far from Bacon's influence. 'He was the last of the Bohemian figures, who would not have been worried by a mortgage or anything which most people worry about: he dedicated his life to his paintings. I will always admire his full Bohemian life.' And Bridget Riley, equally distant from Bacon's example, stressed his difference from his country. 'Bacon cannot be called an English artist. There is little trace of national school tradition in his work and for that alone he was a liberating influence. I admired him for his independence of spirit, for the stringent conditions he set himself, and for his sense of beauty: a terrible beauty perhaps, but one which is measure to what he called "the fact".' Lucian Freud also forgot past differences to remember Bacon as the man who amused and excited him by talking about the paint carrying the form and packing a lot of things into a single brush-stroke – a million miles away from anything he could ever do. The power of paint was Bacon's legacy.

The art critics and the gallery directors joined in the praise. It was not a case of the usual *De mortuis nil nisi* bunkum. It was a genuine appreciation of the leading artist of his age. As his Soho friend, the art critic George Melly said: 'I agree with the clichéd belief that he was the greatest British painter since Turner. He was a charming companion, generous, waspish and a marvellous gossip, not at all gloomy, although his paintings were otherwise. I especially liked the excellent way he was able to use paint not to imitate reality but to make it real.' His opinion had been confirmed by a previous director of the Tate Gallery, Sir Alan Bowness, who had mounted the second retrospective of Francis Bacon there. Bowness specified that Bacon's work set the standard for his time, for he was surely the greatest painter then alive:

> No artist in our century has presented the human predicament with such insight and feeling. The paintings have the inescapable mark of the present; I am tempted to add the word alas, but for Bacon the virtues of truth and honesty transcend the tasteful. They give to his paintings a terrible beauty that has placed them among the most memorable images in the entire history of art. And these paintings have a timeless quality that allows them to hang naturally in our museums beside those of Rembrandt and Van Gogh.

Although Bacon declared that he did not want his dead art to hang in museums, Bowness was correct. Even if Bacon painted for the sensation of the present, he constructed his paintings to serve as the everlasting memorials of his time. He was, in the end, a Platonist. Those who could not create, had children. Those who could, created art. He had an eye on posterity rather than passing fame. His problem lay only in his materials and his methods. His use of acrylic and other inferior paints as well as raw canvas militated against the long survival of his works, although his hemming of them behind thick glass argued a wish for their preservation. Most certainly, Bacon's vanity about his body and his appearance extended to his pictures. They should always look their best.

There was much speculation about where his fortune would go. Even the Chairman of Marlborough Fine Art, the Duke of Beaufort, did not know what his premier artist was worth and was amazed at the way he had lived. 'Of course I had no idea how much he left,' he told reporters, 'but he lived in a filthy little place and led a very simple life. He didn't even have a car.' The Duke was being circumspect. After the Rothko case, in which the relatives and the beneficiaries of the American painter sued Marlborough Fine Art over an estate worth dozens of millions of pounds, he would say nothing until the will was proved and an agreement was reached with the legatees. When he died, Bacon was far too rich for the self he had made.

His last homecoming was to death's door, and he always knew that he would knock there. He had made provisions before he left, trying to avoid the desperate litigation that usually breaks out when a rich painter dies, the fight between the gallery with an exclusive contract, the surviving members of the family, the lovers and other beneficiaries, and the inheritors of paintings, said to be gifts or discarded by the artist, which now could flood the market. Yet his millions and his legacy had always been irrelevant to the artist. His ashes would have stirred with black mirth in his urn to hear the pitiful claims made on his estate. One chance encounter in Soho, Michael Leventis, said that Bacon had promised him the studio door daubed with the whirls of the artist's palette. 'I already have one of Francis's easels and a couple of signed prints. The easel means a lot to me. It has all the colours he used on some of his best-known paintings. I would never dream of using it.'

This supposed bequest would not be answered. Some of the obituaries called on Bacon's clutter of a studio to be preserved for the nation – exactly what he would have hated. He wanted to be born, to paint, to eat and drink and have sex, and to die. To make a monument of his transience was anathema. And yet, it would be done, with that extraordinary English belief in preserving the ephemeral and calling it traditional.

Of the immediate accounts of his life, the facts and the sensations, Brian Sewell wrote the most searching one:

> He took the Crucifixion, stripped it of all its Christian implications, and invested it instead with the universal beastliness of man and abattoir, running with blood, deafened with screams. As a portrait painter he was not the friend with insight but the harsh interrogator, the man outside the ring of light with lash and electrodes close at hand. His prisoners, presidents, popes and old friends squirmed.
>
> He used the ideas of the trap, the cell, the cage, the X-ray and the heavy fall of light to imprison and torment his subjects to distil the violence, and to assault complacent senses with graceless nakedness on the lavatory pan and vomit in the wash basin . . .
>
> Bacon took the vile, sexually and politically obscene, and shudderingly visceral, and lifted them with paint so that we might contemplate ferociously profane images of cruelty and despair and see in them an inheritance from the great Renaissance themes of religious and temporal power.
>
> Titian, Rembrandt and Velázquez might not have cared for Bacon's work but they would have recognized kinship in his astonishing mastery of paint and the profound pessimistic atheism of his images. He was the perfect mirror of the spirit of our age.

Endpiece

What is truth? said jesting Pilate, and would not stay for an answer. Certainly there be that delight in giddiness, and count it a bondage to fix a belief; affecting free-will in thinking, as well as in acting.

'Of Truth'
by Francis Bacon, Lord Verulam,
Viscount St. Albans

Indeed, Bacon did reach his solicitors, Theodore Goddard, and dispose of his fortune in a will. The bulk of the estate in England including the studio in Reece Mews was left to John Edwards, who had already removed all the valuables from the mews for safe-keeping on the news of the artist's death. Its value was first estimated at sixty million pounds, although much of it was said to be in unsold paintings, some of them in the hands of Marlborough Fine Art. The Duke of Beaufort was quick to cast doubt on the worth of the estate, declaring that it could only lay claim to half a dozen paintings. He acknowledged that there might be many unfinished or rejected works scattered around, but he would be surprised if they were very good. 'He left work unfinished when he wasn't pleased with it. All this talk about a million pounds a picture is absolute rubbish.' The final value of the estate in England was proved at less than eleven million pounds, while the major Bacon painting of 1969, 'Study of a Nude with Figure in a Mirror', did not fetch more than £700,000 in the Sotheby's saleroom, in the December of the year of the artist's death.

The Duke could show such confidence because the Marlborough held the whip hand. It had an exclusive contract with the dead artist, who had rarely signed his paintings. It was uniquely able to authenticate any Bacon paintings, because there had been no *catalogue raisonné* for nearly thirty years. The many pictures given by Bacon to the Edwards family and other close friends would have to be verified, and the gifts proved by the recipients. Without that acknowledgement from the Marlborough, the works of art would have a murky provenance and not be worth much on the market. John Edwards did, however, move quickly to show his responsibility for the bequest of the bulk of the artist's estate, whatever its value might turn out to be. 'I am going to keep the house and studio exactly as it is,' he declared. 'I am going to live in it until I die and then donate it to the nation. When I pop off, then it's up to them what they do with it.' Lord Gowrie knew what might happen. It would be difficult to open the studio to the public because of the narrow stairs, which nobody understood how Bacon navigated when he was drunk. But it remained of 'extraordinary interest, because he used it as his palette, he mixed his paints on the walls'.

No static studio could commemorate an artist, who had made painting a process, where his will was overruled by his instinct, and where he was 'a medium for accident and chance'. Equally lost was his method of work, the early rising at dawn, the concentrated attack on the canvas until lunchtime, the sauntering and drinking and gambling for the rest of the day. Bacon had hated the afternoons, saying that 'they're absolutely revolting, they're a wash-out'. But he had felt better again in the evenings, acquiring a hangover for the next morning's session of painting. None of that wild way of work and life could be preserved.

Nor could the way he put his daydreams into paint be left to the nation. He had insisted that he was not gifted or inspired, but merely receptive of the series of images, which his unconscious had acquired during his long life. His job was to 'rivet the appearance' of a picture seen in a passing vision or a glimpse. 'Pictures drop in like slides,' he once said. 'The way I see them is not necessarily related to the way I paint them.' That had to do with the nervous system and with chance. But so many pictures came to him in his daydreams that he had even wanted to make a film from the thousands of urgent images he had never used.

There could be no studio legacy for the British people in how Bacon thought or painted. In a way, he had been correct. His work was dead without the living artist, without the continuing process. He was what he was doing, not what he had done, although that defined his past life. He was an existentialist in that sense, as well as a dandy and something of a nihilist in his 'compulsive attention to the inevitability of death'. In his final interview, he had laughed at his own bleak attitude, saying, 'we've only become civilised towards horror. I mean, we accept it now as an everyday thing. It's sort of ladled out to us like soup.' But his concentration on horror and dying was his contribution to the images of our time.

So powerful were these images that they have become the only legacy worth preserving. They were too raw and sickening for some. As early as 1952, John Berger had complained that we looked at Bacon instead of going to Belsen, and this was not a constructive attitude. Other moralists among the art critics agreed. Peter Fuller recalled that when Pope Innocent X first viewed his portrait by Velázquez, he exclaimed, 'Troppo vero.' To be too true was Velázquez's technique, but even in his paintings of dwarfs and freaks, he had given them a defiant human dignity. But Bacon's pursuit of truth and the fact seemed to owe more to the violence and perversity of his imagination, so that he produced a travesty rather than an extraction. He was a wonderful painter, in the poet Kathleen Raine's opinion, 'But his is a misuse of art. He sets at large in the world images that are a denial of the sacred reality.'

Bitchy and homosexual friends from Soho such as Colin MacInnes could call Bacon 'the Norman Hartnell of the horror movement'. His perverse images became so chic and prevalent that the designer of the film about the cannibal serial killer, *The Silence of the Lambs*, used Bacon's obsessive constructions of foul figures locked in transparent cages as his inspiration for the set of the incarcerated murderer. But even those like Bryan Robertson, who did not believe that Bacon painted the entire human condition, and that a screaming man sitting in an expensive hotel bedroom failed to represent universal suffering, did admit to the power of the artist's iconography.

He was a marvellous painter, 'who caught a nerve in painting as no artist has ever done before.' Acutely sensitive to surface, he created some of the strongest images of the century. 'He had a fantastic feeling for the figure in space: trapped, pinned down or imperilled like a moth or a hunk of meat.'

That was the genius of Bacon. He was receptive to the plethora of images of his childhood and the newsreels and the snapshots which he saw. He even found an engineering book on industrial filters very stimulating. He trawled through such material and transmuted it into a universal perception of his insight. In a way, a Bacon painting does touch an exposed nerve more than a photograph of Belsen and does make the viewer feel sick at human violence. His screaming popes jerk the grandeur of the Velázquez portrait, caged and yelling, into this moment. His reduction of the Crucifixion to a butcher's shop does deny the sacred reality, but it also affirms the negation of God in this century. If Bacon's imagination was perverse, there is a streak of perversity in most of us, and he translated that into a revelation of what we are in secret and may not wish to admit. The nerve he caught in his pictures still twists in mankind, and in depicting his own sensations, he brought to light our hidden desires and our griefs along with his own.

Bacon claimed to have no system of beliefs. 'If I wanted to express philosophy', he once said, 'I would write – use words, not paint.' In point of fact, his philosophy was as consistent and coherent as that of his namesake, Lord Verulam, Viscount St. Albans. He learned it from his experience and from what the French critics wrote of him. They ordered his 'rules of chance' into a logic that disclaimed itself in a gentlemanly show of depreciation and irony. Bacon revealed his philosophy in his paintings and discounted it in his talk, which asserted along with Balzac that 'hazard was the greatest artist'.

Yet he had what W. H. Auden wished for a birthday present, no 'confusion of what we say and do with who we really are'. The sensations of his life were the sensations of his painting. Once he was driving through France with a friend when they came across a bad collision. 'There was blood and glass all over the road,' he recalled. 'But I remember thinking that there was a beauty about it. I didn't feel the horror of it, because it was part of life.' On another occasion he hired a train to take him and a large group of friends to the South of France and back to Paris. The blinds were closed over the carriage windows, caviare and champagne were served, poker and roulette were played, the only stop was to reverse the engine and return. It was a process in sealed spaces of pleasure and risk with companions, which was as futile as the journey through life, signifying nothing. Yet he relented by finally accepting to stay the weekend at Château Lafite with Baron Eric de Rothschild. He had always refused before because he had never owned a *smoking* or dinner-jacket. He had to be reassured that he would be welcome as he was in this new age of the appreciation of genius.

Bacon ended in fear of death, as he always had been, and without reconciliation with God. Yet he had reconciled himself with life as it was. One of Tom Stoppard's characters once said, 'This is the life.' The answer was, 'This is a life, among others.' Bacon's life was a life among others. His genius was his own, he shared it through his pictures with the world, he was unfortunate in love, amoral only by circumstance, generous in fact and to a fault. He was a man who pursued the ultimate truth without fear or favour, and who jested like Pilate about what was truth. He delighted in giddiness in his playing and counted it bondage to fix his beliefs, except in the need to paint. He affected free-will in thinking and in all his actions.

He usually protested that he painted only for himself. He committed to canvas his private visions, expressing his life. His boon companions, such as Daniel Farson, derided the critics who saw a human significance or a historical importance in his works. Yet he spoke otherwise to myself as a social historian and to art historians such as John Russell, who was frequently told by Bacon that he always had a great object at the back of his mind, to paint 'the History of Europe in my lifetime'. To us, he did acquiesce in the proposition that he was trying to depict the violence of his times and the *angst* of his age.

It was not that he was duplicitous or that he did protest too much. More than most men, he spoke exactly what was on his mind and had no pretensions. To avoid being a hypocrite, he stressed that all was personal to him and without significance. He never claimed too much for what he did. In the Anglo-Irish manner of the born gentleman, he ran down his genius and his influence. As his ancestor, the noble philosopher Francis Bacon, wrote 'Of Truth', 'a mixture of a lie doth ever add pleasure'.

To paraphrase what W. H. Auden wrote about 'The Novelist', there could have been a comment on Bacon, 'The Artist', that he:

> And in his own weak person, if he can,
> Must suffer *fiercely* all the wrongs of Man.

The images of Bacon did transmute his personal pain into universal grief. Of course, he was hardly a Christ to absolve our sins, although he painted his crucifixions as dead meat. His *métier* – to use again the only word which gave a meaning to existence in Camus's novel *The Plague* – was to describe human suffering and pain, as he did with his Furies at the base of the Cross. He was certainly conscious of those references. If he insisted later that he performed unconsciously, so be it. He was still a lightning-rod struck by two World Wars. His works were also the erratic flashes of decades of thunderous peace. As a conductor of the force and the agony of humanity, he was the true transmitter of the burned facts of this century.

The most admirable quality in man is generosity of spirit. Sir Michael Levey paid tribute to that part of Francis Bacon. When the National Gallery organised a public appeal in 1971 to acquire Titian's 'Death of Actaeon', Bacon was introduced to Levey by Sonia Orwell. He became involved in a radio appeal and gave a dinner for people who might become significant contributors. He gave a substantial donation himself, although he was not rich at the time. He chose to remain anonymous and provoked this statement after his death from Sir Michael:

> My experiences do not include a comparable instance of such instinctive, imaginative, generous support for acquisition of an old master painting for the nation from a great living painter, but then I am not aware of having met another painter whose greatness seemed to me – seems, rather – so uncontestable.

Francis Bacon was not a violent man, and yet he lived in violent times. To David Sylvester, he told of what violence meant to him, and so gave an insight into his century and his work. He had been accustomed always to live through forms of violence. These had affected him, but they were different to the violence in painting, which had nothing to do with the violence of war. He had tried to remake the violence of reality itself. This was not only the simple violence as when he said that a rose was violent, 'but it's the violence also of the suggestions within the image itself which can only be conveyed through paint.' He conveyed that in his life and violent times.

Notes

I am profoundly grateful to Francis Bacon for taking the time to talk to me with his usual frankness and illumination. I am also indebted to Henry McDowell for his researches on the Bacon family in Ireland, and to the Imperial War Museum for providing me with the military history of Anthony Bacon. Indispensable were the long interviews Francis Bacon gave to Sir John Rothenstein, reported in *Francis Bacon* (intro. Rothenstein, text by Ronald Alley, London, 1964), which also supplies a definitive *catalogue raisonné* of all Bacon's early works, including some which are now destroyed; in *Modern English Painters III: Wood to Hockney* (London, 1974); and in *Time's Thievish Progress: Autobiography III* (London, 1970). Also indispensable are the Bacon interviews given to Hugh M. Davies in 1973, reported in his thesis, *Francis Bacon: The Early and Middle Years, 1928–1958* (New York and London, 1978); also to David Sylvester, reported in *Interviews with Francis Bacon* (London, 1975) and to John Russell, whose *Francis Bacon* (London, 1971 and rev. ed. 1979) is authoritative on his subject. I am further obliged to Bacon's talks with Melvyn Bragg and Daniel Farson. Many of the people I have interviewed do not wish to be identified because of Bacon's wish to have no biography written of him. These confidential sources are protected in the notes, but full references will be provided to qualified Bacon scholars. I am particularly grateful to and have acknowledged Bruce Bernard and Sarah Fox-Pitt and Shusha Guppy and Donald M. Hess and Barry Joule and Pamela Firth Matthews and Kenneth Partridge and Patrick Procktor and John Richardson and Lady Jane Willoughby and Michael Wishart and Sir Peregrine Worsthorne. Unless otherwise attributed in the notes to the text, the comments on his life by Francis Bacon come from my own notes on the conversations I held with him in 1988.

Chapter One

Pamela Firth Matthews has supplied me with many early memories of her cousin, Francis Bacon, who was always most generous and kind to her, even as a small girl. She has also shown me the Firth family albums with the only existing photographs of Francis as a baby and many other extraordinary snapshots of the life and houses of the Protestant Ascendancy. Henry McDowell has interviewed most of those people who still remember the Bacon family and the Bells and the Supples in County Kildare. Michael McConville, *Ascendancy to Oblivion: The Story of the Anglo-Irish* (London, 1986) gives a good general picture of the Protestant Ascendancy. C. S. Andrews, *Dublin Made Me* (Dublin, 1930) speaks of the feelings of Catholics to Protestants, while L. MacManus, *White Light and Flame: Memories of the Irish Literary Revival and the Anglo-Irish War* (Dublin, 1929) was the traveller from Dublin who witnessed the London black-out. Air Commodore L. E. O. Charlton, *War over England* (London, 1938) described the Zeppelin psychosis of the time and the methods used to counter the air threat.

Chapter Two

Francis Bacon's memories of Ireland are taken from the introduction to the catalogue of his exhibition at the Tate Gallery in 1962 and from a conversation with his close friend Barry Joule. Other sources were Grey Gowrie, 'Homage to Work and Love,' the *Guardian*, 29 April 1992, and Shusha Guppy, *Telegraph Sunday Magazine*, 4 November 1984, and Richard Cork in *The Times*, 16 March 1991. The quotations from contemporary sources of the way Ireland was in the time of troubles are taken from 'I.O.', *The Administration of Ireland, 1920* (London, 1921): Joice M. Nankivell and Sydney Loch, *Ireland in Travail* (London, 1922): and Professor W. Allison Phillips, *The Revolution of Ireland, 1906–1923* (London, 1923). Generally useful were Constantine Fitzgibbon, *Out of the Lion's Paw: Ireland Wins Her Freedom* (London, 1968); Richard Bennett, *The Black and Tans* (London,

1976): and Michael Hopkinson, *Green against Green: The Irish Civil War* (London 1986). Henry McDowell contributed, 'The Big House: A Genealogist's Perspective and a Personal Point of View' to *Ancestral Voices: The Big House in Anglo-Irish Literature* (Otto Rauchbauer ed., Hildesheim and New York, 1992).

I have closely followed the masterly analysis of the British reaction to homosexuality during the First World War in Samuel Hynes's *A War Imagined: The First World War and English Culture* (London, 1990). Oscar Wilde's leading biographer is Richard Ellman. I also acknowledge the help of another masterwork, Paul Fussell, *The Great War and Modern Memory* (London, 1975) and of Nicholas de Jongh, *Not in Front of the Audience* (London, 1992). Francis Bacon spoke of homosexuality as an affliction to Shusha Guppy and Grey Gowrie, who was told by Bacon that his nature was to tell everything. Francis Bacon told David Sylvester of his parents' objections to him being an artist. He also told Shusha Guppy about his background of gambling. His opinion on Ireland as a country of literature, not paint, was given to Gérard Regnier of the Picasso Museum in Paris. The information on the patron who took him to Berlin was supplied by Henry McDowell, although Hugh Davies supplied Bacon's evidence in 1973 of his route to Berlin. Lady Caroline Blackwood wrote of Bacon and his friend talking to her about his Irish boyhood in 'Francis Bacon (1909–1992)', *The New York Review*, 24 September 1992.

Chapter Three

I have used Oliver Lawson Dick's edition of Aubrey's *Brief Lives* (London, 1949). Francis Bacon spoke of his early perception of mortality and of the reason he was always helped when he was young to his friend and critic David Sylvester. Christopher Isherwood's remarks on 'civil monsters' are quoted in Samuel Hynes's admirable introduction to the Folio Society edition of Isherwood's novel. *Mr Norris Changes Trains* (London, 1990). *The Temple* by Stephen Spender was eventually published in London in 1988.

Christopher and His Kind, 1929–1939, was published by Isherwood in London in 1977: it contains his description of the West End bars. There are two useful biographies of him, *Isherwood* by Jonathan Fryer (London, 1977) and *Christopher Isherwood: A Critical Biography* by Brian Finney (London, 1979). Auden's *Poems* dedicated to Isherwood were published in

London in 1930. Hugh Davies records Bacon's reactions to the sex booths in Berlin, his vanity as a pretty boy and his reactions to his patron running off with a woman. René Gimpel, *Diary of an Art Dealer* was published in New York in 1966. Peter Sachse, 'Der verkehrte Ball im Eldorado-Kasino', *Berliner Journal* May, 1927, described the Eldorado. Christopher Isherwood, *A Berlin Diary, Autumn 1930* is reprinted in the Folio Society's edition of *Goodbye to Berlin* (London, 1975) with drawings by George Grosz.

Otto Dix is quoted on photography in the brilliant article by Matthias Eberle, 'Otto Dix and *Neue Sachlichkeit*', printed in *German Art in the 20th Century, Painting and Sculpture 1905–1985* (Munich and London, 1985): Eberle also supples the criticism of Otto Dix's work. The commentator on the Weimar Republic was Mrs Seaton Wagner in *Germany in My Time* (London, 1935). Ernst Toller's *Brokenbrow* with illustrations by Grosz was published in London in 1928. He spoke on Berlin to Michael Kimmelman for *The Times*, 2 September 1989.

Francis Bacon spoke to Hugh Davies on 19 May and 26 June 1973, about the influence of the Picasso Exhibition in Paris on him. Maurice Sachs was the Goncourt of Paris in the 'twenties in *The Decade of Illusion: Paris 1918–1928* (New York, 1933). Jean Cocteau told of his experiences with Picasso in *A Call to Order* (London, 1926). He also claimed that Picasso had invented the art of camouflage, which had so impressed the boy Francis Bacon in Hyde Park. He had been discussing a new field uniform with Picasso in 1914, and the Spanish painter had said, 'If they want to render the army invisible at a distance, let them dress their men as harlequins.' Hugh Davies was the art critic of Bacon's early career, when he tried to resolve the influences of Berlin and Paris.

I am indebted to Lawrence Gowing in his text with Sam Hunter on *Francis Bacon: The Human Presence* (London and Washington, 1989) for the correspondence between André Masson's stage set and Bacon's first painting of the Crucifixion. Francis Bacon's remarks on leaving a snail's trail of slime were printed in *The New Decade: 22 European Painters and Sculptors* (New York, 1955), and those on buying a second-hand book on diseases of the mouth were made to David Sylvester. Alice Prin's biography and Ernest Hemingway's opinion of her Montparnasse are quoted from the excellent *Kiki's Paris: Artists and Lovers 1900–1930* by Billy Klüver and Julie Martin (New York, 1989). The details on the furniture design and contemporary architecture which influenced Bacon are shown in Douglas and Madeleine Johnson, *The Age of Illusion: Art and Politics in France, 1918–1940* (London, 1987). Janet Flanner's writings were printed in *Paris*

Was Yesterday 1925–1939 (London, 1973). Janet Flanner was also an habituée of the salon of the extraordinary Natalie Barney, then having an affair with Dolly Wilde, the daughter of Oscar's brother Willie. She bore such a striking resemblance to her uncle, particularly in her wit and drag costumes for masquerade balls, that she said, 'I am more Oscar-like than he was himself' – or certainly, during his last sad months before his death in Paris.

Brassaï's *The Secret Paris of the '30s* (Paris, 1976) is what its publisher claimed it to be, the photographic equivalent of Toulouse-Lautrec. Perhaps one of the more amusing episodes of the time was when the epicene Brian Howard had his clothes stolen in a Parisian male brothel and walked to the Café de Deux Magots, wearing only a stolen maid's frilly apron, which he refused to return with the words, 'My dear, I *like* having a souvenir so *very* inappropriate to that night's adventure.' Lord Gowrie wrote of his conversations with Francis Bacon in the *Guardian*, 29 April 1992. For Buñuel's early films, I have relied on the texts and introduction to *L'Age d'Or/Un Chien Andalou* (London, 1968).

Chapter Four

Francis Bacon's important reflections on the difference of the violence of paint and of war were made in his seminal interviews to David Sylvester. His loathing of his early furniture was expressed to Hugh Davies in 1973, also an admission of early influences on him because he was perhaps in love. Roy de Maistre's youth is excellently recalled in David Marr, *Patrick White: A Life* (London, 1991) and in John Rothenstein, *Modern English Painters II: Lewis to Moore* (London, 1956), who is brilliant on his subject: I use quotations from both these books. Patrick White tells of his relationship with Roy de Maistre and Francis Bacon in *Flaws in the Glass* (London, 1981) which also contains the quotation about his feelings on his homosexual temperament. John Rothenstein tells of de Maistre's education of Bacon in his 'Francis Bacon', *Modern English Painters III*, already cited. Julian Symons, *The 'Thirties: A Dream Revolved* (London, 1960) has written the most illuminating work on the period, only surpassed recently by Valentine Cunningham, *British Writers of the 'Thirties* (Oxford, 1988); from these books, the acknowledged quotations are taken. Bacon also told Hugh Davies of his early motives for painting the Crucifixion.

Francis Bacon told John Russell of his destroyed painting of the beautiful wound, recorded in Russell's book on Bacon. He told his friend Daniel Farson about his petty theft and living off people in *Gallery* (London, 1990). John Rothenstein first stressed the importance of Muybridge's photographs to Francis Bacon and pointed out that many other painters also learned from the Victorian photographer of motion: Thomas Eakins, who was photographed running naked himself, and Meisonnier and Seurat. He spoke often to Bacon about the importance of photographs to the painter's life, as did his other friend and critic, John Russell, whose work on Bacon has been cited. Richard Cork wrote on Bacon's preliminaries to his 'Three Studies for Figures at the Base of a Crucifixion', 1945, in *The Times*, 8 May 1992, as did John Rothenstein in his essential introduction and picture notes to the Tate Gallery catalogue of Francis Bacon's exhibition there between 4 May and 1 July 1962. Sir Roland Penrose spoke to Hugh Davies about his rejection of Bacon's 'Surreal' paintings on 29 March 1973, and Bacon spoke to Davies about Penrose's remarks on 3 April 1973.

The definitive listing of Francis Bacon's early works is done by Ronald Alley in his book with John Rothenstein, *Francis Bacon* (London, 1964), from which Rothenstein's remark on Bacon's painting in the 'thirties is taken. Giacometti remarked on his inability to be satisfied that a work was finished to Alexander Liberman in *The Artist in His Studio* (New York, 1960).

Also useful in verifying Bacon's early exhibitions are Roger Berthoud's two biographies, *Graham Sutherland: A Life* (London, 1982), and *The Life of Henry Moore* (London, 1987). The owner of 'Corner of the Studio' was Mrs Gladys MacDermot, who asked Bacon to design her flat at 98 Ridgemount Gardens. John Rothenstein wrote of Bacon's destruction of 'Abstraction from the Human Form' in his essay on 'Francis Bacon' in his *Modern English Painters III*, while Bacon spoke to David Sylvester about the influence of Eric Hall upon himself and to John Richardson about the appeal of gentlemen in pin-striped suits and of the Bath Club. Philip O'Connor's *Memoirs of a Public Baby* with an introduction by Stephen Spender was published in London in 1958. The culture of Fitzrovia and Soho in the late 'thirties and 'forties is covered in *War Like a Wasp: The Lost Decade of the Forties* by Andrew Sinclair (London, 1989). Jeffrey Bernard told me in The Groucho Club of his first encounter with Francis Bacon and confirmed it in his 'Memories of Francis Bacon', the *Independent on Sunday*, 3 May 1992.

Chapter Five

Malcolm Muggeridge wrote on the Bore War in 'The Beginning of the 'Forties', *The Windmill*, 1946. The quotations from Francis Bacon come from the important interviews he gave to Hugh Davies on 19 May and 13 August 1973. The descriptions of the Phoney War and the blitz conditions are taken from my own book, *War Like a Wasp: The Lost Decade of the 'Forties* work cited, and from William Sansom, *Westminster at War* (London, 1947); Mervyn Peake, 'The Shapes', *Shapes & Sounds* (London, 1941); James Monahan, 'Ludgate Hill – December Night', *Far from the Land* (London, 1944); and Stephen Spender, *World Within World* (London, 1951). Herbert Read denounced the Forces Exhibition in 'Vulgarity and Impotence,' *Horizon*, Vol. V, No. 28, April, 1942. The letter from Peter Watson to John Craxton was quoted in the catalogue to the important neo-Romantic painting exhibition at the Barbican Art Gallery, *A Paradise Lost* (David Mellor, ed., London, 1986), while John Piper's observations from Cardiff were quoted in M. and S. Harris, *The War Artists* (London, 1983).

Anthony Cronin wrote on the English Romantics in *Dead as Doornails* (Dublin, 1970). Francis Bacon talked to me about the late Romantics and his literary tastes, particularly Aeschylus and Shakespeare. John Craxton talked to Virginia Button about wartime London, also quoted in *A Paradise Lost*. Stephen Spender spoke to me about Peter Watson, while Michael Wishart wrote of him and of Francis Bacon in his autobiography, *High Diver* (London, 1977). John Lehmann's *In the Purely Pagan Sense* was published under his own name in London in 1976.

John Rothenstein wrote on Bacon's influence on Lucian Freud and on Bacon's triptych in his seminal *Modern English Painters*, while John Russell made the comment on the promise of Freud's youth in his introduction to the catalogue of Lucian Freud at his exhibition at the Hayward Gallery in January-March 1974. George Melly wrote on pre-War and wartime homosexual behaviour in *Revolt into Style* (London, 1970), while Patrick White told of Roy de Maistre's concentration in *Flaws in the Glass*, work cited. The story of Sir Kenneth Clark's visit to Bacon's studio with Graham Sutherland is recounted in Roger Berthoud's excellent *Graham Sutherland: A Biography* (London, 1982). Richard Cork's important review of 'Three Figures . . .' was entitled 'Face to Face with the Dogs of War', and printed in *The Times*, 8 May 1992. Robert Melville criticised Bacon's paintings and was quoted in John Rothenstein and Ronald Alley, *Francis Bacon*, work cited, while Bacon himself spoke to John Russell, whose work on *Francis Bacon* has also been cited. And Eric Hall wrote to Sir Alan Barlow about his Bacon bequests to the Tate Gallery in the Archives (Francis Bacon, 1953).

Chapter Six

The post-war descriptions of London are again drawn from this author's book on the British culture of the 'forties, *War Like a Wasp*, work cited. William Golding's remarks on Hiroshima came from his review of Paul Fussell's *The Great War and Modern Memory* in the *Guardian*, 20 November 1975. Mervyn Peake's drawings for 'The Rime of the Ancient Mariner' were reproduced in *Poetry London*, X, December 1944, while the *Drawings of Mervyn Peake* were reproduced by the Grey Walls Press in 1949. Graham Sutherland's accounts of the flying-bomb site and painters as the blotting-paper of their time and the crucified holocaust victims, also of his time with Bacon in the south of France, came from Roger Berthoud's fine biography, already cited. Francis Bacon spoke to me about the influence on him of the Belsen newsreels and the brutality of fact and T. S. Eliot's Sweeney and his liking for Patrick Hamilton, while Patrick Procktor told me of the Belsen paintings once owned by Keith Lichtenstein. The leading Australian physicist who commented on the dropping of the atomic bomb on Japan was Mark Oliphant.

John Rothenstein reported his conversation with Francis Bacon on the origins of *Painting, 1946* in his book on Bacon with Ronald Alley, work cited. The quotation from T. S. Eliot is from his poem, 'Sweeney Erect' in his *Poems*, 1920, included in *The Complete Poems and Plays of T. S. Eliot* (London, 1960). Constantine Fitzgibbon's gloom about the Fitzrovians in 1945 derived from his biography, *The Life of Dylan Thomas* (London, 1965). Francis Bacon talked to David Sylvester in his many interviews with him about gambling and its importance to him. He also talked about greed in painting and gambling to the *Observer*, 5 May 1962, while John Russell in his illuminating book on Bacon reported on the artist's admiration for Constable's sketch of *The Leaping Horse*, and on the imperious character of his day-dreaming. John Richardson told me of his relationship with Douglas Cooper and of Bacon's relationship with Graham Sutherland, while Picasso's observation to him comes from his admirable four-volume life of *Picasso*, near whom he lived in Provence for ten years. Patrick White wrote on post-War London in his *Flaws in the Glass*, work cited.

The comment on post-War London was from Douglas Sutherland's

Portrait of a Decade: London Life 1945–1955 (London, 1988), while Alan Ross wrote of the time in his introduction to J. Maclaren-Ross, *Memoirs of the 'Forties* (new ed., London, 1965) and in *The Forties: A Period Piece* (London, 1950). Bacon spoke to the shocked reporter of *Time* magazine, printed in the issue of 21 November 1949. His perceptive critic was Hugh Davies, to whom he talked extensively in 1973, and from whose thesis the quotations about Cézanne and Velázquez are taken. The critic of the Hanover Gallery show was Cora J. Gordon and her London Commentary was published in *Studio*, August, 1950. Robert Melville's article on 'Francis Bacon' was published in *Horizon*, XX, No. 120–121, December 1949–January 1950.

Colin MacInnes wrote of the Colony Room in *England, Half English* (London, 1961), and John Minton wrote of it in his notes, published posthumously in Frances Spalding's biography of *John Minton: Dance till the Stars Come Down* (London, 1991). Minton's old friend reminisced on his liberation of Bacon in a profile on Bacon in the *Independent*, 24 September 1988. The reminiscences of Bacon in the Gargoyle derive from Michael Luke, *David Tennant and the Gargoyle Years* (London, 1991), while John Rothenstein recalled his encounter with MacBryde and Colquhoun in his *Modern British Painters*, work cited. Michael Wishart's entertaining autobiography, *High Diver*, was published in London in 1977. John Richardson told me of Bacon's use of make-up on his face while he was painting. And Lady Caroline Blackwood wrote of her first encounter with Bacon while Princess Margaret was singing in *The New York Review*, already cited.

Chapter Seven

Probably the supreme polymath of his time, the underrated Michael Ayrton writes superbly on art and Francis Bacon in *The Rudiments of Paradise* (London, 1971). The most brilliant chapter in a brilliant book is that on 'The prehensile image', dealing with the impact of photography and film on Francis Bacon, in John Russell's cited study of him. Mark Roskill wrote 'Francis Bacon as Mannerist' for *Art International*, 25 September 1963. Robert Hughes wrote on 'David Hockney' in his penetrating *Nothing If Not Critical* (London, 1990). David Sylvester remains the major source of interviews with Bacon in his books on the artist. Hugh Davies's series of interviews with Bacon in 1973 in his cited thesis remain seminal on the artist's early work, and include his feelings about Rembrandt and Duchamp.

William Gerhardi spoke to me about the significance of open mouths, viewed at a distance. Andrew Hammer wrote on the galvanised popes in 'Exhibitions', *The Architectural Review*, Vol. CXI, February 1952. Sam Hunter wrote 'Francis Bacon: An Acute Sense of Impasse' on inventing the film-strip of pictures in *The Art Review*, Vol. XXVIII, 15 October 1953. Bacon talked to Hugh Davies about '*an absorbed solution*' [my italics] on 13 August 1973, and on the failure of his series of papal paintings. Lawrence Gowing wrote of 'Bacon and Existentialism' in his book on *Francis Bacon* with Sam Hunter (London, 1990). Bacon told Jaschia Reichardt about his interest in monkeys. Lawrence Alloway commented on the Van Gogh series in 'Dr. No's Bacon' in *Art News and Reviews*, 9 April 1960, and on Bacon's new use of colour in *Vogue*, 1 November 1963, while Andrew Forge told of the artist's use of the photograph in 'Bacon: The Paint of Screams', *Art News*, LXII, October 1963. Denys Sutton wrote on Bacon's paintings on Van Gogh in the *Financial Times*, 16 April 1957. And Mark Roskill wrote on 'Francis Bacon as a Mannerist' in *Art International*, 25 September 1963.

Bacon's correspondence with Erica Brausen from southern Africa and Monte Carlo and Henley and Tangier is contained in the Tate Gallery Archives (TGA 863), Hanover Gallery (Francis Bacon).

John Rothenstein wrote of Bacon's remarks on the running crowd in St. Petersburg in his introduction to the Tate exhibition of 1962, already cited, and he further commented on the artist's use of the photograph. Bacon told Hugh Davies of 'visual rivets' and stressed that his paintings were autobiographical and that the barriers of the skin could not be broken, even in love. John Richardson told me about the character of Peter Lacey.

I have taken my accounts of Bacon's life in Tangier and of his meetings with Paul Bowles and William Burroughs and Allen Ginsberg in general from Michelle Green, *The Dream at the End of the World: Paul Bowles and the Literary Renegades in Tangier* (London, 1992) and from Ted Morgan, *Literary Outlaw: The Life and Times of William S. Burroughs* (London, 1991), from which the quotations on Ginsberg's views on Bacon and Burroughs are taken. Michael Horovitz wrote on Bacon and Burroughs in 'Legend and his own Lunchtime', *The Times Saturday Review*, 23 May 1992. Paul Bowles wrote on meeting Bacon in his autobiography, *Without Stopping* (London, 1972), while Christopher Sawyer-Lançanno wrote a biography of Paul Bowles, *An Invisible Spectator* (London, 1991). Lorenza Trucchi was the perceptive critic who wrote on Bacon's eroticism in her *Francis Bacon* (New York, 1975), while Bacon spoke to Cecil Beaton about his rows with Lacey in Tangier and St. Ives in *Self-Portrait with Friends: The Selected Diaries of Cecil Beaton* (London, 1979), and Patrick Procktor spoke to me of visiting St. Ives, while he tells in his memoirs, *Self-Portrait* (London, 1991) of the influence on his life of Bryan Robertson after 1960.

Frances Spalding wrote on Bacon and Minton in *Dance till the Stars Come Down*, work cited. Henry Green's tribute to Matthew Smith is reprinted in his *Surviving: The Uncollected Writings of Henry Green* (London, 1990). John Rothenstein wrote on Bacon in the third volume of his illuminating memoirs, *Time's Thievish Progress* (London, 1970).

Giacometti spoke about smashing up his work to Alexander Liberman, who published the conversation in *The Artist in his Studio* (New York, 1960). Rothenstein wrote on visiting Giacometti in his studio in *Time's Thievish Progress*, work cited. Francis Bacon told me the story of Giacometti's smile from the Roman gutter, and he spoke to Hugh Davies about crucifixions in 1973, work cited. Bryan Robertson wrote on Bacon and Giacometti, and on Bacon and de Maistre and Patrick White in the *Guardian*, 29 April 1992. Daniel Farson wrote of the relationship between Graham Sutherland and Bacon in *Sacred Monsters* (London, 1988) and extensively on Bacon's life in Soho and relationship with John Deakin and Wheeler's and the Colony Room in his evocative *Soho in the 'Fifties* (intro. George Melly, London, 1987). Roger Berthoud was the biographer of *Graham Sutherland*, work cited.

Cecil Beaton described his meeting with and sitting for Bacon extensively in his *Self Portrait with Friends*, his selected diaries, already cited. Keith Vaughan wrote on 3 January 1952, and on 27 January 1955, in his *Journals, 1939–1977*, of his opinions on Bacon's work and of the relationship between Dennis Williams and Bacon. The journals were published in London in 1989. Barbara Skelton described Ann Fleming's fiftieth birthday party for Cyril Connolly in her *Tears Before Bedtime* (London, 1987), as did Cecil Beaton in his diaries. Patrick White wrote to Peggy Garland on 29 September 1958 about meeting Bacon and de Maistre again: the letter is printed in *Flaws in the Glass*, work cited. Michael Hamburger wrote of going to the Colony Room with Bacon in *A Mug's Game: Intermittent Memoirs, 1924–1954* (Cheadle, Cheshire, 1973). Graham Lord, *Just the One: the Wives and Times of Jeffrey Bernard* was published in London, 1992.

The stories about Bacon falling apart with John Minton are recounted in Frances Spalding's cited biography of Minton. Henrietta Moraes spoke of her relationship with Deakin and Bacon on a television programme 'Without Walls', 26 March 1991. Paul Potts wrote to Daniel Farson about his opinion of Muriel Belcher: Farson has written by far the most generous appraisal of her appeal. Bacon spoke about painting the history of the past thirty years to the *Sunday Times*, 5 May 1957. The description of the diaspora of the artist from Soho comes from my own book, *War like a Wasp*, already cited. Erica Brausen heard of Bacon's leaving the Hanover Gallery (TGA 863) and spoke to the *Daily Express*, 25 November 1958. And Rothenstein's admirable analysis of the power of Bacon's vision concluded his chapter on the artist in his incisive *Modern English Painters*, work cited. Bruce Bernard kindly gave me his estimate of his friend, Francis Bacon, while Stephen Spender wrote about his dinner for W. H. Auden and the argument with Bacon in his illuminating *Journals 1939–1983* (John Goldsmith ed., New York, 1986), 9 June 1955.

Chapter Eight

I am indebted to Hugh Davies and Sally Yard in their excellent *Francis Bacon* (New York, 1986) for their comparison of the cracked mirror in the bedroom of Reece Mews to Duchamp's 'Large Glass' of 1915–1923. John Rothenstein writes on Bacon's retrospective at the Tate Gallery and on his catalogue introduction and meetings with Lucian Freud and on Roy de Maistre in his memoirs, *Time's Thievish Progress*, work cited. His piece in the catalogue is printed in *Francis Bacon, 24 May–1 July 1962, The Tate Gallery* (London, 1962). John Russell's book on *Francis Bacon* is a work of art in its own right, and I remain deeply in its debt. Bacon's admission that he painted his second triptych of the Crucifixion under drink was recorded by Ronald Alley in his definitive catalogue of the painter's early works made with John Rothenstein, *Francis Bacon* (London, 1964). Lawrence Gowing's opinion of that triptych is to be found in his work with Sam Hunter, *Francis Bacon* (London and Washington, D.C., 1989).

Daniel Farson wrote of hearing about Peter Lacey's death in the Colony Room in his cited work, *Soho in the Fifties*. Stephen Spender's *Journals* have also been cited: these entries date from 23 May and 29 May and 7 June and 11 August 1962. Patrick White recorded his own wish to become a painter in *Flaws in the Glass*, work cited, and represented much of Bacon in Hurtle Duffield in *The Vivisector* (London, 1970). J. R. Ackerley's comparison of his method of writing to Bacon's in painting is to be found in his biography by Peter Parker (London, 1989). Anita Brookner wrote on

Bacon's retrospective at the Tate Gallery in *The Burlington Magazine*, July 1962, and spoke to me about Bacon on Christmas Day 1989. David Hockney's comments on Bacon are recorded in *Portrait of David Hockney* (London, 1991) by Peter Webb and in *David Hockney David Hockney* (ed. Nikos Stangos, London, 1991).

Kenneth Partridge and others have told me of the influence of Alfred Hecht. Francis Bacon's profile was in the *Observer*, 27 May 1962. *Queer People* by Douglas Plummer was published in London in 1963. Bacon told John Russell of his wish to live in an enormous room of distorting mirrors. John Ashbery wrote on Bacon's travelling retrospective in the International Edition of the *New York Herald Tribune*, 7 November 1963. David Hockney wrote on 'Violence in Art' in *20th Century*, Winter, 1964/65. Bacon spoke to David Sylvester about his Munich 'Crucifixion' of 1965. Bryan Appleyard compared Pinter and Bacon in his important *The Pleasures of Peace: Art and Imagination in Post-War Britain* (London, 1989). Keith Vaughan excoriated Osborne and Pinter in his cited *Journal*, 18 July 1965.

I am indebted to two brilliant books for my understanding of the feelings of homosexual society in the 'sixties, particularly through the theatre: Nicholas de Jongh, *Not in Front of the Audience: Homosexuality on Stage* (London, 1992) and to Simon Shepherd, *Because We're Queers: The Life and Crimes of Kenneth Halliwell and Joe Orton* (London, 1989), an incisive and militant work that makes John Lahr's biography of Orton, *Prick Up Your Ears* (London, 1978) appear out of touch. The British Medical Association published its report on 'Homosexuality and Prostitution' in London in 1955. The anecdotes of Bacon's meetings with Giacometti are well told in his entertaining biography by James Lord, work already cited. Andrew Forge commented on Bacon's portraits in his admirable book with Dawn Ades on *Francis Bacon* (London, 1985). Peter Fuller wrote the chapter on 'The Visual Arts' for *The Cambridge Guide to the Arts in Britain*, edited by Boris Ford, Vol. 9, *Since the Second World War* (Cambridge, 1988). Robert Hughes wrote on Bacon in his incisive *The Shock of the New* (rev. ed., London, 1991), and spoke to me about Bacon.

Chapter Nine

Francis Bacon talked to both David Sylvester and Hugh Davies about his studio in Limehouse; but most of the memories of his being there are contained in *Limehouse Days: A Personal Experience of the East End* by Daniel

Farson, published in London in 1991. The quotations from 'Sweeney Among the Nightingales' is taken from T.S. Eliot, the work already cited. John Russell's analysis of Bacon in his short book on him remains definitive, particularly on his feelings for France. The artist spoke to Sylvester about the significance of the Nazi symbols in the Munich 'Crucifixion' and on annihilating his other pictures, both in *The Brutality of Fact*, work cited, and in his first conversation with Sylvester to appear in print in the *Sunday Times*, 14 July 1963. Bacon spoke to 'Art Class' by John Wayne-Morgan, printed in the *Sun*, 2 November 1965. Bernard Walsh spoke to the *Daily Mail*, 12 January 1966, of his pleasure in receiving a Bacon painting of Lucian Freud, and Bacon spoke of his exhibition at the Galerie Maeght in Paris to the *Evening Standard*, 19 November 1966.

Terence Mullaly compared Bacon's Marlborough show to the napalm bomb in the *Daily Telegraph*, 9 March 1967. Nigel Gosling conducted the brilliant interview and analysis of Bacon's work that same year for the *Observer*, 5 March 1967. John Richardson was my main source for George Dyer's suicide attempt in New York, while Daniel Farson reported on Frank Norman's attempts to write on Bacon and on George Dyer's character and mistaken trip to Devon in *Soho in the Fifties*, work cited. The *Daily Telegraph*, 3 June 1971, gave a full report of Bacon's trial on drugs charges. *The Orton Diaries* was edited by John Lahr and published in London in 1986. Richard Cork did the most important interview with Bacon in early October, 1972, before his Paris exhibition, as he was to do the most significant analysis of his Tate 'Crucifixion' after the painter's death. David Hockney spoke to *The Times*, 29 April 1992, on Bacon's scream for George Dyer at La Coupole. Lawrence Raab's poem, 'Figure with Hypodermic Syringe', was printed in *Encounter*, November 1971. Of course, Bacon with his usual disclaimer of any message discounted the syringe, saying he wanted to nail his subject to the bed. Although people said he was suggesting a drug-addict, he said, 'Not at all. I just put a syringe in.'

Chapter Ten

David Sylvester's interviews with Francis Bacon were first published in the United States of America in 1975 to coincide with the show of Bacon's recent work at the Metropolitan Museum in New York. Nine interviews with Bacon were recorded between 1962 and 1986, when Sylvester published an intercut version in his acclaimed *The Brutality of Fact*, Third Enlarged Edition (London, 1987). When it appeared, Stephen Spender asserted that it might have as great an influence on contemporary painting as the critical writings of Pound and Eliot had on modernism in poetry, while Graham Greene found that it ranked with the journals of Delacroix and the letters of Gauguin. Certainly, these illuminating interviews with Bacon put any researcher deeply in debt to David Sylvester, whose construction of the conversations is as complex and subtle as Bacon's own paintings.

Lorenza Trucci, *Francis Bacon* (Milan and New York, 1975) gives an admirable compilation and dissection of the artist's painting up to the early 'seventies. Michel Leiris wrote his profound analysis of the painter for *Francis Bacon* (London, 1988). Guy Brett compared Léger with Bacon in *The Times*, 27 October 1971, while Pierre Schneider found that Bacon had radically changed modern art in *The Times*, 7 November 1971. Bacon spoke about the offer of a show at the Metropolitan Museum in New York to the *Evening Standard*, 3 November 1971, and *The Times* stated that 'Francis Bacon paintings boost Britain' on 11 January 1972.

Daniel Farson's memories of Dyer's and Deakin's deaths are recorded in his *Soho in the Fifties*, work cited. John Russell's work on *Francis Bacon* has been previously mentioned, as has Hugh Davies's thesis on Bacon, based on his series of interviews with the painter, this one about reacting to one's times on 6 March 1973. I am most grateful to Barry Joule for talking to me about his friendship with Bacon. Stephen Spender wrote on Bacon's views on 'frustration and despair' in his *Journal*, work cited, on 12 March 1974. Jeffrey Bernard wrote on Bacon in the *Independent on Sunday*, 3 May 1992. Tom Driberg's encounter with Bacon at the Colony Room was described in the *Sunday Times Magazine*, 25 August 1974. James Kirkup's poem, 'The Love that Dares to Speak its Name', was published in *Gay News* 96, June 1976. Kirkup objected to the Christian version of the Crucifixion in the *Observer*, 17 July 1976. The summing-up of the judge at the trial is quoted in John Sutherland's penetrating *Offensive Literature: Decensorship in Britain, 1960–1982* (London, 1982).

Bacon spoke to Sylvester about his dislike of the welfare state and a happy society. The critic of Bacon's exhibition at the Metropolitan Museum in New York for *The Burlington Magazine*, June 1975, was Norman W. Canedy. Bacon gave his one-line witticisms before his American exhibition to the *Daily Mail*, 18 March 1975. John Russell again was the recipient of Bacon's liking for flat landscapes.

Chapter Eleven

Bacon spoke at length to me about gambling and risk and abstract art, also to Melvyn Bragg in his admirable programme on the artist, 'Francis Bacon', transmitted on The South Bank Show, 9 June 1985. Barrie Penrose reported on the Bacon forgeries from Italy in the *Observer*, 4 April 1976. Joan Wyndham's *Anything Once* was published in London in 1992. Richard Cork turned against Bacon's exhibition in Paris in the *Evening Standard*, 11 November 1971, and Edward Lucie-Smith denounced Bacon's contempt in the same paper on 5 January 1978.

Gilles DeLeuze, *Francis Bacon: Logique de la Sensation* was published in Paris in 1984. His words about declining to be a Companion of Honour were spoken to Richard Holliday for the *Sunday Telegraph*, 5 June 1977. Hugh Davies reported further interviews with Bacon in his admirable book on *Francis Bacon* with Sally Yard, work already cited. And Bacon spoke about American abstract art and the necessity of the past to Shusha Guppy, the *Telegraph Sunday Magazine*, 4 November 1984.

Chapter Twelve

This chapter is wholly dependent on the incisive work by Gilles DeLeuze, *Francis Bacon: Logique de la Sensation* (Paris, 1984). It is an original and compelling analysis of Bacon's work. As in the previous chapter, I am grateful to Francis Bacon himself for talking to me in 1988 about the DeLeuze book and to Melvyn Bragg in 1985. Bacon's admiration of the early works of Cézanne is attested by Sam Hunter in his excellent essay on Bacon in his book with Lawrence Gowing on *Francis Bacon*, work already cited. John Livingstone Lowes's remarkable *The Road to Xanadu* was published in London in 1927.

Chapter Thirteen

I am indebted again to Pamela Firth Matthews for her reminiscences of her first cousin, Francis Bacon, and particularly to David Sylvester and to Melvyn Bragg for his conversations with them as well as myself. Stephen Spender recorded his conversation with Frank Auerbach in his *Journal*, already cited, and Michael Wishart recorded his thought on seeing the painting of the men coupling in Coombe Priory in *High Diver*, also cited as has been Daniel Farson's *Sacred Monsters*. Graham Sutherland wrote to Wishart about his break with Bacon on 26 February 1978.

The friend's opinion of Bacon's agile arrival in the Colony Room derives from his profile, the *Observer*, 19 May 1985. Elena Salvoni recorded the painter's opinion of her refurbished L'Escargot in *Elena: A Life in Soho* (with Sandy Fawkes, London, 1991). Gaston Berlemont spoke of his feelings about the French Pub to Judith Summers, *Soho: A History of London's Most Colourful Neighbourhood* (London, 1991). Andrew Forge's fine essay in his book with Dawn Ades on *Francis Bacon* has already been mentioned. David Sylvester's culminating live interview with Bacon was transmitted by *Arena* on the BBC on 16 November 1984, while Melvyn Bragg's probing and illuminating interview appeared on Thames Television's The South Bank Show. Bacon spoke to Shusha Guppy, interview already cited, about painting as an old man's occupation. In an afterword, 'Notes on Technique', Sally Yard and Hugh Davies wrote a perceptive analysis of Francis Bacon's methods of painting in their cited book on him.

Bruce Bernard spoke to me about Bacon's increasing dominance in his old age and wish to manipulate the records of his past. Richard Francis spoke on his opinion of Bacon to Shusha Guppy. Brian Sewell's 'The Loaded Brush' on Francis Bacon was published in the *Radio Times*, 10 November 1984. Lord (Grey) Gowrie recorded his opinions on Bacon in the *Sunday Times Magazine*, 19 May 1985. Waldemar Januszczak assessed the Tate retrospective for the *Guardian*, 22 May 1985. Bacon himself took Jane Withers and Anthony Fawcett of *The Times* around his retrospective, and their piece on it was printed on 20 May 1985, while John Russell Taylor's criticism of the show was published two days later. Bacon spoke to Melvyn Bragg about the Rokeby Venus and to John Russell about the Degas, 'Woman Drying Herself'.

Chapter Fourteen

John Richardson gave me his personal opinion of Bacon's later work, while Peter Fuller wrote an essay in *The Cambridge Guide to the Arts in Britain: Volume 9, Since the Second World War* (ed. Boris Ford, Cambridge, 1988). Robert Hughes's opinion of Bacon's work in *The Shock of the New* has already been cited. The critic of the 'purely evil' 'Second Version of

Triptych, 1944' was Richard Dorment, writing in the *Daily Telegraph*, 3 February 1989. Bacon asked Michael Kimmelman of the *Times Review*, 2 September 1989, who was more surreal than Aeschylus, and then proceeded with him to see the Constables in the Victoria and Albert Museum, and then on to the Colony Room. He read from Aeschylus on *The South Bank Show*, already cited.

The reviewer of the Bacon show at the Lelong Gallery in Paris in 1987 was Geordie Grieg for the *Sunday Times*, 4 October 1987. James Birch spoke of his meetings with Sergei Klokov to Geraldine Norman for the *Independent*, 18 March 1988, and Daniel Farson, for the *Daily Mail*, 22 March 1988, while David Sylvester and Brian Sewell spoke of the Moscow show to the writer of the Bacon profile in the *Independent*, 24 September 1988. Bacon spoke to Geordie Grieg again of his reasons for not going to Moscow and of his probable reception there in the *Sunday Times*, 25 September 1988, and saw me shortly afterwards at Groucho's. William Parker reported on 'Russian Taste for Bacon' in the *Financial Times*, 1 October 1988, and Brandon Williams for *The Times*, 12 October 1988, while the reactions of the spectators in the Visitors' Book appeared in the *Sunday Times*, 13 November 1988. Patrick Procktor and Barry Joule spoke to me about the end of Bacon's life.

Daniel Farson wrote of Bacon celebrating his birthday quietly in the *Sunday Telegraph*, 29 October 1989, and Michael Kimmelman received most of Bacon's rehearsed opinions for the readers of *The Times*, date cited. Bruce Bernard wrote an illuminating piece on 'The Book that Bacon Banned' for the *Independent Magazine*, 2 April 1992, and spoke to me at length about the matter. John Minihan's *Photograph of Francis Bacon, Samuel Beckett, William S. Burroughs* was published as a catalogue for the October Gallery, London, February/March, 1990, and the author quoted George Bernard Shaw on photography. Sam Hunter wrote his authoritative essay on 'Metaphor and Meaning in Francis Bacon' for Lawrence Gowing and Sam Hunter, *Francis Bacon*, work cited: both of the extracts are his incisive insights.

Chapter Fifteen

The Homecoming by Harold Pinter was published in London in 1965. Pamela Firth Matthews has been my invaluable guide to Bacon's last years at Long Melford. Richard Sapiro of Wintrust was the banker, who went to dinner in Long Melford. Bacon told Shusha Guppy of his progressive happiness a week before he died, and Barry Joule and Kenneth Partridge told me of the artist's last afflictions. Bacon spoke to Richard Cork for *The Times*, 16 March 1991, about his two versions of the Triptych of 1944, and about his feelings on his future paintings and his life mask and death and homosexuality and money.

The Times, 29 April 1992, reported the premature reports of Bacon's death. He had told Patrick Procktor of his loathing of a gallery for his dead paintings and had spoken on the same theme to Peter Plagens in *Newsweek*, 11 May 1992. Lord Gowrie wrote a moving obituary on Bacon in the *Guardian*, 29 April 1992. John McEwan's brilliant piece on Bacon as a dandy and the heir of Baudelaire was printed in the *Sunday Telegraph*, 3 May 1992. And Richard Francis also perceptively brought in the influence of Baudelaire in his essay 'Memory Traces' for the catalogue of the Francis Bacon exhibition at the Tate Gallery, Liverpool, 20 February 1990–13 January 1991. Bacon's interview with Gérard Regnier, Director of the Picasso Museum in Paris, who writes under the name of Jean Clair, was printed in the catalogue of an exhibition on the theme of Picasso's crucifixions, also in *The Art Newspaper*, No. 19, June 1992.

The artists' tributes to Francis Bacon after his death were printed in the *Sunday Times*, 3 May 1992. Sir Alan Bowness's opinion of Francis Bacon was printed in the catalogue of his second retrospective at the Tate Gallery in 1985. The Duke of Beaufort spoke to the *Evening Standard*, 29 April 1992. Michael Leventis was reported in the *Daily Telegraph*, 29 April 1992. Brian Sewell wrote Bacon's obituary for the *Evening Standard*, 28 April 1992.

Endpiece

The Duke of Beaufort spoke about the value of the Bacon estate to the *Evening Standard* 7 October, 1992. *The Times* reported the net value of the Bacon estate at £10,923,900 and of the Bacon sale at Sotheby's at about £680,000 on 4 December 1992.

John Edwards spoke about the Bacon bequest to the *Sunday Times*, 30 August 1992, as did Lord Gowrie. Bacon spoke to David Sylvester about being a medium for accident and riveting the appearance, and to Richard Cork about afternoons and the car accident in France. Donald Kuspit accused Bacon of nihilism in 'Francis Bacon: the Authority of Flesh', *Art*

Forum, New York, Summer, 1975. The artist's last interview with Gérard Regnier has already been cited.

John Berger complained about Bacon and Belsen in a panel meeting at the ICA, reported by Lawrence Alloway, 'Points of View: Bacon and Balthus', *Art News and Review*, 26 January 1952. Peter Fuller compared Velázquez and Bacon in the *Daily Telegraph*, 28 October 1989. Kathleen Raine spoke of Bacon in *The Times*, 18 April 1992. Bryan Robertson gave his opinion of Bacon's work in his obituary on the painter, the *Guardian*, 29 April 1992. Sir Michael Levey paid his last tribute to Bacon in the *Independent*, 11 May 1992. And if I end on Bacon's talking on violence to David Sylvester in *The Brutality of Fact*, work cited, it is because that book records some of the most illuminating conversations ever held between artist and critic.

Index